REIMAGINING
THE REPUBLIC

RECONSTRUCTING AMERICA
Andrew L. Slap, series editor

Reimagining the Republic

Race, Citizenship, and Nation in the Literary Work of Albion W. Tourgée

Sandra M. Gustafson
and Robert S. Levine,
Editors

FORDHAM UNIVERSITY PRESS
NEW YORK   2023

Fordham University Press has no responsibility for the persistence or accuracy of URLs for external or third-party Internet websites referred to in this publication and does not guarantee that any content on such websites is, or will remain, accurate or appropriate.

Fordham University Press also publishes its books in a variety of electronic formats. Some content that appears in print may not be available in electronic books.

Visit us online at www.fordhampress.com.

Library of Congress Cataloging-in-Publication Data available online at https://catalog .loc.gov.

Printed in the United States of America

25 24 23   5 4 3 2 1

First edition

Contents

Foreword

Carolyn L. Karcher

The publication of the first volume to bring together a set of essays analyzing the literary works of Albion W. Tourgée merits celebration. Among the dozen novels, two novellas, and three collections of short stories Tourgée authored, *A Fool's Errand: By One of the Fools* (1879) sold six hundred thousand copies in his lifetime, and *Bricks without Straw* (1880) sold fifty thousand.[1] Besides earning commercial success, the twin Reconstruction-era bestsellers helped elect a president supportive of African American rights and influenced the policy he outlined to overcome the legacy of slavery.

Despite this record of achievement, Tourgée has suffered shocking neglect by literary scholars. The only book-length overview of his literary corpus is more than a half-century old—and hostile, to boot.[2] The list of articles focusing on his fiction is pitifully short, and the bulk of it has received almost no attention. Both literary course syllabi and anthologies typically omit Tourgée. Yet readers willing to sample his novels will find their plots gripping, their prose style engaging, their characters psychologically complex, their treatment of African American characters far superior to that of most other nineteenth-century white writers, their rendering of dialogue lively, their historical insights profound—especially as regards the American race problem—and in the case of *A Fool's Errand* and *Bricks without Straw*, their depictions of Ku Klux Klan violence and African American resistance unforgettably powerful.

How can we explain the neglect of a novelist with such accomplishments to his credit, who was not only "hailed as the originator of a new school in fiction" but compared in his day to such giants as Charles Dickens and Victor Hugo?[3] The causes, I would argue, are predominantly ideological and conceptual, rather than aesthetic, but they also point to the need for new literary paradigms.

Ideology accounts for both Tourgée's meteoric rise to prominence and his precipitous fall into obscurity. Based on Tourgée's own firsthand observations of Klan violence as a Radical Republican superior court judge during North Carolina's Reconstruction, *A Fool's Errand* intervened at a pivotal moment in the national debate over how to empower the freedpeople to exercise their new constitutional rights as US citizens in the teeth of their former masters' murderous opposition. Contemporaries acclaimed it as the *Uncle Tom's Cabin* of Reconstruction.[4]

A Fool's Errand indeed extended the reach of Harriet Beecher Stowe's masterpiece beyond slavery while similarly fortifying the resolve of white northerners to fight for the freedom of Black southerners, this time from the savage attacks by white southerners aiming to terrorize them into submission. *Bricks without Straw* created further sympathy for the Black liberation struggle by introducing realistically portrayed, three-dimensional Black characters, rooted in an African American community rather than serving as appendages to whites, and by presenting Reconstruction through their eyes as a quest for self-determination that involved formalizing marriages, building churches, purchasing land, pursuing education, and voting. This major literary innovation, which would not be equaled by another white writer until Howard Fast's *Freedom Road* (1944), drew much praise from reviewers, who quoted long passages from the novel.[5]

Tragic events nevertheless doomed Tourgée's attempt to change the course of history. Four months after President James A. Garfield delivered the inaugural address in which he embraced Tourgée's recommendation to promote federal aid to southern public schools as a means of uplifting Blacks and reeducating whites, he succumbed to an assassin's bullet. Garfield's successor, Chester A. Arthur, swiftly retreated from Reconstruction. Meanwhile, as white southern violence against the freedpeople and their white Republican allies raged unabated, the northern public wearied of the seemingly hopeless task of transforming the South into a democratic society.

Sales of the novels that had won Tourgée overnight fame plummeted. By 1887, publishers noted that "his *great* popularity is a thing of the past."[6] Nothing better reveals the ideological reasons for the eclipse of *A Fool's Errand* and *Bricks without Straw* than their replacement as bestsellers by novels that glorified the paramilitary restoration of white supremacy as the South's "redemption": Thomas Nelson Page's *Red Rock: A Chronicle of Reconstruction* (1898) and Thomas Dixon's *The Leopard's Spots: A Romance of the White Man's Burden—1865-1900* (1902) and *The Clansman: An Historical Romance of the Ku Klux Klan* (1905).[7]

Far from admitting defeat, Tourgée kept up his battle against white supremacy for another decade and a half in fiction, journalism, and law. His novel *Pactolus Prime* (1890) blasted the racism and religious hypocrisy of white American Christians and exposed the delusiveness of race itself through a title character who flips from Black to white to Black again. It "succeeded incomparably," judged the African American feminist scholar Anna Julia Cooper, "in photographing and vocalizing the feelings of the colored American."[8] Tourgée's newspaper column for the *Chicago Daily Inter Ocean*, "A Bystander's Notes" (1888-1898), not only documented and denounced racial discrimination, segregation, disfranchisement, and lynching, but broadcast the voices of African Americans (who often reprinted the column in their own newspapers) and set them in dialogue with whites. As a lawyer, Tourgée represented the African American plaintiffs challenging segregation in the 1896 *Plessy v. Ferguson* case, which he argued pro bono and which the US Supreme Court infamously decided in favor of the "separate but equal" doctrine cementing white supremacy.

After the ideological triumph of white supremacy erased Tourgée from literary history, African Americans kept his memory alive. Tellingly, the African American poet and critic Sterling Brown was the first twentieth-century literary scholar to discuss Tourgée's fiction. Brown lauded the African American characters in *A Fool's Errand* and *Bricks without Straw* as people "not before met with in [white-authored] American fiction." Their "dignity" and militancy revealed Tourgée "as well conversant with problems faced by Negroes," Brown underscored.[9]

When the civil rights movement of the 1950s and early 1960s stormed the bulwark of white supremacy, it was not literary scholars but the historians John Hope Franklin, George M. Fredrickson, and Otto H. Olsen who rehabilitated Tourgée's reputation and brought his Reconstruction novels back into print. All three pioneered in debunking the long prevalent white southern view of Reconstruction as a "tragic era" of barbaric "Negro rule" over a "prostrate" aristocracy.[10]

With a few salient exceptions—including Alexander Cowie, whose monumental *The Rise of the American Novel* (1948) ranked *A Fool's Errand* as "one of the most powerful novels of the nineteenth century" and pronounced Tourgée's prose style "among the best, certainly, in his period"[11]—literary scholars did not follow suit. Once again, ideology played a significant role in preventing most from either studying or teaching Tourgée's fiction. On the one hand, the lingering white southern version of Reconstruction, to which literary scholars lent credence well after historians had discredited it, led several to dismiss Tourgée's Reconstruction novels as propagandistic and "biased."[12] On the other hand, the rediscovery of African American writers—thanks partly to the Black Studies programs demanded by radical Black youth and their white allies in the liberation movements of the late 1960s and 1970s—also worked against Tourgée. The dramatically reconfigured American literary canon that granted African American writers long overdue recognition left no room for antiracist white writers like Tourgée. Instead, it encouraged a tendency to pit African American and white writers against each other, both in critical studies and classroom teaching, with the effect of implying that no white writer could ever overcome racism. This approach inevitably resulted in misrepresenting Tourgée as a racist, notwithstanding his decades-long advocacy of African American rights, eulogized by such leaders as Ida B. Wells and W. E. B. Du Bois, as well as by scores of their forgotten contemporaries; his extensive collaboration with African Americans in fighting against lynching and Jim Crow; his voluminous correspondence with them; and their moving tributes to his championship of them.[13]

Lately, however, triggered by the brutal police murder of George Floyd in May 2020, as captured in a video that went viral around the world, a multiracial mass movement against white supremacy has arisen to complete the revolution that Reconstruction and the civil rights movement left unfinished. Racial coalitions and intersectionality are currently supplanting identity politics. Demonstrators of all races have joined in toppling statues of Confederate officers erected after the restoration of white supremacy. Reflecting the composition of an army 40 percent of whose rank and file is now made up of people of color, protesters are also demanding that military bases named for Confederate generals be renamed. Reshaped by these developments, ideology may inspire rather than impede more productive approaches to Tourgée's dialogues with African American writers.

Conceptual as well as ideological factors pose barriers to reintegrating Tourgée's fiction into the American literary canon. Tourgée does not fit comfortably into the school of American literary realism that dominated the era during which he produced his best fiction. While boldly laying claim to his own brand of realism, Tourgée carried on a running quarrel with the school's chief theorist, William Dean Howells, whose "so-called realism" he derided as restrictive and "petty." Howells's definition of realism "set up a false standard of the truth," charged Tourgée, according to which only "average, every-day, common-place happenings" qualified as "true" or "real." It excluded heroism as "exceptional" and therefore unrealistic, mocked "self-sacrifice [as] an attribute to be ashamed of," and stigmatized the "novel with a purpose" as inartistic.[14] Tourgée refused to concede the field of realist fiction to a theory he judged so misguided. "You know I am a realist, in a much broader sense than those who claim the name," he wrote to the magazine publisher S. S. McClure. His realism, he specified, consisted in providing a "true picture" of a particular society at a particular historical moment, drawing on his "knowledge . . . of locality and incident to give verisimilitude, flavor and . . . interest," building fictional characters on "actualities," and capturing people's speech and regional accents accurately.[15]

We can glean additional insight into Tourgée's understanding of realism from his praise of Charles W. Chesnutt's fiction. "Its realism is unique and true," he wrote to Chesnutt, "—true to nature and not to the fettering ideas of the narrow rules which make our so-called realism the falsest and sorriest of fiction" (again a swipe at Howells).[16] Clearly, Tourgée recognized in Chesnutt a kindred writer for whom realism served not as a literary creed but as an artistic tool for undermining the racial prejudices that distorted white readers' perceptions of African Americans.

Tourgée's dissent from the literary dogma of his time suggests the need for new paradigms to help scholars effectively teach and analyze his fiction in conversation with that of Chesnutt and other revalorized African American writers, as well as alongside their canonized contemporaries Howells, Mark Twain, and Henry James. One of these new paradigms should certainly expand the definition of literary realism to encompass many more variants than hitherto—and to consider the ways that traces of romanticism, sentimentalism, and sensationalism surface even in canonical realist texts. Another new paradigm should reclassify the "novel with a purpose"—or novel of political advocacy—not as a subliterary genre that fails to measure up to the artistic standards of canonical works but as a distinctive literary genre that succeeds artistically when it arouses readers' outrage at injustice and gives victims of injustice an authentic voice.

Yet another new paradigm should extend beyond fiction to journalism—a genre to which Tourgée contributed reams of articles in unrivaled prose over more than three decades. Journalism scholars have recently defined "literary journalism" as a genre, elaborated on its characteristics, and tracked its history in the United States from colonial times to the present.[17] Much of Tourgée's journalism falls into this genre, through which he educated the public about race, politics, history, economics, and literature.

In sum, Tourgée's writings offer literary scholars scope for original work of many kinds: reconceptualizing literary realism, theorizing the artistry of novels that advocate political change, identifying the "literary" components of literary journalism, making room in our canons for white antiracist authors, devising approaches better suited to evaluating their writings, and producing a literary biography worthy of Tourgée's astonishing achievements. Once introduced to his vast corpus, much of which lies buried in libraries, scholars will find ample opportunity to explore texts they can be the first to interpret. The essays collected in the present volume greatly advance the process of restoring Tourgée to his rightful place among nineteenth-century America's most important writers.

Notes

1. On sales figures for Tourgée's two bestsellers, see Albion W. Tourgée Papers (hereafter AWTP), obituary clippings AWTP #9907, "Judge Tourgee, the Author, Dead: A Novelist Whose Reputation Was Worldwide," *Baltimore American*, May 22, 1905; and "Specimen Bricks," advertisement excerpted from *Rochester American Rural Home*, available from APS Online.

2. Theodore L. Gross, *Albion W. Tourgée* (New York: Twayne, 1963).

3. AWTP #9907, "Judge Tourgee," *Chicago Daily Inter Ocean*, May 23, 1905; *Baltimore American* clipping.

4. Ten press notices in later printings of *A Fool's Errand* appear under the heading "The New 'Uncle Tom.'"

5. See the reviews quoted in Carolyn L. Karcher, ed., *Bricks without Straw* (Durham, NC: Duke University Press, 2009), 48–49, 61n125.

6. AWTP #2601, Roberts Brothers to Emma Kilbourne Tourgée (hereafter EKT), March 25, 1887.

7. AWTP #9907, "Death of Tourgée," *Gazette*, May 23, 1905.

8. Anna Julia Cooper, *A Voice from the South. By a Black Woman of the South*, ed. Mary Helen Washington (1892; New York: Oxford University Press, 1988), 199.

9. Sterling Brown, *The Negro in American Fiction* (Washington, DC: Associates in Negro Folk Education, 1937).

10. See the reprints of *A Fool's Errand* edited by John Hope Franklin (Cambridge, MA: Belknap, 1961) and by George M. Fredrickson (New York: Harper & Row, 1966) and of *Bricks without Straw* by Otto H. Olsen (Baton Rouge: Louisiana State University Press, 1969). See also John Hope Franklin, *From Slavery to Freedom: A History of African Americans* (New York: Knopf, 1947); George M. Fredrickson, *The Black Image in the White Mind: The Debate on Afro-American Character and Destiny, 1817–1914* (New York: Harper & Row, 1971); and Otto H. Olsen, *Carpetbagger's Crusade: The Life of Albion Winegar Tourgée* (Baltimore, MD: Johns Hopkins University Press, 1965). The phrases in quotation marks refer to Claude Bowers's *The Tragic Era: The Revolution after Lincoln* (1929) and James S. Pike's *The Prostrate State: South Carolina under Negro Government* (1974).

11. Alexander Cowie, *The Rise of the American Novel* (New York: American Book Co., 1948), 535.

12. See Gross, *Albion W. Tourgée*; Ted N. Weissbuch, "Albion W. Tourgee: Propagandist and Critic of Reconstruction," *Ohio Historical Quarterly* 70 (January 1961): 27–44; and Sylvia E. Bowman, "Judge Tourgée's Fictional Presentation of the Reconstruction," *Journal of Popular Culture* 3 (Fall 1969): 307–23.

13. For documentation and analysis of Tourgée's relations with African Americans in the 1890s, see Carolyn L. Karcher, *A Refugee from His Race: Albion W. Tourgée and His Fight against White Supremacy* (Chapel Hill: University of North Carolina Press, 2016).

14. Quotations are from Tourgée's article "The Claim of 'Realism,'" *North American Review* 148 (March 1889): 386–88; and from his Migma column "The Book Shelf," in his magazine *The Continent*, May 23, 1883, 669.

15. AWTP #7748, AWT to [S. S. McClure], n.d. [May 1894]; AWTP #6688, undated draft to unknown correspondent [1893].

16. AWT to Charles W. Chesnutt, December 8, 1888, Chesnutt Papers, Fisk University. For an opposing perspective, see Joseph R. McElrath Jr., "Why Charles W. Chesnutt Is Not a Realist," *American Literary Realism* 32 (Winter 2000): 91–108.

17. William E. Dow, Roberta S. Maguire, and Yoko Nakamura, eds., *The Routledge Companion to American Literary Journalism* (New York: Routledge, 2020).

REIMAGINING
THE REPUBLIC

Introduction

Literary Tourgée

Sandra M. Gustafson
and Robert S. Levine

On November 14, 1905, a remarkable group of mourners came together at the Methodist church in Mayville, New York, on the shores of Chautauqua Lake. Among those gathered to commemorate the passing in May of the writer and activist Albion Tourgée were Ida B. Wells-Barnett, best known for her antilynching crusade, and Charles W. Chesnutt, arguably the most accomplished Black fiction writer before the Harlem Renaissance. Tourgée had died in Bordeaux, France, where he was serving as US consul. The tribute that Wells-Barnett presented included a passage from a letter he had written from Bordeaux to her husband, Ferdinand Barnett, president of the Appomattox Club of Chicago, a civic organization for African Americans.[1] Tourgée's own words in that letter, as they appear in the published "In Memoriam" pamphlet, provide a compelling overview of his career:

> For more than a quarter century, I gave my best thought and energies to a study of race relations in the United States and the effort to establish conditions favorable to the enjoyment of equal rights, equal protection, equal opportunity, political and industrial by the colored citizens of the United States.
>
> My reasons for devoting myself to this subject, to the practical exclusion of other personal interests, were
>
> 1. A love of justice, and a consuming hatred of injustice.
>
> 2. An abiding confidence in the justice of Almighty God as the shaper of National destiny, not by physical and intermittent miracle, but by the development of popular forces through the evolution of general principles.
>
> 3. An overwhelming pity for the inconceivable woes of the colored people in the United States.
>
> 4. A burning desire that American Christianity and American civilization should purge themselves from the shame and stain of such inconceivable atrocities as sprung from the root of slavery.

After quoting these lines from Tourgée's letter, the pamphlet, which contains "Tributes of Respect by Colored Citizens of Chicago," concludes: "Presenting this creed to the American people, as a call to duty by a voice from the dead, we take comfort in the thought that though our friend and benefactor is dead, yet shall he live through the inspiration of his work and words." It is Tourgée's words that are the focus of this volume on his literary engagements and achievements, but as Tourgée himself suggested, those words cannot be separated from his quest for racial justice in the post–Civil War United States.

Albion W. Tourgée (1838–1905) was a major force for social, legal, and literary transformation in the second half of the nineteenth century. His prominence at the time of his death can be gauged from the fact that on the Thanksgiving following the memorial service in Mayville, branches of the Niagara Movement led by W. E. B. Du Bois held memorial meetings for three "friends of freedom": William Lloyd Garrison, Frederick Douglass, and Albion Tourgée. Garrison and Douglass remain familiar names. To the extent that Tourgée is remembered at all today, it is for his Reconstruction novels *A Fool's Errand* (1879) and *Bricks without Straw* (1880) and for his role as lead counsel for the African American Homer Plessy in *Plessy v. Ferguson* (1896), the Supreme Court case on the constitutionality of state-mandated racial segregation in public facilities. Less well known is that Tourgée was a prolific writer who published more than a dozen novels and a volume of short stories, as well as nonfiction works on history, law, and politics.

An Ohio native, the son of a farmer, Tourgée enrolled at the University of Rochester in 1859 and then dropped out in 1861 to enlist in the Union Army. He was severely injured during the Battle of Manassas, but after recuperating he re-enlisted and was captured during the Battle of Perryville, spending four months in Confederate prisons before being released as part of a prisoner exchange. After the war, Tourgée moved to North Carolina with his wife, Emma Kilbourne, and devoted himself to the Reconstruction effort as a judge and politician.

While there he also wrote a number of his major Reconstruction novels, starting with *Toinette* in 1874. In 1881, he moved from North Carolina to the small town of Mayville, located on the train line from Buffalo to Chicago and a few miles from Chautauqua Institution, then emerging as a national arbiter of culture. Known as "the sage of Mayville," Tourgée wrote novels and short fiction on a range of topics, such as early Mormonism and Christian socialism. He also continued to write fiction about slavery and its legacy, including a historical novel, *Hot Plowshares* (1883), on the antislavery movement. In 1882, he launched *Our Continent: An Illustrated Weekly Magazine*, an ambitious periodical that featured fiction, poetry, and nonfiction until it folded in 1884. He continued to publish in

Figure 1. Emma K. Tourgée and Albion Winegar Tourgée, 1865. (Dolph Brothers, Erie, PA. Courtesy of the Chautauqua County Historical Society, McClurg Museum.)

a variety of journalistic outlets, notably the influential *Chicago Daily Inter Ocean*, where his widely read "Bystander" column addressed such topics as lynching, disfranchisement, civil rights, and trends in American literature. The column was reprinted in the African American press, and even as he was involved with developing arguments against "separate but equal" for the Plessy case, he collaborated with Ida B. Wells on her antilynching campaign. He also worked closely with Charles Chesnutt to build support for other African American journalistic and literary projects.

Tourgée has attracted a burst of scholarly attention in recent years. There have been two conferences devoted to his legal career and civil rights activism, as well as a 2019 conference that the coeditors organized at Chautauqua Institution on "Literary Tourgée." The past two decades have also seen two highly influential biographies of Tourgée—Mark Elliott's *Color-Blind Justice: Albion Tourgée and the Quest for Racial Equality from the Civil War to Plessy v. Ferguson* (2006), and Carolyn L. Karcher's *A Refugee from His Race: Albion W. Tourgée and His Fight against White Supremacy* (2016)—along with a volume of his writings and speeches, Mark Elliott and John David Smith's *Undaunted Radical* (2010); Carolyn Karcher's edition of *Bricks without Straw* (2009); Brook Thomas's major study *The Literature of Reconstruction* (2017), which mainly focuses on Tourgée; and Steve Luxenberg's *Separate: The Story of Plessy v. Ferguson* (2019), which looks at Tourgée's career in the context of the *Plessy* case. Much of this scholarship has addressed Tourgée's Reconstruction and civil rights activism. There has been relatively little attention to him as a literary figure or to the strong interconnections between his literary work and his work as a social reformer.

This collection—the first to address the *literary* Tourgée—aims to change the way that we view one of the most important, and still relatively neglected, writers of the nineteenth century by highlighting Tourgée's contributions as a novelist and editor and as a supporter of African American writers. Tourgée is one of the great writers of fiction about the Reconstruction era—arguably the greatest for the wide historical and geographical sweep of his novels and his ability to work with multiple points of view, whether white or Black, northern or southern, rich or poor. As Reconstruction has come to take center stage in our understanding of nineteenth-century US history—with the idea that the nation has failed to live up to the promise of Reconstruction—Tourgée can serve as our literary guide to the racial, political, and economic issues that are a legacy of slavery.

That was certainly the case in Tourgée's own time, when he was celebrated, somewhat in the manner of Harriet Beecher Stowe, as the nation's most important writer on these crucial social topics. According to Carolyn Karcher, Tourgée's *A Fool's Errand* sold several hundred thousand copies during his lifetime. Though he never achieved such popular success again, he continued to be a widely read novelist who was strongly supported by his publisher—Fords, Howard & Hulbert—which brought out his novels and nonfiction through much of the 1880s and into the 1890s. These books came festooned with blurbs culled from newspaper reviews and personal testimony, along with assertions from the publisher (which can't be completely trusted) about Tourgée's wide sales. In the unpaginated ad at the end of Tourgée's 1891 novel *Murvale Eastman: Christian Socialist*, for example, the publisher claimed that readers of Tourgée's novels "number *more than a million* of our people—North and South, East and West." Comparing Tourgée favorably to Shakespeare, Sir Walter Scott, Thackeray, and Stowe, the publisher says of his best-known novel: "It is safe to presume that every intelligent person has heard of 'A Fool's Errand,' even if he has not read that famous book which has made its author's name known all over the land." Shortly before his death in 1885, former president Ulysses S. Grant proclaimed about that novel, in a blurb that Tourgée's publisher affixed to a number of his books: "I read 'A Fool's Errand' with deep interest, and shall keep this volume in my library as a souvenir of the author, whom I remember to have met during the time he so admirably and graphically depicts." Taking advantage of Tourgée's popularity, his publisher marketed his major novels of the period—*Hot Plowshares, Figs and Thistles, A Royal Gentleman, A Fool's Errand, Bricks without Straw, John Eax,* and *Black Ice*—as "an extraordinary line of Novels" that told the story of the nation from abolitionism to Reconstruction."[2]

Reviewers of the time hailed *A Fool's Errand* and *Bricks without Straw* in particular as the two major novels of Reconstruction. The *New York Times* called *A Fool's Errand* "one of the most notable books that have appeared in this country for many years." The *New York Commercial Advertiser* agreed with that assessment and termed *Bricks without Straw* "a greater work than 'Fool's Errand.'" Referring to both of these novels, the Springfield, Massachusetts, *Republican* told its readers: "Scarcely anything in fiction so powerful has been written from a merely literary stand-point, as these books."[3] The reviewer's use of the phrase "merely literary stand-point" is worth noting, for it speaks to a certain prejudice against fiction while failing to see that, for Tourgée, there was nothing "merely" about the "literary standpoint." There is considerable evidence, beyond the many years that Tourgée devoted to his fiction writing, that he regarded the literary as just as important, if not more important, than the work he did as a judge, politician, and lawyer. At the very least, that literary work was integral to what he was trying to accomplish as a reformer.

Tourgée speaks directly to the importance of the literary, specifically fiction writing, in his 1883 *Hot Plowshares*, a novel that begins in 1848 in the Mohawk Valley of New York with the rise of the Free Soil Party and ends with the trial of John Brown. At a time when Tourgée concluded that Reconstruction had failed, he used his novel to remind readers about the main ideals of the anti-slavery struggle, which he believed should remain central to the post–Civil War period. In the preface to the novel, he makes one of his strongest arguments for the importance of fiction as a genre with implications for his current moment. "History," he says, "gives only the outlines of the world's life," and "biography both supplements and obscures History." But "fiction," he maintains, "labors under no such disadvantages. It fills out the outlines History gives, and colors and completes its pictures. . . . It vivifies the past of which History only furnishes the record." But that isn't all. Tourgée's larger point is that fiction can be part of a broader commitment to social activism and the principles of racial equality. Thus, he states that he has been writing novels inspired by "the Anti-Slavery struggle" in order to provide "a truthful picture . . . of the growth of its influence and its character as a preparation for the struggle in which those whose thought had been moulded by its sentiments were destined to engage."[4]

And it is here where Tourgée may have got into trouble with twentieth- and twenty-first-century readers. This is a writer who was doing what the critic Jane Tompkins calls "cultural work" in novels that typically were over four hundred pages.[5] Why read long didactic fiction about race relations and the failure of Reconstruction when we can read the more elusive and suggestive fiction of such writers as Charles Chesnutt and Toni Morrison? The immediate answer is that Tourgée's fiction is not so didactic after all. His best novels address large cultural issues through dialogue and conflict in the tradition of the realist novel, as Carolyn Karcher emphasizes in the introduction to her 2009 edition of *Bricks without Straw*. Amanda Anderson productively challenges today's dominant aesthetic criteria in *Bleak Liberalism* (2016), in ways that could open up new readings of Tourgée's works. His fiction manifests many of the same concerns with ethos and character that Anderson examines in her discussion of liberalism and high realism, and he employs the techniques of dialogue and argument that she identifies as a dominant feature of the political novel.[6] It is worth noting that until 2009, when Karcher brought out her edition, all modern reprints of Tourgée novels were either edited by historians or were simply reprinted in Gregg Press's series called American Novels of Muckraking, Propaganda, and Social Protest. That series included reprints of *Pactolus Prime* (1890) and *Murvale Eastman*, novels deserving close attention from a literary perspective as well. *Pactolus Prime* is one of the most provocative passing novels of the late nineteenth century, while *Murvale Eastman* features a Methodist minister who works to reconcile socialism and Christianity.

The historians John Hope Franklin and George Frederickson brought out editions of *A Fool's Errand* in 1961 and 1966, respectively, emphasizing the novel's importance to rethinking the history of Reconstruction. But what was the source of the novel's literary power? Several of our contributors wrestle with that novel from a variety of literary perspectives. The historian Otto Olsen published an edition of *Bricks without Straw* that, as with Franklin's and Frederickson's editions of *A Fool's Errand*, used the novel to tell the history of Reconstruction.[7] The novel does contribute to our understanding of Reconstruction, presenting, as Karcher emphasizes in her 2009 edition, the importance of Black perspectives and agency to the period. But it also tells a good story, works effectively with dialect, and, as several of our contributors point out, makes use of a number of literary techniques, including biblical typology in the manner of Stowe. Karcher's edition of *Bricks without Straw* is the only extant edition of a Tourgée novel that approaches it as a work of literary art. We could use more such editions of Tourgée's other major novels. We hope that this collection will generate further interest in Tourgée as a novelist, situating him in relation to other major American novelists of the period.

In his best-known statement about writing fiction during the Reconstruction and post-Reconstruction period, his 1888 "The South as a Field for Fiction," Tourgée took a backhanded slap at William Dean Howells and Henry James, claiming that for these writers "trivialities" were "the most important features of real life." He goes on to argue that the "'realists' profess to be truth-tellers, but are in fact the worst of falsifiers, since they tell only the weakest and meanest part of the grand truth which makes up the continued story of every life." The implication here is that, by contrast, Tourgée tells that "grand truth." But the emphasis of the essay is on the future of American fiction, specifically as authored by African Americans, who, he believes, have the most important story to tell about the South. Concerned that Blacks are stereotypically stock characters in much of the fiction of the day, Tourgée laments the inadequacy of racial representation in US fiction: "About the Negro as a man, with hopes, fears, and aspirations like other men, our literature is very nearly silent." For that reason, he encouraged Black authors, and he concludes the essay with a prediction: "The life of the Negro as a slave, freedman, and racial outcast offers undoubtedly the richest mine of romantic material that has opened to the English-speaking novelist since the Wizard of the North [Sir Walter Scott] discovered and depicted the common life

JUDGE ALBION W. TOURGÉE

SOLDIER   JURIST

LAWYER   NOVELIST

Author of "A Fool's Errand," "Bricks Without Straw," "Out of the
Sunset Sea," etc., will Lecture on

"The Race Problem" A Subject of Vital Interest At This Time

AT UNION PARK CONGREGATIONAL CHURCH,
Corner Washington & Ashland Boulevards

TUESDAY EVENING, APRIL 11th, 1893, at 8 o'clock

TICKETS 50 CTS.   NO RESERVED SEATS.

ALBION WINEGAR TOURGÉE, was born in Williamsfield, Ohio, in 1838. He is the son of a farmer of Huguenot descent. After studying at the Rochester University in 1859-1861, he served in the National Army in 1861-1865, was wounded at Bull Run and at Perryville, and was a prisoner in the hands of the Confederates for four months. After the war he settled as a lawyer, farmer and editor at Greensboro, N. C. He opposed the plan of reconstruction that was adopted, favoring instead the establishing of territorial governments in the seceding states. At the Loyalists' convention in Philadelphia in 1866, he prepared the report on the condition of the Southern states. He was an active member of the N. Carolina Constitutional Conventions of 1868 and 1875, and was one of the commission appointed to codify and revise the state laws. In April 1868 he was elected Judge of the Supreme Court for the seventh judicial district of North Carolina. His judicial district included the counties where the Ku-Klux Clan was most powerful and aggressive, and several unsuccessful raids were planned for his capture. In 1866-7 he published at Greensboro the *Union Register* and in 1882 he published *The Continent* a literary weekly in Philadelphia which was discontinued in 1885. His first novel, A Royal Gentleman was published in 1875. Since then he has published: A Fool's Errand; Figs and Thistles; Bricks without Straw; John Eax: Hot Plowshares; Black Ice; Button's Inn; The Veteran and his Pipe; Pactolus Prime; Murvale Eastman; and numerous other professional works, short stories and magazine articles. Since 1886 he has written weekly for the Chicago *Inter-Ocean*, "A Bystander's Notes." In addition to his literary work, he is a popular lecturer and a professor in the Buffalo Law School.

NOTE: Judge Tourgée will reply informally to any questions that may be asked.

Figure 2. Flyer, speaking engagement of Albion Winegar Tourgée on the subject of "The Race Problem," at Union Park Congregational Church on April 11, 1893. (Courtesy of the Chautauqua County Historical Society, McClurg Museum.)

of Scotland."[8] That prediction has been realized and exceeded by subsequent African American fiction writers. As two of our contributors suggest, Tourgée's prediction anticipated and arguably helped inspire the fiction of Charles Chesnutt.

Tourgée may have predicted great things for African American writing, and indeed American writing, of the future, but his own work, starting with his first novel, *Toinette*, had all along been wrestling with issues of racial representation and themes of racial equality. To take one example before turning to the essays in the collection: Tourgée demonstrates a remarkably sophisticated awareness of the cultural obstacles that literary tradition and convention could pose to African American authors in a striking scene from *Bricks without Straw*. The scene features Mollie Ainslee, a white woman from New England who has recently moved to North Carolina to instruct the freedpeople in a town called Red Wing, and Eliab Hill, a disabled Black man who serves as her assistant. Ainslee has been instructing Hill after hours, with the aim of helping him advance from his role as assistant teacher to replace her as head of the school. Despite Hill's ready acquisition of basic literacy skills and his commitment to learning, however, he has unexpected difficulty moving to a higher level of comprehension. Ainslee attributes this slowness to "the momentum which centuries of intelligence and freedom give to the mind of the learner" and reflects on "how unconscious is the acquisition of the great bulk of that knowledge which goes to make up the Caucasian manhood of the nineteenth century"—a description that resonates with Isabel Wilkerson's recent account of how a racial caste system has long been operative in the United States. Hill explains the impediments he encounters when he reads a work such as Tennyson's "The Princess" (1847), focusing on the line "Tears, idle tears, I know not what they mean!" He can read the literal words, he explains, but they do not convey meaning to him in the same way that they do to Ainslee: "I cannot make out what is meant by 'idle' tears, nor whether the author means to say that he does not know what 'tears' mean, or only 'idle' tears, or whether he does not understand such a display of grief because it *is* idle."[9] Ainslee suggests that the line might mean all these things, but Hill remains frustrated by the ambiguity and challenges his teacher to recognize the unconscious knowledge that enables her immediate comprehension. (Tourgée describes this as knowledge of *leges non scriptae* [197], that is, unwritten cultural norms.) She knows the author's "life and ways" as Hill does not; they share a "race and class"; "his thoughts are your thoughts, his life has been your life" (196).

Hill relates his inability to grasp the meaning of the poem to a recent crisis, when the community leaders at Red Wing fail to anticipate the response of a nearby white community to their procession at the election. The newly enfranchised voters from Red Wing thought "it was nice to be free, and have our own music and march under that dear old flag to do the work of free men and citizens."[10] Ainslee is far from embracing an idealized view of the southern past, but she has readily understood how the procession will affect local whites: as a reminder of what some experience as "Death in Life," in Tennyson's apt phrase, after losing the Civil War. The sharply divergent experiences of Black and white southerners produce conflicting hermeneutics, and Hill despairs of bridging the gap, at least among the adults. It is with this in mind that he refuses more of Ainslee's instruction and, unbeknownst to her, proceeds with his own course of solitary study whose aim at first remains mysterious, though its effect is to elevate his authority in the Black community at Red Wing and exacerbate tensions with local whites. This scene offers a nuanced portrayal of slavery's legacy of "caste" and the role of literary culture in both reproducing and challenging it.

But the scene also points to an issue that has troubled some readers of Tourgée and is taken up in some of the essays: the matter of white paternalism. Tourgée's post–Civil War career shows a remarkable commitment to social justice and antiracism. But did he think of himself as a white savior? Consider the letter quoted at the beginning of our introduction, in which he remarks on his "overwhelming pity for the inconceivable woes of the colored people in the United States." A critical reader could view Tourgée's use of the word "pity," along with his lumping together of "the colored people of the United States" into a single body, as condescending. Such a reader might even take the wording to imply that Blacks en masse needed to be rescued by white people like Ainslee—although Eliab Hill's accomplishments after he strikes out on his own suggest a quite different conclusion. As the essays here demonstrate, Tourgée's full oeuvre presents a striking range of Black characters and experiences. Even so, his most popular novel in his own time, A Fool's Errand, could be read as a rescue narrative that played to the beliefs of many white readers that Blacks were essentially helpless. The novel's popularity arguably says more about the limitations of Tourgée's white readership than about his own. Still—and not unlike William Lloyd Garrison—Tourgée was a radical who sometimes could be condescending. As John Ernest suggests in his essay in the collection, some white radicals clearly had limits to how they thought about Black people. But as Ernest also suggests, those limits can be taken as one of the large subjects of A Fool's Errand. We don't make claims for Tourgée's ability to transcend white privilege, but we would emphasize that there were few nineteenth-century white Americans more committed to improving the situation of Black people. Moreover, as a novelist he was committed to developing not a single Black perspective but multiple Black perspectives, sometimes even in conflict. The challenge was to do justice to those perspectives in the larger context of the story he wanted to tell about America. Over a writing career of approximately thirty years, Tourgée's fiction took up that challenge.

We have divided the seventeen essays that constitute this collection into three parts—Race, Citizenship, Nation—that address key concerns of Tourgée's writings, with the understanding that the sections are hardly self-contained. Some of the essays could be placed into different sections, and all are in conversation about what makes Tourgée such a compelling writer of fiction.

Tourgée has been celebrated by Carolyn Karcher for developing a "remarkable alliance with African Americans" in his battles for Black civil rights from his time as a judge in North Carolina to his pro bono legal work in the *Plessy v. Ferguson* case. But as the essays in Part 1 show, Tourgée was also engaged with the literary complexities of racial representation. Toni Morrison famously remarked that African Americans can be regarded as the "ghost in the machine," having an almost unconscious impact on "the choices, the language, the structure" of white-authored US literature even as they are relegated to minor roles when they are present at all.[11] But Blacks are fully present in Tourgée's most compelling fiction, actively involved in the effort to forge their way in a nation that had a long history of regarding them as marginal or as property. As Robert Levine argues in his reading of *Toinette*, Tourgée learned how to evoke that history through his engagement with Nathaniel Hawthorne's gothic fiction, especially *The House of the Seven Gables* (1851). In her essay on *Bricks without Straw*, Nancy Bentley comes at this history from a very different perspective in her exploration of that novel's account of Black kinship. The history of slavery and racism in the United States meant that kinship for the freedpeople in particular had complicated valances at odds with the legal codes of the bureaucratic state. Black kinship is also crucial to DeLisa Hawkes's analysis of Tourgée's great passing novel, *Pactolus Prime*, which may also be the first American novel to make the case that Black people should receive reparations for the crime of slavery. In the gothic mode of *Toinette*, *Pactolus Prime* brings hidden family histories to the surface, with the implied suggestion that maybe all Americans are racially passing.

Tourgée's racial fictions impressed a number of Black readers, perhaps most profoundly the fiction writer and essayist Charles Chesnutt, who, as Tess Chakkalakal shows, developed an instructive literary friendship with Tourgée. Jennifer Greeson also takes up the literary relationship between Tourgée and Chesnutt, provocatively suggesting that the figure of Tourgée himself informed one of Chesnutt's most important white characters. Tourgée deserves greater attention from readers interested in race in American literary history for his depictions of Black characters and his influence on African American writing. But in a useful cautionary essay focused on Tourgée's most famous novel, John Ernest raises questions about Tourgée's subject position as a white man, arguing that we may be going too far in conceiving of Tourgée as somehow able to transcend white privilege in a white supremacist culture. Ernest's reading of *A Fool's Errand* therefore emphasizes the limits of the white radical imagination. However limited the imagination informing *A Fool's Errand*, there is no question that Tourgée in both his fiction and legal work remained committed to the proposition that Blacks should be granted full rights to citizenship.

As the essays in Part 2 show, the nature and contours of citizenship were at the heart of the unsettled postwar nation and Tourgée's fiction. Sandra Gustafson traces the core republican principles that run through his published work, from his earliest political statements to his Reconstruction fiction and beyond. Gustafson's essay concludes with a discussion of Tourgée's depictions of class conflict, religious pluralism, and citizenship in *Murvale Eastman, Christian Socialist*. Kenneth Warren's contribution to the volume offers a fine-grained analysis of Tourgée's approach to realism and romance. The essay situates Tourgée's literary vision vis-à-vis Alexis de Tocqueville's discussion of democratic aesthetics and contrasts it with theories of realism offered by William Dean Howells and Henry James. Warren provocatively concludes that Tourgée was right to perceive a connection between southern culture and romance in terms of class domination. The biblical language of *Bricks without Straw* provides a lens that focalizes the richly detailed treatment of "incomplete emancipation" in Christine Holbo's discussion of that novel. Holbo highlights the novel's portrayal of a racialized caste society in the process of (re)emerging in the post–Civil War years and reveals how Tourgée used the language of the Hebrew Bible to point the nation in a different direction.

Religious diversity presented other challenges to concepts of US citizenship, with the plural marriage practices embraced by the Church of Latter-Day Saints offering a controversial instance. In her essay on *Button's Inn* (1887), Molly Ball follows the thread of Tourgée's complicated plot to highlight nonexclusive notions of marriage, property, and invention. Tourgée's main target in the novel, Ball argues, is the possessive individualism that permeated so many aspects of American society. The final two essays in this section return to the nexus of race, literature, and the law with respect to contested notions of citizenship. Almas Khan's essay connects Tourgée's literary criticism to the rise of legal realism. Drawing on a broad range of work, Khan uncovers the shared roots of literary and legal realism in Tourgée's oeuvre. The section's closing essay, by Brook Thomas, a leading Tourgée scholar, reads *With Gauge and Swallows, Attorneys* (1889) as a "legal romance." Thomas argues that Tourgée rightly saw the potential for law to be more than a contributor to systemic racism; it could be a means to the kind of social reform that would expand the rights of citizenship. The literary form of *Gauge* offers clues as to how the law might be reimagined in the service of progressive values. In Tourgée's words, the novel seeks to imagine "what the law *ought* to be," rather than depict "what it was." These very sentiments became central to Tourgée's support of Homer Plessy in his quest for the full rights of citizenship.

In Part 3, the contributors consider Tourgée's conception of the nation from the Civil War to the late nineteenth century. In the immediate post–Civil War years, rebuilding the nation in a more unified and equitable way was a central aim of the Freedmen's Bureau. Sarah Chinn's discussion of *Bricks without Straw* focuses on the bureau's literal and figurative connections to amputation, specifically the white veteran amputees who were overrepresented among its employees. Noting that the bureau was headed by General Oliver O. Howard, who lost an arm in the Civil War, and connecting Howard to Hesden Le Moyne, the southern veteran in *Bricks* who did as well, Chinn draws out how amputation figured the permanent alteration of both the body and the nation. While missing limbs stood for what had been sacrificed, the developing railroads of the later nineteenth century promised not only the reintegration but the further expansion of the United States. In a comparative reading of Tourgée's *Figs and Thistles: A Romance of the Western Reserve* (1879) and María Amparo Ruiz de Burton's *The Squatter and the Don* (1886), Annemarie Mott Ewing focuses on the mythologies of the West undergirding a certain postwar vision of the United States. Ewing shows that both novels reject these mythological views to instead emphasize imperialist expansion and corporate greed as driving forces tied to the railroad. Tourgée's alternative vision of a more socially just US permeated his ambitious literary periodical *Our Continent* (1882–1884). Mary Hale's essay characterizes the "decidedly nationalist agenda" of *Our Continent* as an inclusive and equitable vision of the nation-to-be. In order to achieve that vision, Tourgée challenged the cynical portraits of US politics offered by Henry Adams and John Hay, whose novels *Democracy* (1880) and *The Bread-winners* (1883) he critiqued in the pages of his magazine.

The last two essays in this section return to the theme of race as it relates to nation. In his provocative discussion of *A Fool's Errand*, *Bricks without Straw*, and *Pactolus Prime*, Gregory Laski teases out how revenge, as mediated by

Shakespeare's *Hamlet,* emerged as a large theme in Tourgée's writings as his hopes for Reconstruction crumbled. Laski concludes with a nod to the revenge theme in Thomas Dixon's white supremacist fiction, and it is Dixon's engagement with Tourgée that Alex Leslie examines in the closing essay of this volume. Leslie calls attention to the way publishers and reviewers paired the novels of Tourgée and Dixon as complementary views of the Civil War and its aftermath. The effect, Leslie emphasizes, was to create a false equivalence that undermined the very racial justice that had emerged as Tourgée's goal during the war and remained central to his life's work for more than thirty years. Sadly, in the opening decades of the twentieth century, Dixon's vision of the Civil War and Reconstruction had captured the imaginations of white America and was taken by many as "true." But interest in Tourgée remained, and there was an initial resurgence of interest during the civil rights period. As Mark Elliott notes in his afterword, recent work on Tourgée, including the essays in this volume, speak to the vitality of Tourgée's fiction. At a time of deep polarization in US culture about race, citizenship, and nation, we need Tourgée's writings more than ever.

Notes

1. The tribute was published as a pamphlet titled "In Memoriam: Tributes of Respect by Colored Citizens of Chicago to the Memory of Judge Albion W. Tourgée. Adopted by the Illinois Division of the Niagara Movement and the Appomattox Club and presented on the occasion of the funeral obsequies at Mayville, NY, by Mrs. Ida B. Wells-Barnett, representing the above named organizations." W. E. B. Du Bois is listed on the back of the pamphlet as general secretary of the Niagara Movement. There is no publication information.

2. This paragraph draws on the unpaginated back pages of Fords, Howard, & Hulbert's 1891 edition of Tourgée's *Murvale Eastman: Christian Socialist.*

3. These reviews were reprinted in the unpaginated front and back pages of Fords, Howard, & Hulbert's numerous editions of Tourgée's novels. For the first two, see the front unpaginated page of the 1881 edition of *Figs and Thistles: A Romance of the Western Reserve;* for the third, see a back unpaginated page from the 1881 edition of *A Royal Gentleman.*

4. Albion W. Tourgée, *Hot Plowshares* (New York: Fords, Howard, & Hulbert, 1883), ii, iv.

5. On literary work as cultural work, see Jane Tompkins, *Sensational Designs: The Cultural Work of American Fiction, 1770–1860* (New York: Oxford University Press, 1985).

6. Amanda Anderson, *Bleak Liberalism* (Chicago: University of Chicago Press, 2016).

7. See Albion R. Tourgée, *A Fool's Errand,* ed. John Hope Franklin (Cambridge, MA: Harvard University Press, 1961); Albion R. Tourgée, *A Fool's Errand,* ed. George M.

Fredrickson (New York: Harper Torchbooks, 1966); and Albion R. Tourgée, *Bricks without Straw*, ed. Otto H. Olsen (Baton Rouge: Louisiana State University Press, 1973).

8. Albion W. Tourgée, "The South as a Field for Fiction" (1888), in *Undaunted Radical: The Selected Writings and Speeches of Albion W. Tourgée*, ed. Mark Elliott and John David Smith (Baton Rouge: Louisiana State University Press, 2010), 205, 209, 208, 209.

9. Albion W. Tourgée, *Bricks without Straw*, ed. Carolyn L. Karcher (Durham, NC: Duke University Press, 2009), 194. On caste and race, see Isabel Wilkerson, *Caste: The Origins of Our Discontents* (New York: Random House, 2020).

10. Tourgée, *Bricks without Straw*, ed. Karcher, 197.

11. Carolyn L. Karcher, *A Refugee from His Race: Albion W. Tourgée and His Fight against White Supremacy* (Chapel Hill: University of North Carolina Press, 2016), xi; Toni Morrison, "Unspoken Things Unspoken: The Afro-American Presence in American Literature" (1989), in *Criticism and the Color Line: Desegregating American Literary Studies*, ed. Henry B. Wonham (New Brunswick, NJ: Rutgers University Press, 1996), 23.

I   Race

1

Gothic Reconstruction

Hawthorne's House in Tourgée's
Toinette *and* A Royal Gentleman

Robert S. Levine

Albion Tourgée began his career as a novelist not too long after the *Atlantic Monthly* initiated a campaign to canonize Nathaniel Hawthorne (who died in 1864) as the nation's greatest writer. The *Atlantic*'s editors printed numerous essays about Hawthorne, along with much of his unpublished writings. Perhaps because of this exposure in the major cultural journal of the day, Hawthorne had a significant influence on Tourgée's emergence as a novelist, especially in providing him with a model for writing historical fiction in a gothic mode. Of all Hawthorne's novels, *The House of the Seven Gables* (1851), a romance about the impact of past crimes in family histories on the contemporary moment, especially helped Tourgée consider how "the wrong-doing of one generation," as Hawthorne put it, "lives into the successive ones."[1] Nowhere was Tourgée more effective in exploring historical continuities, and thus the difficulty of bringing about the social change called Reconstruction, than in his first novel, *Toinette*, drafted during the late 1860s, published in 1874, and then republished in revised versions in 1879 and 1881 (when he retitled it *A Royal Gentleman*). Set mainly in North Carolina, the novel in all three versions is almost entirely devoid of literary references, with the key exception of a bow to *The House of the Seven Gables*. This essay examines the art of the gothic novel of blood, property, and romance as Tourgée learned it from Hawthorne.

Hawthorne was not known for his antislavery views and in fact mocked abolitionists and Abraham Lincoln. But his 1851 *The House of the Seven Gables* depicted a long history of conflict in a "house divided" and indirectly addressed the problem of race as well. Perhaps most important to Tourgée, it underscored connections between the past and present in a manner that helped him better understand the challenges of Reconstruction. Writing at the time when Tourgée first drafted *Toinette*, Frederick Douglass declared: "Let not the connection of the present with the past be ignored nor forgotten."[2] Slavery may have been abolished, but it would not go away quickly. Tourgée came to a similar conclusion while working as a Reconstruction judge in North Carolina, and as a novelist he thought in terms of what I'm calling gothic Reconstruction, seeking to take account of the crimes of the past while imagining a way forward.

A few words on the gothic in Hawthorne's *House*: The novel, set during Hawthorne's contemporary moment, tells the story of how the aristocratic Colonel Pyncheon, during the time of the Salem witch crisis of 1692, appropriated land from the plebeian Matthew Maule by having him executed as a witch. Pyncheon subsequently built the House of the Seven Gables on that land in an effort to perpetuate his "race" for "future generations," only to die under mysterious circumstances on the day he celebrates the opening of the house. Pyncheon's act of violation—of killing for property—haunts the novel and the house itself. The house is troubled by other events as well. One hundred years before the present action of the novel, a Maule descendant, also named Matthew, used mesmerism to make a Pyncheon descendant, Alice, "Maule's slave," and he inadvertently kills her.[3] So there is a history of a double set of violations: the founding Pyncheon's murder of a Maule and then a Maule's killing of a Pyncheon. There are other moments from the past that haunt the house, including a robbery and apparent murder over a missing deed involving members of the Pyncheon family. It wouldn't be too much of a stretch to say that Tourgée, in thinking about how to transpose the terms of this historical romance to pre–Civil War, Civil War, and Reconstruction North Carolina thought of the Pyncheons as representing the master class and the Maules as something like enslaved Black people. In *House*, Hawthorne implies such racialized links by depicting the eighteenth-century Pyncheons as actual slave owners, by having their Black servant/slave Scipio treat the second Matthew Maule as if he were enslaved, by describing some of the Maule characters as "black," and by working with genetic imagery to link the supposedly pure-blood white Pyncheons to their pure-blood (and degenerating) chickens.[4] The conflict between the Maules and the Pyncheons takes place over a nearly 160-year period, but *House* concludes in romance fashion with a marriage between a Maule and a Pyncheon. Consistent with historical romance, the marriage appears to resolve the struggle between the two families, though the gothic mode hints at continued hauntings. The mix of gothic and romance inspired but also confounded Tourgée, leading him to bring out three versions of *Toinette* with three different endings.

Tourgée claimed to have begun *Toinette* in the late 1860s "as a recreation merely, when the Miracle of Emancipation was fresh to the minds and hearts of us all."[5] He published the novel in 1874 under the pseudonym of Henry Churton, after working as a self-described carpetbagger judge in North Carolina who supported the Republicans' Reconstruction programs, which he hoped would bring about racial equality in the former Confederate states. He revised the ending of the 1874 *Toinette* and published the novel under his own name in 1879, the year he published *A Fool's Errand* and had come to lament the naiveté of northern "fools," like himself, who had failed to anticipate that southern whites would resist making changes to their racial caste system. In the wake of the popular success of *Fool's* and *Bricks without Straw* (1880), Tourgée published one more version of *Toinette*, in 1881, retitling it *A Royal Gentleman*, thereby moving the focus, at least in the title, from the slave woman Toinette to her former master.

On the evidence of these three publications and revisions, it seems safe to say that Tourgée regarded *Toinette*, in whatever guise, as worthy of his (and his readers') continued attention. In my view, it is one of the finest gothic novels published in the nineteenth-century United States for the way it shows how the history of property (in people and land) haunts the present moment.[6] The few critics who have studied the novel have done so by contextualizing it in relation to the legal, social, and political debates surrounding Reconstruction. These contexts are important, but in the spirit of a collection on the *literary* Tourgée, I want to foreground his creative use of the gothic, as mediated by Hawthorne, to explore issues of sexual violation and blood at the time of Reconstruction.

Central to my analysis is the gothic trope of haunting, which Hawthorne and Tourgée use in their respective novels to suggest the presentness of the past. In her provocative *Ghostly Matters* (1997), Avery F. Gordon argues for the social resonance and reformist potential of that trope. "Ghostly matters are part of social life," she says. "If we want to study social life well, and if in addition we want to contribute, in however small a measure, to changing it, we must learn how to identify the hauntings and reckon with ghosts." With its hauntings and ghosts, gothic fiction can perform a recuperative sort of history, helping refashion the social landscape by exposing readers to "unresolved social violence."[7] As gothic romancers, Hawthorne and Tourgée share a conviction that fiction can participate in social reform, making clear that any effort to reshape the present requires an honest and sometimes uncomfortable engagement with the violence that continues to haunt it.

Like *The House of the Seven Gables*, *Toinette* is a ghost story about a house that is haunted by past crimes, with at least one such crime being the practice of slavery.[8] The house that is the focus of *Toinette* is Lovett Lodge, which has a vexed history that we learn about in the first half of the novel. The novel begins several years before the Civil War, in 1858, and ends during the immediate post–Civil War years of Reconstruction. Before reaching that ending, the novel focuses on connections between 1858 and events of two decades earlier, with a Hawthornean emphasis on repetition. In the past and present of the novel, that which is repeated is the sexual violation of enslaved Black women.

All versions of *Toinette* begin on Christmas Day, as would Tourgée's later *Pactolus Prime* (1890). Manuel Hunter, a North Carolina lawyer and owner of enslaved people, gives his son, Geoffrey, two holiday gifts: his serving-maid Toinette, a light-complected enslaved woman approximately sixteen years old, and the family plantation at nearby Lovett Lodge. For reasons that become clear later in the novel, Hunter's cook, Mabel, is furious about this development. Initially Geoffrey regards the white-to-the-eye Toinette as potentially bringing a high price at the slave market. But he finds himself increasingly attracted to her, and he devises a plan, in the manner of a Pygmalion, "to make the gal a doll" (40) by buying her nice clothes and educating her. Toinette seems as attracted to Geoffrey as he is to her. This burgeoning interracial romance, it is worth emphasizing, occurs in the corrupt setting of a slave plantation. In that respect, the scene of romance is also a scene of violation, as Tourgée shows when the novel takes a gothic turn.

Soon after Geoffrey begins educating Toinette, he learns that Lovett Lodge has a "secret room" (67). In an effort to provide a "full understanding" (68) of the room's history, the narrator first takes the reader on an architectural tour. Like Hawthorne's House of the Seven Gables, Lovett Lodge has numerous gables, and "each gable was bisected by a huge chimney built upon the outside of the house" (68). The secret room has a hidden entrance and is furnished with "a bed and a small dressing-case" (71). Geoffrey likes the idea that he can educate the attractive enslaved woman in a secret room with a bed; not surprisingly, Toinette soon becomes pregnant.

As subsequent events reveal, the room is haunted by a prior violation that speaks to that pregnancy, for Toinette and other enslaved people at Lovett Lodge begin to see what they believe is a ghost. Toinette informs Geoffrey that she viewed "something like a woman, only so tall and white, an' with eyes that burned like coals of fire, lookin' straight at me, as ef it wanted to jes git hold o' me an' kill me dead" (84). (As Toinette becomes better educated, she stops speaking in dialect.) Geoffrey mocks her fears, while wondering if there's a connection between the sighting of a ghost and his discovery of the secret room. He even comes to feel that "hostile eyes were gazing at him through the window of the sitting-room" (88). And then near-tragedy ensues: Geoffrey shoots at what he now perceives as a ghost, and when he checks on Toinette finds her in a pool of blood lying by her dead dog. They have both been stabbed. Geoffrey staunches the bleeding, and a doctor saves her life. The stabbing initiates a series of chapters in which different characters tell Geoffrey what they know about the historical past as it might bear on the attack. Those who tell their stories about the history of Lovett Lodge include the doctor, a working-class white woman of the neighborhood named Betty Certain, and Geoffrey's father. It soon becomes apparent that what had seemed like violence perpetrated by a "ghost" was in fact a misplaced effort to put an end to a cycle of slave masters violating enslaved women.

While Hawthorne begins *The House of the Seven Gables* with a history of the gabled house, Tourgée provides the history of the gabled Lovett Lodge shortly after the shocking stabbing of Toinette. The story is complicated but basically goes like this: Twenty years or so earlier, Arthur Lovett, at the time around the same age as Geoffrey, fell in love with (or raped) "a young quadroon woman of remarkable beauty" (116) on his father's North Carolina plantation, and they had several children, including Toinette. This woman, named Belle, was legally the slave of Arthur's father. At the son's request, Belle and the children were taken to New York and freed, but when Belle returns to North Carolina to claim their freedom, the town's whites refuse to recognize it, at least in part because of their disapproval of the interracial relationship between Arthur and Belle. At this point, Arthur, who takes on Belle and the children as his trustees, builds Lovett Lodge, making the secret room part of the architectural plan so he can spend time with Belle without raising the enmity of people in his household and community. (It's also a place where the man who was still regarded as a slave master could have sexual relations with the woman who was still regarded as enslaved.) Subsequent events echo the key events of Hawthorne's *House*, as Tourgée clearly intended.

Among the multiple narrators of the history of Lovett Lodge, the doctor, in describing an episode, abruptly makes a surprising and seemingly irrelevant literary allusion, referring to the "king of suggesters" who happens to be "the author of *The House with* [*sic*] *Seven Gables*" (129). Such was Hawthorne's fame at the time of the publication of *Toinette* that Tourgée doesn't have to name the author. But through the doctor's story he moves directly from the allusion to Hawthorne's *House* to an account of Arthur's death that underscores the influence of Hawthorne's novel. For reasons initially mysterious, Arthur plans to marry the working-class woman Betty Certain. The night before the marriage, he retreats into his library, and as the doctor recounts: "There was no disturbance here that night, but as he did not make his appearance at the usual time next morning the door was forced open, and in a great arm-chair, which was his favorite seat, they found him, stone dead" (129). The opening chapter of *House* describes how Colonel Pyncheon had been found dead in his library in "an oaken elbow-chair."[9] Pyncheon died from either a curse from Matthew Maule, an attack by a Maule avenger, or (most likely) a stroke. Lovett dies from a stabbing, supposedly from a ghost. Because many in the community believed Lovett Lodge to be haunted, Geoffrey's crafty lawyer father was able to purchase it at a bargain rate.

Tourgée's storytelling moves back and forth between the present and the past. In the present, Toinette needs considerable time to recover from her wounds. She is briefly visited by Mabel, the cook at her former residence, who lashes out at her, declaring, "Yes jes' Mass'r Geoffrey Hunter's nigger, body an' soul" (155). Mabel's cruelty leads Toinette to think that Geoffrey is the only person who cares about her. But Betty Certain, the woman who years earlier had been on the verge of marrying Arthur Lovett, seems to care, and she remains at the lodge to nurse the wounded Toinette, remarking at one point that she looks somewhat like Belle, who had disappeared after Arthur's murder. As in *House*, which also moves back and forth between the present and the past, there is much in the novel about property and missing deeds. The Pyncheons over a 160-year period search for an Indian deed that supposedly would have given the family thousands of acres in Maine; that missing deed led Jaffrey Pyncheon, at least a decade before he became a respected judge, to frame his cousin Clifford for murder. The deeds in *Toinette* are more about human property but also about the ownership of Lovett Lodge. The details are baroque, but we learn that Arthur Lovett did the paperwork to free Belle and that Betty Certain had a central role in the past relationship between Arthur Lovett and Belle.

Betty eventually reveals all to Geoffrey. She had agreed to marry Arthur Lovett, whom she loved, so that he could use the cover of a marriage between two white people to continue his relationship with Belle. He is killed right before the wedding by a woman wearing one of Betty's dresses, and mystery remains, at least until the present of the novel, about the identity of the killer. As it turns out, Mabel, the cook working for Geoffrey's father, is Belle herself, having returned to the area to watch over her daughter, Toinette (who is legally free, according to papers in a "secret drawer" [205] at Lovett Lodge). In a chilling scene, Belle confronts Betty and wildly declares that she (Belle) is "the ghost, the terrible ghost—the murderer of Arthur—the mutilator of Toinette" (264). Her eyes "two fiercely burning orbs" (265), Belle boasts that she had killed Arthur because he had betrayed her by choosing to marry a white woman, and now, years later, had attempted to kill her daughter "to save her from a worse fate" (278) of being a white man's concubine. In response, Betty reveals that her marriage to Arthur was intended as a façade—a front—enabling the plantation master to continue his romance with Belle. Aghast at the extent of her misunderstanding, Belle runs into the woods with a poniard that had once belonged to Arthur. Betty finds her dead from stab wounds in a nearby cave.

Belle, for good reason, misunderstood the intentions of Arthur in wanting to marry Betty. Misunderstanding is crucial to *House*'s second key event: the descendent Matthew Maule's inadvertent killing of Alice Pyncheon sixty years after the founding of the House because he incorrectly interpreted "her admiring glance" as aristocratic condescension toward a "brute beast" of the working classes. Desirous of revenging himself on Alice for something she didn't do, he metaphorically violates her sexually, using mesmerism to enter what Hawthorne terms her "holy of holies."[10] Alice dies from pneumonia when Maule mesmerically orders her to attend his wedding on a cold, rainy evening; her spirit continues to haunt the House of the Seven Gables in the figure of Alice's posies and the sounds of her harpsichord. The double hauntings (of the elder Matthew Maule and Alice Pyncheon) cast shadows over the relationship developing in the novel's present between Holgrave (secretly a Maule) and Phoebe Pyncheon. However, Hawthorne's romance raises the hope that these descendants can somehow get past the repetitions of history and forge a redemptive romance—that the house divided can, in effect, be reconstructed. Tourgée raises similar hopes about breaking away from the repetitions of his house divided.

In *House*, the Pyncheons and Maules reconcile through marriage. As Walter Benn Michaels and others have observed, the marriage works to secure property.[11] The evil Judge Pyncheon dies in the way of his progenitor Colonel Pyncheon (probably from a stroke), his son dies shortly thereafter, and as a result the Pyncheon property falls to the formerly poor brother and sister Clifford and Hepzibah Pyncheon. They now own the House of the Seven Gables and the judge's country home, to which they retreat with the besotted Holgrave (who reveals himself to be the surviving Maule) and Phoebe Pyncheon. The novel ends with the descendant of the man whose property had been appropriated in the historical past marrying a distant relative of the appropriators, with the promise that all of the land and money will fall to the happy couple once the elderly brother and sister die. Because the novel so pointedly raises questions about claims to property and even, through the Pyncheon obsession with a missing Indian deed, raises the larger question of whether whites had the right to appropriate land from Native Americans, there is something troubling about the happy ending: the romance side of the novel (the reconciliation between the conflicting parties through marriage) seems in conflict with the gothic side (histories of human violations and appropriations of property).

At the end of *House*, Holgrave reveals that papers hidden for nearly 160 years behind the portrait of Colonel Pyncheon are worthless. This was the Indian deed that Judge Jaffrey Pyncheon believed Clifford knew about and that had led him to frame his cousin. By contrast, in *Toinette* legal papers stashed away in the secret room and elsewhere allow Toinette to claim her freedom. We don't see the precise workings of all this, but three or four years after her mother's suicide, with the country in the midst of the Civil War, Toinette lives as a free woman in Oberlin, Ohio, passing as a white widow with a white son. She does not tell her neighbors about her mixed-race status because even "in that part of the nation, which boasted of its freedom and equality," her Black ancestry would have made her "a Pariah" (311).[12]

Working in the mode of Hawthornean gothic romance, Tourgée offers the possibility of some sort of redemption between whites and Blacks, masters and slaves, by following the Toinette-Geoffrey story to the end of the Civil War and into Reconstruction. In a key scene in all three versions of the novel, Toinette, who decides to volunteer as a Union nurse in Virginia, meets up with Geoffrey at an outdoor Civil War hospital. Fighting on the Confederate side, he has been blinded by his wounds. Toinette feels compassion for her former master; Geoffrey, even while lying gravely wounded on a hospital bed, cruelly attempts to reassert his hierarchical power over Toinette. In an improbable turn of events, Abraham Lincoln shows up at the hospital, takes pity on the wounded Confederate soldier and the woman who still cares about him, and arranges to have Geoffrey and Toinette taken to Washington, DC, to consult with a leading eye surgeon. That surgeon restores Geoffrey's sight. Will his new eyesight allow him to see? Will the end of the war allow for a happy marriage between the former master and slave that, in the manner of the happy resolution in Hawthorne's *House*, could somehow redeem the troubled history of the Lovetts, Hunters, and Belle's family, as well as speak to the possibility of the larger national program of reconciliation and reform called Reconstruction? Writing soon after a war that killed hundreds of thousands of Americans yet still seemed not to have resolved the plight of the freedpeople, Tourgée found himself wrestling with the form of gothic romance. In the spirit of what I am calling gothic Reconstruction, his three different endings, in his three different versions of *Toinette*, trace his growing disillusionment with northern Republicans for their failure of historical imagination. In his final version, Tourgée to some extent also takes on Hawthorne.[13]

Tourgée published the first version of *Toinette* in 1874, when he would have had good reason to despair about the failure of Reconstruction. But he asserted in the prefaces to both his 1874 and 1881 versions that he had drafted the novel in the years immediately after the war, when he still believed that emancipation and the Union victory promised to bring about great changes in the nation. Working with literary romance, Tourgée in the first version of *Toinette* expresses these hopes through a marriage between Geoffrey and Toinette that is as improbable as a reconciling marriage between a Pyncheon and a Maule. After fighting for the Confederacy, Geoffrey remains obsessed with Toinette, and he tracks her down in Boston, where she's performing as a chanteuse in a peace jubilee under the name of Madame Lovett (in this way she takes the name of both her father and the property she inherited). When Geoffrey recognizes the singing "white-robed figure" (498) as Toinette, he faints and once again loses his vision. Toinette comes to his aid, and Geoffrey announces that "even with blinded eyes I now see—see that I was blinded with pride and folly before. Only now—now when it is too late—I see how essential to my peace was my love, and how adorable is its object!" (507). But it's not too late: Toinette takes him in with her/their son, and in a plot turn probably taken from *Jane Eyre* (1847), Toinette declares her love to her blinded former master. The novel ends, as does Hawthorne's *House*, with the suggestion that the conflicting parties—the formerly enslaved woman and the former slave master, whose sight slowly returns—will marry, and that as a Jane Eyre figure Toinette will give up her singing career to care for her new husband. As in *House*, property has been secured (Toinette now "owns" herself and Lovett Lodge), and the prospects look good for the beginnings of racial and even sectional reconciliation in the United States. That said, the novel's more problematic suggestion is that Toinette will choose to pass as a white woman in order to serve her former master and that racial hierarchies will remain just as intransigent in post–Civil War America. In that regard, the novel's happy ending seems out of sync with the novel's darker themes. Tourgée took a different tack five years later.

Tourgée brought out a second version of *Toinette* in 1879, the year he published *A Fool's Errand*. With its horse chases and invocations of the past, *Fool's*, too, works with the gothic, making it clear that racial violations and hierarchies from the past live on into the present in a post–Civil War North Carolina society obsessed with upholding the racial caste system. As the title of the novel suggests, Tourgée had become disillusioned with Reconstruction, pointing to the failure of northern Republicans to understand the southern white psyche. That failure, he believed, ultimately hurt Black people. There is no happy ending for the novel's main character, the Fool (Tourgée's version of his own naive self), and no happy ending for the formerly enslaved people of North Carolina. Tourgée's more jaded take on Reconstruction leads to a very different ending for the 1879 *Toinette*, which he published under his own name, hoping for greater sales as a result of the popular success of *Fool's*. In this version, the former master and former enslaved woman fail to reconcile. Toinette emerges as a "musical celebrity" at the novel's end, singing some of the songs she had learned from Geoffrey "when the garlands of love were twined so thick about her life that they quite hid the shackles of the slave."[14] But for most of the novel she was an enslaved woman whose life to some extent was a repetition of her mother's. The novel leaves the reader with a relatively sad account of a light-complected Black singer alone in a northern city who will probably choose to pass.

The 1881 version provides a clearer, more assertive sense of resolution, but not of the romance variety. This version, in the manner of the ending of Hawthorne's *House*, places a greater emphasis on Toinette's acquisition of property. But as is consistent with *A Fool's Errand*, Tourgée seems increasingly interested in exploring the white psyche in order to show, somewhat sympathetically, why it was that southern whites resisted Reconstruction. In an odd and disturbing move, he changed the title of *Toinette* to *A Royal Gentleman*, remarking in a new preface (incorrectly, I think) that Toinette is "not the pivotal person on whom the whole action of the drama turns." That person, he says, is the white master Geoffrey Hunter. Tourgée concludes the preface by warning readers of what he terms the "startling" thrust of the argument he's making in this version through the revised ending: "that the dominant race suffered greater loss from the relation of slavery than the servile one, without any of that compensating development which the latter received."[15] Here Tourgée once again seems to be talking back to northern Republicans for their imaginative failure to understand the perspective of defeated white southerners. Yet the actual ending belies the overall reactionary claims of the preface, for it foregrounds Toinette as the key character of the novel—her mother's daughter, as it were—while indicting southern slave culture for its malevolence and obtuseness.

In this final version, Toinette does not go North, at least not yet. After the war, she returns to her small town in North Carolina to lay claim to Lovett Lodge. Property that had been denied her before the war—in herself and in her rightful inheritance of the lodge—has been restored. She is accompanied by her (and Geoffrey's) son, and shortly after their arrival Geoffrey, who does not initially recognize the boy, rescues him from drowning. That sets the stage for what could have been a hopeful reconciliation between the former master and his former slave in the manner of the romance ending of *House*. In the romance ending of the 1874 version, Toinette appears content to take up the servant's work that she might have performed as an enslaved woman. Here, in a novel that Tourgée says places an emphasis on the Royal Gentleman, Tourgée chooses the gothic over romance. When Geoffrey demands that Toinette live with him in Lovett Lodge as they had in the past—unmarried and with himself in the position of master— she refuses, and in his anger he reveals, in an anticipation of one of Faulkner's great themes, that the past is never past. He proclaims: "Geoffrey Hunter will never demean himself by marrying a nigger!" Realizing that with these words "her 'royal gentleman' was discrowned," Toinette prepares to go North, but not before making one last visit to "the secret room at Lovett Lodge" where she composes a farewell letter to Geoffrey. By writing from within the secret room, she reminds the reader of its history as a space of violations, aligning herself, at long last, with the haunting gothic energy of her mother. In the letter, she talks back to Geoffrey (and white slave culture more generally), celebrating her new freedom, telling him that she refuses to "bend to your entreaty of evil" and bitingly concluding that "her once master is a slave now."[16] Geoffrey is a slave to the past because he has failed to come to terms with the crimes of the past, including his own. A question raised by the ending of this final version of *Toinette* is the extent to which slavery will continue to exert its presence in the post–Civil War United States.

Frederick Douglass regularly maintained that "there is no such thing as instantaneous emancipation," that the "links of the chain may be broken in an instant, but it will take not less than a century to obliterate all traces of the institution." In his preface to the 1879 edition of *Toinette*, Tourgée similarly referred to the false assumptions "that slavery is dead." *Toinette*, he states in that preface, discloses "those *unconscious* influences which shape and mould mental and moral qualities, and through which *Slavery still lives and dominates*." Ten years later, Tourgée declared that "a nation can never bury its past," a sentiment that Hawthorne would have surely agreed with, which is why both found the gothic romance so appealing.[17] But the Hawthornean version of romance in *House* could only take Tourgée so far in his fiction. Even so, Hawthorne remained an influence on Tourgée's later novels, such as *Pactolus Prime*, which depicted the necessity of confronting the past in order to do the work that Tourgée had hoped would have been accomplished by Reconstruction. At his most optimistic, Tourgée believed that change could come about when Americans were prepared to address the painful history of slavery and racism that continued to haunt their social landscape. That is the burden of all three versions of *Toinette*, and that is precisely what Tourgée's Hawthorne-influenced mode of gothic Reconstruction sought to accomplish.

Notes

1. Nathaniel Hawthorne, *The House of the Seven Gables*, ed. Robert S. Levine (New York: Norton, 2020), 5. On the *Atlantic Monthly*'s canonization of Hawthorne, see Richard H. Brodhead, *The School of Hawthorne* (New York: Oxford University Press, 1986), 85–89, 108–10.

2. Frederick Douglass, "The Work before Us," *The Independent*, August 27, 1868, 1. For a reading of *The House of the Seven Gables* in the context of Lincoln's image of a "house divided," see George B. Forgie, *Patricide in the House Divided: A Psychological Interpretation of Lincoln and His Age* (New York: Norton, 1979), 115–21; and for Hawthorne's jaded comments on Lincoln and abolitionists, see his "Chiefly about War-Matters," *Atlantic Monthly*, July 1862, 43–61.

3. Hawthorne, *The House of the Seven Gables*, 14, 149.

4. On race in the novel, see David Anthony, "Class, Culture, and the Trouble with White Skin in Hawthorne's *The House of the Seven Gables*," *Yale Journal of Criticism* 12, no. 2 (1999): 249–68; and Robert S. Levine, *Dislocating Race and Nation* (Chapel Hill: University of North Carolina Press, 2008), chap. 3.

5. Henry Churton [Albion Tourgée], *Toinette: A Novel* (New York: J. B. Ford & Company, 1874), iv. All future references to this edition will be cited parenthetically in the main body of the text.

6. My admiration for *Toinette* is shared by Sharon D. Kennedy-Nolle, who writes that Tourgée's gothic novel is "the most ambitious and daring creative expression of his ideals." Sharon D. Kennedy-Nolle, *Writing Reconstruction: Race, Gender, and Citizenship in the Postwar South* (Chapel Hill: University of North Carolina Press, 2015), 77. Earlier critics turned against the novel's gothic mode. In his pioneering discussion of Tourgée, Edmund Wilson objected to the novel's "murders and attempted murders, secret rooms, the walking of unauthentic ghosts, forced non-recognitions and unlikely coincidences." Edmund Wilson, *Patriotic Gore: Studies in the Literature of the American Civil War* (New York: Oxford University Press, 1962), 533. Otto H. Olsen similarly complained that the novel "unfortunately" relied on a "melodramatic plot" involving "murder, ghosts, secret rooms, and fortunate but unlikely circumstances." Otto H. Olsen, *Carpetbagger's Crusade: The Life of Albion Winegar Tourgée* (Baltimore, MD: Johns Hopkins University Press, 1963), 216. My argument is that the novel's gothic mode, which Tourgée learned from Hawthorne, is what makes the novel so effective.

7. Avery F. Gordon, *Ghostly Matters: Haunting and the Sociological Imagination* (1997; Minneapolis: University of Minnesota Press, 2008), 23, xvi. On connections between the gothic and the history of slavery in America, see also Teresa Goddu, *Gothic America: Narrative, History, and Nation* (New York: Columbia University Press, 1997).

8. In this regard, Tourgée no doubt also drew on the gothic tropes of Harriet Beecher Stowe's *Uncle Tom's Cabin* (1852), especially the figure of Cassie and her ghost story.

9. Hawthorne, *The House of the Seven Gables*, 16.

10. Hawthorne, *House*, 146; Hawthorne to Sophia Peabody, letter of October 18, 1841, rpt. in *The House of the Seven Gables*, 305.

11. Walter Benn Michaels, "Romance and Real Estate," in *The American Renaissance Reconsidered*, ed. Walter Benn Michaels and Donald E. Pease (Baltimore, MD: Johns Hopkins University Press, 1985), 156–82.

12. For an extensive and often brilliant reading of property in *Toinette*, see Kennedy-Nolle, *Writing Reconstruction*, 76–122.

13. For a different perspective on the three endings in the context of debates in American literary studies, see my "'That Grim Sphinx': Literary Historicism and Tourgée's *Toinette* Novels," *American Literary History* 34, no. 1 (2022): 224–36.

14. Albion W. Tourgée, *Toinette: A Tale of the South* (New York: Fords, Howard, & Hulbert, 1879), 478, 476.

15. Albion W. Tourgée, *A Royal Gentleman* (New York: Fords, Howard, & Hulbert, 1881), iii, vii.

16. Tourgée, *A Royal Gentleman*, 443, 446, 461, 463.

17. Frederick Douglass, "Addresses Delivered in New York, New York, on 14 May 1868," in *Frederick Douglass Papers: Speeches, Debates, Interviews*, ed. John. W. Blassingame and John R. McKivigan (New Haven, CT: Yale University Press, 1991), 4:174; Tourgée, *Toinette: A Tale of the South*, vi, vii; Tourgée, "The South as a Field for Fiction" (1888), in *Undaunted Radical: The Selected Writings and Speeches of Albion W. Tourgée*, ed. Mark Elliott and John David Smith (Baton Rouge: Louisiana State University Press, 2010), 204.

2

Tourgée's *A Fool's Errand* and the Limits of White Radicalism

John Ernest

Albion Tourgée stands out as one of the great white radicals of the nineteenth century, one of the very few whose commitment seems equivalent to that of William Lloyd Garrison, and one of the fewer still who seemed capable of a searching self-awareness about his identity and responsibilities as a white man. It would seem, then, that a recovery of his literature would be an important step toward addressing a literary history that includes a horrific and broadly influential tradition of white supremacist literature—the most virulently direct of which was published during Tourgée's lifetime. I want to suggest, though, that Tourgée's novels offer us a different kind of lesson, an opportunity to reflect on the challenges of white radicalism, the ways in which even the most radical white Americans can find themselves grounded in the very systemic racial order to which they claim opposition. I will focus on Tourgée's best-known and most successful novel, *A Fool's Errand* (1879). While it has been argued that Tourgée works beyond the limitations of *A Fool's Errand* in his other writings, specifically doing more to represent African American perspectives (or what he imagined such perspectives to be), *A Fool's Errand* is unique in its self-reflexive approach to racial thought, both highlighting it and calling attention to its apprehensive boundaries. This novel represents well the challenges Tourgée faced, the methods he used to address those challenges, and the means by which he attempted to extend his literary efforts beyond the limitations of his understanding.

In taking this approach, it might seem that I am giving Tourgée both not enough and too much credit. Unusual in his own time, Tourgée remains unusual even for ours as a white writer committed to addressing the world shaped by the legacy of slavery and racial oppression. It can certainly seem unfair, then, to suggest that his success in such endeavors was limited by his immersion in a white supremacist society. On the other hand, it might seem that I'm giving him rather too much credit in suggesting that he was himself aware of these limitations and built that awareness into his approach. Ultimately, though, I'm not able to press either point—whether too little credit or too much—with great confidence, which is, I think, where *A Fool's Errand* leaves us. Tourgée, I believe, struggled to reach an understanding of the central challenges of his day; he struggled for a resolution he could not achieve. But this struggle, and his awareness of his limited success, is what makes his work instructive. When we consider either or both of the two possibilities—that he successfully addressed racial injustice or that he strategically draws attention to his own inability to do so—we find ourselves with questions that get at the heart of the lasting value of Tourgée's work, questions still central to white America's approach to understanding race. His writing, at its best, asks us to reach beyond his work, to recognize the fool's errand inherent in his attempt to think and narrate his way out of a white supremacist cultural order that shaped even the reason and discursive tools he used to craft his work.

Given Tourgée's overall career—and especially his exposure of the Ku Klux Klan, a mission deeply associated with *A Fool's Errand*—it is natural to assume that his most famous novel can be understood as an antiracist work, but in fact it would be difficult to support such a claim. The story of the union between a white northern man and a white southern woman, a narrative that guides the broader story of a carpetbagger confronting the nature and conditions of the social order in the South, *A Fool's Errand* operates in a complex field of post–Civil War fiction devoted to defining the terms of national reunion.[1] While *A Fool's Errand* naturally includes considerations of race in its overall survey of southern culture and national reconstruction, it is more appropriately understood as a novel devoted to social justice. To be sure, Comfort Servosse, the transplanted white northerner who serves as the novel's protagonist, recognizes the Ku Klux Klan as an instrument of terror, one that "might be used so as to effectually destroy the liberty of the newly enfranchised citizen, and establish a serfdom more barbarous and horrible than any on earth, because it would be the creature of lawless insolence."[2] But while he is concerned about the victims of this terrorist organization, his opposition to the Klan is not grounded in an antiracist mission. He opposes the organization because it is lawless, because it is the force behind a reign of terror. Indeed, the narrator expresses a grudging respect for the organization, to the point where he compares it to John Brown. "It was no brave thing in itself," he observes, "for old John Brown to seize the arsenal at Harper's [*sic*] Ferry; considered as an assault on the almost solitary watchman, it was cowardly in the extreme; but, when we consider what power stood behind that powerless squad, we are amazed at the daring of the Hero of Ossawattomie. So it was with this magnificent organization" (254–55). This is certainly a novel that opposes "this magnificent organization," but its claims to antiracist work fall largely to its advocacy for a generalized mass of people usually presented as "poor, weak, defenseless men and women" (254).

The distinction between social justice and antiracist work is important because this is a novel that in many ways accepts and sometimes even depends upon the logic of race. Indeed, our guiding Fool is presented as a specifically racial child:

> That the young lumberman, Michael Servosse,—rich in the limitless possibilities of a future cast in the way which had been marked out by nature as the path of advancing empire, a brave heart and unquenchable energy, to whom thousands of acres of unrivaled pine-lands yielded tribute, and whose fleet of snug schooners was every year growing larger,—that he should capture and mate with the fair bird from the New-England home-nest was as fitting as the most enthusiastic advocate of natural selection could desire. They were the fairest types of remote stocks of kindred races, invigorated by the fresh life of a new continent. (8–9)

Our leading character, our white champion is, one might say, the child of racial logic and privilege—supported by land, power, and bloodlines, which are taken to be, collectively, the very voice of nature. The vision of history presented here as his lineage is a vision of race—far beyond anything that Tourgée signifies by his use of the word itself.

Nothing in the novel challenges us to question this vision of the "fairest types of remote stocks of kindred races" at its moral center. If the novel is at all devoted to antiracist work, it is certainly not devoted to questioning the terms of Servosse's natural ability, the gifts that were his ancestry and his strength. My point is not that Tourgée is identifying Servosse specifically as a white man; his "kindred races" are not identified as white, though of course whiteness is implicit in this portrait. Rather, my point is that it is impossible to imagine the novel functioning without an understanding of "remote stocks" of various races coming together in white America. Everything that Servosse does in the novel depends upon his status as a white man operating in a troubled but still functioning realm of access and authority, the singularly unquestioned racial position in this novel. It can be argued that southern white men of status are recognized as racial. It can obviously be argued that Black men are recognized as racial. It can even be argued that poor whites are recognized as racial. Servosse, however, is both racial and not—identified by his good racial stock but omitted from any consideration of race as a national problem.

What is missing in this novel is an understanding of race as a systemic fabrication, a dynamic presence shaped, reinforced, and continually transformed by law, economics, social position, theology, and virtually every other cultural institution. As David Theo Goldberg has argued, "*race* is a fluid, transforming, historically specific concept parasitic on theoretic and social discourses for the meaning it assumes at any historical moment."[3] By this formulation, race operates even at the level of the discourse Tourgée draws from to tell his story. Clearly, race operates at the level of narrative, as Tourgée deploys a familiar trope of northern and southern romance to speak of a possible (white) national reunion. But this is a race that remains virtually invisible in the novel—apparent at every turn but never identified as racial. One thinks of Charles W. Mills's observation that

> in a racially structured polity, the only people who can find it psychologically possible to deny the centrality of race are those who are racially privileged, for whom race is invisible precisely because the world is structured around them, whiteness as the ground against which the figures of other races—those who, unlike us, are raced—appear. The fish does not see the water, and whites do not see the racial nature of a white polity because it is natural to them, the element in which they move.[4]

This positionality is reflected in the novel's narrative perspective, guiding those moments when race becomes an explicit concern and those other moments when it does not—or guiding those moments, as in the description of Servosse's background, when race is explicitly mentioned but is clearly not intended to function in the same way as it does when we are considering those in the novel that the narrator sometimes refers to as "Africans."

Most of the novel concerns Servosse's encounters with, and his and the narrator's reflections on, upper-class white southerners, and if the novel is clear in its denunciations of social injustices, it is clear as well in its admiration for the white South. "One can not but regard with pride and sympathy the indomitable men," we are told deep into the novel, "who, being conquered in war, yet resisted every effort of the conqueror to change their laws, their customs, or even the *personnel* of their ruling class; and this, too, not only with unyielding stubbornness, but with success" (253). Deeper still, we encounter admiration again for the "infinite patience, matchless organization, unremitting and universal zeal" with which ruling white southerners worked to "foil the design of their foe" (323). "It was a daring conception for a conquered people," our narrator muses; "only a race of warlike instincts and regal pride could have conceived or executed it" (323). As the narrator reflects on the collective effort needed for this resistance, his admiration grows incrementally. "The whole South must be fused and welded into one homogeneous mass," he observes, "having one common thought, one imperial purpose, one relentless will. It was a magnificent conception, and, in a sense, deserved success!" (323). The narrator is very much aware that this magnificent effort includes the insistence "that white and black could not and should not live together as co-ordinate ruling elements" (253), and while he generally leans otherwise, he clearly is drawn to the sheer force of the argument, as if drawn to the manifestation of a superior racial stock.[5]

When the narrator and Servosse express similar admiration for African Americans, they extend their compliments to distinctively foreign communities: the "African" or "Ethiopian" population. To some extent, the novel presents what was at the time a familiar image of postwar African Americans, a group of "freedmen, dazed with new-found liberty," who "crowded the towns and camps, or wandered aimlessly here and there" (130). This is a community educated in the "hard school" of slavery (130) and now facing the challenge of freedom. But Tourgée finds great strength in this aimless community. Graduates of that school, "they had been indurated to want, exposure, and toil" and accordingly "could endure the present better than their old masters' families, and had never learned to dread the future" (130). To be sure, Tourgée joins many other commentators in his belief that African Americans were little prepared for what he viewed as the responsibilities of freedom—responsibilities that, apparently, ruling southern whites met—but he includes poor whites in the formula when looking ahead to a more responsible republic. "Let the Nation educate the colored man and the poor-white man," the narrator states, "*because* the Nation held them in bondage, and is responsible for their education; educate the voter *because* the Nation can not afford that he should be ignorant" (387). Race here is both central and incidental—the reason why this class of people was enslaved but not an active quality that the narrator needs to include in his formulation of the means by which social justice might be achieved. They are notable for what they lack, and their education in the school of absence has provided their only presence, a passive ability to endure.

When accounting for a more active trait, our narrator admires African Americans for the same boldness that inspired his admiration for upper-class southern whites—but the admiration is qualified and on racial terms. Reflecting on Uncle Jerry's views on the needs of the race, the narrator observes, "He had the idea that his race must, in a sense, achieve its own liberty, establish its own manhood, by a stubborn resistance to aggression" (225). Uncle Jerry, we are told, had "infused into his duller-minded associates the firm conviction which possessed himself,—that it was better to die in resisting such oppression than to live under it" (224–25). In short, the narrator finds the same qualities in African Americans that inspire in him such admiration for southern whites, the same determination to maintain one's dignity, the same resistance against the odds. Or nearly so, anyway. While the white community seems broadly capable, the African American community seems hitched primarily to Uncle Jerry's star—and it is a falling star. While it is "altogether probable" that Uncle Jerry's position "would have been the correct and proper one" under normal circumstances, "the odds of ignorance and prejudice" were "decidedly against them" (225). Accordingly, their position "was the sheerest folly, for "when experience, wealth, and intelligence combine against ignorance, poverty, and inexperience, resistance is useless" (225). This is, indeed, a useless mission to which the novel subscribes—"the heroism of folly, the faith—or hope, rather—of the fool" (225), but it never rises to the level of a fundamental characteristic of the race, as it does for elite southern whites or arguably for the narrator himself. Uncle Jerry, an exceptional representative of his race, dies of this folly—in the name of a reasonable position that was, to white southerners, a "monstrous doctrine" of self-defense.

Given this array of forces, these contending races, and given the history of the South, the novel, perhaps understandably, presents prejudice as a reasonable presence in the overall formula that our narrator tries to work out over the course of *A Fool's Errand*. What could be more reasonable, after all, than to conclude that "the social conditions of three hundred years are not to be overthrown in a moment" (24–25)? Any plan for Reconstruction, the novel suggests, would have to take into account "that strange and mysterious influence which ranges all the way from a religious principle to a baseless prejudice, according to the stand-point of the observer, but always remains a most unaccountable yet still stubborn fact in all that pertains to the governmental organisms of the South,— the popular feeling in regard to the African population of that section" (133–34). Accounting for that popular feeling, the narrator emphasizes that such feeling is entirely reasonable. "That a servile race," he explains,

> isolated from the dominant one by the fact of color and the universally accepted dogma of inherent inferiority, to say nothing of a very general belief of its utter incapacity for the civilization to which the Caucasian has attained, should be looked on with distrust and aversion, if not with positive hatred, as a co-ordinate political power, by their former masters, would seem so natural, that one could hardly expect men of ordinary intelligence to overlook it. (134)

It is worth noting again that in these explanations, regardless of what we might take to be the position of the narrator, Tourgée quietly presents African Americans as foreign bodies—Africans—and suggests that they constitute "a servile race," something naturally separate from "the civilization to which the Caucasian has attained." This is a battle of the races in which we are reminded that African Americans have a distinct disadvantage, but here the disadvantage begins to take on the hue of a racial condition.

Tourgée has considerable reason to find fault in the national Reconstruction measures, but when presenting his critique, he echoes and even quietly subscribes to the discourse of race as formulated by white Americans. White southerners fighting against a superior force become "indomitable men" with a plan worthy of success; African Americans become a foreign entity and a servile race, admirable fools, but fools all the same for standing against a superior force. And whereas whites are distinguished between a ruling class and a subordinate class, African Americans remain a community distinguished only by the occasional leader, an Uncle Jerry who sways the community toward ideals but against its better interest. The "African race" is presented as "the ignorant, unskilled, and dependent race—a race who could not have lived a week without the support or charity of the dominant one" (137, 320). When imagining a solution that would involve "an elevation of the blacks," the narrator notes that such a solution would involve a white man willing to be "regarded as putting himself upon their social level in a community where the offender against caste becomes an outlaw in fact" (134). Those who might choose to make such a move can be divided into three classes: martyrs, self-seekers, and fools, "who hoped that in some inscrutable way the laws of human nature would be suspended" (134–35). It is little wonder that "*The Policy of Suppression*," however wrong, might still command Servosse's "unbounded admiration" in "its completeness and success" (326). Given the equation whose construction we witness over the course of the novel, this is not an unreasonable approach.

And that is the problem, for the overriding fool's errand in this novel involves the narrator's unquestioned faith in the power of reason as something that operates independently of the dynamics of race. What is most striking about *A Fool's Errand* is the drive to categorize and explain that presses through its otherwise thin and conventional plot. Scholars have naturally tried to nail down Tourgée's approach to addressing the needs of post–Civil War America and the failures of Reconstruction, and they focus not on the story Tourgée tells but on the reasoned consideration of the different and contending forces barely contained by the story—the many moments when the novel pauses to define important terms;

identify central ideological positions; offer comparative cultural studies of North and South; and explore through syllogisms, charts, and extended analytical musings the reasons why government policy is misconceived. The novel's greatest narrative tension, indeed, has to do with the anticipation of possible solutions, as we follow along this ongoing analysis, complicated by the friendships, alliances, romance, and violence of the novel's action—and we are left with very few choices. As Brook Thomas has observed, the reasonable resolution of these tensions is complicated by the fact that Tourgée's reason was presented to a prejudiced world. "A child of the Enlightenment," Thomas observes,

> Tourgée believed that by embodying right reason in his fiction he could educate public opinion and eliminate prejudice. The problem with that goal is similar to the one he himself noted in the [Supreme] Court's interpretation of the equal but separate law. The texts he hoped would alter racial prejudice could not be interpreted free from the history of prejudice that he would alter. (218)

What chance for success is there when the other white and empowered purveyors of right reason at the time included not only the members of the Supreme Court but also such writers as Thomas Nelson Page and Thomas Dixon Jr., those for whom a reasonable approach to Reconstruction would differ dramatically from that which Tourgée struggles to present? How could this novel hope to reach those most in need of its message?

I have been suggesting, though, that the central problem in Tourgée's approach is even deeper than Thomas suggests, for reason in this novel doesn't simply encounter a world of prejudice. Rather, it operates wholly within a white frame.[6] A child of that frame, one "for whom race is invisible precisely because the world is structured around them," Tourgée is unable to piece together an equation that actually accounts for the realities of US culture.[7] This is a world nearly invisible and wholly unaccountable by the terms of that mode of reason, also central to Enlightenment thought, that had made racial dominance either a reasonable development in a nation that claimed devotion to liberty and human rights or that made race, in effect, a side issue, a contradiction that could be dealt with separately from any conception of the nation's philosophical coherence. To the extent that one could say that race is central to the equations that are themselves central to A Fool's Errand, one would have to add that the concept of race we encounter in the novel is already the product of white reason operating within a white cultural frame. My point is not that Tourgée doesn't see race, for of course he does. He sees it in the "unaccountable African" (328), and his reason operates in a realm apart from that mysterious racial terrain. Reason, the novel seems to suggest, transcends race, but the narrator is unable to recognize the extent to which the tools he brings to reason are grounded in racial premises.

What Tourgée can't reason himself into is an understanding of that unaccountable variable in the formulas that guide his reason, the uncertainty principle undermining his syllogisms, the actual African Americans behind and beyond what Anna Julia Cooper called the "little Tourgees" that populate his fiction.[8] What Tourgée can't account for, and what he would find unaccountable, is the complex performativity of Black life and its entanglement both within and without the logical systems upon which he relies. African Americans had long before been immersed in the gaping irrationality of the American cultural order, its fundamental incoherence—to the extent, as Douglass insisted in his 1852 Fourth of July address, that even language itself had lost its referential power. Forced to confront this national incoherence, African American culture developed a dynamic, inherently theoretic approach to life, one that we have only gradually come to appreciate as an analytical model. Fred Moten, drawing our attention to what he identifies as "the problematics of everyday ritual, the stagedness of the violently . . . quotidian, the essential drama of black life," has defined blackness as "the extended movement of a specific upheaval, an ongoing irruption that arranges every line." In Moten's formulation, this extended movement constitutes "a strain that pressures the assumption of the equivalence of personhood and subjectivity." Accounting for blackness, then, involves, among other things, immersion in the dynamics of what Moten calls the "economy of . . . hypervisibility," which lies "between looking and being looked at, spectacle and spectatorship, enjoyment and being enjoyed."[9] These dynamics nowhere enter Tourgée's analysis, even when he looks through the eyes and speaks through the mouths of his African American characters. And in his inability to account for that dynamic, performative, and complexly interrelational and contingent presence, all of Tourgée's efforts to reason himself and his readers from disorder to order are doomed by a conceptual misapprehension, a design error.

Of course, I'm writing this in a time when we have more conceptual tools to bring to an understanding of race than were arguably available to Tourgée, though I'm also writing this at a time when Tourgée still seems ahead of most white Americans in his determination to understand a social order shaped by race. We are now benefiting from the work of scholars like Moten, Saidiya Hartman, Sylvia Wynter, Stephen Best, Alexander G. Weheliye, Marisa J. Fuentes, Christina Sharpe, and others who are attending to the theories of history and humanity that emerge from an understanding of Black experience. It matters, regardless of historical circumstances, that Tourgée was unable to account for these dynamic understandings of humanity and historical process in formulating an understanding of his time, for without such an accounting, he was unable to come to an understanding of the very machinery—history, culture, and reason— he was so intent on recalibrating. Indeed, Tourgée seems to argue that it matters to consider a more dynamic, and not strictly rational, understanding of the social order. He accounts, for example, for the ways that slavery closed off opposing or even complicating thought "from its inner sanctuary . . . and persecuted with unsparing severity all who rejected its dogmas" (91). Attentive to the limitations of understanding in a closed system, he explores the ways that "the terrible suppressive power which slavery had exercised over liberty of thought and speech had grown into a habit of mind" (147). He accounts for the ways in which perception becomes reality, and he accounts for the ongoing effects of slavery "as a force, a power, a moral element" (380). "Its conscious evils were obliterated," he observes, but "its unconscious ones existed in the dwarfed and twisted natures which had been subjected for generations to its influences,—master and slave alike" (380). He accounts, in other words, for a disordered system and a dynamic, even chaotic historical process—but he was unable to adjust his application of reason to match his model.

While he would continue his efforts to write his way into an understanding of his times, what makes *A Fool's Errand* stand out is exactly what the novel's title suggests—that his attempt to make sense of his world is a fool's errand. His limitations, his ultimate failure, are, in effect, the point of the novel. The world he describes resists the sense-making apparatus he brings to it, and while his methods seem to apprehend that failure, he lacks the perspective that African Americans, those born into and of the system's contradictions and disorder, had developed into a necessary approach to life, even as they themselves struggled to theorize what they were living and transforming into expressive culture. Tourgée himself seems aware of the problem, which he arguably tried to address in subsequent works. I agree with Carolyn L. Karcher, for example, that Tourgée brings race to the center of his analysis in *Pactolus Prime*, a novel in which "Tourgée identifies white racism as the root of the [race] problem, charging that it permeates all aspects of U.S. society and especially contaminates the Christianity preached and practiced by white Americans—hence the subtitle, 'The White Christ.'" [10] More to the point, I agree with Karcher that *Pactolus Prime* is most interesting as a work that Tourgée initially resisted bringing to neat resolution, insisting that readers should be provoked to read between and even *outside* the lines. Tourgée's

attempts to represent Black life and thought in that novel are finally less interesting, and less productive, than his recognition that understanding required something more than he was able to set down on the page. He understood, in effect,
that the nation needed to embark on a fool's errand—and the sense that he tried
to bring to the endeavor did not add considerably to that fundamental message,
that basic need.

Ultimately, I am not saying simply that Tourgée suffers from the limits of
white radical thought; I'm suggesting that he crafts his work to *identify* those
limits, the boundaries beyond which he could not reach. Like a mystic attending
to the limitations of language, ritual, and being, so as to gesture to the beyond
that cannot be claimed, attained, or contained, Tourgée keeps at the forefront
the boundaries of his claims, even as he pushes those boundaries, as if to reach
beyond. What makes *A Fool's Errand* a great work is not that it succeeds in the
reasoned advocacy that it seems to represent but rather because it accounts for
its own failure, provides us with the terms of that failure, and compels us to look
beyond. At a time when we are still drawn to the illusion that we are dealing with
hypocrisy, contradictions, or cancers upon an otherwise healthy national body, *A
Fool's Errand* can press us to the broadly collaborative and reciprocal interracial
engagements needed to address a system that was designed to be incoherent,
designed to work reasonably within the realm of its own unreason, designed to
offer a mockery of the kind of justice that our Fool thinks we should pursue—
within and beyond what we know as our world.

Notes

1. The best studies of this history of narrative reunion are Daniel Aaron, *The Un-
written War: American Writers and the Civil War* (Madison: University of Wisconsin
Press, 1987); David W. Blight, *Race and Reunion: The Civil War in American Memory*
(Cambridge, MA: Belknap, 2001); Kathleen Diffley, *Where My Heart Is Turning Ever:
Civil War Stories and Constitutional Reform, 1861–1876* (Athens: University of Georgia
Press, 1992); and Alice Fahs, *The Imagined Civil War: Popular Literature of the North and
South, 1861–1865* (Chapel Hill: University of North Carolina Press, 2001). As Jay Martin
has observed, Tourgée extends his own narrative of national (white) reunion over the
course of his "American Historical Novels," building to "the last novel of his series, *John
Eax*—a story of the 'New South'—[in which] he could finally conclude: 'If the North and
South are contrasted, it is but to show the fusing potency of love.'" Jay Martin, *Harvests
of Change: American Literature, 1865–1914* (Englewood Cliffs, NJ: Prentice-Hall, 1967),
52. See also Rebecca Skidmore Biggio on the complementary racial politics of Tourgée
and Thomas Dixon Jr., "the reconstruction of" a "racial fantasy" by which "Tourgée
and Dixon redeploy and reconstitute an abstract prewar white national identity for an
internally fractured postwar nation." Rebecca Skidmore Biggio, "Violent Fraternities and

White Reform: The Complementary Fictions of Albion Tourgée and Thomas Dixon," *Arizona Quarterly* 67, no. 2 (Summer 2011): 82.

2. Albion W. Tourgée, *A Fool's Errand, by One of the Fools* (Cambridge, MA: Belknap, 1961), 191. Subsequent quotations will be cited parenthetically.

3. David Theo Goldberg, *The Threat of Race: Reflections on Racial Neoliberalism* (Malden, MA: Blackwell, 2009), 74.

4. Charles W. Mills, *The Racial Contract* (Ithaca, NY: Cornell University Press, 1997), 76.

5. In this regard as in others, Edmund Wilson's 1962 assessment of Tourgée, while dated in some respects, stands out as a balanced and thoughtful reading—accounting for Tourgée's bold advocacy for social justice while also accounting for his clear admiration for white southerners and even his measured admiration for the Klan. Edmund Wilson, *Patriotic Gore: Studies in the Literature of the American Civil War* (New York: Oxford University Press, 1962), 536. See also Robert M. Myers, "'Desirable Immigrants': The Assimilation of Transplanted Yankees in Page and Tourgée," *South Central Review* 21, no. 2 (2004): 73–74; and Bill Hardwig, "Who Owns the Whip? Chesnutt, Tourgée, and Reconstruction Justice," *African American Review* 36, no. 1 (2002): 7.

6. I have in mind here Joe R. Feagin's useful study *The White Racial Frame: Centuries of Racial Framing and Counter-Framing* (New York: Routledge, 2013).

7. Mills, *The Racial Contract*, 76.

8. Anna Julia Cooper, *A Voice from the South by a Black Woman of the South* (New York: Oxford University Press, 1988), 189.

9. Fred Moten, *In the Break: The Aesthetics of the Black Radical Tradition* (Minneapolis: University of Minnesota Press, 2003), 1.

10. Carolyn L. Karcher, *A Refugee from His Race: Albion W. Tourgée and His Fight against White Supremacy* (Chapel Hill: University of North Carolina Press, 2016), 55. Karcher's is the best and most thorough study of Tourgée's views on race. While I obviously believe that his fight against white supremacy was more intimate and less successful than Karcher argues, I am greatly indebted to her study.

3

"Queer Synecdoche"

Tourgée's Bricks without Straw *and Black Kinship*

Nancy Bentley

How do political novels work? A passage from Albion Tourgée's *Bricks without Straw* offers a striking formulation for thinking about that question. The passage comes at the end of the forty-ninth chapter, as one of the white protagonists, Hesden Le Moyne, begins to doubt his ingrained assumptions about "the South." In earlier chapters, the phrase "the South" has been a floating signifier, referring variously to a regional section, a "race," a "people," and a "would-be nation." In this passage, however, the narrator steps back to provide a brief but telling gloss about how the term derives its meaning from a particular figural logic:

> Hesden had only wondered what the effect of these things would be upon "the South;" meaning by "the South" that regnant class to which his family belonged—a part of which, by queer synecdoche, stood for the whole.[1]

A term hitherto used without qualms appears here in scare quotes, a typographical alert that what has previously been a self-evidently meaningful reference, "the South," is something we should not necessarily take at face value—something here may be illogical, or "queer," as the narrator labels it. We are explicitly told, moreover, that this concept of "the South" is an artifact of figural language, created from a synecdoche in which a particular class of (white, propertied) families represents a larger whole.

As a window on this species of synecdochic logic, the passage displays how some political novels generate their meaning: In fiction of this kind, the lives of private *persons* are made to embody the meaning of a public *polity*, in this case, the post–Civil War United States and its still politically contentious sections ("the South," "the North"). The passage also flags for us that a key element in this synecdochic construct is kinship. The romances, marriages, and family tragedies of private individuals are understood to represent the life of a fractured nation—not just the personal travails of Americans themselves but also the fate of a ruptured political body.

This kinship synecdoche was at the heart of the large body of fiction that Nina Silber memorably described as telling a post-Reconstruction "romance of reunion." In this fiction, a happy-ending marriage between a white Northerner and a white Southerner signifies the political restoration of the Union. Eliding the costs to Black Americans, the conventional "romance of reunion" uses marriage and kinship to craft a political allegory channeling the "sentimental culture of conciliation" that prevailed among middle-class white Americans in both the South and the North.[2] These novels operate through a discursive syntax in which the personal relations of kinship articulate the impersonal entity of the nation-state.

Tourgée's novel certainly partakes of this syntax; the fraught courtship between the southerner Hesden and the northerner Mollie Ainslie is one of the sustained plotlines in this sprawling novel, and their romantic friction finally gives way to a marriage that symbolically links two regional populations. Yet in *Bricks*, at the very moment the narrator discloses the allegorical logic of this marriage plot, he also asks us to distrust it, or at least to examine it anew. What if the architecture of a political novel of this kind is in fact a misalliance between the parts and the whole, a "queer synecdoche" that offers up a distorted view of the body politic and its enduring fractures? As much as Tourgée seems to find kinship a meaningful thematics for probing politics, his novel seems equally attuned to the ways that kinship stories might actually obscure or distort—or simply fail to meaningfully signify—what happens at the level of political power. In this essay, I trace the way *Bricks* operates to unravel the kinship synecdoche that structures the post-Reconstruction novel. Tourgée's novel, I contend, actually traces a *disjunction* between kinship and nation, exposing a mismatch in what are supposed to be complementary spheres of private life and public governance. The result is a portrait—or at least the outlines of a portrait—of a sphere of kin life that is incommensurate with the rationality of the liberal state.

Alert to the "queer" construction that would falsely conflate a subset of private families with a larger polity, Tourgée's novel interrupts the implicit racializing operation of the liberal model of the private family and its relation to the nation-state. *Bricks* achieves this, I argue, because it makes a serious attempt to represent the distinctive kin relationality of African Americans in the postbellum South.

With the discrepancies it uncovers in the field of kinship, Tourgée's novel forces a recognition of the racial and political fault lines that would be left untouched in any purely symbolic reunion of white America.

If *Bricks* finally disables the figural links between private kinship and public polity, it is not because Tourgée doubted the value or authenticity of the nation-state, as some critics of liberalism do. On the contrary, Tourgée offers a remarkably detailed portrait of the offices and officers of the administrative state, showing structures of bureaucratic governance in a way that is rare even for political fiction. Within just the space of a few opening chapters, the reader encounters examples of antebellum county courthouses, the tents of federal army officers, references to legislative assemblies, clerks in postwar military districts, the crowded offices of the Freedmen's Bureau, voter registration sites, and more, all of them specific nodes of a vast apparatus through which persons come into contact with state power. Representing these nodes in ways both extensive and intensive, Tourgée finds a way to make that power—real but otherwise intangible—come alive on the page.

Whether motivated by his commitment to a stronger federal government or his first-hand knowledge of Reconstruction officialdom, *Bricks* gives a literary gravitas to these institutions and officials, making legible the way state agencies are part of the infrastructure of everyday family and work life. Consider, for instance, the way *Bricks* depicts the marriage between the Black protagonist Nimbus and his wife, Lugena. There are no extended scenes of the two together, no dramatization of what the narrator calls "the domestic relations of the freedmen" (106). Instead, Tourgée offers a chapter containing a long and almost absurdist exchange between Nimbus and a white county clerk, as the two work through the complex bureaucratic steps necessary for fulfilling what is called the freedman's "sacred responsibility" to enter legal wedlock (107). In the novel, more words are exchanged between man and clerk than are ever shared between man and wife.

This imbalance might well reflect Tourgée's neglect of Lugena, and Black women more generally, relative to the attention he gives to Nimbus and other male characters. But the reason for the imbalance is likely because Tourgée was less interested in marriage per se—its affective dynamics or even its appeal to readers—than in the momentous *event* pertaining to the formal marriages of freedpeople under Reconstruction. In other words, he was most interested in the state's role in an unprecedented project of bringing a vast population into a legal institution from which it was hitherto barred. Tourgée is compelled to explore what his narrator calls "the marriage of a race by wholesale, millions at a time," taking up marriage as a bureaucratic milestone rather than a private affair of couples (107).

One way we might characterize this aspect of the novel is to say that Tourgée shifts the more conventional novelistic focus on the relation of husband and wife to the relation between the couple and the state. But when we recognize that difference, we can also see how it alters the way love, marriage, and kinship operate as a field of signification in his novel. In the typical "romance of reunion" described by Nina Silber, the conjugal family lends its affective weight and its flesh-and-blood reality to the polity. Those novels rely on a vertical transfer of qualities (mutuality, affective belonging, lasting union) from private persons to a higher political body, a symbolic substitution. But Tourgée's narrative operates on a horizontal rather than a vertical axis. He is interested in how persons, in their role as citizens or would-be citizens, make claims on and receive protections—or not—from the very different entity that is the state. In *Bricks*, private couples are not allegorical stand-ins for the nation; they are petitioners before the state. To that end, he places the two relevant entities, persons on one hand and polities on the other, in a relation of *metonymic contiguity* rather than *metaphoric similarity*. Or, to put it in Roman Jakobson's terms, he deploys a poetics of realism rather than the poetics of romance, a choice that pulls him toward a portrait of the concrete apparatus of the state rather than the hazier and more symbolic concept of the nation.[3]

This alternative poetics—horizontal rather than vertical, working through contiguity rather than a symbolic substitution—has multiple effects. One effect is political. With his poetics of the state, Tourgée is able to bring a new specificity to the conundrums faced by the formerly enslaved. By tracing the effects of law and state agencies on everyday life, *Bricks* represents with a remarkable clarity the fractured legal condition, as Tourgée dubs it, of being "free without power or right" (110). Few novels give as detailed a portrait of what it meant for freedmen and freedwomen to negotiate the shifting civil terrain of the post–Civil War era. In multiple scenes and surprising plot turns, Tourgée's Black characters confront a concrete set of new affordances and dangers that emerged in Reconstruction and its aftermath. Nimbus exercises his right to own property and contract labor, only to have local officials prosecute him for "seducing the laborers" of a white planter who had paid rock-bottom wages (405). Attempts by a federal official to register Black voters are slowed by town authorities who block the use of public spaces for the bureaucratic process of registration. As Election Day approaches, a plan by Black voters to "march in a body to the polls with music and banners"

as a festive celebration of "the first exercise of the electoral privilege" triggers opportunistic rumors among the white townspeople, stoking fears that freedmen
intended to "seize the polls" and wreak havoc against the white community (183).
Election Day brings a tense standoff between white and Black residents that gives
way to gunfire and a narrowly averted massacre. Tourgée's portrait discloses how,
for Black men, the capacity to vote is simultaneously both a constitutional right
and a civil disability. Any effort to exercise the legal right triggers the possibility
of violence, and merely possessing the powers of a citizen means exposure to
injury and death. As depicted in *Bricks*, freedom for African Americans is not
a coherent civil status but rather a formal status of nonenslavement that merely
sets the stage for high-risk efforts—efforts often thwarted through violence or
through the law itself—to labor, to buy and sell, to assemble, and to vote without
any secure protection.[4]

Just as significant as this political dimension of *Bricks*, however, is what Tourgée's poetics of the state means for the novelistic space of kinship. As previously
noted, Tourgée shifts the details of quotidian family life into the background
and gives center stage to the zone of interface where kinship comes into direct
contact with the state. With this kinship-state interface in the foreground of the
narrative, *Bricks* ends up portraying a fault line or seam in that zone where kinship meets politics, alerting readers to a significant difference between the way
kinship is defined and regulated by the state and the way it is lived in everyday
life by kin themselves.

Readers become aware of this fault line most sharply when the narrator depicts the "wholesale" entrance of African Americans into legal kinship. Although
the narrator rhapsodizes about the "proud hour" in which "hundreds and thousands . . . crowded the places appointed" for this "first act of freedom," when the
time comes to narrate Nimbus's effort to secure legal recognition for his marriage, the scene is marked by a series of gaps and confusions (107). First, in the
clerk's office Nimbus must absorb the difference between a license to marry and
marriage itself. Nimbus has brought himself and his wife to the county office
because he has heard about the statute requiring them to marry ("I heard der
was a law—"). But the legal office cannot deliver what the law demands: "I can't
marry you," the clerk announces, "You'll have to get a license and be married by
a magistrate or a minister" (108). Next, the clerk is left to grapple with the fact
that the registration form requires him to enter a surname for the spouses even as
Nimbus insists—wholly accurately—that he has but one name. Against Nimbus's
protestation, the clerk enters his former master's last name on the registration

form: "The fact is, a man can't be married according to law without two names." Nimbus's dialect response to the clerk points up the arbitrariness introduced by the demand to adhere to the pregiven contours of a legal form: "Ain't it quare dat I should hev old Mahs'r's name widout his gibbin' it ter me, ner my axin' fer it, Mister?" (109). In this response, Nimbus identifies another queer ("quare") aspect of a process of codification that takes white families as the de facto model for proper familialism, with the result that Nimbus and Lugena acquire a false patronym invented and bestowed by the law itself.

In a final irony, Nimbus points out to the clerk that if one purpose of the law requiring freedmen to formally marry is to give legitimacy to children, the certificate of registration had no space in which to designate them. "'Sure enough,' said the clerk with amusement. 'That would have been a good idea, but, you see, Nimbus, the law didn't go that far.'" To fulfill one of the key aims of the statute, the clerk is forced to improvise and enter the names and ages of Nimbus and Lugena's children "on the back of the paper" (110). In a case where a legally sanctioned marriage was supposed to symbolically instantiate the wisdom, authority, and rationality of the state, Tourgée's scene makes us feel a vexing mismatch between law and lived kinship.

When the novel pulls back to describe this history of mass marriage more broadly, the difference becomes even sharper, for it becomes clear that the state has little ability to recognize freedpeople in their independent relations as kin. Indeed, in passages where the narrator describes kinship from the state's point of view, the preexisting kin relations of African Americans essentially vanish: In the aftermath of emancipation, the narrator says, freedpeople were a "fatherless, childless, nameless" population. "Husband or wife there was not one in four millions" (106). In a telling metaphor, the narrator even describes the Freedmen's Bureau as having "adopted" a "vast family of foundlings," as if there were no such thing as meaningful kinship without legality (158).

In these moments, the novel comes close to ratifying a version of the notion of Black "kinlessness," the idea that enslaved persons and their descendants had such tenuous protections for their status as human subjects as to make their claims on kinship altogether negligible.[5] As a white official says of the newly freed slave, "He could have no surname, because he had no family" (114). The erasure of Black kinship in these passages produces a strange bifurcation in Tourgée's novel. Ventriloquizing the viewpoint of the state, the narrator asserts that "uncle and aunt and cousin, home, family—none of these words had any place in the freedman's vocabulary" (106). Yet the same novel that offers this solemn pronouncement also features Black characters who use an extensive vocabulary of kinship. Kin relations are frequently specified, and we are told the independent Black settlement of Red Wing is a community of "fifty or sixty families" (129).

At the heart of the novel, then, is a kind of formal fissure: the right hand of bureaucracy does not seem to know that the left hand of Black kinship even exists. We might chalk up this difference to a flaw in the novel's construction. But we can ultimately count it as an achievement that *Bricks* suspends together in one novel these two disparate models of kinship. For, in doing so, the literary form of Tourgée's novel captures what historians have described as a striking phenomenon that occurred as the Freedmen's Bureau and other agencies set about bringing emancipated African Americans into the bureaucratic rationality of the state. As agencies like the Southern Claims Commission and the Federal Pension Office attempted to absorb Black families into existing legal frameworks, the result was an event in which "two systems of understanding collided."[6] This moment uncovered a dissonance between white law and Black sociality regarding what kinship actually is, that is, what defines families as opposed to neighbors or strangers.

In his study of archives in postwar North Carolina, the historian Dylan Penningroth shows that when Black petitioners in various court settings claimed people as family members, it was often mystifying to white legal officials. The unwritten rules for why persons qualified as kin or "home people" did not strictly follow bloodlines, and neither biology nor law provided the foundation for what counted as kinship. Instead, flexible rules of belonging enacted a "stretching and bending [of] the lines of blood and marriage" to form families that were recognized as such by the larger community (6). Created in the crucible of enslavement, families included children and adults adopted in particular kin roles ("nephew," "sister") as well as "distant kin," those who were "more than neighbors but not blood relations" and could be called upon to supply resources or labor (85–86). Lacking the sheltering recognition of the law, kinship under slavery was not *private* kinship as that concept operated in nineteenth-century liberal thought. It was a relationality integral to the grammar of a distinctive "extralegal economy," as Black kinship ordered networks of property, labor, and trade that "scarcely registered on the statute books" but that operated in "yards, cities and back roads across the South" (6).

To be clear, my claim is not that Tourgée was able to accurately perceive and record the distinctive nature of the kinship systems that organized southern Black communities in this era. As a white Reconstruction official who migrated to North Carolina from the North, it is likely he was just as confounded as other legal authorities when it came to grasping the unwritten rules that organized Black families and generated the qualitatively different meanings, both spiritual and material, of their kin bonds. At the same time, his portrait of the Black community of Red Wing can be said to provide traces—perhaps inadvertent traces— of an implicit grammar through which particular reciprocities of labor, property, worship, and dwelling, more than blood or law, were the real basis for determining how "home people" were formed and ratified through mutual recognition.

The fictional settlement of Red Wing was modeled on the free-labor farming community of West Green, a community outside of Greensboro, North Carolina, that Tourgée and his wife, Emma, assisted in multiple ways. Most fundamentally, the Tourgées appear to have helped African Americans circumvent the tacit ban that white planters placed on Black land ownership, dividing a portion of their own acreage into small farmsteads in order to sell them to Black families. (For their pains the couple became pariahs in the social world of white Greensboro.) Black ownership and cooperative labor are also the organizing forces in Tourgée's portrait of the settlement of Red Wing. Using money he earned for his services as a Union soldier, Nimbus had purchased undervalued land and offered small plots to other freedpeople in exchange for their labor. The settlement's cooperative tobacco farming begins to flourish, drawing new laborers attracted by the higher wages Nimbus is willing to pay. Although the details are somewhat sparse, the chapters devoted to Red Wing depict a web of relationality that appears to function somewhat like the antebellum "extralegal economy" that had tied persons through specific kin roles and affiliations in that region.

These relations resemble what Tourgée's white officials deem kinship. But, significantly, they are marked by those officials as only an approximation of kinship, something that introduces an internal discrepancy in the way the novel represents the domain of family. An especially vivid instance of this proximate kinship is the tie between Nimbus and Eliab Hill, a bond composed of conjoined strands of habitation, affect, and bodily and economic dependence. A disabled man who cannot walk, Eliab relies on the wheeled chair that Nimbus has built for him. In turn, Nimbus—who cannot read—relies on Eliab to read and write his letters and business communications. Although Eliab lives in a small cabin adjacent to the home of Lugena and Nimbus, he regularly joins them for their evening meal. The narrator most often uses the term "friend" to denote their relation, but the label seems inadequate to the descriptions of how the men are bound by a bodily tie that is both practical and notably tender. Whenever Eliab needs to visit a house or public space where his chair cannot go, Nimbus carries him in his arms or on his back, as he does after he drives Eliab to the "place of registration" to join the roll of local precinct voters. "On arriving there he took his friend in his arms, carried him in and sat him on the railing before the Board," remaining by his side to steady him while Eliab answers the necessary questions (122).

Because the relation between the men exceeds what is expected of a friendship, it gives rise to discomfort among white observers. The two are "always together," white officials complain, finding themselves both mystified by and suspicious of their close relation (122). This unease at the closeness of Nimbus and Elias registers how the two men seem to partake of the "mutuality of being" that Marshall Sahlins finds at the heart of kinship.[7] The narrator intuits the same mutuality, albeit without the consternation felt by the officials. Although the narrator labels the men "friends," whenever he offers extended scenes of physical contact between the two, his figural language tips over into the language of kinship. "Nimbus bent over him as tenderly as a mother over the cradle of her first-born, clasped his arms about him, and lifting him from the bench bore him away" to the evening meal in his house (121). The same language of figural or proximate kinship occurs when the white observer describes their relationship to a federal officer from the North: "'Liab lives in Nimbus' lot, has his meals from his table, and is toted about by Nimbus . . . Nimbus seems to think more of him than he would of a brother—than he does of his brothers, for he has two whom he seems to care nothing about. His wife and children are just as devoted to the cripple as Nimbus, and 'Liab, on his part, seems to think as much of them as if they were his own" (131).

Because Eliab and Nimbus in the eyes of these officials are not kin, they seem to possess a curious relation that only resembles kinship: The two are *like* brothers (or "more" than brothers) because they are *not* brothers. Such a view aligns with what theorists refer to as "fictive kinship," relations among non-kin that still operate pragmatically as if kin relations. But in *Bricks*, the affirmed difference that is the ground for simile—men who behave "as if" brothers—can be said to inscribe within the fabric of the novel a certain understanding of a plurality of kinship systems; a distinct Black relationality that is not kinship may be kinship. Whether or not Tourgée intended to represent Nimbus and Eliab as kin, the language of his novel enacts a syncopated conjunction that hovers in the space between friend and kinsman, marking a difference but giving a definitive status to neither alternative. We know from Tourgée's notes that Nimbus and Eliab were modeled after actual persons who lived in West Green. Those men may have been brothers or shared some other kin relation, or they may not have. But the ambiguity encoded in Tourgée's fictional representation registers the possibility of a literal kin relation that was illegible through the lens of law.

We can profitably (if speculatively) read this syncopated language of relationality as indexing an incommensurable kinship system in Black southern communities that is otherwise labeled as merely *like* kinship. The novel thus displaces the law as the arbiter of what counts as kinship and rejects the notion that nonblood ties are a mere artifice or an approximation of the real thing. As Penningroth observes of Black kinship in the South, it is a mistake to call such ties a matter of "fictive kinship." The qualifier "fictive," like the similes of a merely proximate kinship, gives priority to the understanding of kinship that the state was attempting to impose on the kin relationality of Black southerners. In *Bricks*, in contrast, that meaning of "fictive kinship" is in effect suspended inasmuch as all kin relations are fabricated from a flexible realist poetics and made to share the same fictional world. White officials who regulate kinship are merely human observers who grapple with relations that exceed what they understand, while the families formed at Red Wing emerge as a coeval kinship system that carries the same ontological weight as the kinship backed by the state. The novel's conflicting forms of kinship are both contingent, unable to be reduced to either nature or uniform law.

With its poetics of kinship plurality, Tourgée's novel tacitly recasts the meaning of kinship itself, positioning it as a poetics writ large—a matter of history and human making. Like the process Penningroth describes on plantations, in which "years of making property together helped turn these strangers into a cousin, two sisters, an uncle, and a grandmother," the glimpses of community life at Red Wing orient us to perceive kinship as a language of becoming, a semantics or social vernacular that traces a historical process (86). The work of laboring, worshipping, and sustaining precarious lives together has realized an order the narrator confidently calls "fifty or sixty families." Tourgée's narrator, in other words, does not have the qualms of the federal official in the Freedmen's Bureau who, in describing Black constituents, referred to the "groups *they call* families" (170, italics added). The kinship at Red Wing is not a matter of nominalism; a family is something made real in the lives of those who are its constitutive members. This mutuality of being that is Black kinship becomes especially vivid after KKK marauders launch a nighttime attack on the community. The church and schoolhouse are burned; some residents are killed and injured and others forced to flee their homes, including Nimbus. But even as the attack leads to a scattering of individuals to other towns and states, the novel follows the dispersal of those family members across these new geographic spaces, thereby affirming in its plot and textual language the kinship—the mutuality of being—that has formed the families of the settlement. Persisting across both time and space, the relations forged through mutual labor, time, and blood continue to exist even when violence has ruptured the local world in which they were created.

Whether or not Tourgée's novel manages to limn with much accuracy the reality of Black southern kinship, *Bricks* successfully registers the material difference of that lived kinship from what was formalized and regulated by the state. Whether by design or merely in effect, the novel does not cede a monopoly on defining kinship to the law. As a consequence, some of the sharpest political insights in *Bricks* come from the way the fate of the novel's families actually *fails* to secure a vision of political reunion for the nation as a whole. With its complex, heterogeneous field of kinship, the relations of marriage and family resist being conscripted into a project of symbolizing a political reconciliation that would come at the cost of obviating the facts of Black disenfranchisement.

As if to underscore a disjuncture between kinship and state law, the final chapters of *Bricks* juxtapose the resolution of its marriage plot with the irresolution of postbellum national politics. Tourgée, it should be noted, doesn't forgo altogether the symbolic possibilities of kinship, and the marriage plot of *Bricks* does have the capacity to signify unities that are larger than individual families. The rocky courtship between Mollie Ainslee and Hesden Le Moyne has a resonance with the differences between the cultures of their respective regions. A single woman who has arrived from New England to teach in a Black school, Mollie is initially treated with polite tolerance by the white residents, who see her as a visitor blind to the realities of race in the South. When she emerges as a potential wife for Hesden, however, she is quickly castigated as an interloper tainted by her close association with the Black community. But when the couple finally weds, the marriage is held out as proof to readers that two Americans shaped by "New England Puritanism and Southern Prejudice" can overcome the friction produced by their conflicting regional views and temperaments (295).

White Americans, the marriage plot promises, can eventually restore the fellow feeling that had existed before the different sectional populations had become the constituents of rival polities. But crucially, this successful marriage between a white northerner and a white southerner in no way signals the recovery of an organic political unity. As the novel concludes, the turmoil of the immediate past appears to have receded, bringing a "peace" to counties like Horsford, the novel's primary setting and the place where Hesden and Mollie commence their life as a married couple (392). Rather than let the harmony of a happy marriage signify that ambient peace, however, Tourgée's narrator dwells at length on the specific operations of a "counter-revolution" against the federal efforts at Reconstruction (394). Conflict in Horsford is quelled not by a return to good feeling among all citizens but through wholesale dismantling of the administrative infrastructure that had opened a place for Black political representation. As if to offer a valedictory for lost political possibility, Tourgée's narrator slows his story to name a litany of offices, from the "trustees of the townships" and the "boards of commissioners" of local schools to the "registrars of voters" and "board of inspectors" for elections, all offices from which unnamed agents were expelled or replaced by the top-down directives of a small group of white political "redeemers" (394–95). In making visible the details of this bureaucratic restructuring, *Bricks* tells what few novels narrate: that "peace" in the South really meant that "the vast colored majority, once overcome, had been easily held in subjection" by a "dominant minority" (392, 395).

Political loss is juxtaposed with successful family unity; the personal and the political are conspicuously contrasted rather than symbolically combined. When Hesden and Mollie travel to visit Washington, DC, the happy ending for the couple is set in relief against the fractures in the national polity. Precisely because these chapters foreground the "evil" legacy of slavery for the post-Reconstruction era, the successful union of two white people has no ability to signify whether "national ills" stemming from race can ever be overcome (419, 420). In an extended dialogue, Hesden and a northern senator discuss Hesden's belief that education and widespread political reform could still bring about a democratic "solution" to Black subjugation in the South (419). But whether these measures could bridge the differences in two divergent "political systems" is an open question, and the title of the novel's penultimate chapter, "What Shall the End Be?," marks for readers the uncertainty of the national future (421).

Overtly eschewing symbolic substitution for metonymic juxtaposition, the conclusion brings Hesden and Mollie into contact with the seat of national political power only to underscore at that site the enduring political discord: "So, day by day, the 'irrepressible conflict' is renewed" (432). The union of Hesden and Mollie has no predictive value for any national rectification of racial injustice any more than does the reunion of Lugena with the long-missing Nimbus. In *Bricks*, family bonds are not a map to the territory of larger political realities. On the contrary, in Tourgée's novel the private relations among citizens—ranging from kinship and interracial friendship to extralegal racial violence—are all shown to be conditioned by "irrepressible" conflicts in the realm of the political.

Notes

1. Albion W. Tourgée, *Bricks without Straw*, ed. Carolyn L. Karcher (Durham, NC: Duke University Press, 2009), 288, 352, 291. All future page references to this edition will be cited parenthetically in the main body of the text.

2. Nina Silber, *The Romance of Reunion: Northerners and the South, 1865–1900* (Chapel Hill: University of North Carolina Press, 1997), 2.

3. Roman Jakobson, "Two Aspects of Language and Two Types of Aphasic Disturbances," in *On Language*, ed. Linda Waugh (Cambridge, MA: Harvard University Press, 1995), 115–33.

4. For a close examination of how jurists in the South wrestled with the "state of legal limbo" of recently emancipated persons, see Giuliana Perrone, "What to the Law Is the Former Slave," *Slavery and Abolition* 40, no. 2 (2019): 256–70. See also Perrone's study of how that uncertain legal status required jurists to devise doctrines for addressing the "presumed illegality of the enslaved family" as freedmen and freedwoman made claims that turned on marriage, kinship, and inheritance. Giuliana Perrone, "'Back in the Days of Slavery': Freedom, Citizenship, and the Black Family in the Reconstruction-Era Courtroom," *Law and History Review* 37, no. 1 (2019): 125–61.

5. On Black "kinlessness," see Hortense J. Spillers, "Mama's Baby, Papa's Maybe: An American Grammar Book," *Diacritics* 17, no. 2 (1987): 64–81. The historian Dylan C. Penningroth addresses Black kinlessness from a different angle in discussing the ways that slavery in West Africa—as opposed to slavery in the Americas—relied on imposing new kin ties on those with slave status rather than on stripping all legal kinship. Dylan C. Penningroth, *The Claims of Kinfolk: African American Property and Community in the Nineteenth-Century South* (Chapel Hill: University of North Carolina Press, 2003).

6. Penningroth, *Claims of Kinfolk,* 11. All future page references to this edition will be cited parenthetically in the main body of the text.

7. Marshall Sahlins, *What Kinship Is—and Is Not* (Chicago: University of Chicago Press, 2013), 2.

4

Reparations and Passing in Tourgée's *Pactolus Prime*

DeLisa D. Hawkes

lbion Tourgée's provocative passing novel, *Pactolus Prime, or The White Christ*, was serialized in the *Chicago Advance* from December 13, 1888, to March 14, 1889, and then published as a book in 1890. The novel received mixed reviews, primarily because of its seemingly intimate and too-close-for-comfort critiques of racial injustice done under the guise of Christianity. Tourgée was aware that the novel would touch a nerve. He wrote in his unpublished notes, "I have no defense for [*Pactolus Prime*], don't know whether it is artistically or technically correct or not and don't care. It is a mere vehicle for thought. If it serves that purpose and jams home the idea like a wasp's tail I am satisfied."[1] Although not entirely convinced of Tourgée's literary talent, but aware of the risks he took in the novel, Anna Julia Cooper praised *Pactolus Prime* in *A Voice from the South* (1892), noting not only the novel's success in "photographing and vocalizing the feelings of the colored American" but also in describing the main character, Pactolus Prime, as "Judge Tourgée himself, done over in ebony." Cooper categorized Tourgée as a preacher with an interest in writing, stating that "novel making with him seems to be a mere incident, a convenient vehicle through which to convey those burning thoughts which he is constantly trying to impress upon the people of America."[2] Tourgée's unpublished notes show that he would not have taken offense with Cooper's analysis.

One of Tourgée's "burning thoughts," which he develops in the novel through Prime, is the possibility of reparations for the formerly enslaved. He discusses reparations by focusing on racial passing and raising questions about racialized religion—what Prime calls "White Christianity."[3] Before the Civil War, many white Christians supported the practice of slavery; after the war, many of these same individuals closed their eyes to the damage done to Black Americans through the lingering aftereffects of slavery. In the passing-novel genre, authors usually depict Black characters who appear white as attempting to pass by way of escaping from white characters' hateful gazes and gaining access to a better life, economically and otherwise. The "gains" made from passing often come at the price of being isolated from family and friends. In *Pactolus Prime*, Tourgée moves the passing novel in a different direction, inviting readers to consider the possibility of reparations for the harm done to enslaved Africans and their descendants by staging debates between the novel's main characters.

Pactolus Prime follows the life of Pactolus Prime, the Black bootblack at the novel's center, while uncovering the problematic underpinnings of passing and racial injustice.[4] Born into slavery to a Black woman and a white father who was also a congressman, Prime passed as a white Union officer and eventual lieutenant of a Black regiment after attacking his enslaver upon seeing him make advances towards his love interest Mazy. Years later, Prime reunites with Mazy but discovers that she has had a child with her enslaver, presumably as the result of sexual violence. The narrator later reveals that Prime's apprentice Benny is that child. Prime and Mazy eventually start a family and live comfortably in South Carolina while passing for white. However, Prime returns to a Black identity after suffering from a chemical reaction that changes his skin to a "leaden-gray" color (28). This incident, which Prime refers to as an ailment, makes it impossible for him to maintain his white disguise. His marriage ends abruptly when he discovers that his wife is having an affair with their former enslaver. Prime takes their young daughter, Eva, away to Washington, DC, and begins a new life. Eva grows up to know Prime only as her dear old "Uncle Pac"—her father's former servant—and not as her father. Fearing that "followers of the white Christ were seeking to take [Eva] away" (318) out of suspicion of their close relationship, Prime sends her farther North to be raised and educated as a white woman.

Now, in the novel's present, an older, well-to-do owner of a bootblack business in Washington, DC—a setting that allows Tourgée to speak to the nation's political and social condition as a whole—Prime regularly critiques whiteness as a physical marker of supposed superiority, civilization, and Christian values. In his conversations with white customers, he condemns the US government for not offering reparations for enslavement, which he believes would help end economic disparities and internalized racism among members of the novel's Black community. In this regard, *Pactolus Prime* stands as one of the earliest American novels to make a case for reparations. Cooper takes note of Tourgée's bravery in advocating for reparations, noting, "Not many would have dared, fearlessly as he did, to arraign this country for an enormous pecuniary debt to the colored man for the two hundred and forty-seven years of unpaid labor of his ancestors. Not many could so determinedly have held up the glass of the real Christianity before those believers in a white Christ."[5]

Nevertheless, and somewhat surprisingly given his support for reparations, Prime continues to implore younger members of his community, including

Benny, to pass for white if they can. He believes that appearing white ensures economic stability and generational wealth that would have otherwise been impossible without government-granted reparations. Prime's choice to promote racial passing says less about the actual act and more about the social value placed on racial appearances by self-proclaimed Christians. He (and Tourgée) would much prefer a program of reparations with equal and equitable opportunities over mere lip-service apologies.

Prime displays racial pride that has an impact on some of his fellow Black community members who attempt to dismantle racial injustice in the form of economic independence. At the same time, Prime teaches his white customers at the hotel about the contradictions in their claims to be Christians in a racist society. As Prime puts it simply early in the novel: Followers of a white Christ "have a heap to say about 'jestice and mercy,'" but their lack of action to address the racial crimes of the past and present only convey the idea that Black Americans should "be mighty grateful for [their] *sheer of what's left*" (17). Tourgée's emphasis on "sheer" highlights the view that Black Americans have been offered the bare minimum in terms of equity within the United States.

Prime (or, as Cooper would suggest, Tourgée) clarifies that he mainly aims to criticize what he identifies as *white Christianity*. Prime asserts, "I do not mean . . . to assail Christianity. I know little about it except in the abstract, for my own ideas have become so warped that I can hardly imagine a church which has not one door for black and another for white believers" (297). The fact that Prime knows little of what he alludes to as true Christianity speaks to the fallen nature of white Christianity in US society. These views fall in line with those expressed by Frederick Douglass (whom Tourgée eulogized), who clarifies in his famed 1845 *Narrative* that he also distinguishes between true Christianity and the Christianity of the "*slaveholding region* of this land."[6] Of course, Douglass's comment applies not only to the region labeled as "the South," for slavery existed throughout the nation and was supported by many northern industries, such as shipping and manufacturing. Douglass notes that the Christianity of this land is both "partial and hypocritical" and that to call the United States "Christian" would be "the climax of all misnomers, the boldest of all frauds, and the grossest of all libels."[7] Prime, in many ways, echoes these same views in his debates with his white customers. By offering these critiques, the passing character Prime becomes something like a Black "white" Christ; his physical appearance and racial identities cross society's color line while he seeks to inspire change in the novel's other characters about the racist beliefs and practices that exist within white Christianity.

Prime's initial act of passing, his suggestion that others should pass, and his discussions with his white customers about the need for restorative justice for Black Americans, point to the hypocritical nature of some white Americans' celebrations of the United States as a white Christian nation. Prime aligns slavery with white Christianity when debating with his white customers at the bootblack stand, stating that slavery was "only another name for the worship of the White Christ!" (67). He adds that so-called Christians measure "right and wrong by the color of the skin" (67). Prime depicts white Christianity as *the* dominating institution that fails to offer salvation while seeking to impose a hierarchy based solely on race and color. That hierarchy, Prime suggests, has its roots in the fallen Christianity that white Americans uphold through legal measures.

Consequently, Prime also chastises those Black community members who believe in the so-called Christian nation to the point that they internalize racist beliefs about themselves. Put simply, Prime's analysis of US society and its majority religion imply that such was the psychological pressure on Black Americans to buy into "white Christianity" that those capable of doing so should choose to pass as white. In this formulation, passing proves a tempting choice brought on by a desire to be part of a supposedly Christian nation.

Despite Prime's questionable presentation of his advocacy, the overall novel argues, to the contrary, that the far better solution would be for true Christians, white Christians in particular, to acknowledge the dire consequences and moral evil of slavery and offer reparations to Black Americans. Prime says, "Perhaps . . . the true Christ, not the white Christ whose worship is tainted with apology for lust and greed meant thereby to teach those who would condition His grace and prescribe the method of its operation and extension, that He is no respecter of persons, and will make even their pride and sin to minister to His mercy and love" (139). Although Prime's commentary here does not directly focus on reparations, his interrogation of the color line through passing, here and elsewhere in the novel, demonstrates to his peers on the full spectrum of the color line what true equality entails according to a true Christian believer. He repeatedly contrasts true Christians with white supremacist Christians who fail to offer reparations as a form of repentance. As the Black "white" Christ, Prime performs a ministry intended to show white readers what a truly Christian nation might entail.

Notions of Christianity prove central to the novel from its very beginning. The omniscient narrator sets the scene during a seemingly peaceful Christmas morning in Washington, DC. In many respects, *Pactolus Prime* is a Christmas novel as much as it is a passing novel. The narrator describes an aura that fills the streets and gives life to Black and white Washingtonians alike. More importantly, the narrator carefully notes how such a "Christian capital" of a "Christian nation" filled with a "Christian people" makes these individuals "not as other men" (2) but, surprisingly, as a potentially utopian nation. Despite the many problems that Prime addresses throughout the novel, the narrator depicts US citizens' purportedly Christian character, going so far as to claim that the United States is a "favored nation . . . [f]ounded in justice" (2) and exalted in righteousness. Counter to other nations where "heathens" reside in darkness, states the narrator, the United States basks in the protection of the herald angels because it is "the most Christian nation of the most enlightened epoch of the Christian era" (3–4). Nevertheless, within the novel's first scene, where the narrator introduces the main characters at the bootblack stand in a segregated hotel, readers are presented with how white Christianity has contributed to economic injustice through systemic racism. The overinsistent language that Tourgée uses to describe the United States' claims to religious morality by self-proclaimed Christians highlights the harsh reality of the racial injustice that these same individuals perpetuate.

Prime directly connects white Christianity to calls for reparations despite US society's failure to offer such a program because of its race and color prejudices. Shortly after describing the Christmas morning setting, the narrator invites readers to consider how the lack of support for reparations is rooted in racist beliefs filtered through economic arguments. Prime addresses several popular counterarguments to offering reparations. For instance, he considers the stance that the government freed formerly enslaved people after the Civil War and that freedom alone should be enough compensation. One of Prime's white customers, simply referred to as "the Major," asks, "Didn't the white man give you your freedom?" Prime responds, "Didn't he first deprive us of our liberty?" (97). Language associated with banking, such as "credit," "account," and "debit," occurs throughout this exchange, pointing to the centrality of economic justice to Prime's arguments. The men's discussion illustrates that freedom *was not* enough payment. Prime then raises the ever-present issue of race discrimination, asserting, "In other words, having deprived us of *all* our rights for two hundred and fifty years, we became the debtor of the race as soon as they give us back a *part* of what the laws of God and nature declare to be our own" (97). For Prime, the question of reparations includes both economic justice and full acknowledgment of Black peoples' human rights.

Prime also addresses the argument that Black Americans should be grateful for their ancestors being brought to the United States. The Major brings up this point, to which Prime replies (somewhat in the mode of Phillis Wheatley's famous 1773 poem "On Being Brought from Africa to America"), "I don't deny that it was a great advantage to the colored race to be brought to this country . . . I do not doubt that God did it; but no follower of the white Christ is entitled to any credit for it. It was not done . . . for His glory. . . . It was done in the name of the white Christ, and with the claim of having His sanction and approval" (103). Once again, Prime makes a distinction between the white Christ and the true Christ, thus noting that enslavement and violence were surely not a part of His plan as "*He* is the Saviour of men" (103). Tourgée emphasizes "He" to imply the difference between Christ recognized by true Christians and Christ recognized by those who follow white Christianity. Prime indicates that white Europeans' racist attitudes disguised as religious missions—namely, "the white man's burden"—directed the slave trade rather than any efforts to exemplify the Christian virtues of faith, hope, and love.[8]

To help develop his Christian themes, Tourgée depicts a minister visiting Prime's bootblack stand on this Christmas morning. The two men engage in a seemingly friendly debate up until the point that the minister explains his view that Black Americans are "too impatient" in their efforts to receive equal and fair treatment. Prime then shifts the conversation's focus to economic equality and reparations, stating, "If the amount thus unjustly held from *you* had embraced every cent you had earned in your whole life—the entire earnings of your parents and their parents for two centuries and a half . . . would you think you ought to be called 'impatient'" (71; emphasis added). The minister admits that he probably feels less passionately about reparations because he identifies as white, to which Prime hints at his own personal experience of passing for white. The narrator describes Prime "glancing up with a sardonic grin" as he says, "Well yes . . . I *am* so taken and accepted [as a colored man]" (71). Prime's inflection on "am" points to the fact that his race remains a mystery throughout most of his life (and most of the novel), even after the chemical reaction. His racial ambiguity and economic position enable him to have such candid conversations with white men about Black Americans' current plight. Furthermore, the minister's reason for not sympathizing with formerly enslaved persons and their right to reparations demonstrates that individuals might take certain causes to be limited to certain racial identities.

Prime uses white Christians' racialized view of Black people against them to help further his point that those formerly enslaved and their descendants are owed reparations. He tells Mr. Phelps, another one of his customers, "You're Christian . . . and I am only a black pagan, but we manage to understand each other pretty well" (68). Here, Prime places white Christians and "pagans" on equal footing, noting that they share a similar worldview. Biblical teachings state that pagans worshiped idols and not the true God. By equating white Christians with pagans, Prime highlights white Christians' failure to worship the true Christ. Instead, these individuals exalt a hierarchy that would deny Black Americans "plain and simple justice . . . except [for] the mere fact of [their] color" (129). Prime bases his arguments about US society and the government's failure to offer reparations solely on assumed differences in racial appearances that the white Christians he critiques then attach to racial stereotypes.

Prime concludes his conversation with his customers by suggesting that white Christianity and its followers robbed Black Americans of reparative justice because white Christians' assumptions of racial superiority permeate US social and government institutions. When speaking about efforts to develop educational equality, Prime asks, "Why should not a Christian State that added the labor of the slave—aye even the slave himself, to its taxable aggregate—why should it not have educated his children?" (85). The minister acknowledges Prime's position that Black Americans were to blame for their social and economic plight. However, the minister still cannot understand Prime's criticisms against what he can only see as Christianity; he cannot comprehend Prime's criticism of a specifically white Christianity. Prime explains, "It was Christian men and women who [wronged Black people]—the earthly exponents of the Christian idea,—and they received the advantage" (77). The minister asks himself, "Who would have dreamed there could be such a difference in the views that may be taken of the Savior of Mankind and the Message which ushered in the Christian era! Is Prime right in calling Him the 'White Christ?'" (79). Again, Tourgée offers a textual distinction between "Him" and the "White Christ," thereby suggesting that the minister finally understands Prime's claim that *white Christianity* is at fault. The narrator notes the minister's internal conflict, describing his contemplation of "what would have been his own religious status had the *Man* Jesus Christ been black, and the circumstances of his life and that of Pactolus Prime been reversed" (80). The minister's thoughts signal the reader to consider the golden rule—"So in everything, do to others what you would have them do to you"—in the context of enslavement and reparations.[9] Imagining Christ as Black rather than white forces the minister to reconsider race and color's centrality to white Christian society. Prime's assertion that "the Christian idea of justice never gets across the color line" (93) starts to make sense to the minister.

Eventually, Prime also suggests that even some Black Americans contribute to US society's and the government's denial of reparations because of internalized racism. Prime chastises some members of his community, ironically through his counterintuitive support for racial passing, and sheds light upon white Christianity's ability to influence some Black people to aspire to pass for white. Prime points out that many followers of mainstream American Christianity, or white Christianity, are Black Americans. Thus, these Christians buy into the same beliefs as those individuals and institutions that attempt to oppress them.

Most scenes in which Prime urges other members of his community to pass usually feature conversations between Prime and Benny. Although Benny works for Prime at the bootblack stand, Benny aspires to become a civil rights lawyer. When Prime tells one of his customers about Benny's goals, he does not proudly reveal this information. Instead, he repeats ideas rooted in white racial prejudice, stating that Benny's racial identity will never allow him to make real change for his people through legal measures. Prime says that Benny "wants to be a lawyer like a white man," but "He's got no chance to be anything more or less than a [n——], and a [n——]'s got no call to be a lawyer" (59–60). Furthermore, Prime argues, "What's the good of law to him—or religion either, for that matter? Money's the god he ought to worship" (60). Prime proclaims that the law in the "Christian nation" that Tourgée illustrates in much of the novel does not aim to assist Black Americans; instead, the law works against them.

Prime brings the conversation's focus back to the question of economic justice to underscore his appeal for reparations. By discussing money as a god to be sought and worshipped, he highlights US society's and the government's heightened concerns over wealth for certain races—or certain racial appearances—at the expense of others. For, while Prime brutally discourages the lighter-complexioned Benny's career aspirations, he says, "the whiter a [n——] is, the less a white man cares for him. As long as a man's black he only just despises him; but when he begins to grow white he hates him" (38). Benny's "white" appearance implies two things to Prime: First, it means that some white people harbor hatred for lighter-complexioned individuals who are openly critical of white supremacy, especially considering Benny's goal of becoming a civil rights lawyer; and second, Prime associates wealth with whiteness via his claim that once a Black man "begins to grow white," white men begin to hate him. The threat of economic stability and generational wealth incite fear in those with powerful social status. Thus, wealth and the financial support beneficial to promoting political and social change must stay within certain individuals' pockets. Prime sees money as the dominant force driving US society and skin color as the means to access its power.

Many other passing novels depict the appearance of whiteness as providing characters access to certain privileges that would not be readily available to others without struggle; these include access to better jobs, education, and social standing, for example. Therefore, Prime tells Benny to pass for white to collect the social benefits that reparations would have provided had the government not denied them. Prime advocates for passing because he feels that asserting one's Black racial identity would not bring about the justice owed to those whom white so-called Christians formerly enslaved; the same is true for the descendants of the formerly enslaved, which Prime underscores by noting the generational effects of these systemic inequities. Prime tells Benny that even though he identifies as a Black man, he is a white man by appearance. Thus, he encourages Benny to "get to be a white man as fast as possible" to "get rich" (39–40) and secure the best life possible for his future family. Benny undoubtedly harbors some negative feelings toward his white appearance, to which Prime assures him, "You are not responsible for [your appearance]; and can't change the fact, but you are responsible for the use or misuse you make of it. The question is whether you will give your children the advantage of being regarded as superior beings to whom all opportunities are open, or leave them to struggle with the same difficulties that confront you" (135). According to Prime, Benny's white appearance—not his future in the practice of law—is his and his future children's saving grace. White supremacy practiced by self-proclaimed Christians promotes the idea that certain races are "regarded as superior" and closes off opportunities based solely on racial appearance and racist beliefs. Prime notes the social and cash value of Benny's appearance and urges him to use it to his advantage; otherwise, he will achieve limited success.

In telling Benny that he "is not responsible" for his appearance, Prime signals the sexual violence that occurred during enslavement and resulted in racial codes and laws against interracial marriage that aimed to keep the races separate. These legal measures also formally established a racial social hierarchy. Prime reiterates ties connecting race and color to religion, stating, "Why God gave the white man a right to take all he could get. . . . Perhaps no one is very fond of the evidence of his own evil, and *everyone like you* is a living testimony of the white man's falsehood, treachery, and crime" (39; emphasis added). Here, Prime essentially claims that Benny's lighter appearance represents the embodiment of white men's crimes—what he calls in other passages "sins"—against enslaved Black women. Prime's appeal to Benny to pass gets around the issue that white self-proclaimed Christians fail to atone for these crimes and sins through reparations.

Prime also mentions that although the community widely knows Benny as a lighter-complexioned Black man, he can create a new identity in a different city, while creating a new identity for his future children as well. He tells Benny, "Be grateful you're white an' don't be too inquisitive about how you became so.

It may not do *you* much good, but your children may have a heap better chance in this world" (39). In Prime's view, Benny's appearance, not his expertise in law, can allow him to make changes for future generations. He furthermore suggests that Benny's appearance offers him a simple choice: "Remember . . . when you think of becoming a colored man by choice, or refusing to make yourself a white man, as you might, what a world of unmerited degradation you are bequeathing to your children and their offspring" (46). Ultimately, Prime sees the law as incapable of bringing about the generational equality that reparations from the government would otherwise bring. He takes this position simply because he does not believe the law was created to assist or represent Black Americans.

Benny remains hopeful for the ability to maintain his Black racial identity while making a better life for his future children and fighting for equality for his entire race. He asks Prime, "Don't you think the good Christian men and women who have done so much to enlighten our people, will see that there cannot be peace and prosperity and true Christian feeling without equality of opportunity?" (135). Prime responds, "Christianity is a very flexible idea. It is a religion that runs with popular thought and adapts itself to popular prejudices. . . . Christianity does not demand or require that its followers should do justice to other men if they happen to be [n——s]" (135, 137). In other words, Prime does not believe that society can change its treatment toward Black Americans until it changes the way it uses Christianity to justify white supremacy.

Prime's daughter, Eva, points to how institutions are shaped by beliefs fostered in the private domestic sphere. Prime sends Eva to a convent for her education, alluding to the connections between racialized religion, passing, and reparations. But rather than continue to live as a white woman after learning about her father's ancestry and enslaved past, Eva decides to live as a Black woman and participate in the racial uplift movement. Eva's character provides a nuanced take on the "tragic mulatto/a" figure that can be found in such African American novels as Frances E. W. Harper's *Iola Leroy* (1892) and Sutton Griggs's *Overshadowed* (1901). The main characters in these two novels offer revised versions of the "tragic mulatta" figure to demonstrate an active participation in altering ideas about race and gender. Characters like Harper's Iola and Griggs's Erma take it upon themselves to spread their new ideology to others within their communities, thereby signaling Harper's and Griggs's shared belief in the possibility of changing the hearts and minds of Black and white audiences alike. Tourgée's Prime works in a similar tradition but through an unconventional take on passing that emerges from his critique of white Christianity.

Prime sends Eva away for the same purpose that he wants Benny to pass for white: so that her blackness will not threaten her opportunity to live a life untainted by racial prejudice. This fate, Prime believes, would surely be inevitable given "Christian [civilization's ability] to drive her back into the abyss" (321) should she be stamped with a Black identity. Prime makes clear the problems that Eva faces in passing. He observes that the widely declared view of the "one-drop rule" dominates "Christian civilization" and that although her peers now view her as "white," that will not always be so. He also remains unsure about the racial (or racist) foundations of her faith, saying, "I could not bring myself to have her taught that form of Christian faith which has been so fateful to all colored peoples" (322). The word "fateful" draws attention to the destructive nature of white Christianity's treatment of African-descended peoples, at least in Prime's view. He underscores his sense of the distinction between Catholicism and American Protestantism by having Eva sent to a convent, stating, "She has been educated by the Good Sisters; but they were instructed that no effort to proselyte her would be tolerated . . . I trust she still believes in Christ,—whether she believes in Christianity or not" (322). Once again, speaking of his desire for Eva to pass, Prime turns his sights to demonstrating how racial identity is tied to more significant institutional concerns: "While I wished her to be white, I could not bear that she be taught to despise the race with which she is even remotely allied" (322). Prime takes on the personal responsibility of parentage, albeit remotely because of his now darker complexion.

It is no coincidence that Eva discovers that Prime is her father at the moment when she considers whether to marry a white man. Prime's attorney's decision to tell Eva about her father at this specific moment serves as a reference to the US legal system's attempts to prevent interracial unions, as well as to draw readers' attention back to Prime's concerns over future generations and what is ultimately his self-sacrificial relationship to his daughter. Upon Prime's death, the leading newspaper reports on this selfless old bootblack's dedication to "his old master's daughter" (347), celebrating him as a hero who "had given wealth to the child of another, the daughter of a 'superior race'" (351). However, Eva accepts the knowledge of her father's ancestry and, in some ways, now displays her own racial pride. She rejects the marriage and decides to use her wealth to give back to her Black community, thus offering her own form of reparations under the name "Sister Pactola." Her new life at the convent brings attention to the possible role that white Christians can play in dismantling racist social structures and addressing racist histories.

During each of Prime's appeals for passing, Tourgée has his eponymous character critiquing white Christianity as well. Tourgée uses his novel to illuminate three detrimental factors contributing to the dismal state of inter-/intraracial affairs in the late-nineteenth-century United States: racialized applications of religion (white Christianity), the failure to provide reparations through equal and equitable opportunities, and internalized racism. Tourgée offers an early exploration into how key practices and ideologies such as racial passing and racialized religion influenced or outright led the charge to stop any meaningful attempt at racial reconciliation at the institutional level and through reparations. The novel explores the development of systemic racism—its circulatory and institutional formation—through white citizens' invidious applications of Christian teachings. Prime's critiques of white Christianity and its followers' failures to acknowledge the original sins of racism, slavery, and sexual violence against enslaved Africans and their descendants make an appeal to readers to consider some social sacrifice, such as providing reparations and letting go of social value in white appearances.

At a time when attempts at making amends for historical wrongs tend to take the form of mere statements and lip service without tangible results, Tourgée's *Pactolus Prime* seems ever timelier as it invites twenty-first-century readers to consider what institutional changes need to be made to address the nation's crimes and sins of enslavement, land dispossession, and racial discrimination, to name a few. Take, for instance, the Southern Baptist Convention's 1995 apology for slavery and racism. Anthea Butler notes that although the statement offers a well-written apology, "it does not address restitution for the structural racism within the institution," nor does it address the "the political positions of the denomination."[10] In *Pactolus Prime*, Tourgée calls on white Christianity's followers to make tangible steps toward the ideological shifts and institutional reform necessary to bring actual change rather than mere apologies or empty statements about historical crimes and their persistent afterlives.

Notes

1. Albion Tourgée, "Pactolus Prime," Albion Tourgée Papers, MS 5193, Chautauqua County Historical Society, 4.

2. Anna Julia Cooper, *A Voice from the South* (Xenia, OH: Aldine, 1892), 188–89.

3. Albion Tourgée, *Pactolus Prime* (1890; Upper Saddle River, NJ: Gregg, 1968), 140. All future parenthetical page references from this edition will be supplied in the main body of the text.

4. For more on Tourgée's depiction of passing and debates over reparations, see Carolyn Karcher's chapter "Passing for Black in *Pactolus Prime*" in her excellent study

A Refugee from His Race: Albion W. Tourgée and His Fight against White Supremacy (Chapel Hill: University of North Carolina Press, 2016), 54–90.

5. Cooper, *A Voice from the South*, 192.

6. For more on Tourgée's eulogy for Douglass, see Mark Elliott's essential book on Tourgée, *Color-Blind Justice: Albion Tourgée and the Quest for Racial Equality from the Civil War to Plessy v. Ferguson* (New York: Oxford University Press, 2006), esp. the chapter "The Making of a Radical Individualist in Ohio's Western Reserve," 43–72.

7. Frederick Douglass, *Narrative of the Life of Frederick Douglass* (1845; New York: Signet Classics, 2005), 122.

8. 1 Corinthians 13:13.

9. Matthew 7:12.

10. Anthea Butler, *White Evangelical Racism* (Chapel Hill: University of North Carolina Press, 2021), 93–94.

5

The True Friendship of Charles W. Chesnutt and Albion W. Tourgée

Tess Chakkalakal

Charles Waddell Chesnutt was a child of the Reconstruction era, a period full of great hope and promise for those "Free Blacks," like Chesnutt and his family, eager to put the racial strife of slavery and the Civil War behind them. His southern journals reveal a young man yearning for intellectual conversation and companionship that he could not find in the segregated South.

Long before he left the South for Cleveland, where he embarked on a literary career and became a central figure in the racial uplift movement, Chesnutt dreamed of a "True friendship," finding a friend with whom he has "something in common," a friendship where "there is respect as well as admiration."[1] In the absence of such a friend, Chesnutt turned to his journal for intellectual companionship. Living in the segregated South and working as a schoolteacher in various "colored" schools offered few opportunities for rigorous conversation about the books he was reading and the political issues of the day. Writing in his journal in 1882, for instance, Chesnutt complained that he had "no white friends." He refused to keep company with men who believed themselves to be "too good to sit at table with me, or to sleep at the same hotel" (25). Chesnutt's repudiation of "white friends" was written well after he had read *A Fool's Errand* shortly after its publication on March 16, 1880; he did not know at the time that its author, Albion Winegar Tourgée, would become the kind of white friend he was seeking, a friend who did not think he was too good to sit at table with a colored man like Chesnutt, who respected and admired Chesnutt for his literary abilities, and who shared his interest in literature and politics.

As unlikely as it was, it is not altogether surprising that Chesnutt would find friendship in his early thirties with Tourgée, a white former Union solider from Ohio, twenty years his senior. As Carolyn L. Karcher reveals in her biography of Tourgée, African Americans of the time widely regarded Tourgée as their most reliable white ally.[2] Tourgée's correspondence and friendships with African Americans have figured prominently in recent discussions of his life and work.

Figure 3. Albion Winegar Tourgée, circa 1880. (Courtesy of the Chautauqua County Historical Society, McClurg Museum.)

Figure 4. Charles Waddell Chesnutt at forty years old. Chesnutt Bros. (Cleveland, Ohio). (Courtesy of the Cleveland Public Library, Fine Arts and Special Collections Department.)

But his friendship with Charles Chesnutt, who went on to write *The Marrow of Tradition* (1901), the most important novel dealing with the race problem after the 1896 *Plessy v. Ferguson* decision, was singular. This underappreciated friendship, predicated on a common commitment to literature, is pivotal to imagining the possibility of a friendship that transcends the racial constraints imposed by legal segregation in the United States.

On the surface, the two appear to have little in common. Shortly after the war, Tourgée moved to Greensboro, North Carolina, where he set up a profitable business, "A.W. Tourgée & Co.," with other northern Unionists. Through this collaboration, he operated a nursery and plantation, practiced law, and engaged in other financial ventures. It would not be long before Tourgée entered politics, first serving as an influential delegate to the 1868 state constitutional convention and then as a superior court justice from 1868 to 1874. While Tourgée was steeped in the legal, political, and business worlds of the state, Chesnutt was working as a school teacher at the State Colored Normal School in Fayetteville.

Tourgée's and Chesnutt's paths never crossed in North Carolina. While living about a hundred miles apart, they were moving in very different social spheres. Chesnutt learned of Tourgée in 1879, soon after the publication of his bestselling novel, *A Fool's Errand*, but it was not until December 1888, after Tourgée had paid Chesnutt a highly public compliment, that the two became friends.

"Judge Tourgée has sold the 'Fool's Errand,' I understand, for $20,000," Chesnutt mused in his journal on March 16, 1880 (124). The novel earned another $24,000 in the six months following its initial publication, a sum that would be just under a million dollars in today's terms. The novel's popularity and critical success led to a new edition with a documentary supplement, "The Invisible Empire," detailing the activities of the Ku Klux Klan. Chesnutt could not help but be impressed by the novel's popularity. Unlike novels by Charles Dickens and poems by Lord Byron, which he spent much of his time reading, the scenes and characters of *A Fool's Errand* were familiar to Chesnutt from his experiences in North Carolina. Tourgée's novel raised Chesnutt's hopes that he could have a similar critical and popular success.

Tourgée was forty-one when he published *A Fool's Errand* and was hailed as the preeminent novelist of the Reconstruction era, moving past some of the more familiar luminaries of the period such as Mark Twain and Harriet Beecher Stowe. The novel offers a panorama of Reconstruction, from its hopeful beginning to its bitter end, from the point of view of "a carpet-bagger"—a northerner who moves to the South to capitalize on the cheap labor and land left behind by the devastation of the war. It features a naive protagonist in Comfort Servosse, whose limited experiences fighting in the Civil War lead him to believe that he can have a fruitful career in the newly subdued southern states. The novel, as we are told at its outset, draws heavily on Tourgée's own experiences of his time in Greensboro, and he calls his fiction an "uncompromising truthfulness of portraiture."[3]

Tourgée had first entered the South's literary scene in North Carolina by establishing and editing a radical unionist newspaper in Greensboro called the *Union Register*. Co-edited with A. B. Chapin, a native of Michigan and a recent Union Army surgeon, the paper espoused the principles of Radical Reconstruction, which he developed more fully in *A Fool's Errand*. The novel teeters between romance and political manifesto. Following the adventures of the novel's hero, Tourgée traces his course from his enlistment as a Union soldier following the northern defeat at Bull Run, through his decision to take his wife and daughter to live in North Carolina, to Comfort's death, as he is mourned by friends, family, and former enemies. Along the way, readers are introduced to a number of southern characters who remain so absurdly set in their ways and unable to listen to the reasonable ideas of the Fool that readers are left to marvel at their profound ignorance and to wonder how to bring about change to such a backward-looking society.

The novel argues that what the South needs is education, of a most rigorous kind, one that can only be provided by men with political vision and a sense of justice, like the novel's hero and its creator. As Otto Olsen, Tourgée's first biographer, observes of the novel: "Not only did it offer the populace an astute and entertaining account of the Reconstruction puzzle, but it particularly pleased those Republicans who were reacting against the conciliatory tactics of President Hayes, and it provided the Republican party with a powerful campaign weapon for the approaching election."[4] Olsen, unlike Tourgée's later readers, is quick to point out the partisan appeal of Tourgée's fiction. While Tourgée provides a more sympathetic portrayal of the South than most northerners, the novel makes no secret of its political biases. Tourgée is committed to informing readers how to complete the difficult task of explaining to the South the error of its ways and how to implement a better plan for its total reconstruction.

Chesnutt offers a judicious reading of the novel, focusing less on its political influence than its literary value. Though he has not yet met the author, he reports that "Judge Tourgée is a Northern man, who has lived at the South since the war, until recently" and that "he knows a great deal about the politics, history, and laws of the South." Impressed by Tourgée's powers of observation, Chesnutt notes the innovation of employing "this faculty of observation upon the character of the Southern people" (124–25).

Despite its innovation and observation, the novel's limitations are just as important. Chesnutt goes on to note "something romantic" about the northern interest in the "southern negro" that Tourgée's novel taps into but also that "his necessarily limited intercourse with colored people, and . . . limited stay in the South" make it inevitable that he would leave some crucial things out of his account of the region. Chesnutt traces Tourgée's literary limitations to the narrowness of his experience with the South and its people, so that Chesnutt, "a colored man who knew all this, and who, besides, had possessed such opportunities for observation and conversation with the better class of white men in the south as to understand their modes of thinking; who was familiar with the political history of the country, and especially with all the phases of the slavery question" could correct them. Chesnutt decided he could write "a far better book about the South than Judge Tourgée or Mrs. Stowe has written" (125).

What would a far better book about the South be? Would it be less sentimental than Stowe's *Uncle Tom's Cabin* or based more on authorial imagination than Tourgée's real-life experiences and political commitments? Chesnutt's relatively long March 1880 journal entry on Tourgée is well known among readers of the two men's fiction. As Bill Hardwig notes, "These critics have rightly emphasized Tourgée's influence on Chesnutt's career as a writer, as one of the sparks which ignited his literary aspirations."[5] But Hardwig and like-minded critics have come to view the relationship between Chesnutt and Tourgée as more competitive than collaborative.[6] If we examine the full extent of their correspondence and friendship, however, we can see that their relationship extends well beyond Chesnutt's 1880 journal entry. In fact, it wasn't until Tourgée encountered Chesnutt's fiction when it was published in the *Atlantic Monthly* that we can begin to assess the true nature of their relationship.

Of Chesnutt's seven stories that appeared in the prestigious *Atlantic Monthly*, the first two of these, "The Goophered Grapevine" and "Po' Sandy," were published less than a year apart, in August 1887 and May 1888, respectively. There is an abundance of literary criticism detailing Chesnutt's brilliant amalgamation of the classics with African American folklore and folk culture in these stories; however, the stories are also interesting for their publication history. When "The Goophered Grapevine" appeared in the *Atlantic* in the late summer of 1887, the monthly magazine was considered to be "the organ of the literary craft in the United States."[7] Founded thirty years earlier by a few of the most celebrated authors of the time—Harriet Beecher Stowe, Henry Wadsworth Longfellow, and Ralph Waldo Emerson, among others—the *Atlantic* marked a major literary effort to articulate the North's collective opposition to slavery. Following the Civil War, the *Atlantic* quickly shifted gears and became known as a proponent for literary excellence. Most of the literature printed in the *Atlantic* had been from England or New England, but by the time Chesnutt's work appeared in its pages, it had extended its understanding of what counted as literature to include works dealing with the South. Much of this extension was thanks to William Dean Howells, who served as its editor-in-chief for a decade, from 1871 to 1881. Hailing not from Boston but from rural Ohio, where Tourgée also spent his formative years, Howells made it his business to ensure that all of the nation's regions were represented in the post–Civil War *Atlantic*.

Often referred to as "the first work of fiction by an African-American author to appear in so prestigious a publication as the *Atlantic Monthly*," "The

Goophered Grapevine" might also be read as Chesnutt's first publication that imagines a conversation with Tourgée's *Fool*.[8] The story opens with the voice of a first-person narrator who remains unnamed. All we know about him is that he has a wife called Annie, who is in poor health, and that he has "been engaged in grape-culture in northern Ohio."[9] He relocates to central North Carolina, where he purchases a vineyard that "had not been attended to since the war and had fallen into utter neglect." The similarities between Chesnutt's northern narrator and Tourgée's Comfort Servosse are clear. Comfort, like Chesnutt's narrator, hails from northern Ohio and purchases a vineyard on an old plantation that he finds in a deplorably "deteriorated condition." However, Chesnutt's story moves swiftly from the voice of this Tourgée-like narrator to the voice of a "venerable-looking colored man" called Uncle Julius. The remainder of the story is told in the voice of Julius McAdoo, a former slave who possesses an intelligence and gift for story-telling that dumbfounds the story's northern narrator.

The northern narrator, called John in Chesnutt's later *Conjure Woman Stories* (1899), returns only briefly at the end of Uncle Julius's story to reveal his limited understanding of both the southern land and its people. He is motivated to take Julius's story seriously by the "respectable revenue" he earns "from the neglected grapevines" (43). Whether or not the story was intended to critique or celebrate Tourgée's well-known work of fiction is beside the point. What matters is that the story caught the more established writer's attention, and he was so moved by it that in December 1888 he celebrated its little-known author publicly in an audacious critique of contemporary American literature.

Eighteen eighty-eight was a banner year for Tourgée. In April, Tourgée launched "A Bystander's Notes," a weekly editorial column published in the Chicago newspaper *Inter Ocean*. Considered an exemplary organ of the Republican Party, it was said to have had the largest circulation of any morning newspaper in Chicago. The column was an ideal platform for Tourgée to expound his opinions on all the political issues of the day, from strikes and tariffs to lynchings and literature. With his column, Tourgée became a well-known political commentator reaching as many as two hundred thousand subscribers nationwide. The publication of Chesnutt's stories in the *Atlantic* moved Tourgée to turn to the well-respected northern journal *Forum* to publish "The South as a Field for Fiction," a sustained critical discussion of contemporary American literature. Olsen terms the tone of the column "petty partisanship," but it is fair to say that Tourgée took a more objective study of the literary scene.

"The South as a Field for Fiction" offers one of the first critical appreciations of Chesnutt's works in print. Tourgée argues that the novel as a genre had been defined since its inception by its ability to recognize the complexity of the human condition in those who have been shunned by society:

> The life of the Negro as a slave, freedman, and racial outcast offers undoubtedly the richest mine of romantic material that has opened to the English-speaking novelist since the Wizard of the North [Sir Walter Scott] discovered and depicted the common life of Scotland. . . . The slave's devotion to the master was trite in the remote antiquity of letters; but the slave as a man, with his hopes, his fears, his faith, has been touched, and only touched, by the pen of the novelist.[10]

Departing from the "loyal former slave" caricature popularized by writers such as Joel Chandler Harris, Chesnutt's Uncle Julius is exemplary of "the slave as a man." Tourgée was perhaps the first of Chesnutt's readers to recognize the distinction of his fiction, and this recognition was attributable in no small part to the fact that he could see himself reflected in it. Perhaps recognizing in John the shortcomings of his fellow northern carpetbaggers, Tourgée was able to appreciate all the more the complexity with which Chesnutt renders men like Julius. In Uncle Julius, Tourgée observes an example of a slave as a complex character, "his hopes, his fears, his faith" represented with vivid accuracy. Such a work could only be produced, as Chesnutt well knew, by someone "who has lived among colored people all his life; who is familiar with their habits, their ruling passions, their prejudices; their whole moral and social condition." Unlike northern authors celebrated at the time, Tourgée goes on to explain that the work of writers like Chesnutt is "earnest, intense, full of action, and careless to a remarkable degree of the trivialities which both these authors [Howells and Henry James] esteem the most important features of real life." Tourgée treats William Dean Howells and Henry James, perhaps the most celebrated and prolific authors of the late nineteenth century, with nothing short of disdain. Having read Chesnutt's recent fiction, Tourgée also sees it as superior to the more popular stories of Joel Chandler Harris, whose "genius" has put the "traditions of the freedman's fireside . . . into his quaint vernacular." By placing Chesnutt's fiction above the work of these critically acclaimed and popular writers, Tourgée was attempting to alter the American literary landscape through his polemical literary criticism.

Other literary friendships have commenced with a glowing written tribute or perceptive review. Compared to Herman Melville's "Hawthorne and His Mosses" (1850), Tourgée's comments about Chesnutt appear somewhat understated. His carefully veiled appraisal of Chesnutt reveals much about the racial restrictions of the time that would have inhibited a literary alliance between the two authors. Still, Tourgée's allusions to his work were not lost on Chesnutt; he took the essay as an opportunity to reach out. In a letter sent shortly after the essay's publication, he thanks Tourgée for the compliment paid as if they already knew each other, even though they had not yet met in person. In his response to Chesnutt's letter, Tourgée removes the veil of race separating them to celebrate the younger writer's work freely and warmly: "I have kept track of your work and have noted the growth. Its realism is unique and true—true to nature and not to the fettering ideas of the narrow rules which makes our so-called realism the falsest of fiction." In holding up Chesnutt's work as an example of "true realism" Tourgée takes yet another swipe at Howells and James, who have come to embody the conventional style. Contrary to later critical assessments of Chesnutt's realism, Tourgée declares Chesnutt's fiction to exemplify the form.[11]

Tourgée's letter continues with his views on the central principles of realism: "It involves American liberty—American civilization, and Protestant Christianity" and goes on to speculate that African Americans will become central to our understanding of American literature: "I incline to think that the climacteric of American literature will be negroloid [*sic*] in character—I do not mean in form—the dialect is a mere fleeting incident, but in style of thought, intensity of color, fervency of passion, and grandeur of aspiration." Chesnutt was busy working on new stories that exhibited the full extent of his literary powers and waited until the appearance of his third story in the *Atlantic*, "Dave's Neckliss," before responding to Tourgée's effusive letter. In his letter, Chesnutt pointedly instructs Tourgée how to read his latest publication:

> I take the liberty of sending you a copy of the October *Atlantic*, which contains one ["Dave's Neckliss"] of my stories, which if you read it, I hope you may think the best of the series. I think I have about used up the old Negro who serves as mouthpiece, and I shall drop him in future stories, as well as much of the dialect. The punishment of tying the stolen meat around the thief's neck was a real incident of slavery—in fact I think it hardly possible to imagine anything cruel or detestable that did not have its counterpart in that institution. The setting of that incident is of course pure fiction. I tried in this story to get out of the realm of superstition into the region of feeling and passion—with what degree of success the story itself can testify.[12]

Carolyn Karcher detects a "note of annoyance" in Chesnutt's letter, suggesting that he may have been "irritated" by some of Tourgée's remarks, particularly

his assertion that color was a "curse" (29). Indeed, Chesnutt would complain
in a later letter to George Washington Cable about "Judge Tourgée's cultivated
white negroes [who] are always bewailing their fate, and cursing the drop of
black blood that 'taints'—I hate the word, it implies corruption—their otherwise
pure blood."[13] Chesnutt feels a need to correct Tourgée's racial logic but does so
indirectly, not by telling him but by writing a story that would show him why the
problem is not color but the blindness of men who fail to see the truth. "Dave's
Neckliss" reveals "the simple but intensely human inner life of slavery" in which
a romance between two slaves—Dave and Dilsey—is interrupted by another
slave, Wiley, who wants Dilsey for himself. Falsely accused of stealing a ham,
Dave is tortured by his master, goes mad, and eventually kills himself. By getting
out of "the realm of superstition" and entering "the region of feeling and passion,"
Chesnutt attempts to upset the simple opposition between "colored characters"
and "white characters" that we find in much of Tourgée's southern fiction. Chesnutt proceeds in this letter to call Tourgée's attention to some other of his recently
published works in which he tries "to write as an artist and not as a preacher."
While we might read this remark as Chesnutt's declaration of his aesthetic difference from Tourgée's political fiction, as Karcher helpfully does, we can also see
in Chesnutt's explication of his method an attempt to defuse Tourgée's pointed,
even petty, opposition to writers like Howells and James. These writers, Chesnutt
seems to be saying, are not the enemy; despite being "colored," I am more like
them than you realize. Like them, I too am engaged in the business of literature.

Following these exchanges, Tourgée came to value, even rely, on Chesnutt's
nonpartisan attitude, manifested by his steadfast commitment to literature. As
their correspondence developed and Chesnutt continued to publish stories, his
work would come to represent, in Tourgée's mind, the solution to the race problem in the United States: "Literature rather than politics, science, or government,
is the branch in which the American Negro—not the African, for there is really
but little of the African left—will win his earliest, perhaps his brightest laurels."
The two met several times over the course of their careers. Most notably, in July
1891, Chesnutt spent a good part of his summer vacation away from his family
with Tourgée at Point Chautauqua, New York, where the two spent hours talking
politics, exchanging work, and getting to know each other. In one of the letters
he sent to his wife from Chautauqua, Chesnutt remarks about Tourgée that "he is
a very interesting fellow, and improves on acquaintance."[14] While Chesnutt never
refers to Tourgée as a friend in his letters, perhaps because a friendship between
a black man and white man remained taboo, we can see here a meeting of minds
that was, for Chesnutt, an essential feature of a true friendship.

A couple of years after this visit, on April 8, 1893, Tourgée once again drew the public's attention to Chesnutt, but this time the compliment appeared in his "Bystander" column and carried implicit political overtones. This column, unlike previous ones that focus almost exclusively on questions of politics and civil rights, begins with a rather lengthy review of two books that had been recently published: William E. Easton's *Dessalines* (1893) and Anna Julia Cooper's *A Voice from the South* (1892). Tourgée declares that these books are "practically the first fruits of literary culture of the American negro."[15] Practically the first, but not quite. "Except Mr. Chesnutt" he points out, whose stories "were something marvelous in their unpretentious realism, of which there are no more because prosperity in other fields has smothered his rare gift." Tourgée's claim that Chesnutt has "smothered his rare gift" was a provocation. While writing about other "colored" writers, Tourgée decides to mention Chesnutt's "rare gift." Why? Tourgée proceeds with a provocation or dare, goading Chesnutt to write the book he knows he can: "The slave romance has yet to be written by the slave descended, if indeed any pen can ever depict its lights and shadows. But the great field of first endeavor will not be the story of slavery, but the tale of half-freedom. The great opportunity which waits the pen of the colored novelist is not the plantation of yesterday, but the plantation of today." He concludes the review with a question that some might view as merely rhetorical but I read as a direct challenge to Chesnutt: "Is the [Victor] Hugo born who will give the world the romance of the tenant's or the cropper's life so truly as to stir the world to justice?"

Tourgée devotes the rest of his column to the question of the state's power to compel passengers on trains to be sorted by race. He notes that this question will for the first time be presented "to the Supreme Court in ex parte Plessy, from Louisiana, now pending, wherein the Bystander is counsel for the plaintiff in error." Tourgée goes on to explain the case in order to correct all misconceptions regarding the simple fact that in eight states of the South, it is a crime punishable by fine or imprisonment for a colored man to ride in a car with white people, no matter what rate of fare he pays or is willing to pay.

The shift in tone from the first section, which discusses literature by African Americans, to the second section regarding African American civil rights is striking. In the first, Tourgée is hopeful. He reads the books by Eastman and Cooper as signs of positive change. His discussion of the separate-car law suggests that he is on the losing side, even though he may be in the right. There are too many readers and writers who have no regard for the personal or political rights of the formerly enslaved race. Fearing that he has little chance of winning "in the court," Tourgée turns to literature, particularly to Chesnutt, to win the battle against segregation by writing a novel that could speak to those on both sides of the color line.

Though Tourgée may have received many responses to this particular column of the "Bystander's Notes," he kept two. The first is from Frank J. Webb, who had in 1857 written one of the first novels by an African American, *The Garies and Their Friends*. Referencing his review of Easton's *Dessalines*, he asks Tourgée if he will read "some M.S. of mine, illustrating a phase of the relations of the races here in the south" and to assist him with finding a suitable publisher for the work.[16] There is no evidence that Tourgée responded to Webb's request. The second letter is from Chesnutt. Chesnutt's letter, dated April 18, 1893, thanks Tourgée for mentioning his work in his column and offers evidence that his claim concerning the smothering of his rare gift is false. Chesnutt, like Webb, encloses a new story for Tourgée to read as evidence that his desire and intention to write is stronger even than when he was writing most. "I am simply biding my time," Chesnutt goes on to say, "and hope in the near future to devote the greater part of my time to literary production." Chesnutt would, of course, go on to devote more of his time to literature following the *Plessy* decision. *The Marrow of Tradition* (1901) would serve as Chesnutt's answer to Tourgée's call for "a tale of half-freedom."[17]

Tourgée's political and legal battle against the Louisiana Legislature's 1890 Act 111, also known as the "Separate Car Act," is well known.[18] The law required that all state railway companies provide "equal but separate accommodations for the white and colored races" in the form of "separate coaches or compartments for each." Tourgée's attempt to persuade a majority of Supreme Court justices of its unconstitutionality has been well documented by Karcher and Mark Elliott. Though Chesnutt and Tourgée were in close correspondence when the case emerged, neither mentions it in their letters. Instead, they continue to confine their conversations to literary matters. Their correspondence ended shortly after the *Plessy* decision, but Chesnutt would return to the case and his friendship with Tourgée a few years later in a crucial chapter of *Marrow of Tradition*.

In the novel's fifth chapter, "A Journey Southward," Chesnutt introduces the friendship of Dr. William Miller and Dr. Alvin Burns. Set on a southbound train from Philadelphia, we meet the novel's protagonist, Dr. Miller, when he unexpectedly sees Dr. Burns riding in the same train car. "The two acquaintances, thus opportunely thrown together so that they might while away in conversation the tedium of their journey, represent very different and yet very similar types of manhood."[19] The difference is that one is "white and the second black, or, more correctly speaking, brown ... what has been described in the laws of some of our states as a 'visible admixture' of African blood." Another difference is age. "The white man was perhaps fifty years of age and the other not more than thirty." In all other respects, they are similar: "They were both tall and sturdy, both well dressed . . . both seemed from their faces and their manners to be men of culture and accustomed to the society of cultivated people." More important than their external similarities is that "they were members of the same profession."

This fictional friendship echoes the true friendship between Chesnutt and Tourgée. Though separated by color and age, the two were joined by their literary profession. When the train crosses the line into the South, the friends are interrogated by the conductor, who insists that the *"friends"* cannot sit together because "the law of Virginia does not permit colored passengers to ride in the white cars." Chesnutt emphasizes and repeats the word "friend" throughout the chapter. The word first appears when the conductor suggests to Dr. Burns that Dr. Miller is his servant, perhaps alluding to the famous story of William and Ellen Crafts, *Running a Thousand Miles to Freedom* (1860). In that slave narrative, the dark-skinned husband disguises himself as the servant of his light-skinned wife, who disguises herself as a wealthy white man. In Chesnutt's story, there is room to mistake the relationship between the two men. When asked if Dr. Miller is Dr. Burns's servant, the former corrects the mistake. "'No, indeed!' replied Dr. Burns indignantly. 'The gentleman is not my servant, nor anybody's servant, but is my friend.'" Chesnutt suggests that this public declaration of friendship challenges segregation in the United States in ways that spoke directly to the political and legal arguments Tourgée put forth in *Plessy*. Reading his fictional and real-life friendships together, we see Chesnutt offering up a model of true friendship as perhaps a better way to solve to the problem of the color line than forging a challenge to the law in the Supreme Court.

Following the disappointing decision of the *Plessy v. Ferguson* case and Tourgée's move to France, Chesnutt lost touch with his friend. In his final letter to Tourgée of May 24, 1897, Chesnutt congratulates him on his appointment to the US consulate in Bordeaux, without alluding once to *Plessy* or any other matter relating to race in America. He concludes the letter optimistically, looking forward to reading the "Franco-American literature" that will be produced as a result of Tourgée's move. Even though the nation had not yet dissolved the color line dividing Americans, this last letter between the two writers suggests that they had discovered a way around it. Their friendship was founded on reading and writing literature together, a true friendship that challenged the fiction of race that continues to divide Americans.

Notes

1. Charles W. Chesnutt, *The Journals of Charles W. Chesnutt*, ed. Richard H. Brodhead (Durham, NC: Duke University Press, 1993), 172. Subsequent citations will be noted in the text.

2. Carolyn L. Karcher, *A Refugee from His Race: Albion W. Tourgée and His Fight against White Supremacy* (Chapel Hill: University of North Carolina Press, 2016).

3. Albion W. Tourgée, *A Fool's Errand: By One of the Fools*, ed. John Hope Franklin (Cambridge, MA: Harvard University Press, 1961), 6–7.

4. Otto Olsen, *Carpetbagger's Crusade: The Life of Albion Winegar Tourgée* (Baltimore, MD: Johns Hopkins University Press, 1956), 224.

5. Bill Hardwig, "Who Owns the Whip? Chesnutt, Tourgée, and Reconstruction Justice," *African American Review* 36, no. 1 (2002): 6.

6. For a more recent example of the critical view of the Chesnutt-Tourgée relationship, see Jennifer Rae Greeson's essay "'Their Position Must Be Mined': Tourgée in Charles Chesnutt's Career-Long Engagement with White Readers" (in this volume), in which she considers "Chesnutt's early and outsized focus on Tourgée as a literary figure."

7. Letter from James Lane Allen to Walter Hines Page, May 13, 1896, Walter Hines Page Collection, Houghton Special Collections, Harvard University, MS Am 1090.3.

8. Edward H. Bodie, "Chesnutt's 'The Goophered Grapevine,'" *Explicator* 51, no. 1 (Fall 1992): 28.

9. Charles Chesnutt, "The Goophered Grapevine," in *The Conjure Woman, and other Conjure Tales*, ed. Richard Brodhead (Durham, NC: Duke University Press, 1993), 31. Subsequent citations will be noted in the text.

10. Albion Tourgée, "The South as a Field for Fiction," *Forum* 6 (December 1888): 405.

11. Comparing Chesnutt's fiction, particularly his short stories, to what he calls "touchstones of Realism," namely, *Daisy Miller: A Study*, by Henry James, and *The Rise of Silas Lapham*, by William Dean Howells, McElrath views Chesnutt as a "romancer" who has more in common with writers such as Tourgée and Ambrose Bierce. For a full discussion of this argument, see Joseph R. McElrath Jr., "Why Charles W. Chesnutt Is Not a Realist," *American Literary Realism* 32, no. 2 (Winter 2000): 91–108.

12. Charles W. Chesnutt, *"To Be an Author": Letters of Charles W. Chesnutt, 1889–1905*, ed. Joseph McElrath Jr. and Robert C. Leitz III (Princeton, NJ: Princeton University Press, 1997), 44–45.

13. Chesnutt to George Washington Cable, letter of June 13, 1890, in *"To Be an Author,"* 66.

14. Tourgée to Chesnutt, letter of December 8, 1888, in *"To Be an Author,"* 46; Chesnutt to Susan Chesnutt, letter of July 20, 1891, qtd. in Helen M. Chesnutt, *Charles Waddell Chesnutt: Pioneer of the Color Line* (Chapel Hill: University of North Carolina Press, 1952), 65.

15. Albion Tourgée, "Bystander's Notes," *Chicago Daily Inter Ocean*, April 8, 1893, 4.

16. Frank J. Webb to Tourgée, letter of April 13, 1893, Albion Winegar Tourgée Papers, McClurg Museum, Westfield, New York.

17. See *"To Be an Author,"* 78.

18. Steve Luxenberg offers a recent history of the case in *Separate: The Story of Plessy v. Ferguson, and America's Journey from Slavery to Segregation* (New York: Norton, 2019), in which Tourgée plays a central role. However, the causes and consequences of the *Plessy* case are by now so familiar to the general public that the phrase "separate but equal" is commonly used in everyday speech without any mention of the role Tourgée played in it.

19. Charles W. Chesnutt, *The Marrow of Tradition* (1901; New York: Penguin, 1993), 49.

6

"Their Position Must Be Mined"

*Tourgée in Charles Chesnutt's
Career-Long Engagement
with White Readers*

Jennifer Rae Greeson

Albion Tourgée's visibility as a literary artist has been inextricably bound up with narratives about his interactions with and influence on African American writers. Mark Elliott notes that Tourgée's literary reputation was "kept alive" into the twentieth century, "long after his works fell out of the mainstream canon," by African American writers and critics, particularly Anna Julia Cooper and Charles Chesnutt (and, later, Sterling Brown).[1] Just as surely, the renaissance of interest in Tourgée's literary work attested by this volume follows upon a prior renaissance of interest in fin-de-siècle African American writers. Since Chesnutt holds one of the prime places in narratives of Tourgée's literary relevance, in this essay I will revisit that literary-historical relationship in order to consider two facets of it more comprehensively: first, the North Carolina–based origin of Chesnutt's early and intense engagement with Tourgée's writings, and second, how Chesnutt's literary engagement with Tourgée persisted and evolved across the course of his own literary oeuvre—and to what end.

Chesnutt's early and outsized focus on Tourgée as a literary figure—along with that of his almost exact age-mate Anna Julia Cooper—exceeds any generic observation about Tourgée simply having a broad influence on African American writers of the next generation. Instead, Chesnutt's and Cooper's early perceptions of Tourgée's significance as a writer were grounded locally in their shared home of central North Carolina, during a formative period in their respective intellectual comings-of-age in the mid-to-late 1870s. When they were secondary school students, Judge Tourgée indeed cut an outsized figure on their local landscape, and he catapulted to national prominence for his novels just as both young people were contemplating their own career paths. Their early local awareness of Tourgée perhaps transmuted into Chesnutt's and Cooper's notably intense engagement with him as an author, as opposed to a polemicist or political figure.

(Indeed, the other writer of this generation with an outsized literary engagement with Tourgée, the virulent white supremacist Thomas Dixon, similarly was growing up in the same area of central North Carolina at the same time.)[2]

Both Chesnutt and Cooper were born in 1858, both hailed from long-established North Carolina roots, and by the age of sixteen in 1874 both were substantially involved in higher education in the state. Cooper was a student at St. Augustine College in Raleigh, the state capital. Chesnutt was a teacher first in Charlotte and then at the State Colored Normal School (now Fayetteville State University), beginning at its founding in 1877—a post that put him in regular correspondence with educators and bureaucrats in Greensboro, Raleigh, and Chapel Hill, especially once he assumed the principalship in 1880.[3] (Dixon was at college in Wake Forest in these years.)

Tourgée was inescapable and impossible to ignore in the mainstream periodical culture of North Carolina at this time, and that is of course where Chesnutt and Cooper would first have encountered his writing. (As Cooper put it in 1892, "Mr. Tourgée excels, we think, in fervency and frequency of utterance, any living writer, white or colored.")[4] As a brief example of Tourgée's voluminous local polemical publication in these years, take his "C Letters," a series of wild, cutting, masterfully insulting newspaper columns that he wrote weekly between March and May 1878, under the pen name "C," to indict and embarrass the Democratic slate of candidates for elected judgeships in the state.[5] He takes the Democrats one by one and rhetorically flays them: insulting their cowardly service in the war, calling out their profiteering, mocking their Klan activity and attempts to distance themselves from it, and so on. The columns were published under a pseudonym, but within the first two weeks Tourgée had been outed as their author; they were carried by papers from Salisbury to Wilmington, answered feverishly but ineffectively by Democrats, and ultimately published as a pamphlet at the close of the series. Everyone educated and politically involved in the state was reading these, everyone was talking about them, and Cooper and Chesnutt would not have been any different.

It's interesting to think about what Chesnutt and Cooper, just turning twenty, might have taken from this particular Tourgée performance. On the one hand, especially at that moment in North Carolina politics, it would have been delicious to read Tourgée's takedowns of these Democratic candidates. (Again, as Cooper put it in 1892, "with his whip of fine cords [Mr. Tourgée] pitilessly scourges the inconsistencies, the weaknesses, and [the] pettiness of the black man's persecutors.")[6] On the other hand, Tourgée's portrayal of the North Carolina political landscape betrays gaping lacunae. There are no African American public figures, which Chesnutt and Cooper certainly aspired to become; Tourgée portrays no educated African American population, while both young people were working ardently in that burgeoning field; and he betrays no cognizance of the important presence of generations of free people of color in the state, such as Chesnutt's family and associates. Despite his fiery Republican politics, Tourgée only occasionally, and rather patronizingly, refers to "the colored vote" as an undifferentiated "element" that "will remain for many years solid" and supportive of whichever candidate is "the present dispenser of arms and uniforms and military titles."[7]

Whatever the limitation of his conception of the central North Carolina scene in 1878, Tourgée became an immediate and remarkable model for Cooper and Chesnutt with the success of A Fool's Errand a year and a half later. Via the novel, he had jumped scale from their own provincial locale to nationwide acclaim, and he had done so by melding political commitment with belletristic aspiration. Yet both of the young writers approached Tourgée's authorial achievement somewhat doubly, melding respect for his loud commitment to liberal political principles (and, in Chesnutt's case, frank admiration for his financial success) with hesitancy about the limits of his artistic vision. In her important 1892 essay "One Phase of American Literature," Cooper encapsulates this complicated engagement. On the one hand, she elevates Tourgée as probably no other critic would have done in the early 1890s, considering him at length as one of the most important writers in American literary history. On the other hand, she creates a hierarchical dichotomy between "artists" and "preachers," classing Poe, Bryant, and Longfellow with Shakespeare in the artist category, "myriad-minded" and immortal, and Tourgée (alongside Milton and Carlyle) as the foremost American exemplar of the preacher. "[Mr. Tourgée's] power is not that already referred to of thinking himself imaginatively into the experiences of others," Cooper explains authoritatively. "He does not create many men of many minds." And then referring specifically to the title character from Pactolus Prime as "Judge Tourgée himself, done over in ebony," she concludes: "All his offspring are little Tourgées— they preach his sermons and pray his prayers."[8]

Cooper's assessment of Tourgée's contribution to US literature provides a capsule description of the limitations of his liberal idealism.[9] His judgelike dedication to abstract and presumably universal principles blinds him to the specificities of lived experiences, to material structures of power, to the truth of others.[10] Chesnutt similarly marks the limitations of Tourgée's liberalism in his often-quoted early response in his journal to learning of Tourgée's literary success: "Judge Tourgée has sold the Fool's Errand, I understand, for $20,000," and this financial coup must attest that "there is something romantic, to the Northern mind, about

the southern negro." But "if Judge Tourgée, with his necessarily limited intercourse with colored people, and his limited stay in the South, can . . . make himself rich and famous, why could not a colored man . . . if he possessed the same
ability, write a far better book about the South?"[11] Numerous commentators, beginning with William L. Andrews, have remarked on Chesnutt's epiphany about
the existence of a national market for "local color" here, but the repeated word is
"limited"—however correct his principles, Tourgée's "preacherly" artistic vision
is limited, and Chesnutt immediately can imagine writing a "far better book."

Much less often attended to in Chesnutt's journal response to Tourgée's literary success is his sense of the *promise* of political liberalism. The liberal understands his universal principles to be rational and correct and therefore capable of
winning over the wrong-thinking: thus Tourgée's investment in winning hearts
and minds via polemic as well as through his excursion into imaginative fiction. With Tourgée as his model, Chesnutt vows that he, too, "shall write for a
purpose": "It is the province of literature to open the way for [the Negro] to get
[social recognition and equality]—[by] accustoming the public mind to the idea;
and while amusing them to lead them on imperceptibly, unconsciously step by
step to the desired state of feeling." Indeed, Tourgée's switch to fiction writing
seems just the right tactic to Chesnutt, for American racial prejudice "cannot be
stormed and taken by assault. . . . [White Americans'] position must be mined,
and we will find ourselves in their midst before they think it."[12] In other words,
the promise of Tourgée's liberal example is that discourse is powerful, that if you
have more just ideas and more artistic expressions of them, you can bend the
public perception of universal truths in your direction. Via the medium of fiction, you can undermine white supremacy.

In his earliest stories, calibrated for precisely the national audience he had
seen Tourgée reach, Chesnutt seems to create a literary form for testing the
promising liberal proposition he imbibed from Tourgée's authorial success.
These "conjure stories" structurally dramatize the act of reading and reception—
mind-changing, undermining, and resistance thereto—by staging a frame narrative in the North Carolina present, within which Julius, a formerly enslaved local
African American, relates a tale of the slave past of the area to John, a recently
arrived white northern carpetbagger. At the time and since, Chesnutt's stories
were seen as an adult version of Joel Chandler Harris's *Uncle Remus Tales* for children, a connection Chesnutt underlines by having John refer to Julius as "Uncle
Julius." Yet the recurring structure of the stories treads more directly on the contemporary political ground of Tourgée's North Carolina novels, highlighting the
interaction between northerner and southerner, white and Black. The frame is

narrated by educated, self-possessed John, who has come from Ohio to North Carolina with his wife, Annie, to take over the land and social position vacated by a disappeared planter class, and the nested tale is told in dialect by the elder Julius McAdoo, who was "born and raised" on the plantation John buys in the first story. This structure puts the cultural and knowledge transaction of "local color" fiction front and center and makes each story into an experiment in Chesnutt's avowed authorial mission of writing fiction with a purpose: Can Julius, "while amusing [John] lead [him] on imperceptibly, unconsciously . . . to the desired state of feeling"?[13]

Although Chesnutt seems initially to have thought of his conjure-story form as simply a vehicle for breaking into national publication, soon to be abandoned for his greater ambition of writing novels, he continued to return to the form across his entire literary career. His breakthrough story "The Goophered Grapevine" in the 1887 *Atlantic Monthly* is a conjure story, but so is his last published piece of fiction, "The Marked Tree," in the *Crisis* in 1925. As Chesnutt comes back to this set piece again and again, it becomes clear that what he's coming back to is John. John is the only character whose interiority is on display; he ostensibly is transcribing Julius's narration in the nested tale, so all we get of Julius is his recorded speech. John is the character who potentially can change over time, in response to each tale from Julius for which he is the audience, and that, I believe, is the problematic that brings Chesnutt back to the scene of the conjure story: Can John learn from Julius's tales? Can *his* position be mined?[14]

In the often-quoted first pages of his first conjure story, "The Goophered Grapevine," Chesnutt has John wax prolix in self-introduction. Among other things, we learn that he has come to North Carolina because "our family doctor, in whose skill and honesty I had implicit confidence, [had] advised a change of climate" for his wife and because "labor was cheap, and land could be bought for a mere song."[15] Richard Brodhead has pointed out how "unusually rich in social markers" Chesnutt's characterization of John proves; Chesnutt precisely situates John as elite, educated, reform minded, all for national and capitalist progress, saddled with a neurasthenic wife—the quintessential *Atlantic* reader.[16] Eric Sundquist more explicitly finds Chesnutt's opening introduction of John to "deliberately echo that of Albion Tourgée in *A Fool's Errand*. . . . Like Tourgée's autobiographical narrator, John from the beginning is locked into the mode of foolish naiveté . . . and his position as an outsider to the South . . . is the means for Chesnutt to scrutinize both his moral pretensions and his cultural, racial blindness."[17] Ultimately, via this overloaded introduction Chesnutt alerts the reader that "The Goophered Grapevine" is about John—just as we might say *A Fool's*

Errand is about the "Fool"—not about North Carolina or the previously enslaved people there.

Julius, for his part, immediately pegs John as "de Norv'n gemman w'at's gwine ter buy de ole vimya'd," and in defense of the place where he "'uz bawn en raise'" he offers up his first tale, explaining that the plantation is bewitched and telling the tale about how that came to be during slavery time (6). Julius's presence, his presentation of the history of this place John does not know and that he knows intimately, his demonstrated artistry in weaving the tale—do any of these things change John? In this first conjure story, Chesnutt's answer is a resounding *no*. "I would n' 'vise yer ter buy dis vimya'd," Julius concludes his tale, and John picks up the narration with a jarring switch out of dialect in the next line: "I bought the vineyard, nevertheless, and it has been for a long time in a thriving condition, and is often referred to by the local press as a striking illustration of the opportunities open to Northern capital in the development of Southern industries" (13). Julius's tale of the occult recent history of the plantation does nothing to lessen John's enjoyment of his principled acquisition of it; if anything, his "romantic" tale has added value to John's civilizing foray into the southern wilds.

This story, however, was to be the first in a series, and Chesnutt was already writing the second installment when Tourgée himself entered the picture by mentioning "The Goophered Grapevine"—sort of—in his 1888 essay on the "South as a Field for Fiction."[18] In the opening paragraphs of that essay, Tourgée crows about having been correct when he said at the close of the war that the defeated South would become the center of romantic imagination for American literature. The editors of the *Atlantic Monthly* had scoffed at him at the time, he notes, but it turns out that he was so very right that "that very magazine has given a complete reversal of its own emphatic dictum, by publishing in a recent number a dialect story of Southern life written by one of the enslaved race."[19] Tourgée notes the existence of "The Goophered Grapevine" simply as a proof of his own correctness, as a "striking example" of what he already knew—as value added to his own venture. The parallel between Tourgée's first elliptical acknowledgment of Chesnutt and John's response to Julius's tale within the story he cites is, to my mind, uncanny.

Nonetheless, Tourgée's article opens up a direct correspondence between the two authors for the first time. Although Chesnutt's initial letter has been lost, he seems to have written Tourgée to say "thank you, I think you were talking about me?" for Tourgée replies, "Of course it was to you whom I referred. I did not dare make the reference more explicit lest it should do you an injury" given "the fact of color."[20] Several months later, Chesnutt replies that, contra Tourgée's concern, he thinks that "the fact of color may in the course of time prove to be a distinction instead of a disadvantage" in his literary career. Chesnutt tucks this gentle demurral into a postscript, though, for his main purpose is to solicit Tourgée's response to a copy of his third—and, he thinks, possibly final—conjure story published in the *Atlantic*. Having broken into the national literary scene, Chesnutt is thinking of turning to novels, "dropping" the characters of his conjure formula "as well as much of the dialect." Yet he senses a new achievement with this third story and craves Tourgée's critical opinion. "I hope you may think it the best of the series," he writes. "I tried in this story to get . . . into the region of feeling and passion—with what degree of success the story itself can testify."[21]

The extraordinary story in question is "Dave's Neckliss." It is the culmination of Chesnutt's raising of the stakes of Julius's tales from slavery time dramatically across his first three *Atlantic* conjure stories, almost demanding a response from his in-story audience, John. In the nested tale of "Dave's Neckliss," Julius describes an enslaved man, the respected preacher within his community, being humiliated by an overseer, who forces him to wear a ham chained around his neck while it decomposes. Under this arbitrary punishment Dave ultimately goes mad, decides that he has turned into the ham, and "built a fier, en tied a rope roun' his neck . . . en had hung hisse'f up in de smoke-'ouse fer ter kyo [cure]"—he commits suicide in the form of a self-lynching. John's response to this existentially bleak tale of psychological realism disrupts the frame structure; instead of taking the last word, he seems to be left speechless. "There was a short silence after the old man had finished his story, and then my wife began to talk to him about the weather. . . . I went into the house" (42). What is John thinking? In his letter, Chesnutt asks Tourgée this almost directly: Having read "Dave's Neckliss," what is Tourgée thinking? But, again uncannily, Tourgée gives Chesnutt a response almost identical to the one Julius receives from John: In his reply, Tourgée acknowledges receipt of the story but does not spare a single word as to its contents. He goes into the house.

Clearly, the conjure story has not yet done its office—the position of Chesnutt's reader is not sufficiently mined—and he continues to return to the form. He writes another of his greatest stories in the mid-1890s in the midst of a difficult correspondence with Tourgée about the periodical that would become the *Basis*. Initially Tourgée offers Chesnutt the chance to be listed as "associate editor" of the publication and asks that he put up $2,500 to fund it; Chesnutt agrees that he will "sacrifice somewhat of comfort and leisure" to do the editorial work in addition to his legal job but notes that the solicited sum "is out of the question," as it is almost the price of his family home. Tourgée makes it clear that the offer of editorial cooperation is rescinded if Chesnutt doesn't provide the funding but then continues for more than two years to lean on Chesnutt to front money for shares and sell subscriptions. Throughout, he reminds Chesnutt how deserving he is of support: "I do not believe there is any man who can do it but me."[22]

Around this same time, Chesnutt writes the conjure story "The Dumb Witness," in which John, who I'm proposing is inspired to some extent by Tourgée, takes over narration of the entire story from start to finish—including the internal tale from slavery time—thus dispensing with Julius's voice in dialect. In the opening of the story, John explains that he initially heard the tale from Julius but subsequently has gathered additional "circumstances of which Julius was ignorant" and "woven [it] all together here in orderly sequence" (63). Going it alone, John promises to deliver a more factually accurate and an aesthetically superior story—resonating with Tourgée's contemporaneous "I do not believe there is any man who can do it but me"—but Chesnutt throws a curveball at the close of the frame. John realizes he has gotten the point of the tale wrong, that he didn't actually understand what was going on. He must turn to Julius for the last word: "I give it up, Julius. Enlighten me" (71).

At the close of the 1890s, after a deeply disappointing encounter with the Houghton Mifflin publishing house that resulted in the production of the *Conjure Woman* volume, Chesnutt does seem to put the conjure-story form aside for good.[23] Tourgée may show up in a different way in Chesnutt's writing as the title character of his elegiac 1905 novel *The Colonel's Dream*, as Carolyn Karcher suggests convincingly; this is right at the time of Tourgée's death and Chesnutt's eulogy for him.[24] After a long hiatus, though, Chesnutt returns to the conjure story one last time with "The Marked Tree," his last published piece of fiction, in W. E. B. Du Bois's periodical the *Crisis* in 1925. In Chesnutt's revival of the form, perhaps we see another kind of revisiting or memorialization of Tourgée as author. Though Chesnutt was far from sanguine about the status of race relations in the United States in the 1920s, he reveled in the ascendancy of the Harlem Renaissance, the proliferation of journals like Du Bois's, and the national and international recognition of African American artistic prowess.[25] This evolution in US literature seems a fulfillment of a prophecy Tourgée had made in his very first reply to Chesnutt back in 1888: "I incline to think that the climacteric of American literature will be negroloid in character. . . . Literature rather than politics, science or government, is the [medium] in which the American negro . . . will win his earliest perhaps his brightest laurels."[26]

In his fullest moment of participation in this new movement, Chesnutt reanimates the Tourgée figure John—and we find him much evolved. In "The Marked

Tree," John fully understands that Julius is a true artist and that the "sad fact of race" (echoing Tourgée's comment on the "fact of color" from his opening correspondence with Chesnutt) is a social rather than a biological or personal limitation. John now sees that his own best purpose has been to facilitate and record Julius's feats of "poetic license . . . stories as complete, in their way, as the sagas of Iceland or the primitive tales of ancient Greece" (133). He hears Julius's nested tale of a tree cursed during slavery time, the how and the why of its cursing, and allows it to reshape his own view of his adopted southern home. Rather than questioning Julius's account of slavery time, or ignoring it, or appropriating it to his own use, John works in service of this new knowledge, in the closing frame of this final conjure story, to "have the stump of the Spencer oak extracted," although it is "a difficult task even with the aid of explosives" (144). White supremacy, the cursed roots of slavery, successfully is *mined* at last. I like to think of Chesnutt putting his Tourgée figure here in the 1920s to witness the fulfillment of a literary vision to which he contributed but which he did not live to see.

Notes

1. Mark Elliott, *Color-Blind Justice: Albion Tourgée and the Quest for Racial Equality* (New York: Oxford University Press, 2006), 219.

2. Brook Thomas limns Dixon's intense and enduring focus on Tourgée, ranging from early days when "the ambitious Dixon sought and accepted advice from him" to Dixon's formulation of *The Clansman* as "a self-conscious rebuttal to *A Fool's Errand*," twenty-six years after the publication of Tourgée's best-known novel. Brook Thomas, *The Literature of Reconstruction: Not in Plain Black and White* (Baltimore, MD: Johns Hopkins University Press, 2017), 104.

3. William L. Andrews traces Chesnutt's formative educational years from his earliest schooling in Fayetteville during Reconstruction through his 1880 journal entries about *A Fool's Errand*. William L. Andrews, *The Literary Career of Charles W. Chesnutt* (Baton Rouge: Louisiana State University Press, 1980), 1–16.

4. Anna Julia Cooper, *A Voice from the South* (1892; New York: Oxford University Press, 1988), 190.

5. [Albion W. Tourgée], *The "C" Letters: As Published in "The North State"* (Greensboro: "The North State" Book and Job Printing Office, 1878).

6. Cooper, *A Voice from the South*, 191.

7. [Tourgée], *The "C" Letters*, 25.

8. Cooper, *A View from the South*, 188–89.

9. In his essay in this volume, "Tourgée's *A Fool's Errand* and the Limits of White Radicalism," John Ernest similarly discusses the limits of Tourgée's absolutist approach to liberal principles such as the rule of law: "What is missing from this novel is an understanding of race as a systemic fabrication, a dynamic presence shaped, reinforced, and continually transformed by law, economics, social position, theology, and virtually every other cultural institution."

10. Cooper's concern about Tourgée's investment in his abstract liberal program at the expense of understanding material realities and human complexities presages Du Bois's overarching assessment of Reconstruction-era ideology as "confused" between "Puritan idealism, transformed into a theory of universal democracy" and "the development of industry in America and of a new industrial philosophy," which would have to be understood via materialist analysis. W. E. B. Du Bois, *Black Reconstruction in America, 1860–1880* (1935; New York: Free Press, 1998), 182.

11. Charles W. Chesnutt, *The Journals of Charles W. Chesnutt*, ed. Richard H. Brodhead (Durham, NC: Duke University Press, 1993), 124–26.

12. Chesnutt, *The Journals*, 139–40.

13. Chesnutt, *The Journals*, 140.

14. I am very much influenced in this interpretive direction by my conversations with and reading of Robert B. Stepto's work on the conjure stories. See his Introduction to Charles W. Chesnutt, *The Conjure Stories*, ed. Robert B. Stepto and Jennifer Rae Greeson (New York: Norton, 2012), vii–xxvii; and Robert B. Stepto, "'The Simple but Intensely Human Inner Life of Slavery': Storytelling, Fiction, and the Revision of History in Charles W. Chesnutt's 'Uncle Julius Stories,'" in *History and Tradition in Afro-American Culture*, ed. Guenter H. Lenz (Frankfurt: Campus Verlag, 1984), 33–51.

15. Chesnutt, *The Conjure Stories*, 3. Subsequent citations will be noted in the text.

16. Richard H. Brodhead, *Cultures of Letters: Scenes of Reading and Writing in Nineteenth-Century America* (Chicago: University of Chicago Press, 1993), 197–98.

17. Eric J. Sundquist, *To Wake the Nations: Race in the Making of American Literature* (Cambridge, MA: Harvard University Press, 1993), 361.

18. In her essay in this volume, "The True Friendship of Charles W. Chesnutt and Albion W. Tourgée," Tess Chakkalakal generously interprets many of Tourgée's larger literary pronouncements in his *Forum* essay as stemming from his reading of Chesnutt's story.

19. Albion W. Tourgée, "The South as a Field for Fiction," *Forum* 6 (December 1888): 405.

20. Qtd. in Carolyn L. Karcher, *A Refugee from His Race: Albion W. Tourgée and His Fight against White Supremacy* (Chapel Hill: University of North Carolina Press, 2016), 26–27.

21. Charles W. Chesnutt, *"To Be an Author": Letters of Charles W. Chesnutt, 1889–1905*, ed. Joseph McElrath Jr. and Robert C. Leitz III (Princeton, NJ: Princeton University Press, 1997), 44–45.

22. Letter from Albion W. Tourgée to Charles W. Chesnutt, November 23, 1893, Albion Winegar Tourgée Collection, Chautauqua County Historical Society. Letters on this matter continue through 1896.

23. Chesnutt proposed publication of a novel manuscript and a collection of twenty stories, of which only seven were conjure stories; Houghton Mifflin rejected both proposals but offered to publish a volume of only conjure stories. "Very much disappointed," Chesnutt wrote six additional conjure stories in seven weeks to order for the volume that became *The Conjure Woman*. His daughter Helen provides a detailed account, including voluminous excerpts from the correspondence between Chesnutt and the representative of Houghton Mifflin, Walter Hines Page (also a central North Carolina native), in

Helen M. Chesnutt, *Charles Waddell Chesnutt: Pioneer of the Color Line* (Chapel Hill: University of North Carolina Press, 1952).

24. Karcher, *A Refugee from His Race*, 30–31. On Chesnutt's participation in Tourgée's memorial service, see Elliott, *Color-Blind Justice*, 313.

25. For Chesnutt's commentary on the Harlem Renaissance, see his responses to "The Negro in Art: How Shall He Be Portrayed," *Crisis*, 1926; and his essay "Post-Bellum—Pre-Harlem," *Colophon*, 1931; both in Chesnutt, *The Conjure Stories*, 217–27.

26. Quoted in Karcher, *A Refugee from His Race*, 29.

II

CITIZENSHIP

7

Reimagining the Republic

Tourgée on Citizenship

Sandra M. Gustafson

R epublican citizenship was a guiding principle and orienting goal throughout Albion Tourgée's overlapping political and literary careers. On the
eve of the war, he wrote to his future wife, Emma Kilborn, predicting
the end of democratic republican government in the United States and anticipating that "a *Monarchy* of limited *powers* will be erected on the *ruins of this
Republic*." He had been skeptical of party politics, tweaking Emma as a "black
Republican" for her dedication to abolitionism and the Republican Party. Yet so
strongly committed was he to the causes of free speech and liberty of conscience
that he violated the University of Rochester's prohibition against political groups
and founded a campus branch of the "Wide Awake Club," a Republican youth
organization. He was willing to jeopardize his university education for long-held
and deeply rooted values that remained constant throughout his later career as a
lawyer, civil rights activist, and bestselling author.[1]

The protection and enhancement of republican self-government became
Tourgée's consistent message after the war. During his successful 1867 candidacy
for the state constitutional convention, he printed a broadside address to the voters of Guilford, North Carolina, listing his principles, beginning with a commitment to "equality of civil and political rights to all citizens" and ending with
"the rights of citizenship . . . extended to the present excluded classes whenever
the Congress of the United States shall see fit." "Voters of Guilford," the broadside continues, "two courses are open before you. Shall the new State have an
Oligarchy or a Republic? An Aristocracy or Democracy?" This choice was also
central to his speech to the convention the following year. There, he emphasized
an ongoing contest between oligarchy and republic to the North Carolina Constitutional Convention as he urged the members to provide vigorous support
for Black suffrage. "The war from which we have just emerged was a struggle
between Republicanism and Oligarchy, between the rights of the people and the
usurpations of Aristocracy, between the elevation of the mass and the exaltation

of the few, between feudal theory and free principles," he told the delegates, appealing to them to "follow Congress" and support voting rights for Black citizens. Alluding to Cicero's claim to have "saved the Republic" from the treasonous conspiracy led by the aristocrat Catiline, Tourgée criticized southern elites who even in defeat refused to extend equal "rights and privileges" to "the poor and the oppressed, the humble and the enslaved." He concluded his address to the convention by exhorting the members to fulfill "this greatest, highest principle of government" and "answer like the noble Roman, 'I have saved the Republic.'"[2]

A prominent theme runs through Tourgée's political writings and his fiction: the importance of defining and securing equal citizenship in an American republic struggling to bridge growing class divides and to accommodate multiple races and faiths. These emphases have aesthetic implications. As noted in the Introduction to this volume, his novels manifest concerns with character and ethos and develop techniques for representing political discussion whose literary value Amanda Anderson analyzes and defends in *Bleak Liberalism* (2016).[3] Scenes involving citizenship practices punctuate *A Fool's Errand* (1879) and *Bricks without Straw* (1880), the Reconstruction novels that made him a national figure. Initially Comfort Servosse, the semiautobiographical northern "fool" of the first novel, holds himself aloof from the political life of his adopted southern home, but eventually he decides to attend a political meeting on "the general interests of the country," which significantly is being held not in the town square but in a remote location. In an aside, the narrator sets the historical context. The scene takes place during the first phase of Reconstruction under Andrew Johnson, which left the status of the freed people to be determined by the individual states. The speakers contend over whether Blacks should be allowed to testify in court, with the deciding statement against this measure ending with the proclamation that "Our rights are too sacred" to allow their testimony. As the proceedings are winding down, the same "orator" calls out Servosse, demanding that he address the gathering to clarify his views on social equality. Is he "a *bona-fide* citizen, having the interest of our people at heart?" the speaker asks. Or "has he come to degrade and oppress us"? The condition of being "a *bona-fide* citizen" is here aligned with the interests of the prewar South, where "our people" are understood to be white.[4]

Forced to the platform, Servosse tries to read the audience while revolving the history of significant local opposition to the Civil War in his mind. Some of those present are silent, and he interprets their reticence as dissent from the racist views that have been expressed. He initially refuses to share his political ideas while winning over the crowd with his good-humored "self-possession" (61), until the chairman flatters him and encourages him to speak in the hope that "an interchange of views" between "neighbors" will "do us good" (62). Feeling somewhat safer after this invitation to speak more freely, Servosse proceeds to give the first political speech of his life. He tells the assembled crowd that their options are more limited than they realize. Certain things have already been determined by law (for instance, there will be no repayment of Confederate war debt), while Black court testimony and suffrage, though not yet codified, have advanced so far that it is only a matter of time until they become a reality. If white southerners wish to have a say in the direction of policy, they need to decide not whether to cooperate with the federal government but how to do so. He concludes by urging the audience to think over the best way to accomplish this end.

His remarks are met with a "dull, surprised silence" (66), which the narrator (who is closely tied to Servosse's perspective) parses into a spectrum of reactions ranging from approval, to wonder at Servosse's audacity, to outright amazement. Thanked by the chairman for his "frank and clear statement of his views" (67), Servosse departs for home. On the road he learns what the audience's silence held for him when he meets a pair of poor white farmers and a freedman named Jerry, who have all just left the meeting. They warn him that his life is in jeopardy. Six white men are planning to waylay Servosse and beat him with hickory switches, as Jerry tells him, "jes' tu let him know dat he couldn't make sech infamous speeches as dat in dis region widout gettin' his back striped" (71). The limits to free speech in the South, as they apply even to well-off white people, are a recurrent theme of the novel.

Tourgée never loses sight of the fact that freed people are even more constrained than Servosse. The novel makes abundantly clear that, faced with violent repression, the most basic exercise of citizenship by the formerly enslaved people and their allies amounted to heroic deeds in an invisible war, a "new Reign of Terror" (250). Meanwhile, the nation embraced a false peace that was broken only when "the cries became so clamorous that they could no longer be ignored" (251). Silence contains many voices, as Servosse has learned the hard way, and open discussion in these circumstances is often impossible. As the novel proceeds, its narrative elements are increasingly overwhelmed by documentary references and even wholesale insertions from official texts. At one point, Tourgée alludes to a thirteen-volume committee report documenting "a strange history of peaceful years."[5] He conveys the brutal irony of characterizing these years as "peaceful," detailing what the report describes as a "battlefield" worth of the slain, "all killed with deliberation, overwhelmed by numbers, roused from slumber at the murk midnight, in the hall of public assembly, upon the river-brink, on the lonely woods-road, in simulation of the public execution,—shot, stabbed, hanged, drowned, mutilated beyond description, tortured beyond conception" (251). Tourgée's point is that the official peace that resulted from Lee's surrender to Grant produced the conditions for a covert war that Reconstruction policies had failed to adequately recognize, much less address. The realities of citizenship in the postwar republic were a far cry from the ideals of free speech and liberty of conscience that Tourgée had long espoused.

Bricks without Straw develops these themes with more attention to the experiences of the freed people. One of the most striking scenes in the novel involves an attack on newly enfranchised Black voters as they parade to a polling place in a nearby white community. Their request to vote in their own town of Red Wing has been denied, and they merely wish to enliven what is, to them, a festive occasion with music and pageantry. Local whites perceive their music and banners as a threat and respond with violence. As the next election season approaches, featuring a Black candidate for the legislature on the ballot, Red Wing attracts attention from the Redeemers—that is, the conspiracy of elite whites intent on reestablishing control of the region. Tourgée repeatedly styles the terrorist undertakings of the Ku Klux Klan as a violent "masquerade," drawing attention to the secretiveness and inauthenticity of the white supremacist movement. He contrasts this midnight activity with the civic life at Red Wing, "the center from which radiated the spirit that animated the colored men of the most populous district in the county" (206). With "no room for hope except through the trustfulness of faith," the narrator explains, Black southerners are "the true children of the Covenanters and the Puritans." The intensity of their faith mirrors the piety of the travelers on "the storm-bound 'Mayflower,'" and the preeminently English devotion to both political liberty and the spiritual well-being of their posterity has become "the leading element in the character of the Africo-American" (206). It is in this "spirit" that Red Wing has served as the civic heart of the county's Black population.[6]

With the next election on the horizon, the town leaders Eliab Hill and Nimbus decide to host a "grand rally" at Red Wing (207). Central to the narrative, these characters represent facets of postwar Black experience with nuance and complexity. To this point neither man has involved himself directly in politics. Nimbus resists appeals to run for office, focusing instead on building his agricultural business. Eliab has achieved independence and status in his role as Red Wing's minister, largely overcoming a mobility impairment. But while Nimbus and Eliab thrive as a consequence of their leading places at Red Wing, Black residents of the surrounding area are increasingly vulnerable to white dominance.

In a chapter titled "A Black Democritus," Tourgée introduces Berry Lawson to drive home this point. Berry works as a sharecropper for his former master, and he makes his poverty and lack of opportunity into a subject of bitter humor. When he shares how his employer has tried to prevent him from attending the political meeting, his words trigger an outpouring from other members of the crowd that transforms the event's atmosphere and shifts its focus. A debate ensues about the best course of action and nearly tips into violence, until Eliab takes the platform and, with Nimbus's support, urges the crowd to exercise "moderation and thoughtfulness" and exhorts those present to "work together, aid each other, comfort each other, stand by each other" (217). Only by remaining unified can they hope to succeed, and separation from white society is their best option. Eliab's closing exhortation to "trust in Him who brought us up out of the Egypt of bondage and set before our eyes the Canaan of liberty" (218) echoes Puritan rhetoric.[7]

Nimbus responds to Eliab's call by canvassing the Black voters in the county and urging them to perform their "political duty" (228). Where previously Nimbus held himself somewhat apart from politics, this meeting clarifies the vulnerability of Black citizens and crystallizes the view that "political cooperation" (228) with one another is their only protection. This raising of Nimbus's political consciousness leads not to equal citizenship but to an attack on Red Wing. The narrator observes with sharp irony that this was a "catastrophe that might easily have been avoided had he been willing to enjoy his own good fortune, instead of clamoring about the collective rights of his race" (228).

Tourgée's political ideals emerge most directly in the novel's final chapters, where he presents an extended political discussion between Hesden Le Moyne, the southern aristocrat who has lost an arm in the war despite his skepticism about the cause, and a northern congressman. Speaking in "the shadow of the National Capitol" (419), Le Moyne champions the town meeting as a crucial institution for the reintegration of the South, bringing it into line with northern democratic values. "I sincerely believe that it is to the township system that the North owes the fact that it is not to-day as much slave territory as the South was before the war" (422), he asserts. The South, by contrast, "is to-day and always has been a stranger to local self-government" (424-5), for southern officials are appointed by "some central power in the county" (425) rather than by popular election.[8]

Le Moyne goes on to attribute New England's early abolition of slavery, high levels of education, and greater per capita wealth to the influence of the town meeting. He calls for a federally funded educational system that would alleviate lasting tensions between North and South by proving to southern whites that the aim of the North was not to dominate them but to end racial injustice. Such a system would also help create the essential conditions for self-government in a racially diverse community. The township system, Le Moyne argues, has proven to be "an essential concomitant of political equality" as well as "a vital element of American liberty" (423). Citing Alexis de Tocqueville, he traces the town meeting to the "the little colony upon the Mayflower" (426), whose true southern heirs are the residents of Red Wing.

Tourgée's essay on "The Township System" in the April 5, 1882, issue of his periodical *Our Continent* extends the closing themes of *Bricks*. Citing a recent debate on the apportionment of seats in the House of Representatives, he quotes a line from a speech by Congressman George Tillman: "I firmly believe that when the future historian comes to write the decline and downfall of the American Republic he will have to record that the last and most desperate struggle for liberty occurred in a New England town."[9] Tourgée expresses skepticism that the "decline and downfall" of the Republic is imminent and challenges Tillman's racialist claim that the township system was inherited from English institutions. The assertion that the system was "brought over in the cabin of the Mayflower" was inaccurate, if the statement was taken to mean that the central political organization of New England was modeled on the practices of Old England. Shaped by English culture and institutions, the emigrants bore the mother country's imprint but worked to "avoid copying her forms and adopting her traditions," as they distanced themselves from Old World hierarchies. They achieved something organic and durable by responding to current needs, creating a system that was "indigenous to American soil": "It was the outgrowth of a dire necessity and of the most profound unconsciousness." Tourgée closes this short piece by asserting that the closest analogue to the New England town meeting was "the French *commune*, of which it was the intended and declared model." Political forms, and not racial identities, remained central to his vision of democratic republican citizenship.[10]

The consistency of Tourgée's views can be seen in his late essay "Twentieth-Century Peacemakers" (1899), where he champions the "Anglo-Saxon theory of the state" against the rival authoritarian forms of government then ascendant in France, Germany, and Russia. Tourgée affirms that his definition of "Anglo-Saxons" includes "the seventy-odd millions of people who constitute the American Republic, whether white or black, Celt or Slav."[11] Here, Tourgée describes as "purely American" people from any background who are committed to the republican ideals descended from New England town meetings. It is a view both pragmatic and aspirational. While a spectrum of figures, ranging from George Tillman to Tourgée's friend Charles Chesnutt in his essay "What Is a White Man?" (1889), emphasize white supremacist uses of "Anglo-Saxonism" to consolidate white power, Tourgée insists that "Anglo-Saxon" ideals should be tied to democratic republican political beliefs and practices, not ascribed racial identities.

Tourgée highlights other aspects of the modern American republican in a lecture on "The Christian Citizen" that he delivered at the Chautauqua Institution in 1881, soon after he moved to nearby Mayville. The institution had been founded in 1874 as a Methodist camp meeting, and it remained closely affiliated with Methodism even as it expanded into the nationally recognized interdenominational "Chautauqua Movement" over the succeeding decade.[12] A lifelong Methodist, Tourgée makes an argument for active political engagement that draws on core religious principles without being narrowly doctrinaire. He characterizes modern republican citizenship as both earthly, in the sense of being restricted to the temporal sphere, and motivated by transcendent values captured in the Golden Rule. Those inclined to trace the roots of American citizenship to ancient Greece and Rome mistake oligarchies for real republics, he insists. True republicanism, defined as a "self-governing community" (86), is only as old as the United States. It has at its core the idea that the individual, or "self-directing integer," should be guided by the principle of reciprocal relations—in brief, "Do unto others as you would that they should do unto you" (87). This principle is not meant in a passive sense but demands active engagement, as Christianity is "a *doing* religion" (87). Bound by an "unwritten contract," each American citizen has a "right to good government" (87), and this goal can be achieved only through popular engagement in party politics animated by the Golden Rule.

Tourgée speculates that many audience members, disgusted by the tenor of contemporary politics, preferred to keep their distance from the "dirty mess" that they feared would only taint them. Explaining that the South had lost the war but was winning the peace because of the active political engagement of white elites, he exhorts his audience to make politics the abiding concern of their everyday lives. In a passage that stands out in light of the later *Plessy* case, he notes that "you will hear more politics in half an hour" on a southern railroad than in all the time it takes to travel "from Boston to San Francisco" (90) on northern trains, implying a connection between the rise of Jim Crow cars and the white supremacist politics of the South. Unless the rest of the nation takes immediate action, he warns, the South will "use the ballotorial power of her ignorant masses to uphold her supremacy and advance the ideas which underlie her civilization" (90)—that is, oligarchy. Tourgée responds to the critics then dividing the Republican Party over issues of patronage and corruption, stating flatly that political parties are the only means of conducting democratic republican politics and that the parties could be reformed if "every good man, every honest man, every Christian" would "go into the party with which he is in sympathy and make it his own" (91). Without explicitly discussing race, then, Tourgée sought to better align party politics with the values that he believed should have been secured by the Union victory.

In *Murvale Eastman, Christian Socialist* (1890), Tourgée returned to the themes and images of "The Christian Citizen," developing them in two directions: with a sustained consideration of economic theory and with characters and a plot designed to turn political ideas into an engaging narrative aimed at prompting action. The union of Christian and Jewish progressives around shared principles of social reform is another salient theme in the novel.[13] He spins out the ideological thread that links "The Christian Citizen" to the novel in its preface, returning to the point that the individual is at the core of Christian thought. The free-labor ideology that had broadly informed the abolitionist movement was likewise anchored in a commitment to individual opportunity and responsibility. After the Civil War, the rise of large corporations with monopolistic tendencies had radically transformed the conditions of labor.[14] Tourgée describes an economic transformation leading to diminished possibilities for "self-direction and control" and leaving many "dependent for opportunity upon another's will"—effectively "half a slave" (v).

The results of this new economy and its background in the war are initially portrayed through the character of Jonas Underwood, a disabled veteran turned strikebreaker who has recently been injured in a strike-related accident. Desperate for money, he agreed to drive a streetcar, and, when striking workers overturned the car, he clung to the reins out of habit. His recovery has been slow because of an underlying war injury involving a bullet buried in his lung. The reader learns that Underwood was shot and captured while doing picket duty for a friend during his service in the Union army. The friend was afraid to reveal his own violation of military rule, with the result that Underwood was reported absent without leave. Released and returned to his unit six months later with a debilitating cough, he finds the medical staff and his superior officers are badly disposed toward him, thinking that he had been captured while running away. They refuse to credit his belief that his cough is caused by a bullet lodged in his body and insist that he suffers from consumption. His "naked word" is set against government policy "to esteem every such applicant a knave," government agents are paid to "disprove his allegations" (17), and after a years-long investigation, his application for a pension is denied "in language none the mildest" (18).

Meanwhile, the piece of shrapnel is "steadily eating its way to a vital part" (390)—a striking echo of a passage from *Invisible Empire*. When Tourgée wrote in that work that "under the half-healed scars of the past are hidden malign influences which are even now threatening the Nation's peace and prosperity" (390), he was primarily concerned with the aftereffects of slavery in the South. By the time he wrote *Murvale Eastman*, he had shifted his focus to include the failure of the federal government to treat Union veterans well—a failure whose consequences ramified widely, as embittered former soldiers like Underwood tried to remake their lives. Underwood represents white working people who have struggled in a volatile economy, where another "class has obtained more than their share of power and privilege, and use it to restrict others' opportunity" (25). He looks back on his enlistment as the moment when he "gave up [his] chance in life from a 'sense of duty'" (23), his decision anchored in his religious training. No "providential *good*" (23) followed Underwood's act of self-sacrifice, however. Set back by an economic depression two decades earlier and too proud to take charity, he and his wife have never fully succeeded in getting back on their feet. Underwood traces their individualist values to the *Mayflower* (26) and argues that a properly organized society—by which he means one aligned with natural law and reflecting God's will—would not allow hard-working people to suffer as they have done.

Underwood forms a peculiar pair with Wilton Kishu, a wealthy white businessman whose "illiberal" liberalism is subjected to scathing critique. The lay leader of the Congregation of the Golden Lilies, the church where much of the novel's action is set, Kishu has "a profound belief in Divine power" and has seen "not a few miracles performed in his day" (141). The abolition of slavery proves to him "God's power to do *anything*"—when "the Deity was really in earnest about a thing" (141). But he needs to be convinced that a social transformation of any magnitude is truly God's will. Deacon Hodnutt of the Golden Lilies later reveals that Kishu had hired a substitute during the war, as the deacon acknowledges doing as well. Both men have benefited materially from these youthful decisions, but unlike the complacent Kishu, Hodnutt has regrets and wonders if his religion is "the genuine sort." Echoing the language of "The Christian Citizen," he proclaims that "in the warfare which Christianity and civilization wage with evil, there is no such thing as putting in a substitute. . . . Everybody has got to do his own share of the fighting, and do it himself" (338). Intent on deflecting the deacon's criticism of his recent actions, Kishu ignores the thrust at his judgment.

Kishu's refusal to reflect on his choices continues until late in the novel, when he meets Underwood at a quiet retreat in Hampton Roads, the scene of a decisive northern victory. Kishu has gone there to recover from an illness, while Underwood has come to die. The bullet has finally been removed from his lung, but too late to save him. The two men become "almost inseparable" (515) and, in an extended conversation that bears a strong formal resemblance to the closing chapters of *Bricks without Straw*, they draw together the novel's ideological goals. Kishu agrees to act as a trustee on behalf of Underwood's plan for a social club to ameliorate conditions of urban alienation and poverty, and Underwood inspires Kishu to propose a "temple of trade and industry" (538) that will launch new businesses fostering personal independence. The embittered veteran and the draft evader collaborate to adapt social policy to the free-labor ideology that had previously driven opposition to slavery.

What unites the men are the ideas of the title character, Murvale Eastman, who has overcome his privileges to develop a vision of social equality. Kishu had hired Eastman to lead the wealthy congregation of the Golden Lilies, and the minister plans to marry Kishu's daughter and inherit from a wealthy aunt. The strike that led to Underwood's injury makes Eastman more aware of income inequality and catalyzes his emergence as a religious leader comparable to John Wesley, the Methodist founder (358–59). After long reflection, Eastman determines to speak out against injustice in a series of sermons based on the text "*There were two men in one city, the one rich the other poor*" (52). The language he uses is still new to him, and he hesitates "to speak his own thought" (114) at first because he knows he will meet with resistance, not least from Kishu.

Building slowly to his radical claims, Eastman challenges the church not to leave these questions "in the hands of those who are hostile to Christian belief." It is the church's duty to address social injustices and not be distracted by the anti-Christian tenor of the dominant Marxist critique. In an echo of Tourgée's famous phrase about the Union "as it ought to be," Eastman states that "the Church should be the support of Society—not as it *is*, but as it *ought* to be—the staunch, unflinching champion of all there is of good, and the unrelenting enemy of all there is of evil in it" (123). Returning to one of Tourgée's favorite themes, he emphasizes the active side of Christian faith, defining "Christian Socialism" as the Lord's expectation that "all classes and conditions, shall make the welfare of their fellows the first and highest object in life, after their own wants and the comfort of those dependent on them" (124). Eastman's challenge to the congregation and the entire city makes him a media celebrity—and an object of harsh scrutiny: "Who had ever before heard of a church allying itself with Socialism?" (309).

Skeptics view the effort to join the two sets of beliefs as effectively "a league of devils and saints" (309).

A spiritual revival at the Golden Lilies only heightens the portentous air surrounding these events. Eastman presides quietly over the revival's organizing committee, "counseling patience, deliberation, charity" (313–14). The committee in turn takes its measures to the public for "free and calm consideration," with the only restraint being that "the speaker must be heedful of the feelings of others" (314). The model for the proceedings is "the town meeting on which the American Republic is based" (314); the Golden Rule is among the organization's foundational principles. In this fictional context, the ideas that Tourgée put forward in "The Christian Citizen" achieve greater specificity. Eastman is hopeful that the plan will do no harm. Whether it will do any good depends on "whether God's time has fully come for the extension of Christian principles to collective as well as individual relations" (320). Ripeness is all. The ultimate fruit of Eastman's public initiative is the joint plan that Underwood and Kishu make to build durable institutions of social repair in the novel's closing chapters.

These institutions are to be built in the park neighboring the Church of the Golden Lilies. The land has a tangled history that unfolds in another strand of the plot involving Jewish ancestry and a contested will. Once claimed by Kishu in a deal that made his fortune, the land has recently been awarded to Underwood as the surviving heir of "the celebrated patriot and scientist" Daniel Valentine (421). Mr. Metzinger, the lawyer who represents Underwood in his suit against the city, is discovered to be a relative of the Valentine family. He also represents a non-Christian group that has allied itself with the Christian Socialists and states their joint principles in a long speech at the Golden Lilies (279–83). The collaboration between Underwood and Kishu late in the novel reenacts this public scene of interfaith cooperation. Kishu announces that "the Christian idea of duty and love has been at the bottom of all progress since it was uttered," and Underwood responds that even before Jesus of Nazareth expressed those ideas, they had been "planted in the heart of man" as "the principle of divine and eternal justice to his fellow" (540). These are universal truths, not divisive sectarian principles.

Murvale Eastman demonstrates that even as Tourgée devoted the majority of his life's work to the cause of racial equality, he understood the broad implications of the principles underlying republican citizenship: reciprocity (the Golden Rule) and deliberative self-government (the town meeting). Today these principles inform a large body of academic work by political scientists, including neorepublican thought and deliberative democracy theory. Tourgée's writings couch many of the ideas present in these abstract theoretical texts in an accessible vernacular idiom. His journalistic writings anchor their concepts in the immediate circumstances of the postbellum United States. Even more rewarding are Tourgée's novels, where he brings vividly to life the struggle to extend republican ideals and fulfill their potential. His works deserve to be better known for their contribution to the history of democratic thought and practice, as well as for their considerable literary merits.

Notes

1. Mark Elliott, *Color-Blind Justice: Albion Tourgée and the Quest for Racial Equality from the Civil War to Plessy v. Ferguson* (New York: Oxford University Press, 2006), 72–73. Letter of March 3, 1861, qtd. on 72.

2. The broadside and speech are reprinted in *Undaunted Radical: The Selected Writings and Speeches of Albion W. Tourgée*, ed. Mark Elliott and David John Smith (Baton Rouge: Louisiana State University Press, 2010), 25–27, 35–42. I discuss Cicero in *Imagining Deliberative Democracy in the Early American Republic* (Chicago: University of Chicago Press, 2011), 75–79.

3. Amanda Anderson, *Bleak Liberalism* (Chicago: University of Chicago Press, 2016).

4. Albion W. Tourgée, *A Fool's Errand*, ed. John Hope Franklin (Cambridge, MA: Belknap, 1961), 57, 58–59.

5. The report is identified in *The Invisible Empire*, the companion text that appeared as an appendix to the 1880 edition of *Fool's Errand*, as the Report of the Joint Congressional Committee on the Ku-Klux Conspiracy, from 1872.

6. Albion W. Tourgée, *Bricks without Straw*, ed. Carolyn L. Karcher (Durham, NC: Duke University Press, 2009), 206. Tourgée likely encountered the *Mayflower* theme in abolitionist works. Kenyon Gradert discusses the trope in "The *Mayflower* and the Slave Ship: Pilgrim-Puritan Origins in the Antebellum Black Imagination," *MELUS* 44, no. 3 (Fall 2019): 63–90.

7. Eliab's speech echoes John Winthrop's "Model of Christian Charity," first published in 1838. Lindsay DiCuirci examines the pairing of the Mayflower and the slave ship in "Two Ships, Two Shores," *Early American Literature* 56, no. 1 (2021): 131–56.

8. Tourgée had been closely involved with introducing the township system and the town meeting into North Carolina's postwar constitution. Daniel Farbman highlights Tourgée's role in "Reconstructing Local Government," *Vanderbilt Law Review* 70, no. 2 (March 2017): 413–97.

9. Tillman was a white supremacist Democratic leader from South Carolina who later lost his position when a Republican-majority congressional committee awarded the seat to the prominent Black Republican Robert Smalls. He was the older brother of Benjamin Tillman, a prominent white supremacist politician who served as the governor of South Carolina and later as its US senator.

10. Albion Tourgée, "The Township System," *Our Continent*, April 5, 1882, 120.

11. Albion Tourgée, "The Twentieth-Century Peacemakers," *Contemporary Review* 75 (1899): 888.

12. The text of "The Christian Citizen" appeared in the *Chautauquan* 2, no. 2 (November 1881): 86–91, a periodical of the Chautauqua Literary and Scientific Circle. The CLSC was the main vehicle of Chautauqua's national and international influence, including its widely popular correspondence learning program. A similarly titled essay on "Christian Citizenship" appeared in the *Golden Rule* 7 (August 18, 1892). This later work shared some themes with the 1881 lecture but had a different focus.

13. Tourgée may have been influenced by the works of the German Jewish novelist Berthold Auerbach, whose fiction he praised in the same issue of *Our Continent* (April 5, 1882) where "The Township System" appeared in a neighboring column.

14. An excellent general treatment of the era is Richard White, *The Republic for Which It Stands: The United States during Reconstruction and the Gilded Age, 1865–1896* (New York: Oxford University Press, 2017).

8

Tourgée, Democracy, Romance, and the Art of Fiction

Kenneth W. Warren

U nsurprisingly, in introducing the 1966 edition of Albion Tourgée's *A Fool's Errand*, the historian George Fredrickson held up for consideration the novel's compelling depiction of its historical moment and the light it might shed on the prospects of the modern civil rights movement. At the time of Fredrickson's writing, the Civil Rights Act of 1964 and the Voting Rights Act of 1965 had toppled two of the key remaining legal pillars on which the nation's Jim Crow order had rested since the 1890s. The novel's "greatest interest for our time," Fredrickson averred, "derives from its picture of Reconstruction and its reflections on the persistent problem of how to build a bridge from Negro emancipation to Negro equality." Refraining from any disparagement of *A Fool's Errand* as a literary achievement and of Tourgée as an artist, Frederickson nonetheless made it clear that in meriting our regard, any artistry to be found in the novel stood at least a few notches below the work's political vision. "The author of *A Fool's Errand* deserves our attention as an early and forceful advocate of civil rights for all Americans, and as a thorough-going exponent of democracy, a true believer who did not shy away from the hard choices which history requires of the faithful."[1] Echoing this sentiment in a blurb for Frederickson's edition, the historian John Hope Franklin lauded Tourgée as "an intelligent observer and participant in Southern Reconstruction" and "a pioneer post-war social critic," further cementing the idea that whatever literary talent Tourgée demonstrated, his politics and social vision deserved pride of place.[2] Even Edmund Wilson, the critic who in the early 1960s was most receptive to the literary quality of Tourgée's novels, declared *A Fool's Errand* "a sensation in its day" that "ought to be an historical classic in ours—for aside from its interest as one carpetbagger's narrative, it contains the actual text of many newspaper clippings, threatening letters and firsthand testimony by victims of the Klan."[3]

Tourgée would no doubt have appreciated such unstinting praise for his egalitarian commitments and the documentary utility of his fiction, but his stated view of his own works was far from dismissive of literary concerns. Writing in 1888 he conceded that to readers familiar with his early work he was "generally supposed to have turned his attention" to conditions in the post–Civil War South "more from political bias than from any literary or artistic attraction which it offered." But such assumptions, he cautioned, could have hardly been more wrong. Indeed, "The exact converse was in fact true; the romantic possibility of the situation appealed to him even more than its political difficulty." Tourgée quickly added, however, that in times of "great national crises, the one was unavoidably colored by the other."[4]

It has, understandably, been difficult for scholars to take Tourgée at his word and place his career as a writer and a literary critic (more specifically, as a serious thinker about the mode and place of romance in US fiction) on par with his career as a political actor and thinker. To be sure, to a certain extent Tourgée has only himself to thank for this imbalance—absent his fiction, the roles he played as a Reconstruction-era judge, as a participant in the group that created North Carolina's post–Civil War constitution, and of course as the lead attorney in *Plessy v. Ferguson* would still merit him our admiration. But some of the reasons for this neglect go beyond Tourgée to the period within which he became an author—the rise and fall of Radical Reconstruction. From the standpoint of US historians, the study of the Reconstruction era, although dwarfed by the Everest of studies devoted to comprehending the Civil War, has long been acknowledged as an interpretive challenge for scholars in the discipline and has produced several monumental, if disputed, classics, from William A. Dunning's *Essays on the Civil War and Reconstruction* in 1898 to W. E. B. Du Bois's *Black Reconstruction in America, 1860–1880* (1935) and, more recently, to Eric Foner's *Reconstruction: America's Unfinished Revolution, 1863–1877* (1988). The case has been different for the literature. As Brook Thomas has observed, while fiction from this period "influenced efforts at reconstruction and how those efforts have been interpreted by historians . . . the amount of literary criticism on Reconstruction pales in comparison to the amount of historical analysis."[5] But Thomas's book and many of the recent studies on the literature of the period he cites by, to name just a few, Robert S. Levine, Sharon D. Kennedy-Nolle, and Jeannine De Lombard, indicate a shift in the tide.

While far from unknown by literary scholars of the period, the essay in which Tourgée made his case for literary consideration, "The South as a Field for Fiction," has not generally ranked as a signal essay in literary history alongside other documents from the mid- to late nineteenth century, such as the prefaces and essays produced by Nathaniel Hawthorne, Edgar Allan Poe, Henry James, or even

John William de Forest, whose "The Great American Novel" introduced an idea that served as a lodestar for some practitioners and critics of the novel across the first half of the twentieth century. If considered in terms of predictiveness, the relative obscurity of Tourgée's essay is undeserved. Many of its observations—"A nation can never bury its past. A country's history may perish with it, but it can never outlive its history"; "our literature has become not only Southern in type, but distinctly Confederate in sympathy"; "the Negro race in America . . . may itself become a power in literature"; "the epoch of [the] overthrow" of the South's "deposed sovereigns" will "live again in American literature"—have either been borne out by history or echoed in the sentiments and pronouncements of subsequent writers and scholars. One could hardly imagine the author of such an essay being surprised by the twentieth-century literary prominence of William Faulkner or Toni Morrison. Having predicted that slavery would persist "as a political idea [and] a factor in partisan strife" long after its existence as a "condition of society," Tourgée would likely hear nothing off-key in the recent chorus of voices insisting that the nation has yet to confront the way that slavery continues to inform and shape ongoing inequalities.[6]

For the purposes of the inquiry I'm pursuing here, though, I'm less interested in celebrating Tourgée's prowess as a prophet than in elucidating his account of literary form and genre, both in their determinations and effects. My hope is that in understanding what Tourgée means by "romantic possibility," we can better describe Tourgée as a literary artist and critic. Of course, as Tourgée himself admits, for a writer of the sort that he was there is no divorcing the literary from the political, and so part of my consideration here will be that of casting some light on how Tourgée's notions of political efficacy and political ethics articulated with literary form during the postemancipation era, thereby illuminating the relation of "romantic possibility" to "political difficulty."

In broader terms, such questions were far from unique to Tourgée. A major preoccupation of American literary production and scholarship has been to determine whether fine or high art, in whatever medium, was compatible with or an obstacle to democratic governance, a vein of speculation represented perhaps most prominently by Alexis de Tocqueville's observations on democracy and the arts in *Democracy in America*, which, among other things, postulated a strong correlation between democracy and literary values—a correlation that did not necessarily bode well for literary taste or literary achievement.

For Tocqueville, American democracy and the triumph of market values went hand in hand. "Democracy," he wrote, "not only infuses a taste for letters among the trading classes, but introduces a trading spirit in literature." As a people who tend to be "engaged either in politics or in a profession that only allows them to taste occasionally and by stealth the pleasures of the mind," Americans become accustomed "to the struggle, the crosses, and the monotony of practical life," and as a consequence "require strong and rapid emotions, startling passages, truths or errors brilliant enough to rouse them up and to plunge them at once as if by violence, into the midst of the subject."[7] For his part, Tourgée likewise noted among his fellow countrymen a similar hunger for literature that made strong appeals to the emotions. He differed from Tocqueville, however, in associating that desire not with the vitiation of literary taste in America generally but with the way that political circumstances in the South had conspired to create the conditions necessary for literary greatness and the failure of most serious writers in the North to recognize and respond to that sensibility.

Although Tourgée appeared to embody Tocqueville's characterization of the American author/reader as a man whose involvement in politics and a profession would produce indifference to literary taste and lofty ideals, he embraced what Mark Elliott in a recent biography calls "a public-spirited ethos."[8] Individualist though he was, Tourgée believed that individuals could make their lives meaningful only through commitment to a larger mission. And in Tourgée's view, by going South after the war, he had plunged himself into a society very different from the democratic ethos described by Tocqueville. He might have agreed with Tocqueville's description of democratic life "as a state of incessant change of place, feelings, and fortunes" where "the mind of each is therefore unattached to that of his fellows by tradition or common habits," if the picture were confined to much of life above the Mason/Dixon line.[9] But in Tourgée's view, these circumstances were almost exactly reversed in the postwar South, where, according to Tourgée, the military defeat of the Confederacy had, at a stroke, created a common tradition and a shared sense of mission. He noted,

> The generation which has grown up since the war not only had the birthmark of the hour of defeat upon it, but has been shaped and molded quite as much by the regret for the old conditions as by the difficulties of the new. To the Southern man or woman, therefore, the past, present, and future of Southern life is the most interesting and important matter about which they can possibly concern themselves. It is their world. Their hopes and aspirations are bounded by its destiny, and their thought is not diluted by cosmopolitan ideas.[10]

When it came to literature, "cosmopolitan ideas" of the North were potentially as vitiating as the heterogeneity and agitation that Tocqueville decried in democracies generally. In Tourgée's estimation, the absence of such forces in the South enabled the writers of that region to maintain the kind of cohesiveness that Tocqueville had associated with literary production in monarchical or aristocratic societies. Acknowledging some uncertainty as to "whether self-absorption is an essential requisite of literary production or not," Tourgée nonetheless insisted

> it is unquestionably true that almost all the noted writers of fiction have been singularly enthusiastic lovers of the national life of which they have been a part. In this respect the Southern novelist has a vast advantage over his Northern contemporary. He has never any doubt. He loves the life he portrays and sincerely believes in its superlative excellence. He does not study it as a curiosity, but knows it by intuition. He never sneers at its imperfections, but worships even its defects.[11]

The difference between the two men surfaced as differences in the way each articulated the social with the literary. For Tocqueville, the demand for strong and powerful emotions, whether attached to truth or error, arose from the cultural entropy of democracy; for Tourgée, the same emotions attached to the power of conviction in a society soldered together by tradition. The South's literature betokened a condition of social cohesiveness produced by the amalgamation of poor and landowning whites. In Tourgée's estimation,

> The dominant class itself presents the accumulated pathos of a million abdications. "We are all poor whites now," is the touching phrase in which the results of the conflict are expressed with instinctive accuracy by those to whom it meant social as well as political disaster. It is a truth as yet but half appreciated. The level of Caucasian life at the South must hereafter be run from the bench-line of the poor white, and there cannot be any leveling upward. The distance between its upper and lower strata cannot be maintained; indeed it is rapidly disappearing.[12]

By contrast, the elite literary practices of the North, which Tourgée identified with the rise of literary realism, had veered sharply away from the tastes of the general reader. Neither of realism's primary avatars, Henry James and William Dean Howells, had yielded to the prevailing demand to "identify himself with Southern types," Tourgée wrote.

Southern life does not lend itself readily to the methods of the former. It is earnest, intense, full of action, and careless to a remarkable degree of the trivialities which both these authors esteem the most important features of real life. Its types neither subsist upon soliloquy nor practice irrelevancy as a fine art; they are not affected by a chronic self-distrust nor devoted to anti-climax.[13]

However just or unjust were Tourgée's characterizations of realists, he misleads us somewhat in placing himself on the other side of the line he draws between realism and romance. That is, his account of romantic possibility posited the identification of the novelist with the life he depicted, an identification he describes as available to southern and not northern writers like himself, despite his lengthy sojourn in North Carolina. For however deep Tourgée's understanding of the southerners he depicted may have been—and Tourgée was a keen observer of social behavior—he was, and he understood himself to be, an outsider to the social world he devoted so many pages to depicting. The romantic interest provided by a society "not diluted by cosmopolitan ideas" could not be a point of departure for Tourgée as a novelist. The challenge he faced was to convey the intensity and integrity of the organicism necessary for romance from a standpoint that was alien to it.

Tourgée's remarks in "The South as a Field for Fiction," along with his novelistic practice, did not, then, simply constitute a brief on behalf of romance but also stood as an effort to solve the problem of producing the charge of romance within the domain of the real. Framed in this way, Tourgée was less an outright antagonist of the realists, whom he decried as "the worst of falsifiers, since they tell only the weakest and meanest part of the grand truth which makes up the continued story of every life,"[14] than a fellow experimenter, whose solutions sometimes resembled, sometimes varied from those pursued by his novelistic contemporaries as they sought to come to terms with what Georg Lukács describes as

> the fact that reality no longer constitutes a favourable soil for art; that is why the central problem of the novel is the fact that art has to write off the closed and total forms which stem from a rounded totality of being—that art has nothing more to do with any world of forms that is immanently complete in itself. And this is not for artistic but for historico-political reasons: "there is no longer any spontaneous totality of being."[15]

For Tourgée, the South as a field for fiction represented the unexpected return of a lived, rounded totality within the historical triumph of the real. Tourgée's criticism of Howells's insistence that the literary models that had been appropriate for the tempestuous conditions of antebellum society were no longer needed given that "all troubles that now hurt and threaten us are as crumpled rose leaves in our couch" rested on the charge of Howells's parochialism—he had taken the North, and not the South, as the basis for novelistic representation.[16] But in implicitly conceding that realism may have been adequate for certain portions of reality, Tourgée also credited the idea that fiction writing needed, at the very least, some source of renewal.

Howells and most especially Henry James had argued that such a renewal could be produced by attention to technique and form. Those novelists who could loosen the grip of the marriage plot on the form of the novel would do a great service to the enterprise of fiction writing, Howells had avowed, by forcing novels to find their form through their engagements with heretofore overlooked dimensions of human life. Contra one of Tourgée's criticisms, expansiveness, not restriction, was Howells's goal for novel writing. But Tourgée was closer to the mark in describing another of Howells's aims. To the extent that Howells coupled his plea for greater expansiveness of possible subjects with a pedagogical effort to shift the preferences of readers from the sensational and overly dramatic to the everyday, he was construing fiction as "meaner," which is to say, as the more common undertaking that Tourgée censured.

Tourgée's disagreements with James, however, were more complex and subtle. James joined Howells in granting writers the freedom to range across any number of possible subjects but parted from him in the presumption that this freedom should come at the sacrifice of intensity. In his novelistic prefaces and in such essays as "The Art of Fiction," James argued that by bringing to bear rigorous powers of observation and a disciplined attention to treatment, a novelist could find a full measure of adventure in a story of a "Bostonian nymph [rejecting] an English duke" rivaling or surpassing that conjured up in a tale of a young woman riding valiantly through the night to save her father from would-be assassins. Urging would-be writers not to "listen either to those who would shut you up into corners of [life] and tell you that it is only here and there that art inhabits," James exulted that there "is no impression of life, no manner of seeing it and feeling it, to which the plan of the novelist may not offer a place."[17] For his part, Tourgée gave due consideration to whether or not literary technique could restore enchantment to the world, only to reject the possibility. "Method," he insisted, "is but half of art—its meaner half. Homer's heroes made his song undying, not his sonorous measures; and the glow of English manfulness spreads its glamour over Shakespeare's lines, and makes him for all ages the poet from whom brave men will draw renewed strength and the unfortunate get unfailing consolation."[18] It was of what these writers wrote, and not the ways in which they wrote, that mattered most for literary art.

Even on this point of profound difference, however, Tourgée and James came down together momentarily before once again striking off in different but related directions. For all the importance that James attached to treatment and form, he placed the greatest responsibility for the success of literary art on the writer, affirming that

> the deepest quality of a work of art will always be the quality of the mind of the producer. In proportion as that mind is rich and noble will the novel, the picture, the statue, partake of the substance of beauty and truth. . . . No good novel will ever proceed from a superficial mind; that seems to me an axiom which, for the artist in fiction, will cover all needful moral ground.[19]

Having eschewed strictures that novelists should write only out of their experiences, James counted on the genius of the individual novelist or artist to create works of artistic and moral depth. His expatriation to Europe indicated his doubt as to whether the United States could reliably produce such individuals, but his return to the United States in the early years of the twentieth century indicated his willingness to put his doubts to the test by traversing the country, including the South, to see whether the conditions of his native country had as yet conspired to cultivate a garden for the flourishing of literary art. His reflections in *The American Scene* contained more doubt than conviction, and he was especially disappointed that what he saw in the South seemed to bear no relation to the romantic world projected in the literature from that region.[20]

Tourgée in his 1888 essay was all conviction. Agreeing with James that authors themselves, rather than the techniques they employed, were the ultimate guarantors of literary success and power, Tourgée, as we have seen, felt that conditions in the South were optimal for producing them. He concluded his essay by reiterating his confidence "that the South is destined to be the Hesperides Garden of American literature." He continued, poetically:

> The history of literature shows that it is those who were cradled amid the smoke of battle, the sons and daughters of national woe or racial degradation who have given utterance to the loftiest strains of genius. Because of the exceeding woefulness of a not too recent past, therefore, and the abiding horror of unavoidable conditions which are the sad inheritance of the present,

we may confidently look for the children of soldiers and slaves to advance American literature to the very front rank of that immortal procession whose song is the eternal refrain of remembered agony, before the birth-hour of the twentieth century shall strike.[21]

Although he was perhaps premature in singing the praises of southern literature as a whole from the 1890s, his embrace of experience and identity in contradistinction to cosmopolitan genius placed him in line with praising what was even then, and would continue to be, a tendency to point to regional and ethnic identity as a way of accounting for American literary excellence. A not-yet-modernist nativism underwrote Tourgée's hopes for the revitalization of American literature.[22]

But to return to an earlier paradox: In delineating the conditions that would secure the near- and long-term success of American literature, Tourgée had appeared to cut himself off from the wellspring that he had uncovered. His fictions proceeded from a deep knowledge of the political and social conditions about which he wrote and derived much of their authority from his considerable experience in the South. His affinity with the subject was such that Wilson had declared him "a special case . . . a Northerner who resembled the Southerners: in his insolence, his independence, his readiness to accept a challenge . . . his romantic and chivalrous view of the world in which he was living."[23] Nonetheless, while Tourgée frequently wrote with sympathy and understanding about southerners, he did not write *as* a southerner. Nor did he write as a quintessential northerner. Mark Elliott has argued that the young Tourgée had "absorbed the individualistic ethos" of the abolitionist movement that had prevailed in the "Western Reserve region of Ohio," from which he derived "a particular notion of the self" that Elliott termed "*radical individualism* . . . not an ideology or a political creed, but an ontological notion of the self."[24] At odds with his allies as often as his enemies, Tourgée was not properly at home anywhere. And it is partly for this reason that notwithstanding his deprecating remarks about method, his novels are distinguished by the way they foreground literary tone and mood, particularly satire and irony, within which were also embedded scenes and episodes of intensity and pathos. In styling Comfort Servosse, the protagonist of *A Fool's Errand*, a fool whose trials one nonetheless also feels deeply, Tourgée had adopted something of the posture of a romantic ironist, producing a work that was simultaneously "a spectacle to be observed . . . as well as a story in which to become engrossed."[25] Whether his novel would turn out to be an account of genius or a "narrative of one of Folly's failures" would be revealed by the unfolding of history.[26]

On this count, Tourgée's sense of alienation—from the North that had nurtured him, the postwar South whose future he'd tried to make his own, and even from the literary profession through which he tried to project his vision of American politics and social life—plunged him fully into the main current of modern authorship, and most particularly American authorship, which from Henry James forward would flow into various forms of literal and spiritual expatriation. Indeed, when one considers Martha Banta's description of James as suffused by that "sense of aloneness that besets the one 'dispossessed' of the confidence of a people who 'have' a self and a place into which that self fits with full comfort," Tourgée and the literary contemporary he was most inclined to disparage appear to be complementary rather than antagonistic spirits.[27] To pair James's Civil War veteran, Christopher Newman, whose most indelible impression of the war in which he had fought was the "waste" it had produced, with Tourgée's account of Comfort Servosse and his apparently quixotic mission to create a true democracy in the South is to get a fuller view of the historical dilemma of Reconstruction than would be possible from regarding each author in isolation from the other.

Tourgée's alien spirit also moved him toward the model of Black authorship that would flourish in the 1890s and give rise to African American literature. The image of the Negro author whom Tourgée had imagined in "The South as a Field for Fiction" as "slave, freedman, and racial outcast" seemed to be drawn along the lines he had used to sketch the figure of Eliab Hill in his 1880 novel *Bricks without Straw*.[28] Eliab, unable to walk since childhood and the best friend of the novel's virile protagonist, Nimbus Ware, becomes a teacher and an intellectual, advancing over the course of the novel from a rudimentary grasp of literacy to an eloquent command of the language. Roughly midway through the story, in a chapter instructively titled "A Child-Man," Eliab movingly detaches himself from the tutelage of Mollie Ainslee, the white northerner who has embraced the educational mission of Reconstruction, saying:

> We're only just past the Red Sea, just coming into the wilderness, and if I can only get a glimpse from Horeb, wid my old eyes by and by, 'Liab'll be satisfied. It'll be enough, an' more'n enough, for him. He can only help the young ones—lambs of the flock—a little, might little, p'raps, but it's all there is for him to do.[29]

Although Mollie interprets Eliab's decision as an abdication of intellectual ambition, the situation is entirely opposite what she supposes. Fully ready to devote "himself to his studies with a redoubled energy," Eliab's withdrawal from school

allows Mollie to direct more of her energies to the education of his younger fellow
students, whose work will be needed for the long haul. Later, after having been
brutally attacked during a Klan raid that virtually destroys the bustling Black
community that Nimbus has established at Red Wing, Eliab, through the aid of
the reconstructed southern gentleman Hesden Le Moyne, leaves the South to
complete his education before returning to continue the work he'd commenced
before the raid.

In a letter he writes to Mollie toward the end of the novel, updating her on
his fortunes, Eliab becomes a spokesperson for Tourgée's views about the necessity of education to remove racial prejudice ("I now see, more clearly than ever
before, that we must not only make *ourselves* free, but must overcome all that
prejudice which slavery created against our race in the hearts of white people").
As importantly, despite a life journey that, for a while, has taken him outside of
the experiences of many of the people he grew up among, he ultimately speaks
as one of them without a sense of having to overcome any distance from them in
order to do so. When he admits to a desire to leave the South, he does so in terms
suggesting that his feelings are theirs—"If I were one of those . . . I wouldn't stay
in this country another day. . . . But I know that they cannot go."[30]

Many early Black novelists shared Tourgée's ambition to give literary voice to
the illiterate, semiliterate, and the recently educated freedmen, who still made
up a large portion of the South's Black population. They also expressed similar
beliefs about the necessity of romanticism to this endeavor. Frances E. W. Harper
concludes her 1892 novel *Iola Leroy, or Shadows Uplifted*, which Brook Thomas
suggests was "likely influenced by Tourgée's *Pactolus Prime*,"[31] with the hope that
the stories arising from the freedmen would glow "with the fervor of the tropics
and . . . the luxuriance of the Orient."[32] Charles Chesnutt, whose literary ambitions were partly spurred by the belief that Tourgée's success had only scratched
the surface of what was possible in writing fiction about Black Americans, touted
the freedmen as "a people whose life is rich in the elements of romance."[33]

But as was the case with Tourgée, many of the writers who sought to represent
the race as a whole produced instead works that subsumed the interests of Black
laborers into the political priorities of Black elites who could not accept them as
social equals. So, for example, while the eponymous heroine of *Iola Leroy* signals her commitment to "the race" by declining an offer of marriage from the
white Dr. Gresham, citing the shadow of racial prejudice as an "insurmount-
able barrier" between them, the novel also forecloses any possibility of a union
between Iola and the heroic but illiterate freedman Tom Anderson, describing
his profound love for her as something akin to the way "a Pagan might worship

a distant star and wish to call it his own."[34] The novel then takes the additional step of killing him off before he might get the idea that he could possibly win her hand. From the standpoint of the novel, the proper relation of its elite well-spoken characters to its vernacular-speaking southern workers is that of tutelage.

But when Tourgée wrote "The South as a Field for Fiction" in 1888, the most significant political consequence of Reconstruction was one that the Fifteenth Amendment, notwithstanding the limitations surrounding enforcement that Tourgée had ably described in his essays and fiction, had made possible, namely, the Populist movement. Tourgée's article had claimed "that the line of separation between the races, being marked by the fact of color, is as impassable since emancipation as it was before," but the larger story in the South from Reconstruction forward had been more nuanced. As Jane Dailey has pointed out, subsequent to the passage of the Fifteenth Amendment "interracial coalition parties did surprisingly well [even] where partisan divides were expected to parallel the color line, and they contributed to the volatility of late nineteenth-century Southern politics. The success of each of these factions depended on the ballots of African Americans, who voted in most places throughout the late nineteenth century."[35]

And through the late 1880s and early 1890s, Populism was the most dramatic example of the efficacy of political cooperation. Indeed, Judith Stein has argued that by "1895 the most effective means to struggle against discriminatory practices, disfranchisement and racism, all of which affected prosperous black Southerners as well as the poor—was Populism. Where black Republicans succeeded in challenging racial practices, it was through alliance with the Populists."[36] Black participation in labor efforts throughout the period was extensive. Adolph Reed Jr. notes that in "the 1890s, the Colored Farmers Alliance, the black expression of the Populist insurgency, had 1,250,000 members, and in 1894 an interracial Populist-Republican Fusion alliance won statewide power in North Carolina as well as in several municipalities in the state and was re-elected by a larger margin in 1896."[37]

This level of political contestation did not indicate a society united by the "halo of romantic glory" that Tourgée had described in his essay. In fact, the wave of disfranchisement that swept over the South from 1890 into the first years of the twentieth century was an attack not only on Black political and economic aspirations but also on interracial solidarity. It left most Blacks without a vote by the turn of the century while disfranchising a sizeable proportion of poor whites. The effects were devastating: For Blacks, violence and Jim Crow segregation imposed severe limits on civic participation and social well-being. For "poor whites, cut off from the black working and agricultural classes by disfranchisement and Jim Crow, mass politics became impossible. They drifted into apathy and individual quest for survival, which sometimes involved opportunistic practices against blacks."[38]

The South's political solidarity—the unified vision that Tourgée saw as underwriting the region's romantic power—did not rest on a shared sensibility across class lines but on the successful suppression of challenges to the region's political order. Even as "Southern politicians proclaimed white solidarity," they subscribed to an economics that left many whites almost as impoverished as their Black class peers.[39] In essence, Tourgée had been right in discerning a relation between literary romance and political power in the South. But what he saw was not an expression of the romantic sensibility of a "people" but rather the grim reality of class domination.

Notes

1. George M. Fredrickson, Introduction to *A Fool's Errand: A Novel of the South during Reconstruction*, by Albion W. Tourgée (Long Grove, IL: Waveland, 1966), xiii, xxv.

2. John Hope Franklin, cover endorsement for Tourgée, *A Fool's Errand: A Novel of the South during Reconstruction*.

3. Edmund Wilson, *Patriotic Gore: Studies in the Literature of the American Civil War* (New York: Farrar, Straus and Giroux, 1962), 536.

4. Albion W. Tourgée, "The South as a Field for Fiction," *Forum* 12 (1888): 404.

5. Brook Thomas, *The Literature of Reconstruction: Not in Plain Black and White* (Baltimore, MD: Johns Hopkins University Press, 2017), 2.

6. Tourgée, "The South as a Field for Fiction," 404, 405, 411, 412, 404.

7. Alexis de Tocqueville, "De Tocqueville on Democracy and the Arts," *Daedalus* 89, no. 2 (Spring 1960): 408, 407.

8. Mark Elliott, *Color-Blind Justice: Albion Tourgée and the Quest for Racial Equality from the Civil War to Plessy v. Ferguson* (New York: Oxford University Press, 2006), 10.

9. Tocqueville, "De Tocqueville on Democracy and the Arts," 406–7.

10. Tourgée, "The South as a Field for Fiction," 407.

11. Tourgée, "The South as a Field for Fiction," 407–8.

12. Tourgée, "The South as a Field for Fiction," 412.

13. Tourgée, "The South as a Field for Fiction," 406. As I noted in 1993, Tourgée's criticism of James had overlooked his depiction of the Mississippian Basil Ransom in the *Bostonians*. Kenneth W. Warren, *Black and White Strangers: Race and American Literary Realism* (Chicago: University of Chicago Press, 1993), 5.

14. Tourgée, "The South as a Field for Fiction," 411.

15. Georg Lukács, *The Theory of the Novel: A Historico-Philosophical Essay on the Forms of Great Epic Literature*, trans. Anna Bostock (Cambridge, MA: MIT Press, 1971), 17–18.

16. William Dean Howells, "The Editor's Study," in *Editor's Study*, ed. James W. Simpson (Troy, NY: Whitson, 1983), 41.

17. Henry James, "The Art of Fiction," *Longman's Magazine* 4, no. 23 (September 1, 1884): 517, 520.

18. Tourgée, "The South as a Field for Fiction," 414.

19. James, "The Art of Fiction," 520.

20. Henry James, *The American Scene* (Bloomington: Indiana University Press, 1978), 374.

21. Tourgée, "The South as a Field for Fiction," 413.

22. Walter Benn Michaels, *Our America: Nativism, Modernism, and Pluralism* (Durham, NC: Duke University Press, 1995), argues for crucial distinctions among the "major writers of the Progressive period—London, Dreiser, Wharton—[who] were comparatively indifferent to questions of both racial and national identity"; novelists like Thomas Nelson Page and Thomas Dixon, who were "deeply" concerned with those issues but not as a commitment to cultural identity; and the major writers of the modernist 1920s, for whom such questions were central and manifested in the formal commitments of their work (8–9). Tourgée is most closely aligned with the second group.

23. Wilson, *Patriotic Gore*, 537.

24. Elliott, *Color-Blind Justice*, 7.

25. Marilyn J. Blackwell, "Friedrich Schlegel and C. J. L. Almqvist: Romantic Irony and Textual Artifice," *Scandinavian Studies* 52, no. 2 (Spring 1980): 129. In Blackwell's account, the romantic ironist embodies a host of competing qualities: "creative and critical, enthusiastic and realistic, emotional and rational, unconsciously inspired and conscious artist." Such a writer could "be both detached and involved, serious and playful about his art" (129).

26. Tourgée, *A Fool's Errand*, 6.

27. Martha Banta, *Henry James: An Alien's "History" of America* (Rome: Sapienza Università Editrice, 2016), 4.

28. Tourgée, "The South as a Field for Fiction," 411.

29. Albion Tourgée, *Bricks without Straw*, ed. Otto H. Olsen (Baton Rouge: Louisiana State University Press, 1969), 149–50.

30. Tourgée, *Bricks without Straw*, 390.

31. Thomas, *The Literature of Reconstruction*, 289.

32. Francis E. W. Harper, *Iola Leroy, or Shadows Uplifted* (Mineola, NY: Dover, 2010), 219.

33. Quoted in Richard O. Lewis, "Romanticism in the Fiction of Charles W. Chesnutt: The Influence of Dickens, Scott, Tourgée, and Douglass," *CLA Journal* 26, no. 2 (December 1982): 160.

34. Harper, *Iola Leroy*, 96, 40.

35. Jane Dailey, *White Fright: The Sexual Panic at the Heart of America's Racist History* (New York: Basic Books, 2020), 8.

36. Judith Stein, "'Of Mr. Booker T. Washington and Others,'" in *Renewing Black Intellectual History: The Ideological and Material Foundations of African American Thought*, ed. Adolph Reed Jr. and Kenneth W. Warren (Boulder, CO: Paradigm, 2010), 33.

37. Adolph Reed Jr., "Black Politics after 2016," *nonsite.org* 23 (February 11, 2018), https://nonsite.org/article/black-politics-after-2016.

38. Stein, "'Of Mr. Booker T. Washington and Others,'" 42.

39. Stein, "'Of Mr. Booker T. Washington and Others,'" 42.

9 Exodian Allegories of Incomplete Emancipation in *Bricks without Straw*

Christine Holbo

*B*ricks without Straw, Tourgée's 1880 sequel to his bestselling *A Fool's Errand* (1879), extended both the legal and literary dimensions of the earlier novel's project. It was on the pages of *Bricks* that Tourgée first rehearsed a radical claim about the interpretation of the Thirteenth Amendment that would be pivotal to the argument he presented to the Supreme Court in the *Plessy* case fifteen years later. More self-reflexively concerned with problems of literary genre than *A Fool's Errand*, *Bricks* was also interested in how the failure of Reconstruction required a concept of minority identity and a literature capable of addressing the African American experience. This essay will be concerned with how Tourgée's choice of the Hebrew Bible as the epic framework over which to stretch a tragicomic plot of failed emancipation created a point of articulation between these concerns, allowing him to advocate for an expansive legal definition of slavery even as he explored the way the problem of incomplete emancipation required a transformation in the imaginative genres of heroic struggle.

Bricks without Straw represents, in the first instance, an effort at documenting the ways in which African Americans remained effectively enslaved in the years after emancipation. Drawing on events Tourgée had witnessed and on language he claimed to have transcribed verbatim, the novel heaps example upon example of how the emancipation process had been undermined by the freedpeople's former owners and oppressors, by their erstwhile northern allies, and by the African Americans themselves. Chronicling the exemplary individual and collective efforts of the freedpeople and celebrating the emergence of leaders within the community, *Bricks* also, nonetheless, depicts the way even the most clear-sighted of the freedpeople struggled against internalized prejudice, self-doubt, and habits of speech or action that marked them as a subordinate caste, left them vulnerable to the predations of the dominant class, and often confounded their attempts to come to terms with the problems they faced.

Tourgée's choice of the Hebrew Bible as a polysemic framework for transforming this experience into narrative was both political and literary. Standing in the background of all Tourgée's work was the precedent set by Harriet Beecher Stowe's *Uncle Tom's Cabin* (1852), which grounded the social novel's appeal to universal humanity on the Gospel story of persecuted innocence. Stowe's slaves suffer the fate of true Christians living in a wicked world; Stowe's slave owners, Calvinist backsliders all, know they are engaged in evil but keep postponing the moment of conversion toward the good. Though Tourgée certainly viewed slavery as a sin, his creativity as a novelist had developed through a negation of Stowe's technique and of the Higher Law jurisprudence it implied. *A Fool's Errand* was an extended, apophatic riff on the idea that truth and justice were transparently obvious but empirically unavailable in an unequal world; the fool was the one who acted as if self-evident truths were governing in a society distorted by domination.[1] *Bricks without Straw*'s Hebraism took this negation of the ideal one step farther. The Hebrew Bible offered a story of the law, and of course this meant revelation—the Burning Bush, the ascent to Mount Sinai. But insofar as it also meant Leviticus and Deuteronomy, the Hebrew Bible offered Tourgée a metaplot that, oscillating between the inadequacy of the individual to law and the inadequacy of the law to the individual, allowed him to consider how people live in a world where moral absolutes are neither given nor even necessarily felt. A realist novel for a secular age, *Bricks* presents the struggle to know what slavery is (and thus how "freedom" is to be achieved) as a form of exilic improvisation in a postrevelatory world. Fragmented, misinterpreted, and even mythological, the law nonetheless represented the only possibility of salvation—the only route to freedom; seeking a right relation to law, however, required working through the tensions between law as guiding ideal, as ordinary practice, and as objective domination.

Badges and Incidents and Bricks and Straw

The focus of *Bricks'* exploration of the problem of law as symbol and practice centered on the interplay between a biblical metaphor and a legal phrase that was becoming more important as Americans debated whether Reconstruction was over: "bricks without straw" and the "badges and incidents of slavery." In antebellum legal language and in Republican usage at the time of the Thirteenth Amendment's passage, the "incidents" of slavery described the complex of laws required to sustain the institution, including limitations on the rights of both slaves and some "free" men to move freely, to vote, to own weapons, to read, preach, or marry. "Badges" were the demeaning symbols that marked the slave as part of a separate caste, subject to the legal impairments of slavery, and included habits of dress or speech, practices such as the bestowing or withholding of honorific titles, or characteristics of the person, such as skin color, which could not be laid aside. Rooted in Roman law's *macula servitutis* ("stain of slavery"), the idea of "badges" implied a society in which the mere fact of being liberated from slavery did not imply being "free" in the sense of being an equal citizen.[2] In exploring the tangle of unfreedoms facing the freedpeople, *Bricks* extensively documented the ways the persistence of these "badges and incidents" represented the positive extension of slavery into the era of freedom. "Bricks without straw," conversely, addressed the negative extension of slavery through the lack of economic, institutional, or political support for the freedpeople's endeavors. Just as "slavery" was a complex structure of laws and symbols, so "freedom" could not exist without its constituent rights, symbols, and practices—the "straw" that held bricks together.

Concern for the "badges and incidents of slavery" had been integral to Tourgée's career since the Civil War. Tourgée had been one of those northerners who saw the war not as a fight to save the Union or even to end chattel slavery per se but as a struggle between republican liberty and oligarchy, and his political efforts in the postwar period had been shaped by this vision. In 1868, in a speech before the North Carolina constitutional convention, Tourgée used the phrase "badge of servitude" to attempt to mobilize voters to side with "the principles of free labor, free speech and free truth [against] oligarchy." Addressing himself to working-class white southerners, Tourgée declared that the essence of the Old South, the "basis principle of the Rebellion," was "not Slavery." Rather, the Confederacy embodied the "damnable principle" that "a few are born to rule, the rest of mankind to obey":

> Color was nothing, caste was everything in the theory of the rebellion. It was builded upon the principle that labor was the badge of servitude, that a nation was composed of two classes only, the ruling class and the serving class.[3]

Defining slavery not in terms of property but of dignity, the division of society into rulers and ruled, the leisure class and the working class, Tourgée believed that only a cross-racial alliance could uphold republican liberty.

Tourgée's hopes for such alliances did not prevail. By 1880, Tourgée had largely stopped railing against oligarchy. But his confrontation with the persistence of slavery through its "badges" had deepened as his career became entwined with the struggles of African Americans. The beginning of the 1880s marked, indeed, a pivotal moment in the strange career of this language as a term of art in American law. In 1883, the Supreme Court would use the phrase "badges and incidents of slavery" to paraphrase the meaning of the Thirteenth Amendment when, in the Civil Rights Cases, it affirmed that Congress had "power to pass all laws necessary and proper for abolishing all badges and incidents of slavery in the United States."[4] This paraphrase, confirming Tourgée's interpretation by acknowledging the language of the Thirteenth Amendment's original Republican sponsors, seemed to presage a broad reading of the amendment as prohibiting not only slavery but all the practices and symbols that contributed to maintaining a racialized caste society. Justice Marshall Harlan's dissent interpreted it this way, asserting that Congress's power to remove the "badges of slavery and servitude" required protecting African Americans against all discrimination, public or private.[5] But in a perverse twist worthy of one of Tourgée's novels, the majority concluded that the only "badges and incidents" subject to congressional action were those imposed by state (rather than private) actors, thereby using the Thirteenth Amendment to hamstring federal action on civil rights.

Tourgée could not have known, when he was writing Bricks, that the Civil Rights Cases decision would turn out as it did. But he was fully aware of the general jurisprudential trend, and anticipatory resistance against narrow readings of the Reconstruction Amendments is written into every page of the novel. Crucial to this resistance was the moment when, at the end of A Fool's Errand, Tourgée first set his Fool to meditating on the fact that African Americans drew upon the Hebrew Bible for expressing their own experience. Comparisons between the Egyptian captivity and America, generative for Bricks, would appear in Tourgée's work for years, culminating in his Plessy brief, where Tourgée cited the Mosaic story to support his argument that slavery, strictly defined, was not chattelism, the ownership of one person by another, but rather was more properly negative, "a caste, a legal condition of subjection to the dominant class":

> The bondage of the Israelites in Egypt . . . was unquestionably "Slavery," but it was not chattelism. No single Egyptian owned any single Israelite. The political community of Egypt simply denied them the common rights of men.[6]

This argument is notable for its radical adherence to the ideal of human equality that had inspired his earlier rhetoric. In looking to the Egyptian captivity as the original model of slavery, Tourgée insisted that the Thirteenth Amendment had not yet been implemented: Slavery still existed. Harlan would find this argument convincing, as he did Tourgée's other arguments, but the majority was provoked into explicit rebuttal. Justice Henry Billings Brown, writing for the majority, would argue that slavery ended with the ban on "the ownership of mankind as a chattel."[7] Tourgée did not witness the Supreme Court's gutting of the Thirteenth Amendment in *Hodges* (1906), but the pattern of using Thirteenth Amendment chattelism to mutilate the Fourteenth Amendment was clear in *Plessy*. Twentieth-century jurisprudence would retain the assumption that the Thirteenth Amendment had exhausted its force in codifying the emancipation, a one-time event. As recent legal scholars have returned to viewing slavery not as a single thing but "a bundle of disabilities"—and have thus reopened the door to understanding tolerance of racial hierarchy as the reimposition of slavery—it is important to recall that Tourgée believed that the original, republican intent of the amendment required an end to caste distinctions and all other barriers to substantive equality before the law.[8]

Law as Myth and Disenchantment

Tourgee's invocation of the Hebrew Bible to fend off Thirteenth Amendment chattelism reminds us that, in court as without, the legitimacy of the law has a literary dimension. While the *Plessy* majority was not convinced, Tourgée's claim that the definition of slavery implied by the sacred text should carry weight in court spoke not only to the fact that the language of the law is always porous, always affected by nonlegal discourses and sources of authority, but also to the fact that Tourgée was writing for the court of public opinion, seeking to shape the way the public would interpret the law. Throughout his writings of the 1880s, when Tourgée appealed to the Hebrew Bible, he was attempting to move a public whose common sense was defined by Christian universalism while also developing a new line of political-narrative inquiry into the way slavery shaped minority identity.

Standing between these two endeavors—to frame African American experience in terms familiar to general readers and to understand how an African American minority was being shaped *as different*—was, as so often the case with Tourgée, the figure of the fool. *Bricks without Straw* signals its approach to the Hebrew Bible as foolish by prefacing its narrative with an invented biblical paratext, supposedly translated from an "ancient Egyptian Papyrus-roll," the story of a jester in the court of Pharaoh. Egypt, in this retelling, was no longer antebellum slavery but Reconstruction: Pharaoh represented all those elites, North and South, who had grown impatient with the freedpeople. In Tourgée's allegory, the fool mocks Pharaoh for having declared that "the children of Israel should deliver the daily tale of bricks, but should not be furnished with any straw wherewith to make them."[9] Pharaoh punishes the fool by sending him to talk with an owl (apparently to imbibe some of its proverbial wisdom), and the fool revenges himself by bringing back his own tale—an absurd, recursive retelling of his own interactions with Pharaoh, which threatens to go on ad infinitum until Pharaoh abruptly ends the farce by throwing the fool in jail. The immediate message in the passage was clear enough to readers in 1880: The United States was acting against its own interests in failing to support the freedpeople through the hard work of emancipation. However, a second, more reflexive message accompanied this call to action, an argument about minorities, domination, and genre—the speech of the oppressed, of fools and of slaves. The word "tale," used in the King James Bible to indicate the number of items to be counted, was increasingly dated and was increasingly being used in ways that merged accounting back into narrative, as in phrases such as "a tale of years," which indicated both a *count* of years and an account, a storyline. The pun behind the fool's "tale" imagined transforming domination by numbers into resistance through narrative.

A Nietzschean reading of the Hebrew Bible would suggest that a people not allowed to be free will produce not law but literature. And this literature will be entwined with the duality of unachieved values: Their stories will be cyclical, recursive, tragic, tricksterish, and also, possibly, funny, charged with painful humor. Taking scripture as a source for both tragic and comic retellings of Reconstruction allowed Tourgée to heap layer upon layer of interpretation onto his core hermeneutic concerns: questions of what made a minority literature and what made a minority political consciousness, of how narrative expectations of freedom shaped law's ideals, of how embedded practices and failures to see the common good led to a frustration of shared ideals, and of how the struggles of a minority could define an inclusive majority's sensibility.

Names: Inheritance and Individuality

The rewriting of Exodus in the mode of repetition, framed by the pseudoscroll, continues in the first chapters of the novel with a farcical rewriting of the litany of names in Exodus 1:1–7. In Exodus, names link the world of the patriarchs to the world of the Hebrews in Egypt, serving as a map of relationships among the Israelites and their descendants; indeed, the book Christianity calls "Exodus" is titled in Hebrew *shemot*, or "names." In *Bricks*, by contrast, names represent nonidentity, the first stumbling block on the road to freedom. Chapter 1 finds the freedman Nimbus puzzling over the problem of his own name as a signifier of personal and social identity. In the world of both the ante- and postbellum South, as Tourgée represents it, the ability to determine one's name was a sign of full citizenship. Nimbus's former owner, P. Desmit, had himself been baptized "Potestatem Dedimus" by a working-class father in celebration of his sense of enfranchisement, having worked and married his way up and into the exalted position of justice of the peace. The surname "Desmit," however, is pure fantasy, a Frenchified translation of the common "Smith" undertaken to satisfy the aristocratic pretensions of his fiancée. Having renamed himself in order to marry into the first families of the county, Desmit moves into that phantasmagoric and proto-Faulknerian world of the antebellum upper class where signifiers of military rank (colonel) and kinship (cousin) circulate without any reference to military service or biological reality. This right of self-naming is reinforced by the authority he exerts—and the business sense he displays—in naming his slaves, giving each slave child on his plantations a unique, singular name, which serves as a mnemonic device for himself and a guide to no further relations.[10]

"Nimbus," the name bestowed on the novel's lead character, testifies to Desmit's success in making badges of slavery adhere to his property. Nimbus, upon becoming first contraband and then a freedman, requires a legal name in order to exist before the law, but virtually every solution to his problem threatens regression into subjection. Nimbus's motives regarding names echo those of the Israelites: He wishes to have his children legally recorded as his own and understands that family begins with the recognition of marriage. Yet his name poses a paradox: The mononym, which is the mark of social death, is also, for him, a personal identity, and being named by one white man seems no different than being renamed by others. In the course of six chapters, he is renamed three times in order, by turns, to become a soldier in the Union Army, to register his marriage, and to register to vote. The final name he is given, "Ware," speaks all too clearly to continuities between his old status as chattel and his new status as a second-class citizen. The first hero of the novel, Nimbus is also the butt of its first joke. Where the names of Exodus marked generations, the multiplication and flourishing of the descendants of Isaac, in *Bricks* names themselves multiply, proliferating conditions of dubious legitimacy and redoubling the nonidentity of the recently emancipated.

Yet the doubleness of Nimbus's name has still another dimension. The word "nimbus" has two primary meanings: A "nimbus" is a dark cloud; it is also a halo. If *Bricks* is a retelling of the Hebrew Bible, Nimbus is not merely one of the patriarchs chronicled at the beginning of Exodus but the most likely candidate for the role of Moses, that leader who sometimes donned a veil to appear to his people and sometimes appeared with the light of holiness shining from his face (or, by quirk of St. Jerome, with horns on his head). Nimbus, like Moses, bears a single name given him by a ruler of the dominant group. He shares Moses's sometimes fiery temper and like him struggles for words, needing a more fluent Aaron to speak for him in the person of Eliab Hill. And, like Moses, he kills a man and has to escape across state lines for a period of time before coming back to find that charges have not been filed. In making Nimbus the most plausible analog to Moses in the novel and assigning him many of Moses's more problematic, more human traits, Tourgée was deploying a virtuosically "foolish" reading of the biblical figure to invoke the widespread sense among African Americans in the Reconstruction years of an urgent need for "a Moses." That Nimbus occasionally appears humorous in the role of Moses captures something latently funny, because flawed, about Moses himself; that Moses was not perfect as a leader of the Hebrews illuminates the debate over whether African Americans needed political or religious leaders, businessmen or educators. The question as to whether Nimbus is indeed Moses, or whether Eliab might not be Aaron but Moses himself, feels at once authentically grounded in the leadership struggles of the Hebrews in the wilderness and realistic as a depiction of the American South in the 1870s.

Every retelling implies a difference. The uncertainty about whether Nimbus should be seen as a comic shadow of a prophetic leader or as a faithfully imagined embodiment of a modern Moses unbalances attempts to stabilize the novel's Exodus leitmotifs, and it initiates one of the major themes in *Bricks*, namely, the intertwinement of myth with its own disenchantment. The Hebrew Bible, a national epic, is an empowering myth. As the Fool had argued, the flight into the wilderness was not an expression of religious belief; rather, the religious belief was a response to oppression, a projection of the "aspirations of independent manhood."[11] In order for an emancipatory myth to do its work, however, it must overcome other myths, create a disenchanted space in which its own narratives may be effective. As the novel progresses, the doubling of Nimbus as both a heroic and a foolish Moses leads to a recursive multiplication of the Exodus narrative itself. The Exodus story appears not once but repeatedly in the novel, as the question of "who is Moses?" amplifies the question of "who is Pharaoh?" and "where is Canaan?" In the process, the fact that the disenchanting work of monotheistic myth is subject to reenchantment underscores the novel's central investigation of the lived problems of slavery and freedom.

First Exodus: Red Wing

Let us consider the straight story, or the closest thing to it that the novel presents. In this reading, the Exodus narrative offers the outlines of a national epic—one in which the Hebrew myth has been remodeled for the American imagination. In the figure of Nimbus, the leader as soldier and yeoman farmer, the theocratic republicanism implied by the Hebrew model fully merges with civic republicanism and with American individualism in the Lockean mode: Nimbus seeks to buy land, improve it through labor, and thereby build a free community. This story about free labor, rugged individualism, and the common good implies that the Civil War had indeed produced a "second founding," that a second revolution had been required to banish the contradictions in the American system, and that the role of Nimbus and his generation involved nothing less than the fulfillment of the American promise, the restoration of the nation to itself.

This merger of Locke and republicanism is itself mythological, but for it to rule, there must be a disenchantment: The world of aristocracy must be displaced, and hierarchies of privilege give way to equality, before the self-made man may build his world of property. *Bricks* enacts this disenchantment in a subtle citation of the Hebrew Bible, a restaging of the contest of the staffs between Moses's brother Aaron and Pharoah's court magicians. Recognizing that this was one of the biblical texts where the religious narrative wobbles off its own straight path and indulges in magic and myth, Tourgée plays upon the mystical quality of walking sticks as emblems of citizenship in southern culture, totemic objects forbidden to slaves (and in many places, free African Americans) in part because they could be used as weapons and in part because they symbolized mastery. When the aging Desmit raises his "heavy walking stick" in the air to strike Nimbus, he is invoking all of these properties of a "badge of mastery"; when Nimbus, bemused rather than intimidated, throws his former *master* to the ground, he breaks the object's spell. This act makes it possible for Nimbus, in the next scene, to purchase the land at Red Wing from Desmit, under the disenchanting gaze of a Union officer, and enter the world (as he thinks) of fee-simple property ownership.[12]

Second Exodus: Eviction

But though the magic of the staff is broken, the magician has more tricks. Desmit resorts to the highest (or lowest) magic, namely, contract fraud, and thus sets up a plot by which law, which should be the source of rationality and transparency, becomes the medium of mystification. As Nimbus seeks to build community on land he has paid for but doesn't own, he is beset by opponents who are still enchanted. His southern neighbors believe in a different story than the Lockean republicanism Nimbus is pursuing, and as Nimbus encounters their resistance the Exodus story fractures and multiplies. When Moses goes out into the wilderness, he meets God and brings back the law. Although it is true that on Nimbus's first escape into the wilderness he meets up with the US Army, Nimbus's extraterritorial ventures largely occur in a space that, profane but not demythologized, utterly distorts the quest structure of the Exodus narrative.

Take, for example, what is, after the gathering at Red Wing, the second most important of the many exoduses in the novel. Threatened by the Klan, Nimbus's neighbor, the community clown and cynic Berry Lawson, offers a definition of exodus as eviction in which a disenchanted view of their supposed rights mingles with resignation before the mystical authority of white society: "I'se gwine ter move on ebbery time dey axes me to," says Berry, "'kase why, I can't help it."[13] While Nimbus first rejects this as cowardice, Berry's statement proves prophetic. The community successfully fends off the Klan assault, but Nimbus and Berry are forced to leave the state. This second exodus, a departure from community, also represents a departure from the biblical model and moral. Here, indeed, the narrative structure of the novel undergoes chiasmatic reversal. What had initially appeared as an American national story (Nimbus as self-made man and community leader) has split. For the first half of the novel, the storyline centering on the white allies of the Red Wing freedpeople appeared as a kind of disorganized supplement to the Red Wing story, a frame for the narrative of community self-determination. Thereafter, the white story moves to the fore, coalescing in a romance of sectional reunion. The Yankee schoolteacher Mollie Ainslie proves to be the legitimate owner of the estate of her southern love interest, Hesden Le Moyne. Le Moyne insists, with a display of selfless principle that strains credulity, on documenting her otherwise unprovable claim, and Mollie restores his title through the surrender of marriage. Where Le Moyne, as his last name indicates, had originally seemed fated to a monkish sterility, love and an insistence on scrupulous legality restore to him the possibility of reproductive futurity. Meanwhile, the African American story dissolves into a spiral of accelerating violence only halted by Mollie's success in the West and the founding of Eupolia as a refuge for white and Black refugees from southern lawlessness. The novel's two plots are, thus, both stories of community bound to narratives of law, and they are arrayed across an inverted structure of legality. Where the white story falls into place through supererogatory legality, the Black story is about the collapse of the legal guarantees that create the very possibility of individual effort and a sense of social selfhood. A fantastic story of how law both grants and gains legitimacy through love plays against an "exodus" story that has been converted into a realistic, if compressed, representation of the violence of "redemption" in the form of two disorganized narratives—torrents of traumatic incident—delivered, in the last two chapters featuring African American characters, by Nimbus and then Berry.

Exodia

One of the elements for which *Bricks* has been praised is its representation of African American voices and the central place it gives to African American efforts at self-determination. Mark Elliot, for example, states that the achievement of *Bricks* lies in its attempt "to tell the story of Reconstruction from the vantage of the freedpeople."[14] For a reader hoping for such a story of a nation rising, the disintegration of Nimbus's storyline is disappointing. This disappointment culminates in a moment in which biblical narration is displaced by another genre altogether.

By the end of the novel, the parallels of character between Nimbus and Moses have reversed. At Moses's death, he is an acknowledged prophet without parallel, undiminished in his strength (Deuteronomy 24:7); Nimbus, by contrast, says "I'se an ole man . . . an' ole man, ef I is young." Mortal and defeated, he is no longer a mythic leader but one of many refugees entering Mollie's Kansan Canaan. Nimbus's last words, to be sure, are in the mode of secular prophecy. Promising to help his friend Eliab in the task of "gibbin' light ter our people, so dat dey'll know how ter be free an' keep free forebber an' ebber. Amen!," he outdoes Moses in describing emancipation as the ability to *remain* free, to escape the cyclical dynamics of social domination as reenchantment. But Nimbus does not get the last word. The last Black voice in the novel is that of Berry, who, delivering a quasi-monologue in the form of a vaudeville give-and-take with Hesden as his straight man, is described as a "light hearted exodian."[15] Though "exodian" might seem to be the adjectival form of exodus, the exilic genre has in fact been displaced by the Roman genre of the "exodia"—short, comic pieces, often in the form of improvised exchange, performed at the end of tragedies. Intended to lift the mood after the catastrophe at the end of the performance, these plays were the literature of slaves in the double sense of reinforcing social hierarchies by directing derision at slaves and of giving voice to slave perspectives through role reversal, revenge plots, and moral inversion. Playing with the affinities between the ancient genre of slave improvisation and the nineteenth-century world of minstrelsy, Tourgée's positioning of Berry at the end of the novel signals the objective regression that has overtaken Nimbus's dream of freedom forever. The hero breaks, his destiny unfulfilled; the weak reed, resilient because flexible, survives, hiding his true thoughts, whatever they are, beneath the mask of clownish mimicry.

Fifteen years later, Tourgée would, in his *Plessy* brief, ask the Supreme Court to respect the authority of the Bible to define slavery beyond chattelism. *Bricks*, however, undermines that authority through the slippage between the exodic and the exodian. This fact—that the epic aspirations of the freedpeople have been swallowed by slave comedy—is tragic. It is also historically accurate, and Tourgée was clearly, in *Bricks*, working through the implications of Reconstruction's reversal for American literature and law. Throughout the 1880s, as Tourgée thought about the Egyptian captivity as a model for a more robust concept of slavery, he also used the Hebrew Bible to think about the shaping of African American identity through memory of suffering and oppression. Repeatedly, he compared the way African Americans related to slavery to the anger the Hebrew scriptures expressed—retrospectively—about the experience of captivity: Not only were African Americans not going to be willing to forget slavery in a generation or so (as Tourgée's nineteenth-century interlocutors expected), but they were still gathering their intellectual resources to count their dead and tell their stories. White Americans were deceived in believing that they understood their African American fellow citizens. In "The Negro's View of the Race Problem," for example, Tourgée argued:

> No doubt Pharaoh and the more intelligent and cultivated classes of Egypt believed they fully understood the character of the degraded tribes they had held in bondage for four hundred years; but it is doubtful if one of them dreamed of that fierce tide of theocratic nationalism which burst from Moses' lips as he gazed upon the waves that engulfed Israel's pursuers.[16]

Slavery—a caste system, systematic inequality—created barriers to knowledge of self and others and eroded the mutual recognition that, as a republican, Tourgée believed was a prerequisite for political equality. Continuing by comparing the situation of the Israelites and African Americans to that of the Irish, he nonetheless affirmed that these misrecognitions constituted, negatively but necessarily, the beginning of national consciousness. The problem of a nation that was not quite a nation and of expression that was neither individual nor collective required revision of his earlier republicanism and thus the articulation of narratives based on more Nietzschean conceptions of negativity and ressentiment.

Who could tell such a story, of a consciousness yet to come? Not, surely, one of the dominant nation, not even if he were among the "more intelligent and cultivated classes." Only a fool would, indeed, attempt such a thing. The opening figure of the jester, the storyteller who transforms simple truth into nonsense through repetition, suggests that Tourgée doubted his powers as an epic poet and sought refuge in the role of the clown mocking power by refusing to get to the point. Where Pharaoh, the voice of power, claims to desire wisdom, he grows impatient when he receives incomplete storytelling instead. This incompleteness, for all its entanglement in myth, is where the story of freedom must tarry so long as the blur of events recounted by Nimbus—from escaping a work gang to surviving a version of the Colfax massacre—are mere chronicle not yet usable. More than a decade before Paul Laurence Dunbar and W. E. B. Du Bois, Tourgée was beginning to work a vein that would become central to twentieth-century African American literature: the exploration of the veil between the minority and "the world," the historical dynamic that requires the recognition of minorities to begin with an acknowledgment of misrecognition.

To go further would require a narrator other than a Yankee fool, and the novel's final switch from Nimbus to Berry speaks to the ramified challenge of finding a Black voice for a national consciousness. The novel had invested heavily in the mononymic Nimbus's Mosaic potential to fuse the horizons of sacred history with national liberation. Berry Lawson, who has accepted the name the law has given him—who is, indeed, the law's very ("berry") son—points toward a different solution. Though Berry's status as the suffering clown attests to the problem that freedom cannot be achieved either within the law or outside it, his resilience shows how clowning compliance informed by slave memory is a way of interpellating one's experience into a law that is not yet justice. A comic complement to the Deuteronomist's injunction to "remember that you were a slave in the House of Egypt," Berry's form of historical memory is weak and unstable, but it nonetheless bears witness to the secular availability of the Hebrew Bible. The Israelites were a nation ex negativo. Neither the flight from Egypt, nor the trek into the wilderness, nor even the promulgation of the law made them free. Rather, the dream of the law's future possibility, conjoined with the devotion to remembering their time in slavery, defined the exilic meaning of their narrative. Berry's gift for turning narratives of suffering, negative identities, and marks of servitude into badges of liberation is wholly of the Mosaic tradition, inclusive of its aspirations, incompleteness, and occasionally stumbling quality. The American story of emancipation cannot be about a chosen people, their divinely ordained leader, and the giving of law but about the elusive horizons of freedom in secular time.

The storytelling of emancipation thus involves both Exodus and exodia, the process by which human beings learn to express their own historical coming-to-be with the legal and narrative tools available to them.

Notes

1. Christine Holbo, *Legal Realisms: The American Novel under Reconstruction* (New York: Oxford University Press, 2019), 22–24, 31–41.

2. See Jennifer Mason McAward, "Defining the Badges and Incidents of Slavery," *Journal of Constitutional Law* 14, no. 3 (February 2012): 561–630.

3. Albion Tourgée, "Speech on Elective Franchise (1868)," in *Undaunted Radical: The Selected Writings and Speeches of Albion W. Tourgée*, ed. Mark Elliott and John David Smith (Baton Rouge: Louisiana State University Press, 2010), 39.

4. 109 US 20.

5. Harlan's dissent is 109 US 26-62, at 35.

6. Albion Tourgée, "Brief of Plaintiff in Error. In the Supreme Court of the United States," in *Undaunted Radical: The Selected Writings and Speeches of Albion W. Tourgée*, ed. Mark Elliott and John David Smith (Baton Rouge: Louisiana State University Press, 2010), 323.

7. 163 US 542.

8. Darrell A. H. Miller, "The Thirteenth Amendment and the Regulation of Custom," *Columbia Law Review* 112 (2012): 1848.

9. Albion Tourgée, *Bricks without Straw: A Novel*, ed. Carolyn L. Karcher (Durham, NC: Duke University Press, 2009), 81.

10. Tourgée, *Bricks without Straw*, 91–92, 94.

11. Albion Tourgée, *A Fool's Errand: By One of the Fools* (1879; London: George Routledge and Sons, 1883), 303.

12. Tourgée, *Bricks without Straw*, 153.

13. Tourgée, *Bricks without Straw*, 260.

14. Mark Elliott, *Color-Blind Justice: Albion Tourgée and the Quest for Racial Equality from the Civil War to Plessy v. Ferguson* (Oxford: Oxford University Press, 2006), 153.

15. Tourgée, *Bricks without Straw*, 406, 409, 418.

16. Albion Tourgée, "The Negro's View of the Race Problem," in *Undaunted Radical: The Selected Writings and Speeches of Albion W. Tourgée*, ed. Mark Elliott and John David Smith (Baton Rouge: Louisiana State University Press, 2010), 156.

10

The Business of Marriage, Pluralized

Mormonism and Money
in Button's Inn

Molly Ball

*B*utton's Inn (1887) may seem like a curious outlier from the rest of Albion Tourgée's work. A historical novel set in 1839 near Tourgée's Mayville, New York, home, *Button's Inn* lacks any overt discussion of race or of politics more broadly. Instead of advancing the antiracist work that defined Tourgée's career, the novel tracks a young inventor's rise from obscurity. That inventor, Ozro Evans, resembles a young Thomas Edison in his creativity, work ethic, and humble origins.[1] Yet unlike Edison, who cultivated a capitalist mythos of individual achievement, Ozro ascends through cooperation. Strikingly, Ozro's cooperative ethic extends beyond his professional life and into his domestic relations. By suggesting that cooperation trumps competition in public and private affairs, the seemingly apolitical *Button's Inn* speaks to changes that Tourgée perceived in postbellum northern culture—specifically, the Gilded Age's celebration of human greed. Mark Elliott has tracked Tourgée's concern with economic inequity, demonstrating that Tourgée viewed laissez-faire capitalism in much the same way that he viewed the abandonment of Reconstruction: as a nationwide abdication of civic responsibility. This essay argues that *Button's Inn* challenges the notion that "the unsentimental pursuit of economic self-interest [is] . . . the best means of serving the public good."[2] Against attempts to cast greed as a social virtue, *Button's Inn* champions a less possessive economic ethic in which virtue involves striving to earn but not to accumulate.

Similar economic ideas are present elsewhere in Tourgée's writings. During the 1880s, Tourgée penned several novels concerned with economic reform. However, while those novels register clearly as political interventions, *Button's Inn*, with its emphasis on courtship and marriage, masquerades as a simple romance. Yet *Button's Inn*'s political message is inseparable from its treatment of domestic matters. We see this in the introduction of Mormons into an already crowded plot. Despite nineteenth-century perceptions of the Latter-Day Saints as an ungovernable, polygamist enemy within the nation's borders, this novel deploys the figure of Mormon plural marriage to suggest that socially generative capitalist relations can only exist if the nation approaches marriage less possessively. Read as a simultaneous critique of economic and domestic norms, *Button's Inn* intimates that social change—economic and otherwise—necessarily involves the domestic sphere. In so doing, the novel indicates the need to reassess the place of domestic relations in Tourgée's body of work. While Tourgée (with good reason) has been remembered largely as an antiracist advocate, *Button's Inn* suggests that the fullest picture of his advocacy should also address his engagement with gender and domesticity.

Tourgée's Antipossessive Ethic

Possession is central to the plot of *Button's Inn*. At the novel's outset, the inn's proprietors—Lonny Button, Lucy Button, and their daughter, Dotty—seem poised to lose their property. Business has languished for the past eighteen years, ever since a guest died at the inn under mysterious circumstances. Her name was Matilda Evans, and though she was wealthy, she apparently left little behind for her orphaned son, Ozro (who was subsequently raised at the inn). Locals speculated that Lonny, the innkeeper, stole the dead woman's fortune, keeping it from Ozro. Even Lonny's wife believes this, leading Lonny to drink too much and loudly resent Ozro, who he claims brought bad luck to the inn. Although Lonny blames the orphaned boy for the inn's decay, Ozro has in fact worked diligently to keep it afloat (in addition to secretly patenting his own inventions on the side). In spite of Ozro's efforts, however, the family will likely lose the inn unless Dotty Button marries a wealthy man. Although Ozro loves Dotty, she is also being courted by Dewstowe, a successful young peddler. Dewstowe can easily support the Buttons, while Ozro lacks an independent fortune—Dotty has feelings for Ozro but fears that marrying him would tie him to laboring at the inn for life. She proclaims: "I tell you, Ozro, you've had enough of hard times, and I ain't going to have anything to do with making your lot any worse. I'd jump down the bank there, before I'd marry you and be a drag on you, as I'd have to be."[3] This love triangle drives the novel, as Ozro and Dewstowe compete to win Dotty's hand.

The courtship plot highlights how marriage organizes and is organized by property relations; Dotty's romantic options are entwined with her financial ones. The novel does not present this as a problem, however. Rather than trying to separate love from monetary concerns, the text asserts that the two have a necessary and positive relationship. For instance, while Dotty's mother reviles her daughter's interest in the showy merchant, Dewstowe, accusing Dotty of "lov[ing] his money and his fine clothes and his horses, perhaps even his dog" (106–7), the novel never suggests that Dotty risks sacrificing love for money by entertaining Dewstowe's suit. Rather, Dewstowe is presented as genuinely likable. According to the narrator: "There was . . . a strong commercial flavor in his love . . . yet it was true and honest and would stand the test far better than the 'wild-cat' money of that day" (94). Dotty's "admiration for the rich trader" combines with "her desire to serve her parents" in such a way that she registers as neither a martyr nor a fortune hunter (95). Instead, she appreciates Dewstowe and rightly values his wealth. Her monetary sense becomes an expression of filial love and exemplifies how to understand wealth's practical value without becoming covetous or antisocial.

Dotty's other suitor, Ozro, embodies these same prosocial qualities. He consistently refuses to profit at others' expense—a trait the narrator contrasts to Gilded Age Americans' rapacity. We see this early on when Dewstowe offers his rival a ride to town. The narrator makes much of Ozro's reticence to accept the favor, presenting him as an emblem of the nation's vanishing virtue. According to the narrator: "American life, *until the worship of wealth took from it much of its distinctiveness*, was characterized by a hesitancy to accept favor at another's hands" (119; emphasis added). In this account, "the worship of wealth" has stripped present-day Americans of their unique character as greed threatens national identity. Although Ozro manfully hesitates to accept a ride from Dewstowe, the narrator implies that such virtue has vanished in the decades between Ozro's youth (the 1830s) and the novel's publication (1887).

The narrator continues to expand on this theme, lengthily describing the waning integrity of Americans. He casts earlier Americans' reticence to use others for their own benefit as "indicative . . . of an inherent hospitality, which offered without reluctance, gave without expecting thanks, and apologized only for causing discomfort or inconvenience to others" (119). Further, he notes "the modest shame-facedness of a people who thought the acceptance of a favor hardly consistent with that wonderful self-reliance which is the mainspring of American life" (120–21). In these examples, the narrator hammers home the point that Americans once were—and should remain—uncomfortable accepting even a freely offered favor if they alone stand to benefit from it.

The sheer length of this discussion of Ozro's hesitance to accept a ride from Dewstowe may seem peculiar, yet the themes the passage treats are hardly anomalous in Tourgée's work. Several of his novels from this period express concern over American attitudes toward profit and argue that greed is a social menace, not a fact of nature. Mark Elliott has shown that Tourgée joined other Progressive reformers who "refuted the popular notion that individuals were motivated solely by economic self-interest . . . and advocated a radical application of Christian ethics."[4] Novels such as *Eighty-Nine; or The Grand Master's Secret* (1888)[5] and *Murvale Eastman: Christian Socialist* (1890) advance a reformist vision, arguing that "rampant selfishness and greed by corporations were at the root of working-class poverty and social unrest" and, further, that corporations must reform themselves. Thus, the discussion of Americans' increasingly covetous character in *Button's Inn* contains an implicit critique of Gilded Age capitalism that links this novel to Tourgée's more overtly political fiction from the period. Seen in this light, *Button's Inn* participates in Tourgée's efforts "to imagine the possibility of a moral awakening on economic injustice akin to the one that swept over the North in the 1850s in opposition to the extension of slavery."[6]

Of course, Tourgée presents this "moral awakening" as arising from individual consciences, not governmental action. Elliott notes that Tourgée and his cohort "called on capitalists to reform their own business practices" rather than demanding external regulation.[7] For example, in the Preface to *Murvale Eastman*, Tourgée asserts that, given the stark divisions of the Gilded Age, "the social bases of the past are too narrow for the demands of the present. The domain of personal duty has been enlarged. The area of mutual obligation has been amazingly increased."[8] Here, Tourgée asks capitalists to recognize a "personal duty" and "mutual obligation" to end exploitation. He goes on to say that *Murvale Eastman* will not propose a programmatic plan but instead will "point out the spirit which must animate and precede any successful effort at ameliorat[ing inequities]."[9] Tourgée does something similar in *Button's Inn*; Ozro's steadfast refusals to benefit at others' expense serve to illustrate "the spirit" that might reform the greed-stricken nation. While Ozro wants financial success, this never outweighs his desire to maintain ethical relationships. He possesses an enterprising spirit yet refuses to quash others' opportunities.

We see this as Ozro repeatedly earns, then refuses, significant amounts of money when that money benefits no one but himself. The first instance occurs after Ozro wins a bet with his rival, Dewstowe. While showing off his bulldog, Turk, Dewstowe places his pocketbook on the ground next to the dog; he boldly declares that anyone can have the pocketbook's considerable contents if they can get it from Turk. Ozro manages the feat handily. However, when Dewstowe acknowledges defeat, saying, "Keep it . . . I vow you've earned it. I wouldn't take the risk you did for all the money that ever was in it," Ozro refuses, intimating that he took the risk not for the money but to impress Dotty (163). Here, Ozro demonstrates that he values relationships over wealth.

Similar values surface in the next scene. Following the excitement with Turk, a small group of men decide to explore the room in which Ozro's mother, Matilda, died—they wish to investigate rumors that her ghost haunts the chamber. However, their investigation yields surprising results. When Dewstowe, a German immigrant, and a mysterious Mormon convert named Abner Jackson all burst into the room, they find only Ozro at work on an ingenious machine. As Ozro explains, he has spent his evenings for the past year inventing two machines that will streamline the process for manufacturing pins.[10] As the others soon realize, Ozro's "natural mechanical turn" will make him a fortune (170); it will also help him win Dotty's hand by making him financially secure. Still, Ozro's individual achievement solidifies social ties rather than fostering competition. Despite being Ozro's romantic rival, Dewstowe compliments his machines and offers to go into business with him. Abner Jackson also wishes to invest. Instead of hoarding this opportunity, Ozro full-heartedly agrees, and the papers binding the three men's partnership are drawn up a few days later.

At the end of this scene, Ozro's economic and romantic fortunes seem secure. Dewstowe gamely admits that Dotty will likely favor Ozro's marriage suit not only because of Ozro's newfound financial stability but also thanks to his mastery of Turk. Fortune, however, proves fickle. Not long after the three men partner together, technological advances render one of Ozro's machines obsolete. This moment crucially demonstrates the novel's economic ethic. Ozro has asked Dotty to give him until Christmas to show that he can win her hand by becoming financially independent. While his talents make it likely that he can invent other machines and make other fortunes, he does not have time for that now—the clock is ticking on his romantic prospects, and he needs *this* venture to succeed. Still, in spite of this tremendous pressure, Ozro immediately releases his partners from what now seems to be a bad deal. Ozro avows: "I don't want any man to pay me for what I haven't got, or to put money in what is not likely to yield a good return" (189–90). He throws their contract on the fire, refusing to profit from others' losses.

Holy Ghosts and Plural Marriages

Button's Inn clearly valorizes Ozro's behavior. Yet Ozro is not the text's primary example of ideal attitudes toward property. That role belongs to Abner Jackson, the Mormon man who joins Ozro and Dewstowe's business partnership. If Ozro exemplifies virtuous economic behavior, then Abner takes that behavior to a utopian extreme. This becomes apparent as Ozro selflessly offers to release Abner and Dewstowe from their financial obligations to him. Even as Ozro throws their contract on the fire, Abner warns: "Burning a paper don't destroy a contract, young man." (191). Unwilling to let go of what appears to be a bad deal, Abner declares:

> "The Lord moved me by His holy sperrit to take part in the worldly enterprise in which you were about to engage, an' I did it. I don't know why—it may be for your good or my ondoin'—it don't matter to the servant of the Most High. I felt a call I didn't dare neglect, an' jest went forard where it led. . . . It wasn't because I looked for gain, though I don't deny I thought there was money in them; but the sperrit of the Lord spoke with my lips, an' the contract I made was signed with the seal of the Almighty. I *can't* renounce it nor go back on it, now." (191–92)

While Abner admits that he hoped to profit from the contract he signed, profit was not his primary motive. Rather, he signed the contract because he felt moved by God to do so. Thus, the contract and the relationship it cements must remain unbroken. Here we see that while Ozro believes business dealings should be *honorable*, the Mormon Abner regards such dealings as *holy*. From this perspective, contracts become much more than a tool by which individuals advance their own interests. In Abner's account, contracts assume spiritual significance by consecrating relationships. This suggests that, in *Button's Inn*, business is not a transaction between self-interested individuals; instead, it functions much as marriage does, uniting participants in eternal, sacred bonds.

This conflation of business and marriage appears at several key moments in *Button's Inn*. For instance, in the novel's dénouement, Abner reveals his past, describing his involvement in a relationship that mixes love and business. We learn that Abner—supposedly a stranger to the inn—is actually innkeeper Lonny Button's long-lost son. As a brash young man, Abner loved Ozro's mother, Matilda Evans, the woman who died at the inn. In a convoluted series of plot twists, Abner's infatuation inflames the jealousy of Matilda's estranged husband, Mr. Evans. The two men fight, and Abner seemingly kills Matilda's husband. Learning of the fight, Matilda falls down dead of shock and—just when things seem unable to get more baroque—Abner finds himself haunted by the murdered man's ghost as he flees into the night. Intriguingly, though, the guilt is not

Abner's alone. While Abner was "reckless, careless, [and] selfish" in not conceal-
ing his love for Matilda, Mr. Evans is also culpable as his own "jealous, fanatic
nature" led him to doubt his wife's virtue (320). In relation to Matilda, then, *both*
men exhibited precisely the possessive attitude that the novel seeks to reform.

Eventually, Abner's attitude *is* reformed, but in a most unusual way. Mr. Evans's
ghost haunts Abner for a full eighteen years. Over that time, he and the ghost
become (by his own report) "the best of friends" (329). Their relationship not
only transforms the feckless Abner into a regenerate man but also enriches him.
Abner concludes that the ghost "must have been a very good business man in
his day, for nothing pleases him so well even yet as to have me do a good thing
in that line" (329). By following the ghost's business advice, Abner returns to the
inn a wealthy man.

Abner and the ghost are linked not only by business, however, but also by
matters of the heart. In the following passage, Abner explains that he and the
ghost are bound together by their mutual love for Matilda and their shared need
to make amends for their possessive behavior toward her:

> Strange as it may seem . . . I think the fact that we were partners, as it were, in
> the wrong that was done your mother, lies at the bottom of our association. . . .
> This it is that links your father and me together,—the tie of endless expiation.
> Not alone here on earth, but during the endless ages of eternity shall we be
> united. Forever and forever we shall walk the plains of heaven together, doing
> the will of the Almighty. (330–32)

Although Abner dwells on the men's crimes—namely, their possessiveness—he
dwells at least as much on the union those sins produced. He speaks of being
"link[ed]" and "united" to Mr. Evans, repeatedly using the words "forever" and
"endless" to describe their connection. By emphasizing a spiritual union that per-
sists after death, the passage evokes precisely the kind of bond marriage is supposed to effect. In light of this, the "association" between Abner, the ghost, and
Matilda combines elements of both a business partnership and a marriage. And,
unorthodox though it is, the bond that links these three characters seems largely
positive. Through this relationship, Abner ends his "reckless, careless, [and] selfish" behavior and learns to earn without jealously possessing (320). In this way,
he embodies the text's most-lauded virtue: the ability to value wealth without
hoarding it. More surprising than this virtue, however, is the fact that it is cultivated by a plural union—a bond that unites not two but three parties.

On Latter-Day Virtues: Wedded Interests, Wedded Bliss

Perhaps Abner's exemplary nonpossessive attitude explains why his sister's relationships mirror his own. At the novel's end, Dotty follows her heart and marries Ozro. However, Abner's intervention means that this marriage unites the couple with Dewstowe as well. Abner gives a third of his fortune to set Ozro up in business with Dewstowe; Abner grants another third to his sister, Dotty, making her the financial equal of both her suitors. In this way, the couple's marriage morphs into a partnership of all three. And, lest we be tempted to see not one threesome but two separate partnerships—a business partnership between Ozro and Dewstowe and a marital partnership between Ozro and Dotty—the novel's final chapter places all three characters together in a setting that mingles the commercial with the domestic.

That chapter finds Dotty, Ozro, and Dewstowe together "in a sunny room overlooking one of the great hives of industry" (416). The room faces an industrial landscape: "Red fires leaped from . . . furnace doors" below, while "the clang of mighty engines jarred the solid walls" (416). Still, an air of domestic calm pervades the scene as "the two men lea[n] against the mantel," at ease in the homey space (416). All three characters have retained their youthful vigor despite the decades that have passed. Ozro is "strengthened yet refined"; Dewstowe has "grown full and sleek, but yet alert and resolute"; and Dotty is "sober and matronly, but not less fair" (416). In addition to aging gracefully, all three have clearly prospered.

Yet although they possess more, they seem less possessive of one another than ever before. We see this not only in the easy comfort they share but also in their commentary on their relationship. As Dewstowe discusses Ozro's original invention, affirming that it set them all on a prosperous path, he exclaims: "It is a wonderful machine! It has made 'Dewstowe & Evans' famous wherever a wheel turns on an iron rail, built up a city, made half-a-dozen fortunes, and—kept me a bachelor!" (416–17). While Dewstowe's bachelorhood may seem like a negative outcome, Dotty's reply mitigates this: "'Don't be too sure about the last,' said the lady, with an arch smile, as she came and leaned against her husband's arm and gave her hand to his friend" (417). While this moment hardly affirms that the three share a consummated marriage, it clearly indicates that, in Dotty's eyes, Dewstowe is not quite a bachelor. While some might read her "arch" remark as an indication that he may still marry, the specifics of the exchange suggest otherwise. Dewstowe declares that the machine "has kept" him a bachelor—in other words, he has never married. When Dotty disagrees, she disputes the claim that he never married, not that he will *remain* single. More tellingly, the gesture that follows her statement—leaning against Ozro while offering Dewstowe her hand—indicates that it is the union between the three of them, not with some prospective wife, that negates Dewstowe's bachelorhood.

This ending showcases the novel's attempts not only to rethink economic attitudes but also to highlight the role domestic relations play in shaping those attitudes. By picturing Dotty, Ozro, and Dewstowe's virtuous participation in industrial capitalism, the novel treats marriage as a route to more moral capitalist relations. Yet rather than casting marriage as a softening influence on commercial activity, this ending suggests that marital relations must themselves be transformed if capitalism is to improve. Dotty, Ozro, and Dewstowe's virtue lies in their nonpossessive relationship; the rivalry for Dotty's hand is resolved successfully because all three lovers have one another in the end. Indeed, as they discuss "the universal miracle" of progress that unfolds outside their window, the greater part of that miracle seems to lie not in the fires of industry but rather in the nonpossessive attitude that allows Dotty to claim that Dewstowe is not, in fact, a bachelor (417). Thus, if marriage offers resolution in this text, it does so by undermining possessive couplehood and favoring more plural formations.

Such a resolution is surprising coming from Tourgée. An unabashed iconoclast on race relations, Tourgée is not known to have been outspoken regarding gender roles, sexual relations, or domestic matters more broadly. Still, although Tourgée's attitudes toward gender remain largely unexplored, elements of his biography suggest an openness to gender parity. For instance, Tourgée's wife, Emma, insisted that she wanted a life beyond motherhood, and Tourgée agreed. Similarly, Elliott notes that Tourgée encouraged his daughter—and only biological child—to pursue a public career, observing that "Albion often showed a keen interest in women's professional advancement."[11] And, while not focusing explicitly on Tourgée's understanding of gender, Carolyn Karcher discusses his collaboration with Ida B. Wells.[12] Yet despite these snippets of personal history, many questions remain regarding Tourgée's stances on gender, marriage, and sexuality. *Button's Inn* may not provide full answers, but by persistently figuring plural unions, this work intimates that revising economic attitudes requires revising domestic arrangements to make them less possessive. In turn, this emphasis on reforming domestic relations sheds light on an even more perplexing feature of the text: its focus on Mormonism.

For any number of reasons, it is strange that Mormons feature so prominently—and so positively—in this text. Tourgée was not Mormon, and in the

period when *Button's Inn* was written, Mormons were a reviled group under intense pressure from the federal government. The historian Paul Reeve notes that
"during the forty-seventh Congress [which ran from March 1881 to March 1883],
lawmakers introduced no fewer than twenty-three bills or constitutional amendments aimed at solving the Mormon problem." Of these, the Edmunds Act of
1882 is notable. It outlawed "unlawful habitation" in order to prosecute Mormons
in plural marriages. This was followed by the 1887 Edmunds-Tucker Act, which
stripped Utah women of voting rights (gained in 1870 in that territory), seized
church assets, prohibited illegitimate children from inheriting, and more.[13] These
bills not only demonstrate that Mormons were perceived as a threat to the nation
(one serious enough to merit federal attention) but also show that the "Mormon
menace" lay at the intersection of economic, political, and domestic relations.
The fact that the Edmunds-Tucker Act attacks Mormon political and economic
power in order to dismantle plural marriage illustrates a recognition that marital
norms undergird economic and political relations; thus, the disruptive force of
plural marriage extends well beyond the domestic realm. In light of this, plural
marriage proved decisive to Mormons' place in the nation. Their willful disruption of Anglo-American marital norms fueled the belief that they were "a population fallen away from the civilizing destiny of whiteness" and therefore existed
as "*expendable life.*"[14] By the 1880s, violence and vigilantism had driven the Mormons into the western territories. Mormon territory would not be admitted to
the Union until polygamy was repudiated, and even then, a linked sexual and
racial taint clung to them, limiting their inclusion in the nation.

In spite of their tainted status, however, *Button's Inn* presents a positive view of
Mormons. Although the novel paints Mormon leaders as avaricious, most Mormon converts are treated sympathetically.[15] Indeed, as we have seen, the Mormon
convert Abner Jackson stands as the text's moral center. His attitude toward property is exemplary, as is his chaste and ghostly plural marriage. Additionally, he
generates wealth by replacing competition with cooperation *and* inculcates this
ability in the next generation by turning Ozro and Dewstowe from rivals into successful partners. Tellingly, Abner is not cast as an exception to the rule of disrepu-
table converts. Instead, Tourgée positions the mass of Mormons as virtuous—and
perhaps exemplary—citizens. In the Preface, for example, Tourgée approvingly
asserts that "the whole movement was purely American in character" and speaks
of his own "acquaintance [with] some very intelligent believers" (vii).

Why might Tourgée offer such a rosy view of a reviled religious minority in
a novel primarily aimed at critiquing Gilded Age greed? The answer may lie,
in part, with early Mormons' experiments with communalism. In the 1830s, the

Mormon prophet Joseph Smith sought to establish "a radical new economic order." Citing divine revelation, Smith declared "the law of consecration," a system
under which converts would deed their property to the church and "receive back
'stewardships' proportionate to the needs of their families, thus equalizing property." Growing up near Kirtland, Ohio, where Smith announced this revelation,
Tourgée may have been aware of these attempts at communalism. Still, these attempts were short-lived. Being asked to deed all their possessions to the church
rankled converts. By 1840, Smith decreed "that 'the Law of consecration could
not be kept here, & that it was the will of the Lord that we should desist from
trying to keep it.'"[16]

In spite of this failure, Smith would later embrace plural marriage, a practice that also disturbed Anglo-American property practices. Indeed, Coviello
observes that polygamy "assemble[s] social forms" that differ dramatically from
the "arrangements of genders, sex, and property" seen in traditional Anglo-
American society.[17] In this formulation, "gender" and "sex" are inextricable from
"property." If property ownership in mainstream Anglo-American culture is
structured by dyadic marriages that pass wealth from one generation to the next
by producing legitimate heirs, then polygamous Mormons represent an alternative economic order. Insofar as their marital arrangements destabilize Anglo-
American modes of property ownership and inheritance, polygamous Mormons
offer Tourgée a useful figure for showing how economic and domestic norms are
reciprocally structured. We see this as Abner Jackson, a Mormon convert who is
bound to a ghost and a dead woman, helps bind his sister to a profitable business
venture *and* her two suitors. These plural unions—which, crucially, are financial
and romantic—emblematize the nonpossessive spirit Tourgée champions.

That said, *Button's Inn* modifies Mormon plural marriage in several important
ways. First, the novel never suggests that the plural unions it depicts are consummated. Second, and more importantly, both Abner and Dotty's relationships are
not properly polygamous—they involve multiple husbands rather than multiple
wives. The politics of these polyandrous unions are ambiguous. On the one hand,
this arrangement positions women—both Matilda and Dotty—as property to be
shared by men. In both relationships, men are rivals who must learn to share.
Thus, men are subjects who learn and grow, while women remain objects: the
human analogue of wealth. On the other hand, however, both Dotty and Matilda
are fleshed-out characters with their own motivations. Moreover, the polyandrous nature of their respective unions erases the trope in which a polygamous
wife is chattel, her access to patriarchal power diminished by sharing a man. In

the novel, neither Matilda's nor Dotty's power flows from her husband; Matilda seems to be independently wealthy, as is Dotty by the novel's end. As a result, the relationships that resemble plural marriage in this novel disrupt the flow of patriarchal power and wealth in ways that Mormon plural marriage was not assumed to do. While *Button's Inn* adapts the institution of Mormon plural marriage, invoking it as a fungible figure rather than portraying polygamous unions as practiced by nineteenth-century Mormons, the novel's plural unions serve a clear purpose in its quest to reform economic attitudes. Instead of simply urging people to be less greedy, *Button's Inn* uses Abner and Dotty's plural relationships to suggest that economic reform begins at home, with altered domestic structures—structures that do not rest on one person claiming exclusive possession of another.

Written in a moment of accelerating capitalism, *Button's Inn* deploys the figure of Mormon plural marriage to explore how to diminish possession's structuring role in US society. In so doing, the novel suggests that domestic institutions are inseparable from economic ones and, further, that both are implicated in any movement toward greater social equity. Seen in this light, *Button's Inn* also suggests the need to examine how sexual politics inform Tourgée's major novels—works that have often been viewed through the lens of racial politics alone.

Notes

1. In fact, Tourgée may well have met Edison through his involvement with the nearby Chautauqua Institution. Edison, in 1886, married Mina Miller, daughter of the Institute's cofounder, Lewis Miller, and began spending time there. Randall E. Stross, *The Wizard of Menlo Park: How Thomas Alva Edison Invented the Modern World* (New York: Penguin, 2007), 148.

2. Mark Elliott, *Color-Blind Justice: Albion Tourgée and the Quest for Racial Equality from the Civil War to* Plessy v. Ferguson (New York: Oxford University Press, 2006), 11.

3. Albion W. Tourgée, *Button's Inn* (Boston: Roberts Brothers, 1887), 81. Subsequent quotations will be cited parenthetically.

4. Elliott, *Color-Blind Justice*, 222.

5. Like *Button's Inn*, *Eighty-Nine* contains a Mormon interlude, but the latter novel casts Mormonism far more equivocally than *Button's Inn* does. While in *Button's Inn* Mormons function as a potentially exemplary minority group, in *Eighty-Nine*, Mormons ally with Mexican forces against a US invasion. Yet while the novel's narrator (in keeping with mainstream nineteenth-century perceptions) characterizes Mormons as a barbarous threat to the nation, *Eighty-Nine*'s narrator is hardly Tourgée's surrogate. Moreover, the novel's Mormons—perhaps heroically—oppose tyrannical attempts at American empire-building.

6. Elliott, *Color-Blind Justice*, 223.

7. Elliott, *Color-Blind Justice*, 223.

8. Albion W. Tourgée, *Murvale Eastman: Christian Socialist*, excerpted in *Undaunted Radical: The Selected Writings and Speeches of Albion W. Tourgée*, ed. Mark Elliott and John David Smith (Baton Rouge: Louisiana State University Press, 2010), 142.

9. Tourgée, *Murvale Eastman*, 142.

10. One may well wonder if this particular invention hearkens back to Adam Smith's famous description of a pin factory in *The Wealth of Nations*. With this invention, Ozro eliminates the need for the division of labor that Smith uses the pin factory to illustrate and can be read as a subtle jab at Smith, whose work popularized laissez-faire capitalism.

11. Elliott, *Color-Blind Justice*, 68–69, 209.

12. Carolyn L. Karcher, *A Refugee from His Race: Albion W. Tourgée and His Fight against White Supremacy* (Durham, NC: University of North Carolina Press, 2016), 212–14.

13. Paul Reeve, *Religion of a Different Color: Race and the Mormon Struggle for Whiteness* (New York: Oxford University Press, 2015), 166–68.

14. Peter Coviello, "Mormon Polygamy and the Biopolitics of Secularism," *History of the Present* 7, no. 2 (2017): 220, 221.

15. Near the novel's end, an unscrupulous Mormon leader tries to have Abner hanged in order to inherit his fortune. While this moment conflicts with the novel's generally positive portrayals of Mormons, it offers Abner an opportunity to give a rousing defense of his faith in spite of this perfidy. Additionally, this negative presentation of Mormon leadership gives Tourgée cover—by casting aspersions on Mormon leaders, he can valorize Mormonism without seeming to embrace outright polygamy (which, importantly, was only publicly avowed *after* the period in which *Button's Inn* is set, even if Tourgée's readers would have associated it with the religion).

16. Richard Lyman Bushman, *Joseph Smith: Rough Stone Rolling* (New York: Knopf, 2006), 154.

17. Coviello, "Mormon Polygamy," 235.

11   Tourgée's New Realism

*Disciplinary Reparation and the
Quest for Racial Justice*

Almas Khan

So he [Comfort Servosse] talked, forgetful of the fact that the social conditions of three hundred years are not to be overthrown in a moment, and
that differences which have outlasted generations, and finally ripened into
war, are never healed by simple victory,—that the broken link can not be
securely joined by mere juxtaposition of the fragments, but must be fused
and hammered before its fibers will really unite.

—ALBION TOURGÉE, *A Fool's Errand* (1879)

During a lifetime spanning from the growth of the abolitionist movement
to the rise of the Jim Crow regime, Albion Tourgée was a professional
polymath: Union veteran, judge, civil rights lawyer, diplomat, and literary author. Underlying his work in these domains was a preoccupation with
history conceived as "the story of the world's outward happenings" and a chronicle of "the world's thought." In *A Fool's Errand* (1879), his best-known novel,
Tourgée implied that legal and political reforms during Reconstruction merely
juxtaposed broken links of the nation when unaccompanied by an intellectual
welding process. For him, the white supremacist ideology ingrained in slavery as
an institution dating to the colonial period may have been "even more dangerous
and inimical to the nation than the institution itself,"[1] and meaningful national
reunification required eliminating caste-based thinking more broadly. Tourgée's
literary writing, coupled with his advocacy for egalitarian public education and
curricular reform, represented a sweeping intellectual effort to forge the new nation into being.

Tourgée's fiction sought to "examine with . . . care the foundations on which
the new superstructure must be reared" in order to actualize the Reconstruction
Amendments' formal promise of a "*new citizenship*." Ratified between 1865 and
1870, the Thirteenth, Fourteenth, and Fifteenth Amendments provided the first

significant expansion of citizenship since the founding. With notable limitations, they respectively abolished slavery, established equal citizenship, and extended the franchise to men of color. These legal gains soon proved illusory, though, as white supremacist terrorism, racist legislation, and judicial decisions constricting the federal government's enforcement powers enabled "the old ideas" to "reassert[] their power."[2] Tourgée believed that the democratic system's vitality rested on cultivating the citizenry's critical thinking skills. His literary work expressed this noblesse oblige for intellectuals through marrying seemingly insular disciplinary and professional critiques with progressive racial and socioeconomic politics. Tourgée saw literary authors, lawyers, and doctors as the vanguard of a massive public reeducation initiative during the late nineteenth century, which was a time of disciplinary and professional revolutions.

The postbellum period witnessed the development of US academic disciplines in their current forms, with the founding of the Modern Language Association and the American Historical Association taking place near the apex of Tourgée's literary career in the 1880s. Major dissenting intellectual movements in American law and letters—legal realism and literary realism—also evolved in the Civil War's wake. Inspired by William James's theory of pragmatism, proponents of the movements defined themselves in opposition to legal formalism and literary romanticism, respectively. The movements, led by social acquaintances William Dean Howells and future Supreme Court justice Oliver Wendell Holmes Jr., distrusted received wisdom, particularly in an era of dramatic legal and social changes. Both movements emphasized experiential methodologies, and many realists relied on insights from the rising discipline of sociology to advance racial and economic justice. Legal realists propelled the New Deal and the civil rights revolution, both of which accorded with Tourgée's social justice commitments.

Tourgée's literary oeuvre and legal writings manifest his belief in disciplinary reparation as a precondition for political and social reconstruction. Moreover, much of Tourgée's fiction can be situated within the cross-racial genre of professional novels about Reconstruction's aftermath. Such texts, including Charles Chesnutt's *The Marrow of Tradition* (1901) and Sutton Griggs's *Pointing the Way* (1908), analyzed racism through the lens of characters' professional struggles for equal rights. Tourgée's writings sympathize with the liberal reformist agendas of literary realism and legal realism, although he is typically not affiliated with either movement.[3] Tourgée nonetheless critiqued realists' lack of idealism, instead proposing a "new realist" aesthetics and jurisprudence that would match his expansive vision for equal citizenship. In literature, Tourgée meshed realism with the earlier tradition of romanticism that many African American authors at the time also drew upon. In jurisprudence, he combined positivist (i.e., socially constructed) conceptions of law with natural- and divine-law theories that could be more conducive to racial equality. Tourgée used a law-and-literature methodology to illuminate his intellectual interventions, anticipating a field that in contemporary times often follows Tourgée in challenging conventional legal epistemologies and vivifying the experiences of oppressed groups.

Tourgée's final novel evaluating the legacy of Reconstruction exemplifies his new realism through a narrative about professionalism and reparations during the nadir of race relations. As a state-of-the-nation text, *Pactolus Prime* (1890) attests to literature and law's reparative disciplinary capacities through addressing a question of ongoing significance for citizens: "In all collective as well as individual matters, the first inquiry of the Nineteenth Century American, in whatever juncture of private or public affairs, would naturally be, 'What do justice and equity toward my fellow-men require that I should do?'"[4] For a doctor in the novel, only a man unworthy "of a place in the great republic of science" would climb "the ladder of success and remain[] indifferent to those upon the rungs below him" (331). Tourgée endorsed this principle from the healing profession of medicine as modeling best practices for lawyers, literary authors, and other professionals seeking to reconstruct the republic, and his literary writings demonstrate the importance of disciplinary reformation for national inclusion.

Creating Law and Literature:
Tourgée's Interdisciplinarity and Racial Justice Activism

Tourgée's literary compositional process suggests a fluidity between his legal work and literary work, beginning from his time as a North Carolina judge who upheld African American rights during Reconstruction. Discussing the origin of his novella *John Eax* (1882), which depicts the renegade son of a white slave-owning family, Tourgée reflected on how a local anecdote "echo[ed] in my ears amid the routine business of a country court" and eventually became part of his "docket." With mischievousness about disciplinary propriety, he continued: "It was a queer 'record' to be 'made up' there, and I could but laugh at the odd admixture of fact and fiction in the consecrated domain of law." Tourgée's literary writings during his most productive literary period (circa 1874–1898) were symbiotic with his legal writings, notably his brief in *Plessy v. Ferguson* (1896).[5] The Supreme Court's upholding of separate-but-equal laws there entrenched the Jim Crow regime, and a disillusioned Tourgée soon ceased literary publication, becoming the US consul to France until his death in 1905.

Tourgée's writings evidence early attempts to theorize the relationship between law and literature, an interdisciplinary field that was founded by progressive jurists. Future Supreme Court justice Benjamin Cardozo's essay "Law and Literature" (1925) cited legal and literary realists, including Holmes and Henry James, in arguing for a greater infusion of literary style into legal discourse, which he believed could transform the law itself. He praised Justice Benjamin Curtis's dissent in *Dred Scott v. Sandford* (1857), the notorious Supreme Court decision that barred African Americans from citizenship. Cardozo saw judicial artists like Curtis as visionaries when dissenting from unjust majority decisions, writing in a passage that resonates with Tourgée's career: "The voice of the majority may be that of force triumphant, content with the plaudits of the hour, and recking little of the morrow. The dissenter speaks to the future, and his voice is pitched to a key that will carry through the years." Even before Cardozo, however, Tourgée's hero in law and letters, Sir Walter Scott, had commended literature's value for law in his novel *Guy Mannering* (1815). An attorney there characterizes literary volumes as his "tools of trade," asserting that a "lawyer without history or literature is a mechanic, a mere working mason; if he possesses some knowledge of these, he may venture to call himself an architect."[6]

Tourgée's prefaces portray his interdisciplinary aesthetic as a form of communal bridge building between the North and the South, African Americans and whites, and lawyers and the public. In the preface to *John Eax and Mamelon; or, The South without the Shadow*, the former of which is narrated by a lawyer, Tourgée claimed to contrast the North and South, "but to show the fusing potency of love or the solvent power of manly friendship." Love, for Tourgée, could also unify "the Master and the Slave," who were otherwise "separated by the whole diameter of the social sphere." The preface to his short-story collection *With Gauge & Swallow, Attorneys* (1889) meanwhile expresses Tourgée's hope to entice "both the professional and non-professional reader," uncovering the inner workings of legal practice for a diverse audience.[7] Tourgée embodied many of the binaries his fiction negotiated, dwelling intellectually in law and letters and geographically in the North and South.

Tourgée's literary writings could be seen to humanize abstract laws, which many law and literature scholars identify as the field's main virtue, but Tourgée also theorized similarities between the disciplines. For example, he speculated that law was a more creative discipline and literature a more constrained one than may appear at first blush. In his novel *A Royal Gentleman* (1881), a lawyer describes common-law reasoning in creative terms, finding "something in the intricate subtlety and ever-varying analogies and differences, agreements and conflicts, of the common law, which gave it an unfailing charm to his mind." Traditional creative arts are in turn not realms of pure freedom. Of patriotic songs, a character in Tourgée's essay collection *The Veteran and His Pipe* (1885) ruminates: "I used to accept the ancient apothegm about the maker of a people's songs being able to bid defiance to the maker of its laws, at par; giving no heed to the farther fact that the song-maker himself is bound by inflexible conditions, which imperatively curtail his influence and domain."[8] Rather than positing a hostile relationship between law and literature, such as in assuming literary discourse is more authentic and humanistic than legal discourse, Tourgée aimed to integrate the disciplines at the substantive and formal levels to promote racial justice, as illustrated in *Pactolus Prime*.

Thematically, the novel foreshadows Dr. Martin Luther King Jr.'s "I Have a Dream" speech (1963), where Dr. King affirmed that in drafting the Declaration of Independence and Constitution, "the architects of our republic were signing a promissory note to which every American was to fall heir." As the nation had unfortunately "defaulted on this promissory note" for citizens of color, March on Washington protestors endeavored to cash a check "that will give us upon demand the riches of freedom and the security of justice."[9] Like Dr. King's address, *Pactolus Prime* is set symbolically in the nation's capital and centralizes the issue of reparations for slavery. The novel takes place largely on a Christmas Day in the late 1880s, with Christ's birth being a metaphor for the national rebirth Tourgée predicted during Reconstruction. A generation after the war, however, *Pactolus Prime* depicts national complacency on racial justice: "The denizens of the city slept; some pillowed on pleasant memories, some happily oblivious of evil deeds, and all expectantly dreaming of tomorrow's joys" (2). An image of the People's House in "dark outline[]" begins the text (1), eerily anticipating the January 6, 2021, Capitol coup attempt. The insurrection, in which white supremacists flaunted symbols including Confederate flags, could be viewed as the grim converse of the March on Washington.

Pactolus Prime is divided into three sections, commencing at the ironically named Best House hotel, where the mixed-race and disabled title character works as a bootblack in the basement. There, Pactolus; his biracial assistant, Ben; and their white customers debate about reparations (chapters 1-11). From this predominantly legal register, the novel shifts to a more literary register in portraying the sentimental relationship between Pactolus and his daughter Eva, who suspects her Black ancestry but has been passing as white (chapters 12-21). Following Pactolus's death, the final mystery section untangles an interracial inheritance plot that sparks a dialogue between a white lawyer and doctor about their professional obligations in the Jim Crow era (chapters 22-28). The novel offers no panacea to cure the soul of a diseased body politic, cutting off a conversation between the lawyer and doctor as they are starting to discuss remedies (264). Yet in a later colloquy where the doctor is asked to give "permanent form" (343) to his theory of racism's causes, Tourgée metatextually references his novel's objective to inform policy making based on a more accurate diagnosis of racism's roots.

Analyzing how racism is embedded in the American legal system, *Pactolus Prime* alludes to fields including constitutional law, contracts, trusts and estates, and family law; more affirmatively, it casts Ben as a nascent civil rights attorney. Ben's entry into a white-dominated profession promises to be substantively and symbolically significant. He is at first demoralized while reading a law book, "noting regretfully one chapter after another" (132) during a period when textbooks often presented cases about slavery descriptively and at times failed to acknowledge emancipation. The necessity of self-help in surmounting racist pedagogy and laws explains why Tourgée saw Black lawyers as a lodestar for the race. He observed that "never one of them opens his lips in court that his example does not inspire some colored boy that listens to do as he has done."[10] Impressed by Ben's intelligence, Pactolus remarks that he would cast a presidential ballot for his assistant if Ben happened to be white (168), unable then to imagine a future in which an African American could inhabit a White House built by enslaved people.

In addition to foregrounding legal subjects and characters, *Pactolus Prime* formally entwines law with literature through chapter titles, Socratic dialogues, and analogical reasoning. The reparations section of the novel is framed as a hypothetical case African Americans could bring against the nation, and over half the chapter titles contain legal references, including "An Assessment of Damages," "Some Expert Testimony," and "Counterclaim and Set-Off." Within chapters, dialogue is frequently in Socratic form, reflecting what would become the signature pedagogical method in US law schools. Instead of lecturing, law faculty in the late nineteenth century were increasingly asking probative questions about cases and uncovering erroneous assumptions in students' reasoning process. Thus, for example, when a minister in the "An Assessment of Damages" chapter chastises African Americans for being "too impatient" in their demands for equal rights (70), Pactolus responds with a series of questions about how the minister had felt when being defrauded. Pactolus then extends the scale of inquiry from the individual to communal level, anticipating Dr. King in asking the minister: "If the amount thus unjustly withheld from you had embraced every cent you had earned in your whole life—the entire earnings of your parents and their parents for two centuries and a half, depriving them of every luxury, every opportunity, every privilege, every right . . . would you think you ought to be called 'impatient,' if you began, after waiting uncomplainingly so many years, to speak a little roughly of your debtor?" (71).

Reasoning by analogy is a hallmark of common-law analysis in the United States, and the novel compares the function of Tourgée's literary jurisprudence to that of equity. Equity was historically a body of law intended to rectify the common-law system's shortcomings by providing justice in individual cases. Equitable remedies extend creatively beyond traditional monetary damages to include injunctions and a defendant's specific performance of an action.

In advocating for reparations, Ben argues that "our case" is not in law, namely, in a racist common-law system, but in equity (86). At a time when a Supreme Court majority had held that African Americans must "cease[] to be the special favorite of the laws"[11] despite centuries of enslavement, *Pactolus Prime* testified to literature's sociolegal reparative powers.

Reconstructing Law:
The Birth of Legal Realism and Tourgée's Literary-Legal Imaginary

Given the judiciary's precipitation of the Civil War through decisions like *Dred Scott*, reformist postbellum lawyers scrutinized their discipline and laid the groundwork for the legal realist movement, which was the most influential jurisprudential movement in twentieth-century America. Most expansively, the movement existed from 1870 to 1960, with the last decades of the nineteenth century constituting a protorealist period, after which early legal realism flourished through World War I. The interwar years were legal realism's high period, but "new legal realism" today evidences the movement's enduring intellectual impact.[12]

Three years after Tourgée's death, the popular legal magazine *The Green Bag* published a legal realist essay he wrote titled "The Unwritten Law and Why It Remains Unwritten." The piece critiques the US common-law system and was likely drafted between 1881 and 1896, thereby coinciding with the publication of two cardinal legal realist texts by Oliver Wendell Holmes Jr., *The Common Law* (1881) and "The Path of the Law" (1897). In *The Common Law*, Holmes expressed legal realists' future cri de coeur: "The life of the law has not been logic: it has been experience."[13] Legal realists sought to dethrone the primacy of the text in understanding how law operates and to unmask the discipline's subjectivity, revealing how nonlegal factors like individual biases and group customs could affect legal decision-making.

Although legal realism is often credited with importing the social sciences into law, many eminent figures in the movement relied on literature in developing their legal theories. In a 1910 article on "Law in Books and Law in Action," for instance, the early legal realist (and later movement critic) Roscoe Pound began by recounting a scene from Mark Twain's *The Adventures of Huckleberry Finn* (1885) to concretize the realist/formalist debate in law. In the scene, Tom Sawyer and Huckleberry Finn argue about whether to use a case knife (as books Tom read would recommend) or a pickaxe (as Huck thinks is a more practical instrument) to rescue Jim, an enslaved man. While Huck comments about Tom's being "*Full of principle*" in avowing to use the case knife, Tom ultimately chooses the pickaxe. Holmes had also read Twain and was invited to be honorary vice president of the Mark Twain Society.[14]

Tourgée was an important jurisprudential contemporary of Holmes and a precursor of Pound, who called for a "sociological jurisprudence" to replenish legal theory and promote economic justice soon after the century's turn. With its title of "The Unwritten Law and Why It Remains Unwritten," Tourgée's essay emphasizes the "unwritten law" at the heart of the US judicial system. The essay evokes Holmes's claim in "Path" that "the logical method and form flatter that longing for certainty and repose which is in every human mind. But certainty generally is illusion, and repose is not the destiny of man. Behind the logical form lies a judgment as to the relative worth and importance of competing legislative grounds, often an inarticulate and unconscious judgment, it is true, and yet the very root and nerve of the whole proceeding." Suggesting the partiality of judicial opinions, Tourgée contended they "are properly termed 'opinions'—the opinions of experts. They hold good in the cases determined and are what we term authority in certain others, but their foundations are always open to assault." Tourgée and Holmes implied that the judicial branch was no loftier than the political branches, being equally steeped in the "common life" of a citizenry varying in rectitude. The common-law system was accordingly a mixed inheritance for Americans, being a "most efficient agent of oppression" but also a "guarantor of liberty."[15]

In narrating the lives of marginalized populations at the nexus of the Jim Crow era and Gilded Age, Tourgée's literary writings delineated jurisprudential theories that would later be seen as core to legal realism. For example, *Pactolus Prime* is methodologically legal realist in presenting several disciplinary perspectives (e.g., economics and medicine) on reparations, in addition to emphasizing Pactolus's experiential knowledge of the issue (111). Furthermore, legal realists distinguished between normative and descriptive analyses of law, which *Pactolus Prime*'s narrator does as well in asserting that "angelic opinions," as of law, "are at a discount in this age. Even what our neighbor thinks is of far less consequence to us than what he does" (4). Substantively, legal realists sought to expose the inefficacy of legal forms, paralleling Pactolus's response to a white major who claims African Americans owe whites for citizenship: "You gave us a *legal* right to exercise the power of the citizen—so you said at least—and then permitted its exercise to be made a matter of mortal peril to the colored man who seeks to benefit himself or his people, thereby" (98). Relatedly, the arbitrariness of legal categories was a leitmotif of realist jurisprudence, and inconsistent racial classification standards across states epitomized this insight. During the Civil War, a colonel encourages Pactolus, who has fled slavery, to become white, refusing to "condemn you to death for an act which all civilized codes justify" (309). The colonel's magnanimity points to a silver lining in realist thought if citizens subvert unjust laws or campaign for more equitable legislation. Such actions could demonstrate how "Liberty is a growth—an evolution—not an instantaneous fact," as Pactolus avers (312).

At the end of the reparations section, Pactolus responds to Ben's question about the prospects for racial equality by expressing realist skepticism about the public in the religious context: "Christianity . . . is a religion that runs with popular thought and adapts itself to popular prejudices" (135). Where Tourgée may have diverged most from mainstream legal realists was his residual faith in natural law and divine justice. *Pactolus Prime* describes the United States as a "Christian nation" (2), and in casting Pactolus as a Christ figure whose death may save the body politic, the novel endorses the idea of a higher law transcending human-made laws. God is depicted as a judge who "has a strange way of keeping his accounts—the debit and credit of right and wrong between races and peoples—and settling them according to His own notions. He holds the scales between them as courts do between man and man, only a great deal steadier" (91). With even supreme secular laws like the Constitution doing little to mitigate African Americans' plight in the late nineteenth century, Tourgée's brand of legal realism may have sought to tap into the religious fervor that had motivated abolitionists. *Pactolus Prime* thus captures a transitional phase in American jurisprudence, reflecting Tourgée's belief in law and literature as forces by which God seeks to uplift humanity, "if we will but use them aright."[16]

Reconstructing Literature:
The Realism Wars and Tourgée's New Realist Aesthetics

Like legal realism, American literary realism arose from the embers of the Civil War, with the lawyer Clarence Darrow proclaiming the aims of many activist realist writers to bring about the "coming dawn when true equality shall reign upon the earth; the time when democracy shall be no more confined to constitutions and to laws, but will be a part of human life." William Dean Howells defined literary realism as "nothing more and nothing less than the truthful treatment of material," and he urged authors to "let fiction cease to lie about life; let it portray men and women as they are." Realism was seen to reject qualities associated with pre–Civil War American literature, including fantastical plots, abstractions, and stylized language. Vernon Parrington would later link romantic literature with a nondemocratic political system, harnessing debates about literary genres to political debates. The literary "realism wars" of the nineteenth century, in which Tourgée figured prominently, could therefore be construed to have political repercussions. In the racial justice context, many African American authors who wrote fiction about Reconstruction and its aftermath blended romantic and realistic conventions, as did Tourgée. While Howells lauded "that republic of letters where all men are free and equal," suggesting that an egalitarian literary community could foster political inclusion, the African American lawyer-author Charles Chesnutt (Tourgée's correspondent) was among those questioning Howells's arguably racialized view of disciplinary excellence.[17]

Much as legal realism's deconstructionist theories of law caused it to be deemed the "jurisprudence of despair," Tourgée's attack on "high" literary realism stemmed from his belief that it was a genre of despair. The most ubiquitous criticism of legal realism was that after it had razed such ideals about law as certainty, uniformity, and objectivity, it proposed no superior normative legal vision. Tourgée critiqued literary realism on similar grounds, first defining realism as "a philosophy in life," "a method in art," and "a trick of trade." Philosophically, he saw realism as a forerunner of twentieth-century existentialism, representing "the aimless *ennui* of a purposeless existence." According to Tourgée, realists believed that the "average life" was permeated by "suffering and cowardice," "duplicity and despair," and "self-distrust," as opposed to hope in humanity. Literary realists' method reinforced their philosophical orientation, Tourgée said, as they described commonplace occurrences through an accumulation of detail. Amid the postbellum commercial boom, including in literary publishing, Tourgée also speculated that the "realist" label was a gimmick to garner readership.[18]

Tourgée's appeal to the romantic tradition in American letters, exemplified by James Fenimore Cooper and Nathaniel Hawthorne, could be criticized as a marketing device as well, though, and his characterization of the literary realism branch led by Howells may be hyperbolic. Harold Kolb Jr. notes literary realism's congruities with its predecessor: "The realists could not accept romantic transcendentalism and its narrative corollaries, but they did acknowledge their debt to the romantic emphasis on personal experience, the individual, particularized description, democracy, and morality."[19] Moreover, in placing scare quotes around "realist" and "realism," Tourgée signified literary realism's contested nature as modernism was emerging. In 1894, he declared his new realist aesthetics: "I am a realist, in a much broader sense than those who claim the name, and *my* realism compels me to represent men talking as they really do—."[20]

Pactolus Prime and many of Tourgée's other fictional writings combined realist, romantic, and naturalist conventions. Tourgée used realist techniques, including characters based on actual figures, detailed descriptions, and vernacular speech. In *Pactolus Prime*, the protagonist resembles Tourgée, being an injured Union veteran devoted to his profession and racial justice. A chapter titled "The Professor of the Black Art" discusses Pactolus's work in depth, with the next chapter, "Master and Disciple," presenting Pactolus's speech in dialect as he converses with Ben (20-50). Plotwise, however, the novel is romantic, with allusions to angels observing events, coincidental meetings between characters, and a complex inheritance storyline that dominates the narrative after the reparations sequence. Given its melding of realist and romantic conventions within an "allegorical framework that permit[s] the expression of abstract ideas about the human condition,"[21] *Pactolus Prime* is a quintessential naturalist novel whose determinism challenges American Dream ideology. With Pactolus dying prematurely and his daughter renouncing a romantic relationship with a white man to become Sister Pactola, the novel has a conventionally tragic ending. Pactolus is even honored by whites for reverse reparations in bequeathing his estate to Eva, who is thought to be his former master's daughter. *Pactolus Prime* thus concludes with a critique of the plantation fiction tradition, which romanticized antebellum race relations as a model for racial reconciliation.

The novel ultimately espouses a guarded hope that professional desegregation, motivated by compliance with gentlemanly norms, will pave the way for social and political equality writ large. A Christmas meal between Pactolus and his white lawyer, Willard Phelps, "the courtly leader of the bar of the capital city of the most Christian nation" (164), is from this perspective symbolic. The episode also presages the controversial 1901 dinner between President Theodore Roosevelt and Booker T. Washington, who was the first African American invited to dine at the White House. Yet Phelps invites Pactolus for a mere "snack" and "securely" locks the door to his office while the men are dining, "to save his guest from embarrassment, quite as much as to screen himself from reproach" (165). Phelps's racial epiphany only comes sentimentally, from meeting Eva: "It was the first time he had ever realized the process through which the intelligent young colored American must always go, before our Christian civilization reduces him finally to his proper level of 'essential inferiority'" (206). Phelps stands in for the novel's most privileged readers, whom Tourgée strove to persuade through an emancipatory aesthetic fusing disciplines and philosophical traditions at the nineteenth century's close.

During the civil rights revolution, Tourgée's intellectual reparative work in law and letters was a beacon, and his ideas resound with Black Lives Matter activism in the twenty-first century. Justice Robert Jackson framed the issue before the Supreme Court in *Brown v. Board of Education* (1954), the landmark decision striking down Jim Crow laws in public education, as a redux of *Plessy*, and he contemplated whether Tourgée would attain "a post-mortem victory."[22] The establishment of law and literature as an interdisciplinary field and legal realism and literary realism's lingering influence suggest Tourgée's intellectual victory, even as racial justice remains an elusive goal. Today, Tourgée's intellectual heirs in literature include Black lawyer-authors like Evie Shockley and Reginald Dwayne Betts, who have penned formally audacious poems that critique inequitable laws in contexts including voting rights and criminal justice.[23] Judge Carlton Reeves's creative nonfictional opinion in a 2020 case involving a potentially racist police stop meanwhile shows how Tourgée's disciplinary renegadism in law manifests now. The opinion begins by cataloguing the supposedly suspicious activities that ultimately led to police killing African Americans like George Floyd, with the defendant in the case triggering scrutiny as "a Black man driving a Mercedes convertible." Later, discussing the Reconstruction-era origins of a key civil rights statute, Reeves asserted: "If the Civil War was the only war in our nation's history dedicated to the proposition that Black lives matter, Reconstruction was dedicated to the proposition that Black futures matter, too."[24] Tourgée's disciplinary reparation efforts over a century ago shared this futuristic vision for equal citizenship, and as an intellectual architect, he continues to inspire lawyers, literary writers, and other activists in the Third Reconstruction.

Notes

1. Albion W. Tourgée, *A Fool's Errand: By One of the Fools* (1879; Prospect Heights, IL: Waveland, 1991), 107, 343. The epigraph is on 24–25. I thank Robert Levine and Sandra Gustafson for organizing the 2019 Literary Tourgée conference, which showcased Tourgée's intellectual agility. My gratitude also extends to Kenneth Warren and Brook Thomas for "enlightened scepticism" that has enriched the essay. See Oliver Wendell Holmes Jr., "The Path of the Law," *Harvard Law Review* 10, no. 8 (March 1897): 469.

2. Albion W. Tourgée, *An Appeal to Caesar* (New York: Fords, Howard, & Hulbert, 1884), 63; Albion W. Tourgée, "Brief of Plaintiff in Error" (1895), in *Undaunted Radical: The Selected Writings and Speeches of Albion W. Tourgée*, ed. Mark Elliott and John David Smith (Baton Rouge: Louisiana State University Press, 2010), 317; Edgar Henry [Albion Tourgée], *'89* (1888; New York: Cassell & Co., 1891), 337.

3. But see Christine Holbo, *Legal Realisms: The American Novel under Reconstruction* (New York: Oxford University Press, 2019), 9.

4. Albion W. Tourgée, *Pactolus Prime* (New York: Cassell, 1890), 53. All subsequent citations to the novel will be in the text.

5. Albion W. Tourgée, preface to *John Eax and Mamelon; or, The South without the Shadow* (New York: Fords, Howard, & Hulbert, 1882), vii–viii; Brook Thomas, "The Legitimacy of Law in Literature: The Case of Albion W. Tourgée," *Elon Law Review* 5, no. 1 (April 2013): 171-97.

6. Benjamin Cardozo, "Law and Literature," *Yale Law Journal* 48, no. 3 ([1925] January 1939): 505; Sir Walter Scott, *Guy Mannering; or, The Astrologer* (1815; London: Thomas Nelson & Sons, 1910), 314.

7. Tourgée, preface to *John Eax and Mamelon*, ix; Albion W. Tourgée, preface to *A Royal Gentleman and 'Zouri's Christmas* (New York: Fords, Howard, & Hulbert, 1881), vii; Albion W. Tourgée, preface to *With Gauge & Swallow, Attorneys* (Philadelphia: J. B. Lippincott, 1889), 7.

8. Tourgée, *A Royal Gentleman*, 10; Albion W. Tourgée, *The Veteran and His Pipe* (1885; Chicago: Morrill, Higgins, 1892), 219.

9. Martin Luther King Jr., "I Have a Dream," speech, Washington, DC, August 28, 1963, National Public Radio, https://www.npr.org/2010/01/18/122701268/i-have-a-dream -speech-in-its-entirety.

10. K-Sue Park, "The History Wars and Property Law: Conquest and Slavery as Foundational to the Field," *Yale Law Journal* 131, no. 4 (February 2022): 1080; Tourgée, *Appeal*, 105.

11. *Civil Rights Cases*, 109 US 3, 25 (1883).

12. Victoria Nourse and Gregory Shaffer, "Varieties of New Legal Realism: Can a New World Order Prompt a New Legal Theory?," *Cornell Law Review* 95, no. 1 (November 2009): 61-137.

13. Albion W. Tourgée, "The Unwritten Law and Why It Remains Unwritten," *Green Bag* 20, no. 2 (January 1908): 8-17; Oliver Wendell Holmes Jr., *The Common Law* (1881; Boston: Little Brown, 1923), 1.

14. Roscoe Pound, "Law in Books and Law in Action," *American Law Review* 44, no. 1 (January/February 1910): 12; Cyril Clemens to Oliver Wendell Holmes Jr., March 4, 1930,

Harvard Law School Library Digital Suite, http://library.law.harvard.edu/suites/owh/index.php/item/36675178/1.

15. Roscoe Pound, "Liberty of Contract," *Yale Law Journal* 18, no. 7 (May 1909): 454-87; Holmes, "Path," 466; Tourgée, "Unwritten Law," 9-14.

16. *Murvale Eastman, Christian Socialist* (New York: Fords, Howard, & Hulbert, 1890), 269.

17. Clarence Darrow, "Realism in Literature and Art," in *Realism in Literature and Art* (1893; Girard, KS: Haldeman-Julius, 1899), 20; William Dean Howells, *Criticism and Fiction* (New York: Harper, 1891), 73, 104; Vernon Louis Parrington, *The Beginnings of Critical Realism in America* (New York: Harcourt, Brace, 1930), 248-49; William Dean Howells, "The Psychological Counter-Current in Recent Fiction," *North American Review* 173, no. 541 (December 1901): 882; Charles W. Chesnutt, "Letter to Houghton, Mifflin & Co. [December 30, 1901]," in *The Marrow of Tradition*, ed. Werner Sollors (New York: Norton, 2012), 208-9.

18. Philip Mechem, "The Jurisprudence of Despair," *Iowa Law Review* 21, no. 4 (May 1936): 669-92; Albion W. Tourgée, "The Claim of 'Realism,'" *North American Review* 148, no. 388 (March 1889): 386-88; Albion W. Tourgée, *An Outing with the Queen of Hearts*, ill. Aimée Tourgée (New York: Merrill & Baker, 1894), 65-68.

19. Harold H. Kolb Jr., *The Illusion of Life: American Realism as a Literary Form* (Charlottesville: University of Virginia Press, 1969), 136.

20. Qtd. in Carolyn L. Karcher, Introduction to Albion W. Tourgée, *Bricks without Straw*, ed. Carolyn Karcher (1880; Durham, NC: Duke University Press, 2009), 31.

21. Frank Norris, "A Plea for Romantic Fiction," in *The Responsibilities of the Novelist* (1903; New York: Haskell House, 1969), 220.

22. Otto H. Olsen, *Carpetbagger's Crusade: The Life of Albion Winegar Tourgée* (Baltimore, MD: Johns Hopkins University Press, 1965), 354.

23. For an analysis of Shockley's and Betts's poetry, see my essay "Black Lives Matter and Legal Reconstructions of Elegiac Forms," in *Revisiting the Elegy in the Black Lives Matter Era*, ed. Tiffany Austin et al. (New York: Routledge, 2020), 120-37.

24. *Jamison v. McClendon*, No. 3:16-CV-595-CWR-LRA (S.D. Miss. August 4, 2020), 4, 15, https://www.documentcloud.org/documents/7013933-Jamison-v-McClendon.html.

12

With Gauge and Swallow, Attorneys

Tourgée's Legal Romance

Brook Thomas

*W*ith Gauge and Swallow, Attorneys (1889) is Albion W. Tourgée's novel about a Wall Street law firm that almost imperceptibly connects racial with economic injustice. The novel's Preface contemplates the challenge of portraying the law in literature. Whereas authors trained as lawyers risk being too technical, authors lacking legal training too often depend on "miracles performed by the phenomenal practitioner who manipulates courts, juries, and witnesses."[1] The latter is exemplified by the climatic scene in Mark Twain's *Pudd'nhead Wilson* when Pudd'nhead theatrically and anachronistically uses fingerprints to identify a "black" murderer. The former may partially explain the dearth of criticism on *Gauge* since 1948, when Alexander Cowie praised it for containing "some of [Tourgée's] most delightful writing" but worried that its legal detail was "too 'technical' to be popular."[2]

There are, however, other reasons for neglect. Tourgée's most celebrated explosion of literary activity was sparked by hopes of renewing momentum for Reconstruction by influencing the 1880 election. *A Fool's Errand* (1879) and *Bricks without Straw* (1880) are compelling cases for racial justice. The hero of *Figs and Thistles* (1879) is based on Tourgée's friend James Garfield, who became the Republican nominee for president. Less attention has been paid to Tourgée's flurry of activity before and after the election of 1888. Intent on unseating Grover Cleveland, who had dismantled many Reconstruction policies, Tourgée wrote *'89* (1888), which implicitly blames Cleveland for a conspiracy between its southerner narrator and a northern monopolist to suppress the working class in the North and control the race problem in the South. After Cleveland's defeat, Tourgée tried to influence the incoming administration of Benjamin Harrison. In December 1888, he penned "The South as a Field for Fiction," urging writers to stop portraying Confederates as heroes and to start depicting freedmen accurately. He followed with *Pactolus Prime* (1890), addressing the race problem, and *Murvale Eastman: Christian Socialist* (1890), addressing monopolies and the labor problem.

Employing Tourgée's polemical flair, the essay and these two works have gar-
nered some recent attention.[3] Written at the same time, *Gauge* has not. One reason may be that a story about a Wall Street law firm seems unlikely to condemn
either racial injustice or monopoly capitalism. Another may be that Tourgée's
champions have been so intent on defending his "novels with a purpose" from
ridicule by what he called "our over-refined dilettanti" that *Gauge*, lacking polemic, has fallen by the wayside.[4] Tourgée's tale of Wall Street will never receive
the accolades accorded Melville's "Bartleby, the Scrivener," but it deserves attention as his most ambitious attempt to link racial and economic injustice by showing, not telling.

In Tourgée's polemical works, plots, no matter how complicated, are driven by
his message. In contrast, *Gauge*'s plot is episodic. Like TV serials, *Gauge* introduces new legal problems and characters each episode while providing continu-
ity through the firm's personnel. The firm is staffed by Gauge, the senior partner;
Swallow, the junior partner; Mr. Minton, a decorated Union veteran; Mr. Burrill, an elderly immigrant from England; and the young Gerald Fountain, a law
school graduate from New England and the story's narrator. There are episodes
on mistaken identity, a rich monopolist, racial justice, and disputed marriages
and wills. This episodic form simulates the experience of the lawyer who "rarely
knows, or cares to know, the whole history of any life. He sees specific episodes
and catches fleeting glimpses of many as their orbits intersect the plane of his
duty" (5). Occupying a similar position, most readers are likely to consider episodes in isolation. But Tourgée's implied reader is modeled by characters with an
almost miraculous capacity to see hidden connections. Readers paying scrupulous attention to tiny details of seemingly unrelated incidents can discover links
between economic and racial justice.

If *Gauge*'s form is episodic, its literary mode is best described as a romance,
defined by Hawthorne in the preface to *The House of the Seven Gables* as portraying the possible as well as the probable.[5] For Tourgée, romance also involves, as
it did for medieval writers, the intersection of the miraculous with the everyday.
"The romance which the practice of his profession reveals to the lawyer is of the
most intense and fascinating character. . . . To him the days of romance are by
no means a thing of the past. . . . He is the one man who realizes how generally
romance underlies the life we foolishly call 'common,' and is above all others
charitable to apparent evil and suspicious of claims to special excellence, since he
knows how often kindly motive is hidden by the one and sinister design veiled
by the other" (5–6). Although the lawyer rarely confronts legal miracles, "he believes in miracles because they are daily wrought within his knowledge. He hesi-

tates about believing anything impossible, because what cannot be done he has so often seen achieved" (5).

Throughout his career, Tourgée's literary imagination was unleashed by contemplating unrealized possibilities within the law, while his legal imagination had free rein in literature. Those possibilities do not always lead to improvement. For instance, the plot in *'89* hinges on a loophole in the Twelfth Amendment's provision to have Congress decide unresolved elections. In an unlikely but possible scenario, the conspirators prevent election of both the president and the vice president, allowing the South peacefully to secede. But *'89* is a dystopian romance. Expressing Tourgée's love affair with the law, *Gauge* is a legal romance, with a happy ending generated by possibilities in the law. For instance, the action starts with the expert witness Professor Cadmus winning a case by dazzling the courtroom with photographed and enlarged signatures to establish handwriting as an undeniable marker of identity while miraculously authenticating an allegedly forged note. Tourgée even makes a connection with *Bricks without Straw* (1880) when Cadmus reveals contested wills by rival cousins, the plot device that makes the New England schoolteacher Mollie the legitimate heir of her southern lover's estate.[6] More miracles come when the supernatural "orbits" of new characters "intersect the plane of [the lawyer's] duty" (5). The firm's first typist makes herself rich by locating a lost document through a spiritualist trance.

Incidents like these stretch the limits of probability, but they are anchored in details of everyday life in the firm. For instance, typing changed the law's relation to documents previously handwritten. It also made scriveners, like Bartleby, obsolete while altering the gendered dynamics of the workforce. Hiring the typist, Fountain notes, "took the bread out of the mouths of three or four able-bodied clerks for a stipend shockingly insignificant in comparison even with the salary of an embryo lawyer. The 'type-writer girl' was a new institution then. The time had not yet come when one desiring such a position found youth and beauty a disadvantage, and ours could never have advertised among her qualifications 'middle-aged and plain'" (123). Proud father of a talented daughter who illustrated some of his later books, Tourgée was aware of gendered double standards. His point is not to deny women a place in the workforce but to emphasize the vulnerability of wage laborers. Female characters fit his ideal of those whose ingenuity gave them control over their means of production.[7] Some manage estates with uncanny business sense. Professor Cadmus's daughter establishes a school for chirography. A woman novelist captures the heart of Fountain while changing the course of the narrative.

Until he meets his beloved, Fountain primarily relates stories of others. To be sure, the second episode, about Minton's heroism as a soldier, deflates his pretensions to be descended from the de Fontaines of Virginia when we learn that the family's progenitor committed bigamy and forgery. But even that detail foreshadows the book's ending, when both crimes take on added importance as Fountain's love affair dominates the action while becoming intricately linked to the book's story about a monopolist. Using that end as my beginning, I will trace the thread that Tourgée weaves to help attentive readers make connections with earlier episodes about racial justice. Working inductively, not deductively, I try to do justice to Tourgée by showing how, lacking polemic, *Gauge*'s literary method becomes a form of discovery.

Monopoly and Love

In the ninth of thirteen episodes, Fountain falls in love with Mrs. Murray, a young woman writer he thinks is a widow. He is heartbroken to discover that she is going abroad but agrees to become her attorney and learns her story. She met her supposed husband when she and her invalid mother were in dire financial difficulty. He provided mother and daughter with a house and financial security. In return, she was to act as his wife, even though he would frequently be in the West and was already married. She knew what this meant sexually, but he never forced himself on her even after the mother died. He only sought calm from his busy life. Later, letting her in on his secret, he fakes his death in a western railroad accident to give her independence and ownership of the house. When poor health requires him to leave the country, however, she realizes her love and agrees to accompany him. The man turns out to be Swallow's best client. Andrew Murray Hazzard is based on Isaac Singer, of sewing machine fame, owner of one of the first multinational companies and an infamous bigamist. Hazzard married young but had no time for his wife or daughter, who left him while he devoted all of his time to his invention. Rich, he married again even though his first wife was alive. The second wife is unfaithful but continues to have designs on the fortune. Mrs. Murray is not the only "other wife." As Burrill puts it, "A rich man can have as many families as he likes, or as he thinks he can afford. Society doesn't mind it much, and if he is very rich there is not much danger of prosecution for bigamy. There is one thing society is a little peculiar about; each family must have a different name. This is a little troublesome to the man, no doubt, and apt to make difficulty after his death" (138).

Hazzard's multiple marriages become a metaphor for his monopolistic empire. Like Thomas Pynchon's Pierce Inverarity in *The Crying of Lot 49*, he has a hand in almost every segment of the economy. He even has the mysterious power of inhabiting the mind of Swallow, who can then duplicate Hazzard's handwriting. Nonetheless, like the monopolist in *'89*, who makes decisions that ruin the lives of millions, Hazzard is "not only just but equitable in his dealings with his fellows."[8] He never forces his attorney to do something against his will.

Concerned about Hazzard, Swallow sends Fountain to Europe to put himself in the monopolist's service. Jumping at the chance to be close to his beloved, Fountain obeys, only to learn that the "widow" married Hazzard on landing in England, a valid marriage because the first wife had died, although the second "wife" was sure to contest it. Fountain's hopes rise when Hazzard reveals his plan to have the new wife marry him when she truly becomes a widow. But Fountain is told to stay away until that time comes. Supported by the monopolist, he enjoys two years of cultured life in Europe, with Hazzard taking powers over him akin to those he has over Swallow. When Hazzard dies, Swallow is named executor of the will on condition that he leave the firm, which is reorganized, with Fountain made a partner on his return to the United States. According to plan, the widow and Fountain marry immediately after Hazzard's death, but she stays in London, needing time to mourn before they can live together. Two years later, Fountain receives a telegram stating "Venez," and the couple lives happily ever after.

Hazzard's name suggests chance, but unlike William Dean Howells's realistic *A Hazard of New Fortunes*, published the following year, *Gauge*'s economic chance world produces good fortune, not tragedy. Indeed, the lover's "Venez" recalls *Bricks without Straw* when, after keeping her lover waiting, the Yankee schoolteacher finally writes, "Come." Combined with the initial allusion to *Bricks*' inheritance plot, *Gauge*'s union of lovers marks another happy, if contrived, ending. Unlike *Bricks*, however, *Gauge* seems to end with no reference to racial justice. Nonetheless, as Hazzard's will is untangled, one thread suggests a connection. In the dystopian *'89*, the monopolist retains control over the entire economy. In *Gauge*, Hazzard's fortune is divided among multiple individuals and charities. One bequest is for the granddaughter of John Godman, an abolitionist who sought the aid of Gauge in the days of slavery.

Episodes of Racial Justice

The book's episodes devoted to racial justice are foreshadowed by its dedication to Samuel F. Phillips. Tourgée met Phillips in North Carolina where, despite Union sentiments, he served in the state's Confederate government. During Reconstruction, Phillips became a Republican and was appointed the nation's second solicitor general. He was charged with arguing most civil rights cases. That record helped turn him into a fictional villain in Ruiz de Burton's *The Squatter and the Don* (1885), which sympathizes with the South. For Tourgée, however, as "a lawyer worthy of the highest honors of a profession he has abundantly adorned," he is a model for Gauge and Swallow (4). The senior partner first gained notoriety in an 1851 fugitive-slave case initiated by Godman, who knew that Gauge's father kept a station on the Underground Railroad. Risking a boycott by many of his clients, Gauge prevailed by arguing that the slave was not a fugitive since he had been brought voluntarily into a free state. The junior partner's case of racial justice comes in a chapter called "A Conflict between Church and State."

Gauge's case is based on a decision rendered by Melville's father-in-law; Swallow's explores possibilities through a case Tourgée imagines. During the Civil War, Swallow's son ran away to join the Union army under an assumed name, only to be captured, imprisoned, and wracked with consumption. Managing to escape, he made his way to northern Virginia before collapsing. Confederate deserters in hiding tended him while being secretly fed by Elena, the slave of Abiah Wilkens, who served in the Confederate army until he lost an arm. Discharged, Abiah, with Elena's aid, worked the undeveloped land given to him by his father, a former overseer. When the deserters have to flee, they leave Swallow's son with Elena. Rather than throw him out, Abiah gives him his bed and cares for him. The son recovers enough to write an account of his wanderings until consumption takes over and he dies as fighting ends. Abiah sends for Swallow who retrieves the body and writes the farmer to get in touch if he needs legal advice. Twenty years later, the former Confederate needs it.

After the war, despite his lost limb, Abiah worked diligently to make his farm profitable. He succeeds thanks to efficient management by Elena, now free. After a while, the two start producing children as well as crops. Scandalized, neighbors send a minister to instruct the former soldier to put a halt to his immoral ways. For the minister this means paying Elena money to leave. But Abiah has come truly to love his housekeeper and thinks that the Christian act is to marry Elena and make an honest woman of the mother of his children. Virginia, however, has an antimiscegenation law, forcing them to marry in Washington, DC. On their return, they are promptly arrested for violating the Virginia statute. When Virginia's Supreme Court upholds their arrest, Abiah's brother enlists Swallow's aid to appeal to the US Supreme Court. But "a lawyer's business is to serve his client rather than settle legal questions" (178). Filing a writ of error, Swallow arranges to free the prisoners if they agree to leave the state. The couple goes west, leaving undecided whether "those lawfully wedded in one State may still be adjudged malefactors in another" (178).

In addition to exposing the hypocrisy of the church, Abiah and Elena's arrest makes a variety of legal points. One is that racially discriminatory laws, such as antimiscegenation laws, are linked to the heritage of slavery. Antimiscegenation laws are also unnatural. As Tourgée frequently argued, interracial love is bound to happen. Laws banning interracial marriage make love a crime. In addition, Tourgée points to the arbitrariness of the color line by making Elena an albino and thus the whitest character in the episode. Most explicitly, more than a conflict between church and state, the episode is about a conflict between state and national jurisdiction. Why is a marriage recognized in the nation's capital illegal in a state of the Union?[9]

This episode takes place before the chapter in which Fountain becomes the widow's attorney. In the chapter that follows, Fountain goes south to handle another case and learns the story of the African American "Missionary Joe." To understand that story, however, we have to go back to the chapter "A Shattered Idol" about a case Burrill takes at the end of the Civil War involving African Americans' claim to property in the South. The case tests Burrill's love affair with the common law, which he worshipped as the "essence of right" (116). The British immigrant initially had little sympathy for Blacks or concern about the fate of the republic, but he was interested in the legal aspects of slavery, assuming that, even if the common law did not contain a remedy for slavery, it did not support it. For him, the law's relation to slavery was the same as its relation to extralegal activity that "they call 'business' on the exchanges—stocks and produce and petroleum. . . . The law doesn't encourage or protect it . . . but the law doesn't stop it" (111). Research on his case, however, shatters his idol. The law "not only tolerated, but regulated, enforced, and strengthened" slavery (116).

Burrill's case forces readers to confront issues left unresolved because of three incommensurate legal regimes: the antebellum Union, the Confederacy, and the postbellum Union. In 1857, a slave owner tried to take care of his Black kin by sidestepping existing law and selling his children and their mother to someone who took them to New York and freedom. When the original owner died, he left his estate to the mother and children, but they could not take physical possession without being reenslaved. During the Civil War, white relatives bought the estate when the Confederate government auctioned it for back taxes. After surrender, the Blacks sued for ownership, but the white heirs claimed that the sale of the slaves was invalid for lacking consideration, rendering the will void because slaves could not own property. Burrill's clients maintained the validity of the will and contended that an auction by the Confederacy should not be recognized by US law. Nonetheless, in *Texas v. White* (1869), not mentioned in *Gauge* but criticized in Tourgée's "The Right to Vote" (1890), the Supreme Court ruled that because an indestructible Union consisted of indestructible states, southern states had never legally seceded.[10] Thus, although states' actions supporting rebellion were invalid, those "sanctioning and protecting marriage and its domestic relations, governing the course of descents, regulating and conveying the transfer of property, real and personal" were valid.[11] Because slaves were property and considered a domestic relation, the plaintiffs' claim would seem invalid. But wasn't paying taxes and selling the property to put money in Confederate coffers aiding the rebellion?

Burrill is convinced that the case will go to the Supreme Court. "The Dartmouth College case, the Chesapeake Canal case, the Dred Scott decision, the Legal Tender cases, and the Slaughter House cases, all put together, did not present as many nor as difficult constitutional questions as *my case*" (115). Tourgée, however, delays the case. In the delay, Burrill is asked to adjudicate a suit in equity that demonstrates Tourgée's respect for honorable southern lawyers who disagreed with him politically. During the war another southerner wanted to free his children but was legally forbidden from doing so. Before dying, he created a secret trust giving Esquire Bagster his children and financial support with the purpose of freeing them when possible. Bagster loyally invested the money in Confederate bonds, now worthless. Though still committed to the lost cause, Bagster feels he has betrayed his trust as a lawyer and brings suit against himself for recovery of the loss, which requires him to sell his home. Deciding in Bagster's "favor," Burrill is so impressed with his honor that, called back to New York, he leaves the southerner in charge of his case with $5,000 to cover costs. Bagster rightly calculates that his clients might lose and settles for more than they hoped for. To Burrill's dismay, the settlement keeps the Supreme Court from hearing his case. The settlement also forces readers once again to ponder how to resolve legal questions generated by racial inequities.

Nonetheless, a new case emerges. In lieu of a cash payment, Bagster accepts a claim the white heirs have against a railroad. They allege that the railroad violated an agreement by building businesses on property bought from the heirs. Episodes later, Fountain goes south to argue *Burrill v. The Railroad*, where he meets the former slave Missionary Joe.

Once a year while a slave, Joe was loaned to a local inn to tend to the comforts of judges and lawyers when court was in session. Hard work after emancipation leaves him financially flush. Nonetheless, he annually resumes his duties for the pure joy of making people happy. He tells Fountain his story when the lawyer spends two nights at the inn waiting for his train home after his case is held over to next year. As Joe recounts, his owner, perhaps his father, constantly promised to free him and his wife, Elsie. But someone in debt could not free slaves, and Joe's owner was always in debt. The two concoct a plan for Joe to join the California gold rush to pay off the owner's debts and buy his freedom. To get around a law forbidding slaves of people in debt from leaving the state, Joe was sold to a neighbor who held the mortgage on the estate (including slaves), with the proceeds of the sale coming out of the mortgage. Two years later, Joe returned after striking it rich and making $20,000 running a restaurant. But new debts had accrued, and Joe's desire for freedom remained unfulfilled. Elsie died of disappointment, and Joe, restored to his original owner, became overseer, finally making the plantation profitable. He also insisted on selling a portion to a railroad, whose line increased the land's value. When the owner and owner's wife died, the estate descended to the wife's relatives, and Joe was willed to the church under the assumption that it would free him. Instead, he was sold to finance a missionary, which explains his name.[12]

As tragic as Joe's story is, Fountain's knowledge of the law generates a happy ending. Because Joe had not gone west as a fugitive, his residency in California established his freedom, giving him control of the estate's mortgage. Fountain asks him if he wants to dispossess the owner's wife's heirs, but he declines, stating that two wrongs do not make a right. He can, however, document the mortgage with a date prior to any transaction with the railroad. Fountain buys the mortgage for $1,000 to prove that the railroad violated its agreement.

Missionary Joe is one of numerous examples of Tourgée establishing a dialogue with works by himself and others. Forgiving and good-spirited Joe was created in tandem with Tourgée's bitter and angry Pactolus Prime. Pactolus's venom against white prejudice caused Joel Chandler Harris to brand Tourgée a "refugee from his race."[13] In contrast, speaking in dialect, Joe, "a born servitor," seems like Harris's fictionalized former slaves (197). In fact, Pactolus and Joe have similarities. Just as Pactolus calculates how much African Americans are owed for their uncompensated labor as slaves, Joe says, "Ef I hed my way, I'd take from 'em every cent they eber made offen the colored man's work—every cent, sah,—an' then what would be lef'? . . . Jestice is jestice!" (209). Indeed, Tourgée's Joe is a subtle response to Harris's popular "Free Joe and the Rest of the World" (1887), published just before work on *Gauge* began.

Unlike Missionary Joe, Harris's Joe is freed by his owner only to find out that he is worse off than most slaves. In contrast, Tourgée's Joe leaves no question about his and his wife's desire to be free. In addition to challenging the substance of "Free Joe," Tourgée appropriates Harris's preferred form. In 1887, Chesnutt published his first conjure woman tale, which quietly challenges Harris's and Thomas Nelson Page's formula of having a former slave nostalgically reminisce in dialect to a white man about days on the plantation. Tourgée encouragingly wrote Chesnutt while commenting that the dialect form was "a mere fleeting fancy," a sentiment Chesnutt would share.[14] Nonetheless, with Missionary Joe telling his story in dialect to Fountain, Tourgée, like Chesnutt, gives a view of the past and present different from Harris's and Page's while demonstrating his mastery of the form. Even so, when, after this chapter, Tourgée turns back to Fountain's love story, it would seem that *Gauge* ends with questions of racial justice dealt with only in isolated episodes. But Tourgée plants evidence that allows attentive readers to follow an almost invisible narrative thread.

Interweaving Racial Justice and the National Economy

The case against the railroad, which cannot be understood properly without Joe's story, is one example of race haunting multiple aspects of national life. But recognition of the full extent to which racial justice is interwoven with the overall plot comes from unraveling the mystery of the granddaughter of the abolitionist John Godman, related in an early episode. Because of a dispute with her father before the war, Luella Godman went south, married, and had a daughter. Abandoned by her husband, she leaves her daughter with a woman and is reported dead from drowning. In fact, another woman drowned. Luella unsuccessfully searches for her daughter, assumes a new identity, and "marries" a plantation owner, even though her husband is still alive. Unknown to her, the spiritual, if not legal, husband discovers her past when she talks in her sleep. He realizes that the only way to save the honor of the woman he loves is, without telling her, to fake his death and bequeath his estate to her. When the will is contested by relatives, Luella hires Gauge by invoking her father's name. Gauge goes south, wins her case, and is told her secret, which includes the capacity to duplicate her beloved's handwriting and the belief that she can communicate with him beyond the grave. Retaining Gauge for legal advice, Luella frees her slaves, sells the estate, and goes to Chicago, where she makes a fortune in real estate following advice she thinks is coming from her beloved but is in fact her own. Eventually the legal husband dies, although the daughter remains lost. When war breaks out, the spiritual husband, who had also moved to Chicago, enlists in the Union army. On leave in New York, he wanders into Gauge's office and asks him to verify his will, which leaves everything to his beloved. Gauge reveals all he knows, and the two go to

Chicago, where the lovers marry. The husband survives the war but later dies. Luella, through Gauge, asks for Minton to come—with his wife—to handle the will. Minton resigns from the firm to become her attorney with the implication, never made explicit, that Minton's wife is the lost daughter.

Gauge's relation to Godman's daughter mirrors Swallow's to Hazzard. Both involve faked deaths, illegal marriages, spiritual communication, and the ability of someone to duplicate another's unique handwriting. These and other bizarre marital situations make those involving African Americans the most traditional in the book other than Gauge's, Swallow's, and Minton's. Even more striking, the stable relation between Joe and Elsie comes despite the disruption of kinship generated by slave owners fathering their own slaves. In polemical works, Tourgée decries the injustice of Black offspring being denied their just inheritance. In *Gauge*, however, African Americans get enough to satisfy them, even if it is not all they are due. Tourgée also refashions the standard romance of reunion in which a sympathetic northerner marries a southern belle to help her retain her family estate. In *Gauge*, the daughter of an abolitionist marries a southerner who abandons her, while the southerner who loves her makes it possible for her to free his slaves. After the two marry, he joins the Union army to defeat the Confederacy. Adding to the romance, the monopolist divides his estate, leaving part of it to the granddaughter of an abolitionist.

Offering a national vision in stark contrast to the dystopia of "89, *Gauge* dramatizes Tourgée's belief that, exposed to the possibilities of life, the lawyer "is rarely a pessimist" (6). With Cleveland's defeat, Tourgée hoped that Republicans were ready to join Gauge in never forgetting "what the law *ought* to be, in trying to find out what it was" (112). The law may have been complicit with slavery, but, like Burrill, Tourgée felt capable of tracing "the little thread, the golden thread, that runs through all the law, is stronger than all the coarsely-knotted ligaments of human desire, and runs back to truth, to essential truth, absolute truth" (113). The nation, however, was out of step with Tourgée's legal imagination.

An Unrequited Romance

Gauge dramatizes Pactolus's belief that, although compensation for past wrongs "cannot be expected," preventing "injustice, pertains only to the future and is always possible."[15] With Republicans in control, Tourgée directed his imagination to preventing injustice. "The Right to Vote" (1890) creatively interpreted the Fifteenth Amendment to keep states from altering standards that enabled

African Americans suffrage in the early days of Radical Reconstruction. Tourgée also proposed two laws minimizing states' power to control the lives of African Americans. In education, he invoked national security to advocate eliminating illiteracy via federal funds going directly to school districts most in need. For voting, he drew on article 1, section 4, of the Constitution, which allows Congress to alter the "Times, Places, and Manner of holding elections for Senators and Representatives," and proposed giving the federal government, not states, control of federal elections. Unfortunately, Republicans replaced both bills with ones retaining state powers. The Blair Bill funneled federal aid for education through the states, many of which would not support Black schools equally. The Lodge Bill provided a mechanism for national supervision but left states in control of all elections. Like previous measures, this plan was likely to fail without military force and risked jeopardizing the lives of Blacks lodging a complaint. Hope for even compromised reform vanished when both the Blair Bill and the Lodge Bill met defeat, with Tourgée opposing the former and reluctantly supporting the latter.[16] Also in 1890, Mississippi passed the first massive disfranchisement measures. The same year, the Supreme Court undercut Tourgée's hope for national control over marriages when it ruled that "the whole subject of the domestic relations of husband and wife, parent and child, belongs to the laws of the states, and not to the laws of the United States."[17]

Despite these setbacks, Tourgée agreed to help a group from New Orleans challenge an 1890 Jim Crow law for railroads. The Supreme Court retained a number of justices who in 1883 had ruled against the 1875 Civil Rights Act. Nonetheless, Tourgée thought success was possible if a campaign to alter public opinion could pressure existing Supreme Court justices and influence new appointments. Instead, two justices appointed by Republican Harrison and two appointed by Cleveland, reelected in 1892, were almost sure to support the doctrine of separate but equal. That left only Justice John Marshall Harlan to agree with the arguments made by Tourgée, who was joined by his friend Samuel Phillips to represent Homer Plessy.

Plessy v. Ferguson (1896) ended Tourgée's romance with the law. Never again did he turn to literature to imagine possibilities in the law. Instead, by calling the collection he published in 1897 *The Man Who Outlived Himself*, Tourgée suggested that the time for his vision of justice had passed. *Gauge*, however, has not outlived itself. Reading it today, we need to cultivate the capacity to imagine legislation and possibilities lurking within existing laws to remedy the racial and economic injustices that persist, despite the efforts of those like Tourgée.

Notes

1. Albion W. Tourgée, *With Gauge and Swallow, Attorneys* (Philadelphia: Lippincott, 1889), 6. References will appear within the text.

2. Alexander Cowie, *The Rise of the American Novel* (New York: American Book Co., 1948), 531.

3. On *Pactolus Prime*, see Brook Thomas, *American Literary Realism and the Failed Promise of Contract* (Berkeley: University of California Press, 1997), 191–230; and Carolyn L. Karcher, *A Refugee from His Race: Albion W. Tourgée and His Fight against White Supremacy* (Chapel Hill: University of North Carolina Press, 2016), 54–90. See also DeLisa D. Hawkes's essay in this volume. Otto H. Olsen calls *Murvale* "the Judge's greatest new achievement in fiction." Otto H. Olsen, *Carpetbagger's Crusade: The Life of Albion Winegar Tourgée* (Baltimore, MD: Johns Hopkins University Press, 1965), 289.

4. Albion W. Tourgée, *Our Continent* 3 (May 23, 1883): 669. Relying on his pen to make a living, Tourgée wrote nonpolemical works of local color. In this volume, Molly Ball discusses *Button's Inn*'s (1887) treatment of Mormons. Tourgée returns to the Mormons in *'89*. He did not condone polygamy, but he used persecution of the Mormons to highlight contradictions within US society. *Gauge*'s fascination with bigamy should be read in this context.

5. Nathaniel Hawthorne, *The House of the Seven Gables*, in *The Centenary Edition of the Works of Nathaniel Hawthorne* (Columbus: Ohio State University Press, 1965), 1.

6. Cadmus's courtroom theatrics anticipate Twain's *Pudd'nhead Wilson*. Unlike Pudd'nhead, however, Cadmus is not a lawyer performing stunts. Also, unlike Pudd'nhead's fingerprints, Cadmus's handwriting is not a bodily marker revealing racial identity. Thomas, *American Literary Realism*, 191–230, compares *Pudd'nhead*'s and *Pactolus*'s characters who can pass as white.

7. Tourgée denounced monopolists but promoted small, self-employed entrepreneurs. "The conflict [in the North] is not, as so many shortsighted theorists have averred, between the capitalist and the mere laborer, but between the over-gorged capitalist and the great host of enterprising self-employers, whose hope is at best to secure a modest competency." Albion W. Tourgée, *'89; or, The Grand Master's Secret* (New York: Cassell, 1888), 413.

8. Tourgée, *'89*, 413.

9. For a previous discussion of "A Conflict between Church and State," see Brook Thomas, "The Legitimacy of Law in Literature," *Elon Law Review* 5 (2013): 171–97.

10. Albion W. Tourgée, "The Right to Vote," *Forum* 9 (1890): 78–92.

11. *Texas v. White* 74 US 700 (1869) at 733.

12. Joe and his owner are both Masons. The subplot about this secret order adds another dimension to the story, especially when Joe makes a punning reference to the Klan: "I'm 'clined ter think you white folks are de rale 'clan *destins*,' a'ter all" (201).

13. Karcher, *A Refugee from His Race*, xiii.

14. Mark Elliott, *Color-Blind Justice: Albion Tourgée and the Quest for Racial Equality from the Civil War to Plessy v. Ferguson* (New York: Oxford University Press, 2006), 220.

15. Albion W. Tourgée, *Pactolus Prime* (New York: Cassell, 1890), 117.

16. On the Blair and Lodge Bills, see Karcher, *A Refugee from His Race*, 13–17. Karcher highlights Tourgée's tensions with African Americans over the Blair Bill. But also in early 1890 the Convention of Colored Americans endorsed Tourgée's election bill, condemned Jim Crow railroad laws, and welcomed collaboration of whites like Tourgée: "We regret that there exists in certain parts of our country a condition of affairs which renders it necessary for the colored American citizens to meet in a separate body for the consideration of important questions, national in character." Wm. A. Dunning, "Record of Political Events," *Political Science Quarterly* 5 (1890): 371.

17. *In Re Burris* 136 US 586 at 593–94 (1890).

III   NATION

13

"I Don't Care a Rag for the *Union as It Was*"

Amputation, the Past, and the Work of the Freedmen's Bureau in Bricks without Straw

Sarah E. Chinn

No institution represented the radical possibilities of Reconstruction more than the Freedmen's Bureau. Although it was hamstrung from the beginning and was in danger of dissolution more than once during its seven-year run from 1865 to 1872, the bureau sparked the imagination of white radicals, who saw in it an instrument for deep and lasting change as much as a clearinghouse for the needs of freedpeople. Officially called the Bureau of Refugees, Freedmen, and Abandoned Lands, the bureau's brief was both broad and deep; it had a raft of responsibilities, including (but hardly limited to) feeding and clothing thousands of freedpeople, tracking down lost relatives, creating antiracist tribunals, and overseeing labor relations between formerly enslaved people and white landowners. In addition to these, although it was not officially part of the initial charge, the bureau took on the massive task of providing education for the mostly illiterate population of freedpeople.[1]

This essay uses Albion Tourgée's *Bricks without Straw* to explore together two seemingly disparate phenomena: the Freedmen's Bureau and the representation of amputation in the years after the Civil War.[2] I argue that they are articulated to each other through a commitment on the part of Tourgée and his pre–civil rights counterparts toward a radical analysis of the war and its aftermath. For many radical Republicans, the Freedmen's Bureau represented the kind of federally initiated program that could transform the South, providing not just physical resources but also education, initiation into the world of politics, and inclusion in all elements of civil society. I connect this rebuilding to a rethinking of the amputations that were commonplace results of the Civil War, linking the shattering of limbs on the battlefield to the shattering of the slave-holding nation and the necessity of reimagining both physical and national bodies in the wake of life-changing reinvention. The bureau is, in many ways, the limit case for irrevocable change, especially in its education campaign. Unlike the distribution of lands, literacy cannot be rescinded (a point that was especially important at a time in which the territory initially awarded by William T. Sherman to freedpeople was reclaimed for white ownership under Andrew Johnson). Education was an abstract possession whose ownership was invisible but profoundly empowering for freedpeople.

The larger project of the Freedmen's Bureau connects to the phenomenon on several registers. The Freedmen's Bureau was grounded in the experience of amputation from the top down: It was overseen by General Oliver O. Howard, who had lost an arm in the Civil War. Howard is a fascinating figure, by turns energized and frustrated by the work of the bureau, shocked by and incredulous of the violent responses from white southerners, and inspired and irritated by the bureau's clients. The story of Howard and the bureau dovetails with *Bricks without Straw*, in which the Freedmen's Bureau and representations of amputation are combined to offer a radical understanding of what the new nation might look like. As we shall see, for Tourgée, also seriously wounded in the war, it was appropriate that the bureau be staffed by amputees, whose visible sacrifice and commitment to permanent change in political, economic, and social relations were literally worn on their (empty) sleeves.

Although there's no evidence that they actually met, Tourgée and Howard saw Reconstruction in general and the Freedmen's Bureau in particular as intervening not only in freedpeople's lives but also in white and Black Americans' relationship with the history of slavery, the challenge of the present moment, and the promise of an egalitarian future, which the bureau and the white radicals who supported it would help midwife into existence. As white radicals immersed in the experience of the Reconstruction South, Tourgée and Howard saw nostalgia for the antebellum past as a threat to real change. Opposing appeals to "the Union as it was," they argued against any representation of the preemancipation South that minimized the horrors of slavery and that denied the importance of the reworking of the body politic, so powerfully represented by the corporeal losses endured by Civil War veterans. For Tourgée, amputation signaled not just the individual sacrifice of a specific body—although it certainly meant that. Rather, amputation forcefully represented the necessity to acknowledge and embrace the unchangeable alteration of the body and the nation in the wake of the Civil War.

Shattering "the Whole Previously Existing Social System": Amputating the Antebellum Past

Amputation appears again and again in discussions of the Freedmen's Bureau, and in *Bricks without Straw* the Freedmen's Bureau agents are either amputees or otherwise disabled. As I will argue, both Howard's and Tourgée's political development into radical Republicanism was accompanied by serious injury and witnessing the injuries of others. Howard had lost an arm at the Battle of Fair Oaks, and Tourgée suffered a significant back injury from a bullet to the spine at the first Battle of Bull Run (an injury that plagued him for the rest of his life), and he was wounded again at Perryville.

Howard traced his empathy with Black Americans to his own childhood in Maine. When he was six, his father "befriended a little negro lad and brought him to our house." Howard describes himself and his siblings playing, eating, and learning with him—and he "believed it a providential circumstance that I had that early experience with a negro lad, for it relieved me from that feeling of prejudice which would have hindered me from doing the work for freedom which, years afterwards, was committed to my charge."[3] It is hard to trace the accuracy of this account—the vagueness with which it is narrated might strike the reader as suspicious. But at the very least, Howard's desire to include this nameless "negro lad" in the story of his own growing up shows the importance to him of constructing a solid autobiographical rationale for his commitment to Black independence and equality.

Howard's passion for transforming the Union into a nation without slavery was sparked by the trauma and loss he witnessed and experienced firsthand at Fair Oaks and later in almost every major engagement. After a short convalescence to recover from his loss of an arm, he returned to duty in August 1862, in time to fight at Antietam, Fredericksburg, Chancellorsville, and eventually Gettysburg, before joining William T. Sherman's march to the sea. Although Howard was profoundly committed to the Union cause, he was not a booster for war itself, seeing it as a series of wounds both in the bodies of the men fighting and in the soul of the nation. A veteran of many brutal battles, Howard rejected the criticism that writing about war glamorizes it, focusing in his autobiography on the shock, sorrow, and distress he and others felt on the battlefield. It is one thing to imagine war, he argued, but

> it is another thing to see our comrades there upon the ground with their darkened faces and swollen forms; another thing to watch the countenances of

friends and companions but lately in the bloom of health, now disfigured, torn, and writhing in death; and not less affecting to a sensitive heart to behold a multitude of strangers prone and weak, pierced with wounds, or showing broken looks and every sign of suppressed suffering, waiting for . . . the relief of the surgeon's knife or death.[4]

Howard's characterization of the "surgeon's knife" as a relief maps onto his own experience of amputation. Wounded in the right forearm while approaching the front lines at Fair Oaks, he pushed forward. Later in the battle, "though I was not then aware of it, I had been wounded again, my right elbow having been shattered by a rifle shot." After it became clear that his arm could not be saved, and infection threatened, the surgeon, Dr. Palmer, "kindly told me that my arm had better come off. 'All right, go ahead, I said. Happy to lose only my arm.'" In contrast to many later representations of the scene of amputation as excruciatingly painful in the absence of anesthetics, Howard remembers his own surgery as painless thanks to "a mixture of chloroform and gas. . . . When I woke I was surprised to find the heavy burden was gone."[5]

Howard's relief after his amputation is echoed by his later commitment to transforming the South in the wake of the Civil War. The reimagining of his place on the battlefield and in the world aligns with his increasing conviction that slavery itself was a kind of shattered limb of the nation that had to be excised. This belief is played out in a speech he gave in Springfield, Massachusetts, after the bureau's first year. Responding to former enslavers' "glowing accounts of the blessedness of slavery in its prosperous and patriarchal days . . . [and] curses [toward] that freedom which he believes to be the occasion of so much restlessness and suffering," Howard repudiates any nostalgia for the past. "But you and I know," he declares, "that the real cause of the desolation and suffering is *war*, brought on and continued in the interest and from the love of slavery." Itself a "heavy burden," this longing for the old ways not only maintains the fiction of slavery as intrinsic to the regional identity of the South and the economic health of the nation but acts as a roadblock to Black emancipation. The more white southerners (and perhaps members of his white northern audience as well) hold onto nostalgia for the antebellum Union, the more difficult it will be to maintain the work of Reconstruction. As Howard explains, "the rights of the freedman, which are not yet secured to him, are the direct reverse of the wrongs committed against him."[6] For Howard, Black civil and human rights were at their root reparations for the physical, political, psychological, and economic harm done to enslaved people, even if they did not make up for the massive "wrongs" of slavery and discrimination.

In Howard's view, the collapse of the Confederacy, and the attendant result of "making emancipation an actual, universal fact, was like an earthquake. It shook and shattered the whole previously existing social system." Strikingly, Howard uses the same word—"shattered"—that he used to describe the injury to his arm at Fair Oaks. The shattering of the entire social and economic system that was infused by slavery from root to branch is metonymically linked to the change in his own body, as though his own injury makes way for and is the forerunner of the larger act of breakage. Both Howard's physical alteration and the changes in the political system represent the necessity of moving forward in new, as yet unknown ways. And, as he found, "the Bureau constantly stirred up all social life where its operations touched the field."[7]

In a direct critique of aristocratic southerners for whom the losses during the war signified their social, economic, and political demotion, Howard argued that only with the profound changes of war and Reconstruction that were necessary to secure emancipation could the sociopolitical fabric of the South be rewoven. After all, he argued, the cutting off of slavery and the remaking of the nation in its absence brought new advances to the South that no one could have imagined: "It is a wonderful thing to recall that North Carolina had never before that time [i.e., 1865] a free school system even for white pupils. . . . The death of slavery un-folded the wings of knowledge for both white and black."[8] For Howard, the Union Army's occupation of the South and its enforcement of racial equality guarantees education for all North Carolinians—the kind of sweeping social change he hoped Reconstruction in general and the Freedmen's Bureau in particular could make.

Howard's celebration of integrated, free public education invokes not just human but divine (or semidivine) agency. The angel of knowledge unfolds its wings to embrace the people marginalized by slavery: enslaved people, of course, but also poor whites, whom Reconstruction could help understand that their interests lay in identifying with their emancipated Black counterparts and not with the plantation-owning southern oligarchy.

"It Was Most Fortunate and Providential That the Confederacy Had Failed": *Bricks without Straw* and the Drama of Radical Reconstruction

In what follows, I bring this focus on amputation and its metaphorical connection to the radical possibilities for Reconstruction depicted in Tourgée's *Bricks without Straw.* In my reading, Tourgée connects commitment to Reconstruction with the phenomenon of wartime amputation. While some critics have read amputation as a sign of tragic loss, in my analysis, this bodily loss is for Tourgée an entry point for rethinking and reworking the national body.

Bricks without Straw is a remarkable chronicle of Reconstruction in many ways, not least in its representation of Red Wing, a self-sustaining, Black-owned southern community built on land bought by the novel's Black protagonist, Nimbus. Strikingly, at the novel's beginning, Nimbus raises the specter of amputation in his desire to buy the land, introducing the reader to Tourgée's intertwining of lost limbs and the promise of Black self-determination. Nimbus announces his desire to buy the land in the Red Wing section of town, which he sees as "jest de berry place we wants, an' I'm boun' to hev it ef it takes a leg." Here Nimbus enacts the logic of the Civil War itself, in which the loss of limbs is the necessary prerequisite to ensuring Black emancipation. However, for him, amputation is only hypothetical, since his losses caused by slavery—of his liberty, of bodily integrity, of a claim to family or property—have already been tallied in Tourgée's imaginary balance sheet. For the white male protagonist of the novel, however, amputation is very real. Hesden Le Moyne, the scion of the leading family in town, is a Union sympathizer but is pressured to join the Confederate Army to prove that he is not a traitor to the South. Despite his antipathy to the Confederate cause, he fights valiantly and loses his left arm in battle. This loss does not endear the Confederacy to him. Quite the opposite: Hesden returns from the war "with a bitterer hate for war and a sturdier dislike for the causes which had culminated in the struggle than he had when it began."[9]

Hesden's amputation does not align him with the South. In fact, by making him an amputee, Tourgée implicitly places Hesden in the company of the local branch of the Freedmen's Bureau, which was run by agents "chosen from among the wounded veteran officers of our army. Almost every one of them had won honor with the loss of limb or health." In this formulation, the work of transforming freed slaves is best suited to amputees, who embody the promise of the postwar period. Defending the bureau against accusations that it was populated by "corrupt and unprincipled agents of undefined power,"[10] Tourgée points to their altered bodies as proof positive of their commitment to honesty, fairness, and Black liberty:

> It must be said that this [claim of corruption] cannot be true; that thousands of men selected from the officers of our citizen-soldiery by the unanswerable

certificate of disabling wounds . . . a class of men in physical, intellectual, and moral power and attainments far superior to the average of the American people—it may be said that such could not have become all at once infamously bad.[11]

The bureau agents' injuries are more than the inevitable damage done by military conflict. In Tourgée's formulation, they are an "unanswerable certificate"—a diploma of graduation from the slave economy to a nation organized around liberty. Tourgée's use of the modifier "unanswerable" intensifies the power of this visible proof. It cannot be debated or argued away, answered as in a verbal disagreement. But "answer" here can also mean responded to in kind, matched, or equaled. Implicitly, Tourgée is drawing a contrast between the wounds of a Union soldier, who struggled for the Union's new dispensation, and those of his Confederate counterpart. Their injuries may look the same—a lost arm, leg, hand, eye, and the like—but the latter does not "answer" the former. The bureau agent's loss speaks a different language, makes a different argument, based on a logic of radical transformation; the Confederate veteran's injury is a certificate of a very different kind, supporting a superannuated system of violence, tyranny, and duress.

Tourgée was partially correct about the composition of bureau agents, if not their motivations. Many were selected from the Veteran's Reserve Corps, a unit of men disabled by the war but still able to function in a bureaucratic capacity. In Georgia alone, almost half of the assistant bureau commissioners or assistant inspector generals (the regional directors of the bureau) had lost limbs or hands. Moreover, it is striking how many of the amputee bureau employees were outspoken supporters of Reconstruction, from agents up to regional commissioners. One, for example, who had lost an arm and was injured in the other hand was described by a contemporary as "a *splendid man, heart and soul* in the cause."[12]

Tourgée was actively involved in the work of the Freedmen's Bureau in Greensboro, and while the bureau agents and the task of teaching formerly enslaved people make up only a small part of *Bricks without Straw*, the trope of the amputee warrior for Black self-determination infuses the novel. Tourgée returns again and again to the amputated bodies of Union soldiers and sympathizers as the agents of reparation and justice for Black citizens. But this justice is not just the work of white radicals and sympathetic northerners like the female protagonist of the novel, Mollie Ainslie, a young woman who comes to the South after the wartime death of her brother to work as a schoolteacher in Red Wing. Justice is struggled for by Black characters, who lay claim to the rights accorded them by the Reconstruction Amendments—the Thirteenth, Fourteenth, and Fifteenth. When Nimbus takes a complaint to the bureau against Desmit, the man who had enslaved him before the war and was suing him for encouraging a friend to leave his employ, his case is heard by "a captain of the United States infantry, [who] was a man of about forty-five years of age, grave and serious of look, with an empty sleeve folded decorously over his breast. His calm blue eyes, refined face, and serious air gave him the appearance of a minister."[13] The captain decides that forcing employees to remain in a job because of exploitive contracts runs counter to the emancipation amendments and finds for Nimbus.

This unnamed officer combines military heroism, physical suffering, dignity, and spiritual purity. His "empty sleeve" is a sign not just of his bravery and loss but also provides another mode of expression for his calmness and refinement: It is "decorously" folded, imbued with seriousness and gentility. The empty sleeve also seems to intensify his "serious air," which "gave him the appearance of a minister," as though his physical sacrifice in war analogizes to the spiritual commitment to service shared by clergy. Nimbus himself links his new rights with national transformation and "was glad that there was a law for him—a law that put him on the level with his old master—and meditated gratefully, as he rode home, on what the nation had wrought."[14]

The agent's decision in favor of Nimbus intensifies the white townspeople's already powerful opposition to the bureau. In Tourgée's narration, at the core of white southern resistance to Black equality are both racism and a mistaken belief in southern superiority overall, the belief that the Confederacy had been "in all things utterly innocent and guileless." Unlike their pro-Union counterparts, southerners regard the damage and losses they have sustained as disabling the possibility that the nation could return to its former condition, whose disappearance they mourn: They experience injury without a vision of redemption (or, rather, they regard the virtual reenslavement of Black citizens *as* redemption). As Tourgée argues, they see Reconstruction as a vindictive punishment "done solely and purposely to injure the master, to punish the rebel, and to further cripple and impoverish the South."[15] Given Tourgée's use of injury and disability as tropes for remaking the nation along egalitarian, antiracist lines, it is hard not to see the use of "injure" and "cripple" here as undergirding the novel's condemnation of white supremacy: Not only do white Southerners not accept Black humanity and dignity, but they appropriate the very terms, the bodily sacrifices that underwrite a reconstructed Union.

For Tourgée, then, the error that white southerners commit is not just a refusal to see that slavery was wrong or that formerly enslaved people deserve human and civil rights. Rather, it's that they fundamentally misunderstand the meaning of the damage done by the war itself, both to the nation and to the bodies of the soldiers who fought in it. For them, injury is another reason for resentment and holding onto the past, instead of looking toward the future. Moreover, they wholly ignore the centuries-long injury done to the people they enslaved, whom they left totally impoverished and saw as their right to punish.

Over the course of the novel, Hesden's growing refusal to celebrate the past and his investment in an egalitarian future gives his physical injury greater meaning. He becomes increasingly convinced of the need for this work of remaking and rebuilding. A Ku Klux Klan raid on Red Wing intensifies Hesden's antipathy toward the South, aligning him with the Black citizens of the area. As well as being characterized by the brutal violence typical of Klan attacks, this incident is marked by an attack on the disabled preacher Eliab Hill. Eliab's disability is significant—his legs have been withered by illness. Before Mollie Ainsley comes to Red Wing, he has been the sole teacher for the community. Equally important, he supports Black self-reliance and self-determination.

The Klan raid culminates with the (implicit) rape of Lugena, Nimbus's wife, and an attack on Eliab. Given that the loss of the use of a limb by white characters in *Bricks without Straw* signifies the promise of progressive change, it is significant that the violence toward Eliab is a cruel parody of the healing of his disability and of amputation of a leg:

> There was a fall upon the cabin floor—the grating sound of a body swiftly drawn along its surface, and one of the masked marauders rushed out dragging by the foot the preacher of the Gospel of Peace. The withered leg was straightened. The weaken sinews were torn asunder, and as his captor dragged him out into the light and flung the burden away, the limb dropped, lax and nerveless to the ground.[16]

In this passage, Eliab's body is resected—"the withered leg was straightened"—and dissected—"the limb dropped"—by Klan aggression. The attackers pervert the logic of bodily loss in the service of racist violence, which transforms Hesden's relationship to the community of Red Wing and the work of Reconstruction.

Up until this moment, Hesden had subscribed to the efficacy of Reconstruction and the efforts of the bureau, but within a pragmatic, legalistic frame in which Black rights existed because of the power of the federal government to secure and enforce them, not for intrinsic constitutional, ethical, or justice-oriented reasons. After the attack, however, he

> had begun to question—God forgive him, if it felt like sacrilege—he had be-gun to question whether the South might not have been wrong—might not still be wrong—wrong in the principle and practice of slavery, wrong in the theory and fact of secession and rebellion, wrong in the hypothesis of hate on the part of the conquerors, wrong in the assumption of exceptional and un-approachable excellence.[17]

Given the logic of the novel and its representation of amputation as a result of the inequities of the slave system as well as a conduit to undoing those inequities, it's not surprising that Hesden, the sole amputee protagonist in the text, becomes increasingly disillusioned with the South's claim to superiority and opposed to the exercise of white supremacy via the violence of slavery or of Klan vigilantism.

Hesden's body becomes the nexus of the various antiracist, Black emancipa-tion impulses of the other characters in the novel. As the switchpoint between white radicalism and Black self-determination, his lost arm the sign of his even-tual rejection of the Confederacy, Hesden ends up believing that "it was most fortunate and providential that the Confederacy had failed."[18] By extension, he recognizes the bodily loss suffered by Confederate troops as not doing the work it should have—representing a microcosm of the larger defeat of the South, which had failed to convince many southerners that their cause was wrong. Ultimately, he sees southern resistance to Reconstruction as a rejection of American identity tout court: "There was nothing his class could gain [through Reconstruction] except a share in the ultimate glory and success of an enlarged and solidified nation" (322). Whereas the amputated Freedmen's Bureau agents give meaning and a kind of nobility to self-sacrifice, to have lost so much yet still believe in the Confederate cause is not just disloyal—it is to squander the opportunity to participate in the rebuilt nation's "ultimate glory and success."

Such a commitment to a newly constituted nation requires the abandonment of any nostalgia for the past: past political systems, past racial hierarchies, past bodies. Hesden "regarded the experiment of reconstruction, as he believed, with calm, unprejudiced sincerity; he had buried the past, and looked only to the fu-ture."[19] As I've argued, amputation forces readers of *Bricks without Straw* to focus on the present and move beyond the past, in recognition that the past of the intact body is irrecoverable and that the past of an ostensibly intact nation—held together by the ligaments of slavery—was diseased from the very beginning. This echoes Tourgée's own goals for Reconstruction. He rejected the goal simply of preserving the Union, avowing, "I don't care a rag for '*the Union as it was*.' I want and fight for the *Union better* than '*it was*.'"[20]

Tourgée's radical declaration of an emancipated future was, if we credit Oliver O. Howard, a common belief among northerners a few years into the Civil War. In 1860 to 1861, when the war was still in its early days, "military operations were influenced very much in the interest of slavery by purely political considerations. Plans were modified by the endeavor not so much to conquer an enemy under arms, as to restore the Union or preserve the Union." By 1862, according to Howard, this had changed, and "the majority [of northerners] evidently inclin[ed] to the belief that 'the Union as it was' could never be restored."[21]

The phrase "the Union as it was," which characterized the retrospective narratives of Tourgée and Howard, was also part of political speech during the Civil War that did important imaginative work.[22] Although Lincoln famously refused to see the Confederacy as a separate or seceded government and insisted that the Union was simply putting down an insurrection, the phrase "the Union as it was" when uttered in 1862 or 1863 suggests a sharp break with the recent past, relegating a Union economically and socially defined by its inextricability from slavery, and grammatically as something that has already disappeared, to the past.

Of course, the hope that the sacrifices of the war would lead to a reconstituted, reconstructed nation was not fully realized, even during the years of Radical Reconstruction. As African Americans were finding their way to schools and polls, to literacy and even elected office, the backlash against formerly enslaved people claiming their freedom was violent and omnipresent. In every report of the bureau, in every region where the bureau had offices, there are records of murders, rapes, whippings, beatings, shootings, and lynchings attempted and actual, as well as the exploitation of Black workers by planters and employers more generally. As Oliver Howard observed, "The reports of murders, assaults, and outrages of every description were so numerous and so full of horrible details, that at times one was inclined to believe the whole white population engaged in a war of extermination against the blacks."[23]

As Howard realized later, though, the goal was not genocide (although it may have often felt that way) but a desire to reconstitute "the Union as it was"—to ignore the meaning of amputation that Tourgée and Howard embraced. Howard recognized that white southerners were playing a long game, waiting for the opportunity to turn back the clock on emancipation and racial equality. In the form of the Ku Klux Klan and other white vigilante groups, "the main object from first to last was somehow to regain and maintain over the negro that ascendancy which slavery gave, and which was being lost by emancipation, education, and suffrage."[24] This extreme violence is a kind of bitter repetition compulsion, a white supremacist melancholia, in which the lost object of slavery is replayed by white southerners within the new context of emancipation. If for Howard, and in *Bricks without Straw*, amputation and loss provide a language for accounting for the damage slavery did to African Americans and imagining a reconstituted, reconstructed nation forged in the context of that language, the viciousness with which the gains of Reconstruction were clawed back through damage to Black bodies are a kind of inverse: reparations to white southerners for the losses they believed that Black liberation visited upon them.

At this moment in which we are now living, in which the symbolic amputation of memorial statues to Confederate leaders (among others) is being effected by popular action, it is worth remembering *Bricks without Straw* and the work of the Freedmen's Bureau. Once again, white Americans are forced (or, in the best-case scenario, are choosing) to recognize that eradicating the legacy of enslavement requires experiencing a meaningful and important loss: that of the unacknowledged advantages of white supremacy. We might look to Tourgée to strategize how best and most lastingly to embrace that loss for the benefit of a newly made nation. Not "the Union as it was" but "the Union as it might be."

Notes

1. For a detailed discussion of the work of the Freedmen's Bureau, see Eric Foner, *Reconstruction: America's Unfinished Revolution, 1863–1877* (New York: Harper Perennials, 1989).

2. Albion Tourgée, *Bricks without Straw* (1880), ed. Carolyn L. Karcher (Durham, NC: Duke University Press, 2009).

3. Oliver Otis Howard, *Autobiography of Oliver Otis Howard*, 2 vols. (New York: The Baker and Taylor Company, 1907), 1:12–13.

4. Howard, *Autobiography*, 2:441.

5. Howard, *Autobiography*, 1:247, 250.

6. Howard, *Autobiography*, 2:314, 315.

7. Howard, *Autobiography*, 2:363–64, 423.

8. Howard, *Autobiography*, 2:338.

9. Tourgée, *Bricks without Straw*, 140, 247.

10. Tourgée, *Bricks without Straw*, 157, 158.

11. Tourgée, *Bricks without Straw*, 158. Tourgée's uncritical estimation of Freedmen's Bureau agents is only partially true, of course. The bureau was a decidedly mixed bag in which agents "brought to their posts a combination of paternalist assumptions about race and sensitivity to the plight of blacks, the precise mixture varying with the indi-

vidual." Foner, *Reconstruction*, 142. In addition, there was quite a bit of turnover both in leadership positions and of agents at the local level: An egalitarian former abolitionist could be replaced by a more conservative and pragmatic agent more inclined to conform to the dictates of white supremacy, and vice versa. Finally, as Eric Foner has shown, bureau leadership largely subscribed to free-labor politics, which did not take into account the exploitive nature of the work contracts freedpeople were pressured to sign and saw any kind of distribution of aid in the form of food, clothing, and the like as charity that could make them dependent upon government aid. Many bureau employees mostly believed in the laissez-faire economic policies dominant at the time and were convinced that freedpeople would achieve economic mobility through hard work and self-denial.

12. Paul Cimbala, *Under the Guardianship of the Nation: The Freedmen's Bureau and the Reconstruction of Georgia, 1865–1870* (Athens: University of Georgia Press, 1997), 53, 51.

13. Tourgée, *Bricks without Straw*, 160. In fact, leaving the employment of a person with whom one had signed a labor contract, or convincing someone else to leave, was a crime under many of the notorious "Black Codes" of the mid-1860s. See Harold Woodman, *New South, New Law: The Legal Foundations of Credit and Labor Relations in the Postbellum Agricultural South* (Baton Rouge: Louisiana State University Press, 1995), for a detailed description of the Black Codes related to employment policy.

14. Tourgée, *Bricks without Straw*, 160.

15. Tourgée, *Bricks without Straw*, 156, 320.

16. Tourgée, *Bricks without Straw*, 276.

17. Tourgée, *Bricks without Straw*, 291.

18. Tourgée, *Bricks without Straw*, 312.

19. Tourgée, *Bricks without Straw*, 377.

20. Qtd. by Karcher in the Introduction to *Bricks without Straw*, 8.

21. Howard, *Autobiography*, 1:191, 202.

22. An August 27, 1862, letter to the *New York Times* invokes the distinction between "the Union as it was" and "the Union as it ought to be," dismissing the debate between the two as "bosh." According to the writer, "H.R.R.," "Slavery is already dead—beyond the possibility of resurrection." At the end of the letter, the author reiterates the central point: "Slavery is dead—past surgery—and the cry about restoring the Union with Slavery, or without it, amounts to nothing." The Democratic Party slogan for the 1864 election was "The Union as it was, and the Constitution as it is."

23. Howard, *Autobiography*, 2:370.

24. Howard, *Autobiography*, 2:375.

14

Tracking Redress in the West

The Railroad in Tourgée's
Figs and Thistles *and Ruiz de*
Burton's The Squatter and the Don

Annemarie Mott Ewing

S et in the postwar South, Albion Tourgée's most popular novels, *A Fool's Errand* (1879) and *Bricks without Straw* (1880), depict the fraught racial politics of the reuniting nation. Tourgée intended his provocative novel *Figs and Thistles: A Romance of the Western Reserve* (1879) to be read alongside *A Fool's Errand* and *Bricks without Straw* and three other historical novels as a series.[1] Set in the area of Ohio known as the Western Reserve, *Figs and Thistles* reveals Tourgée's geographically expansive intervention into Reconstruction politics and depicts the tensions of a country whose "Star of Ambition as well as Empire takes its course to the Westward."[2] A critical look at this rarely studied novel offers an opportunity to consider the role of the West in Reconstruction politics. Reconstruction did not just attempt to reunite the nation or rebuild the South. Instead, as the historian Heather Cox Richardson argues, Reconstruction also solidified national identity and positioned the United States as an empire. The national identity emerging during Reconstruction rooted itself in mythologies of the American West and was closely linked to both the emerging definition of citizenship and to government's changing relationship to its citizens. Attending to the West, therefore, elucidates the paradox of "nineteenth-century Americans justify[ing] expansion of government activism and still retain[ing] their wholehearted belief in individualism."[3] During Reconstruction, this paradoxical ideology was deployed to exclude some from the rights of full citizenship while aiding others, including corporations, who then falsely appeared to succeed on the basis of merit alone. To better illuminate the potency of this emerging ideology, we might consider another novel with a purpose set in the West, María Amparo Ruiz de Burton's *The Squatter and the Don* (1885), which similarly revolves around depictions of the railroad's construction and expansion. Set a decade after *Figs and Thistles*, *Squatter* portrays the longer-term consequences of the corporate and governmental corruption that Tourgée exposes.

Tourgée's and Ruiz de Burton's novels powerfully delineate the role of the West in Reconstruction politics and its lasting effects on national identity and citizenship. These novels critique both the commonplace of the West as a land of self-made opportunity and the railroad as a symbol of American progress and prosperity. Instead, they frame the railroad's construction and westward expansion as the government's capitulation to the seductive power of imperialism and corporate greed. Moreover, these novels depict citizenship's emerging ideological definition in this period as one located in congressional politics related to westward expansion, and they are both deeply concerned with reparative justice. Written after the injustices they identify, they invite readers to picture the moment of error, imagine an alternate future, and subsequently envision redress. By looking closely at several key moments in these novels, I show that Tourgée and Ruiz de Burton trace plotlines that begin with misdeeds and resolve in regret, confession, and reparative action. In so doing, they allegorize a call for national repair related to the injustices they expose.

The American West and the railroad that spanned it played a critical role in the nineteenth-century American imaginary. The rendering of the American West as a land of prosperity and adventure was ubiquitous by the time Tourgée and Ruiz de Burton penned their novels. The railroad, long figured as a symbol of progress and conquest, raced from each coast to meet at Promontory Point, Utah, in 1869. Some claimed that the golden spike connecting the westbound and eastbound sections of track just four years after the Civil War's end represented the victory of a unified nation and the promise of opportunity and interracial democracy. In fact, the end of Tourgée's *Bricks without Straw* (1880) locates hope for a prosperous, interracial community during Reconstruction in the fictional Eupolia, Kansas, along its new railroad track. In *Bricks*, Tourgée grapples with the devastating need for ongoing federal intervention in the South and asserts that without it, the opportunity for an interracial democracy will lie only in the "ever-welcoming far West"[4] and no longer in reconstructing North Carolina.

While acknowledging the benefits of the economic growth surrounding the railroad, Tourgée resists representing the railroad as an uncontested symbol of national unity or hope. His later writing links the railroad's development directly to imperialist expansionism and white supremacy. In 1885, the same year Ruiz de Burton published *Squatter*, Tourgée's description of those moving west has become less rosy than in *Bricks*. He describes those settling in California as

Anglo-Saxon invaders . . . inflamed with lustful greed [who] have dammed the rivers, tunneled the mountains, and chained the torrents to the unseemly task of leveling the hills and scarifying the valleys. The adventurous hordes have already founded an empire facing the western sea, and bound it to the East with bands of iron along which civilization—*our* civilization—throbs and pulses like a mighty fever.[5]

Rather than portraying westward expansion under what the scholar Manu Karuka calls the "colonialist alibi of 'improvement,'" Tourgée implicates it in the destruction of nature and likens the railroad to chains imprisoning the land. He characterizes the West as a place of freedom and majesty threatened by settler colonialism. In a reversal of common racialized depictions of nineteenth-century Chinese immigrants, Tourgée describes the white settlers as feverish "adventurous hordes" and "invaders." Far before US acquisition of overseas territories, he identifies the imperialist aims of the United States in its railroad expansion and pinpoints how the transcontinental railroad "symbolically finalized the industrial infrastructure of a continental empire where none had existed before."[6]

More than just a static symbol, Tourgée depicts the railroad in *Figs and Thistles* as having agency and being capable of seduction. Its success depends in part on the railroad corporations' ability to convince lawmakers to overlook their personal ethics to support the railroad's construction. To portray this seduction, Tourgée writes a semiautobiographical morality tale. The novel opens with a humorous prologue categorizing each character as either a beneficial "fig" or an obstructive "thistle." [7] Tourgée lists his self-made protagonist, Markham Churr, as a "fig-bearing thistle," a category recognized as an oxymoron by the biblical allusion from which these epithets originate (i). A "poor man's orphan" (i), Markham rises to fame as a soldier in the Union Army. After being injured in the Battle of Bull Run, Markham is elected to Congress, where he faces both the temptation and blackmail of the railroad corporation's lobby. Steadfast, Markham and his wife, Lizzie, comprise the moral compass of the novel. They jointly and repeatedly remind others of small-town ethics, are undeterred by the temptations of wealth, and remain faithful to the end.

Tourgée incisively exposes the dangers of the imbricated interests of government and the railroad corporations through Markham's friendship with his benefactor-turned-foe Boaz Woodley. Woodley, predictably identified by Tourgée as "one of the thistles" (ii), is instrumental in Markham's career and supports his election to Congress. Markham relies on Woodley's expertise and knowledge in his early days as a congressman. When "appointed as the chairman of the special committee in regard to the charter of the T.C.R. Co," Markham tasks Woodley with research and mastery of the charter (354). Eventually Woodley, who has become colonel and chief of military railway transportation and president of the Transcontinental Railway Company, pressures Markham to vote in favor of a bill to amend the charter and create a new company making the "Mississippi an impassable barrier to rival enterprises" (359). Unbeknownst to Markham, Woodley has been investing Markham's money heavily in the railroad. When it comes time to vote, Markham finds himself in an ethical bind. While he believes the railroad to be "a good thing for the country, and the best use [for] the public lands" (443), he finds the bill's "provisions unwise" (364), as they will increase debt and disproportionately benefit the corporate owners. Markham faces the threat of financial and personal ruin from Woodley if he votes his conscience. Despite this, he unwaveringly acknowledges the clear ethical violations involved in the government's role in the construction of the railroad. He votes with the minority, against his own interests.

In stark contrast to Markham's resistance, Woodley's seduction by the railroad better represents the majority of the congressmen's reaction. Their unbridled support incriminates the lawmakers. Woodley finds the railroad irresistible. He is "charmed" by it as he "grasp[s] its vastness" (365). The scale of its ambition was "a conception of such magnificent audacity that [he] yielded at once to its fascination" (356). "The Trans-Continental had entered into his soul . . . the thirst of the conqueror filled him" (357). Tourgée's narrator describes the railroad's power as able to spiritually possess its patrons and inspire insatiable desire. The sheer scale of the "new worlds to subdue" bewitch Woodley into full-throated support without any regard for public good and without posing a challenge to the corporation's right to profit from the rails. "What reward was sufficient . . . what terms should be proffered to those who offered to found empires? Why speak of chaffering with them?" For a dream so "kingly," the "recompense" should be "regal. . . . So said the committee; so said the nation; and so the Congress enacted!" (356). Blinded by the scope of the conquest, Tourgée suggests, civic leaders broadly authorized the rights of the railroad and eschewed any restraint to protect the public good. Tourgée portrays this ambitious project as one driven by an Ahab-like obsession, with no sound reasoning, no "chaffering" over the budget or scope or consideration of whom it benefits. Who haggles over an opportunity to "defy Boreas and conquer the desert" (357)? Only Markham Churr.

Tourgée's portrayal of Congress's capitulation to the railroad links the government's land grants directly to the seductive power of imperialist continental expansion and Indigenous dispossession. Woodley notes that "the land the government has given it alone is almost an empire" (427). He imagines that the railroad will "project that line through the wilderness which the foot of the trapper had never trodden, to climb the mountains where the Indian had found no thoroughfare" and "fill the silent space between with the voice of many peoples" (356). The railroad will conquer and multiply, populating a vast emptiness as it "wrest[s] an empire from savagery" (356). Here the text acknowledges the US government's duplicity as it disregards its treaties recognizing Indigenous lands in order to offer those same lands to railroad corporations. In 1862, the Pacific Railroad Act extinguished Indigenous land titles and redesignated land contiguous to the railroad as public land.[8] Tourgée cites racism as the justification for such dispossession, arguing in "Study in Civilization" that "race prejudice is so intense that no considerations of justice, humanity, or religion have hitherto been sufficient to compel us to recognize the civil or political equality of the Indian."[9] Tourgée represents the refusal to recognize Indigenous rights as imbricated with the imperialistic, expansionist compulsion to expand the railroad.

For Woodley, and by extension perhaps for Congress, the allure of the railroad lies not just in the conquest of the land but in the very opportunity to advance the progression of time itself, ushering in a mode of imperialistic time.[10] In the nineteenth-century imaginary, the railroad often symbolized the outpacing of traditional modes of time, both in the way it changed the regions it connected and one's temporal experience onboard. Traveling by train had a "jarring effect . . . on the senses" as vast distances were covered in a day in ways both exhilarating and disorienting to passengers and onlookers alike.[11] Woodley's contemplation of the railroad's rapid development mirrors the experience of train travel. As he considers the railroad project, enabled by rapid industrialization, time blurs, disorienting him, and it seems as if the "hands upon the dial of Time were about to be moved forward a century in a single decade" (356). His thoughts collapse time, betraying a temporality disrupted by imperialistic ambition. He expects to "add to his laurels the subjection of Time" (357). Carried away in his own reverie, he "for[gets] that his thought had outrun the present, and had leaped the barrier of time" (356). Additionally, because of the competition between the railway companies, the very construction of the railroad is characterized by an urgent impatience. As Woodley "swe[eps] his finger . . . rapidly" across the map, he notes that "time is the essence of . . . success" in this endeavor (367).

Woodley's imperialistic time is echoed in Ruiz de Burton, who, as Brook Thomas argues, saw railroads as effecting a "temporal transformation."[12] In *The Squatter and the Don*, this same mode of imperialistic time allows the law to be "much disregarded and sadly dilatory" in the protection of the Mexican American ranchers' land while expedient in its funding of railroad corporations.[13] Unlike the railroad standard time that was eventually established in 1883, the imperialistic time of Tourgée's and Ruiz de Burton's novels is anything but standard.[14] Instead, it unreliably slows and advances, persuades and seduces, leading to dispossession and unchecked corporate power.

Like *Figs and Thistles*, Ruiz de Burton's novel critiques the commonplace of the West as a land of self-made opportunity. She decries the seductive power of wealth and unscrupulous business dealings in the construction of the railroad. Her censure, however, pertains less to the corrupt nature of the railroad's funding, which is Tourgée's main concern, and more to the effects of the railroad's unchecked corporate power and lack of oversight as it expands west. *The Squatter and the Don* tells the story of Mexican American ranchers who continue to face the devastating consequences of the California Land Act of 1851. This act allowed settlers to claim Mexican land grants, thereby dispossessing Mexican Americans of their land while the claims were reviewed in a lengthy investigative process.[15] Opening in 1872, *Squatter* portrays the devastating effects of both this ongoing expropriation of land and the railroad's unkept assurances about its expansion to San Diego. Just as in *Figs and Thistles*, the novel portrays the allure of the railroad as it tempts many to unethical activity, "subverting the fundamental principles of public morality," and "*lead[ing] others* into the commission of the same crimes."[16]

Ruiz de Burton depicts the wealth gained by railroad officials as having come at the expense of Mexican American ranchers and exposes the misguided attempts to claim the railroad's success as the result of their own entrepreneurial efforts. At the end of the novel, a wealthy railroad magnate offers a toast at a wedding to this enterprising spirit. "Inflated with pride" and attempting to "wax eloquent and didactic," he encourages the young men listening to be "plucky and persevering, and go ahead" to make their fortunes and rise from poverty as he has done. As one guest observed, one could easily be "*plucky and persevering* if [he] had an associate in Washington with plenty of money to bribe people" to eliminate competition from another railroad. Another man responds that he, too, would be plucky if the government had given him "millions of money and more millions of acres to build two railroads," without taxes, with no intent to repay. Ruiz de Burton's wedding guests condemn the same unchecked power that Tourgée's protagonist decries: Congress's complete abdication of its responsibility to hold corporations to their commitment to the public good. This lack of oversight awards public land to companies that will, in turn, profit exclusively. Ruiz de Burton quotes directly from a letter written by Collis Huntington, one of the Big Four, in which he admits that he was able to "fix up a railroad committee in the senate . . . just as [he] wants it."[17] One might imagine this committee with Tourgée's Boaz Woodley at its helm.

Tourgée depicts railroad corporations' coercion of Congress with promises of wealth and a legacy of imperial conquest. Disrupting the notion of the West later characterized by Frederick Jackson Turner as "dominant individualism,"[18] Tourgée's novel suggests that many who succeed in the West are bolstered by government aid at the expense of others left unaided, dispossessed, and disenfranchised. Ruiz de Burton's novel more directly exposes the railroad magnates not as self-made entrepreneurs but as frauds funded by government grants. She unmasks the mythology surrounding these pioneers of industry, revealing the corporations and their unethical ties to Congress as the true power. Additionally, in Tourgée's highly stylized novel the railroad's agency blurs the line between person and corporation.

These two novels reveal the hypocrisy of a nation offering full rights of personhood and support to corporations while denying them to many people. In so doing, they illuminate the Reconstruction period's emerging definition of citizenship, which was contested even as the Reconstruction Amendments sought to clarify it. The Fourteenth Amendment, ratified in 1868, granted citizenship rights to those born or naturalized in the United States and declared that no state should "deny to any person within its jurisdiction the equal protection of the law." While the amendment still excluded many from citizenship, including women and Indigenous people, it did enfranchise African American men and protected their rights. This amendment, however, had the unintended consequence of establishing "corporate personhood."[19] Previously, the Supreme Court decision in *Dartmouth v. Woodward* (1819) defined a corporation as "an artificial being, invisible, intangible, and existing only in contemplation of law." Because corporations could only exist with state sanction, for the first half of the nineteenth century their charters often ensured the public's protection. Over the next decades, however, corporations began to be considered "aggregates of individuals" rather than "imaginary being[s]." Corporations existed in this slippery middle ground until 1882, when the argument was made in *San Mateo County v. Southern Pacific Railroad* that they deserved to be covered by the Fourteenth Amendment's equal protection clause.[20] Incongruously, the very amendment that expanded rights of citizenship to include African Americans also eventually endowed these same privileges to corporate bodies. These strengthened corporate rights enabled imperialistic westward expansion and Indigenous and Mexican American dispossession, as depicted in both Tourgée's and Ruiz de Burton's novels.

Having served as an elected member of the North Carolina Constitutional Convention of 1868, Tourgée was well versed in the politics surrounding corporate rights with regard to the railroad. Tourgée recognized the benefits of railroad expansion, if done ethically with an emphasis on local control. As noted earlier, in *Bricks without Straw* (1880) he wrote enthusiastically about the opportunities the railroad offered newly emancipated African Americans who followed it west into Kansas. He also recognized the dangers related to expansion, however, and passionately defended the necessity of curbing corporate and industrial rights. He opposed government bailouts to railroads because he believed they would unfairly tax those who did not own land.[21] Instead, he supported the National Anti-Monopoly Cheap-Freight Railroad League and Lorenzo Sherwood's proposal for the government to build the railroad itself.[22] Tourgée defended a township system of local control that would protect the landless, incubate democracy, and promote universal education to unite the North and South. He repeatedly appealed to the notion that public land should be used for public good, just as his protagonist Markham does.

In their personal writings, both Tourgée and Ruiz de Burton claim to write fiction to intervene in the politics of their moment. Both of the novels considered here critique the mythology of the West and expose the image of self-made success, showing how it is enabled by government. They highlight the inconsistencies regarding citizenship in this period, one in which the government grants corporations far-reaching privileges and protections while refusing the same to many people. They reveal the racialized and exclusionary politics with regard to the expanding West and depict how those politics allowed for citizenship's ongoing exclusions as the prevailing ideology cast the dispossessed as a special interest group and exhorted them to pursue opportunity through self-reliance. They unmask the myth of the United States, metonymized here by the West, as a meritocracy by instead depicting its unjust partiality. But to what aim are these exposures made? What intervention might these novels suggest? It is my contention that these novels are deeply concerned with reparative justice and demand it by featuring narratives of theft, confession, and redress.

Allegorizing a call for national repair, *Figs and Thistles* traces parallel plotlines of restitution. The action of *Figs* begins in earnest with a bank robbery that shocks the small town of Aychitula. Tourgée's protagonist, Markham, determines that Frank Horton, the son of the bank's cashier, is the thief. Upon being confronted, Horton confesses and flees to serve in the Civil War, hoping to redeem himself as a Union soldier. He promises in a letter confessing his crimes that if he can "redeem the past, [he] will" (210). Horton's personal redemption is acknowledged sometime later, on the battlefield in 1863, where he requests a meeting with Markham. Markham greets Horton warmly and admits he is glad to see that he has not "throw[n] away a future which might easily be made to atone for the past" (308). In Markham's estimation, Horton's rise in the ranks of the Union Army has proven that he is an honorable patriot.

In the ensuing conversation between Markham and Horton, Tourgée theorizes an ethics of redress. Horton has sought the meeting to "begin the work of reparation" (308). He admits that he can never "compensate his father for the suffering [his] act has cost him, but [he] can make good on the loss" (309). He offers Markham a check to repay his debt. But Horton extends far less grace to himself, arguing that he must not ever return to Aychitula and will instead continue to live an honorable life under an assumed name. In this exchange, through Markham, Tourgée depicts what complete restitution for wrong entails. Markham rejects the harshness of Horton's self-condemnation. He urges him to return to their town and "resume his name and abandon the idea of hiding from a fault which had already been amply expiated" (313). By the end of the novel, Markham maneuvers circumstances to ensure that the entire town warmly receives Horton in a touching scene of restoration.

Squatter also features themes of restoration and repair. Early on, the novel depicts Mrs. Darrell in a domestic act of repair, darning her husband's socks while exhorting him to be "guided by . . . past history" and avoid his recent error of misappropriating land he thought was available for settlement in Sacramento. On the eve of his departure to southern California, his wife begs him not to locate a homestead claim without buying directly from a Mexican grantee "on fair conditions and clear understanding," regardless of what the government allows. In the marital dispute that ensues, Ruiz de Burton masterfully interweaves what will be the concepts at the forefront of her novel: discrepancies between what is legal and ethical, concepts of public and private property, and the government's role in land grants and subsidies both to settlers and the railroad. This domestic scene also portrays repentance and reinstatement, much like Horton's example in *Figs*. As Mr. Darrell asks his wife if she can "forgive [his] past wickedness" because he'll "try to do better," she rejects his apology and reframes his actions as an unintentional "misappl[ication] of [his] rights."[23] More radically, she implies that the only meaningful repentance is the avoidance of further acts of injustice.

Ruiz de Burton invites the consideration of how the United States might repair its relationship to Mexican American ranchers by showing an example of a contrite and regretful squatter whose family makes restitution. Despite his promise to his wife, Mr. Darrell does settle on land that belongs to Don Mariano. Without her husband's knowledge, Mrs. Darrell instructs her son Clarence to pay the Don for the land. She passionately prevails upon the other homesteaders squatting on his land, which has been "claimed as Mexican land grants," to ascertain the difference between legal and moral right. Lawmakers may intend well, she argues, but "through lack of matured reflection . . . or lack of unbiased thought" they have "legislated curses upon this land of God's blessings."[24] Though the homesteaders are "deeply impressed by her words," Mr. Darrell remains unmoved.

Ruiz de Burton's portrayal of Mr. Darrell's eventual moment of regret gestures powerfully toward the concept of redress and its relationship to nostalgic imagination. Because of Darrell's ruptured relationship with the Don, his son Clarence will no longer marry the Don's daughter. One evening, Darrell spies a squatter who is now the Don's son-in-law "carrying his baby boy in his arms, kissing him at every few words." Watching the scene causes Darrell to feel a nostalgic happiness that turns quickly to regret. He "tremble[s] with the strength of his keen remorse—remorse which now constantly visit[s] him, invading his spirit with a relentless fury, like a pitiless foe that gave no quarter." Darrell's nostalgia quickly turns to grief in the face of the imagined present and future that he has forestalled. "In another year" a grandchild could have been a reality if he had acted differently. [25]

The nostalgic gaze in each of these novels invites reparative action. As Paul Saint-Amour argues, "counterfactual narratives of the present" share "a homesickness for a different present" in a way that is deeply connected to "reparation's backward look." Just as "reparation and admonition idealize the status quo ante," courtrooms often employ counterfactual thinking to calculate redress. [26] Darrell's recognition of future loss prompts him to look backward in order to find the cause of his misfortune and begin to consider repair. What could have been mutually gained had Mexican ranchers been treated in practice as American citizens by the squatters? The symbolic futurity of this imagined child, born of the union between an American settler and Mexican rancher family, compels readers to imagine new possibilities, including redress. On the final pages of the novel, Darrell confesses his wrongs to his son. He admits that his "wickedness . . . brought infinite misery upon this innocent family." He commissions Clarence to "devote [his] life to repair as much as it is possible the wrong [his] father did."[27] Confession leads to the commissioning of reparation, perhaps in the same way Ruiz de Burton hopes the United States will regret and repair its "legislated curses." Tourgée's Woodley eventually experiences this same nostalgic regret on his deathbed when he begs Markham and Lizzie to "Forgive!" (502).

Both *The Squatter and the Don* and *Figs and Thistles* boldly place the West at the center of Reconstruction politics. From this vantage point, they frame the politics of citizenship, including that of the postwar South, in the larger context of the imperialistic practices of westward expansion enabled by corporate power. They expose the myth of the United States as a meritocracy and incisively reveal the hypocrisy of a nation that grants personhood to corporations while excluding persons from citizenship. Ruiz de Burton makes her claim for redress clear. Openly characterizing the railroad as a thief, she argues that it must return the property it has stolen but believes this will only occur if "the people of California take the law into their own hands, and seize the property of those men, and confiscate it, to reimburse the money due the people." Otherwise, "the arrogant corporation will never pay."[28] Throughout his novel, Tourgée strikes a more hopeful tone, acknowledging the potential for the nation to provide restitution, a path he hopes might be taken for the nation of thistles to become fig bearing. But exactly what figs might the nation bear? What fruitful form of redress might Tourgée's novel suggest, either in its moment of publication or now? Perhaps redress could come in the form of a recalibration of how the government grants and protects citizenship as it expands. Perhaps it could take the form of curtailing corporate rights. Offering examples of what full restoration and ethical governance could look like, Tourgée ultimately leaves it up to his readers, who, like Frank Horton at the end of *Figs*, must find a way to reach the "remoter heirs" who have not yet been found or restored. In an era facing its own fraught debates about citizenship, reparative justice, and the ethics of corporate personhood, this conjuring of nineteenth-century speculative solutions represents a promising step toward contemporary solutions of repair.[29]

Notes

1. Albion Tourgée, *Hot Plowshares* (New York: Fords, Howard, and Hulbert, 1883), xiv.

2. Albion Tourgée, *Figs and Thistles: A Romance of the Western Reserve* (New York: Fords, Howard, and Hulbert, 1879), 98. All future page references to this novel will appear parenthetically in the main body of the text.

3. Heather Cox Richardson, *West from Appomattox: The Reconstruction of America after the Civil War* (New Haven, CT: Yale University Press, 2007), 4.

4. Albion Tourgée, *Bricks without Straw*, ed. Carolyn L. Karcher (Durham, NC: Duke University Press, 2009), 410.

5. Albion Tourgée, "Study in Civilization," *North American Review* 143, no. 358 (1886): 247.

6. Manu Karuka, *Empire's Tracks: Indigenous Nations, Chinese Workers, and the Transcontinental Railroad* (Oakland: University of California Press, 2019), xi, xiv.

7. Tourgée's categories originate from the warning in Matthew 7:16 that people will be known by their deeds—"You will recognize them by their fruits. Are grapes gathered from thornbushes, or figs from thistles?"

8. The Pacific Railroad Act of 1862, signed into law by President Lincoln, incorporated the Union Pacific and the Central Pacific railway companies. Among other provisions, it granted ten contiguous square miles of public land for each mile of track. In order to designate this land as public, the act stated that the "United States shall extinguish as rapidly as may be, the Indian titles to all lands falling under the operation of this act and required for the said right of way and grants hereinafter made." The Pacific Railroad Act, 37th Congress, 2nd. sess., chap. 120 (1862), 491–92.

9. Tourgée, "Study in Civilization," 265.

10. For more on the role of Indigenous temporalities and settler time, see Mark Rifkin, *Beyond Settler Time: Temporal Sovereignty and Indigenous Self-Determination* (Durham, NC: Duke University Press, 2017.)

11. William Deverell, *Railroad Crossing: Californians and the Railroad, 1850–1910* (Berkeley: University of California Press, 1994), 25.

12. Brook Thomas, *Literature of Reconstruction: Not in Plain Black and White* (Baltimore, MD: Johns Hopkins University Press, 2017), 213.

13. María Amparo Ruiz de Burton, *The Squatter and the Don* (1885; Houston, TX: Arte Publico, 1997), 279.

14. Richardson, *West from Appomattox*, 208.

15. Sharada Balachandran Orihuela, *Fugitives, Smugglers, and Thieves: Piracy and Personhood in American Literature* (Chapel Hill: University of North Carolina Press, 2018), 110.

16. Ruiz de Burton, *Squatter*, 367.

17. Ruiz de Burton, *Squatter*, 363, 369.

18. Frederick Jackson Turner, "The Significance of the Frontier in American History" (New York: Henry Holt and Co., 1920), 37.

19. Lisa Siraganian, *Modernism and the Meaning of Corporate Persons* (New York: Oxford University Press, 2020), 2. As a result of these Supreme Court rulings, corporations were granted the status of corporate personhood, which they still enjoy today. As Siraganian persuasively argues, however, "before Emancipation, African Americans and corporate persons were understood analogously in law: not as real persons . . . but as artificial creatures granted some of the characteristics of property and some of the qualities of persons. Because of this prior entanglement and the amendment's 'expansiveness and ambiguity,' the amendment allowed for the establishment of corporate personhood."

20. Thomas, *Literature of Reconstruction*, 230. The notion that this clause should apply to corporations appears again in a reporter's headnote to the Supreme Court's 1886 decision in *Santa Clara County v. Southern Pacific Railroad Company*. Hsuan L. Hsu, *Sitting in Darkness: Mark Twain's Asia and Comparative Racialization* (New York: New York University Press, 2015), 95.

21. Mark Elliott, *Color Blind Justice: Albion Tourgée and the Quest for Racial Equality from the Civil War to Plessy v. Ferguson* (New York: Oxford University Press, 2009), 131.

22. Thomas, *Literature of Reconstruction*, 234.

23. Ruiz de Burton, *Squatter*, 3, 5, 4.

24. Ruiz de Burton, *Squatter*, 236.

25. Ruiz de Burton, *Squatter*, 282.

26. Paul Saint-Amour. "Counterfactual States of America: On Parallel Worlds and Longing for the Law," *Post45* (2011): 4.

27. Ruiz de Burton, *Squatter*, 358, 358.

28. Ruiz de Burton, *Squatter*, 367.

29. In his 1890 *Pactolus Prime*, Tourgée addresses the question of reparations for slavery. See DeLisa Hawkes's discussion of that novel in this volume.

15

The Literary Lost Cause of Albion Tourgée

The Project of Our Continent

Mary B. Hale

O nly the supply of available talent will constrain the ambitions of the newly launched literary magazine *Our Continent*, Albion Tourgée and his assistant editors Daniel Brinton and Robert Davis promise their readers in the magazine's first issue in February 1882. "What the best brain procurable can furnish and the best taste may demand we shall do our 'level best' to supply,"[1] they announce, and indeed, from the start its pages are brimming. The first issue alone offered new fiction by Rebecca Harding Davis, a custom-designed masthead by Louis Comfort Tiffany, and an original poem by Oscar Wilde. Short book reviews cover an omnivorous selection of genres: a dictionary of quotations, a Parisian travel guide, a biography of Cardinal Newman, Herbert Spencer's latest theoretical writings, and even a new edition of the New Testament. In addition to its explicitly literary content, these dense weekly issues also included regular columns on an array of topics such as etiquette, scientific discoveries, home design, education, politics, fashion, cooking, and humor. The tremendous breadth of the magazine can make it difficult to ascertain who the intended audience was, other than to say that Tourgée and his editors clearly sought readers with at least some education and abundant curiosity. But while the magazine's breadth might initially make it sound like an unfocused hodge-podge, a close examination of its short run (1882–1884) reveals that a strong editorial point of view oversaw this project.

While inclusive of a range of topics, *Our Continent* is, as its stated commitment to the "best brain procurable" suggests, not without an evaluative or curatorial impulse. This discernment is most immediately apparent in the magazine's highly stylized design. For its first six months, *Our Continent* was published as a quarto rich in custom engravings and ornamental typefaces;[2] in this large-scale format, it announced itself as a significant newcomer on the literary scene. Tourgée considered the magazine the rival of prestigious monthlies such as *Harper's*, the *Atlantic*, and the *Century*, and given its weekly publishing schedule, it attempted even more than these well-established publications. It was, as Tourgée says, "the first serious attempt ever made to put into a weekly, the attractions and excellences of our great monthlies."[3] But the design and illustrations of *Our Continent* are more than just competitive adornments. These features are indicative of the cohesive aesthetic vision that sought to bind the magazine's large assortment of authors and subjects. Nothing like the tacked-on extras—such as a small cameo of an author in profile—common in other magazines, the images of *Our Continent* are more often pairings conversant with the text itself; intruding into the linear columns, they wind into and around the stories, bringing the reader on a complementary visual journey through a detailed setting, an assemblage of examples, or a tour of a spectacular landscape. Tourgée employed a large team of illustrators to create this effect, and so prevalent is this interplay between the illustrations and the texts that they become a part of what mark the work as uniquely of *Our Continent*.[4]

Where precisely this overarching visual arrangement points is suggested by the title itself. From its masthead, *Our Continent* signals a decidedly nationalist agenda; the name "is designed to express the idea that we desire to be American," the editors explain.[5]

The assumed collective of this plural first person recurs throughout the magazine's columns. This common nationalist point of view connects many otherwise disparate elements of the publication—for instance, the etiquette column promises to provide advice on courtesy specifically applicable to the "freer" American way of life, essays on the higher-education curriculum call for the inclusion of American studies, and pieces on design offer histories in the material culture of the Americas. Visually and textually, *Our Continent* brings its readers through a multidisciplinary tour of the reunited country. It is not, of course, of incidental significance that Tourgée, who was so long committed to a certain vision for the post–Civil War union, chose to use his fame and fortune to attempt such a comprehensive portrait of American identity and culture at this moment in the early 1880s. In his 1882 Fourth of July poem "Yesterday and Today," itself surrounded with characteristic *Our Continent* engravings, Tourgée signals the nature of his particular vision; naming some of those not yet incorporated into the national story—the "half-freed Slave," the Indian forced from his land, the rejected Chinese immigrant—he calls for a renewed force to "shake to the midsummer sky" and realize a fuller form of independence.[6] The nationalist vision offered by Tourgée's *Our Continent* is not a dispassionate snapshot of what America is so much as a comprehensive vision for what he believes it should be.

VOL. I. No. 16. - - MAY 31, 1882.

Copyright 1882 by Our Continent Publishing Co., Philadelphia.

OVR CONTINENT

TEN CENTS A COPY.
FOUR DOLLARS A YEAR.

LES BRAVI.
AFTER PAINTING BY MEISSONIER.

Figure 5. The front page of the May 31, 1882, issue of *Our Continent*. (Image courtesy of The Newberry Library.)

OVRCONTINENT.

SANTA MARIA

VOL. 1. — No. 15

COPYRIGHT 1882 BY
OVRCONTINENT
PVBLISHING CO.

PHILADELPHIA

MAY 24 1882

TEN CENTS A COPY
#4.00 A YEAR
#2.00 SIX MONTHS

THE ANGLER.—After Painting by Nicol.

Figure 6. The front page of the May 24, 1882, issue of *Our Continent*. (Image courtesy of The Newberry Library.)

Most of the critics who have assessed the short-lived *Our Continent* project separate in some way Tourgée's artistic and political outputs, despite the fact that the magazine is structured around their alignment. Writing retrospectively of the *Our Continent* experiment in the 1890s, Jeannette and Richer Gilder, editors of the *Critic*, wonder, "What could have started out more auspiciously than *Our Continent*?" Praising the wealth of authors and artists retained for this "high-class illustrated" publication, they conclude that Tourgée squandered his deep bench of artistic talent for his politics. Recognizing but not liking Tourgée's political vision, they warn the next person who wants to attempt such a venture to "keep out of politics." As the Gilders note, when Tourgée launched *Our Continent*, he was "at the height of his popularity"[7] following the success of his Reconstruction novels. Many subsequent critics have blamed the precipitous collapse of the magazine on the very artistic ambitions the Gilders admire. Noting Tourgée's reluctance to solicit advertisers and his taste for costly additions like the illustrations, Tourgée's biographer Mark Elliott explains that investors became "alarmed at Tourgée's propensity for extravagance and his high-minded inattention to the bottom line."[8] Rather than singular sticking points, both of these factors—controversial politics and impractical artistic ambition—are intrinsic to the *Our Continent* project, and recognizing this relationship is central to understanding Tourgée's broader intervention into the cultural moment of the 1880s.

As Tourgée gained increasing control over the magazine, its political voice grew louder. In July 1882, six months into the *Our Continent* run, Tourgée's assistant editors sold off their stake in the venture, and Tourgée assumed full editorial control. After this change in leadership, Tourgée gave full voice to his literary-political vision through two primary vehicles: the launch in *Our Continent*'s pages of the final novel in his Reconstruction series, *Hot Plowshares*, which tells a story about the rise of the abolitionist movement in US politics, and the launch of his weekly editorial columns, or "Migma." This title, "Migma," draws on the Greek word for mixture, and in these opinion pieces, which often span pages of the magazine, Tourgée expounds upon a mix of current events and questions of the day. In these dense columns, literary and political commentary sit juxtaposed, often separated by nothing more than a paragraph break. While some critics describe the increasingly political and editorial turn of *Our Continent* as at odds with its artistic goals, for Tourgée, resisting an indiscriminate plurality of thought was at the heart of the project. In an early editorial, he condemns the growing interest in journalistic independence and nonpartisanship: "To be 'independent' now, it is claimed, is to be without party, without sect, without aim, except to secure and hold a circulation."[9] Eschewing popular calls for new forms of objectivity, right from the start of the endeavor, Tourgée promises to exercise editorial judgement, to take aim, and to say what he believes is right. This impulse comes in direct response to a danger Tourgée perceived in an emerging strain of nonpartisan thought at work in both the elite fiction and politics of this moment.

To imagine Tourgée's fall from literary celebrity as a matter of personal mismanagement or political indiscretion is to obscure the social trends—in fiction and politics—that his magazine wrote against. Although Tourgée later refers to this moment as his "Icarean plunge,"[10] it is clear from the pages of *Our Continent* that he had not wanted his flight to be a solo mission—he had hoped to build up the collective "we" so often invoked in his pages. He found common cause in his regular contributors, many of whom had roots in the antislavery and civil rights movements, figures such as Louise Moulton, George Washington Cable, and, of course, Harriet Beecher Stowe.[11] But despite this august company, even as *Hot Plowshares* appeared serially in the magazine, Tourgée began to write about "today's fiction" as though he were an outside observer. His "Migma" columns become rife with skeptical references to "modern fiction" and the beliefs of the "so-called realists," while the book reviews, where he pans the work of fellow novelists Henry Adams, John Hay, William Dean Howells, and Henry James, carve out a space separate from the emerging literary establishment. Given the extent of his publishing ambitions, this move to distinguish his own work from the trends and interests of what was coming to be considered serious postwar fiction is a curious one and suggests that Tourgée's exile may have been at least in part self-imposed.

Tourgée's insistence on his alienation from the literary elite at the very moment when he was trying to establish his magazine as a permanent fixture sparks a few questions about what he feared in the cultural landscape of the early 1880s. How did he become so quickly convinced that his considerable fame would not end up shaping the "fiction of today?" It is certainly not Tourgée's penchant for writing political fiction that makes him unusual in the literary landscape of the Gilded Age. In fact, the appearance of the politicians he jokingly calls the "wise men" in *A Fool's Errand* comes at a moment when the workings of government were increasingly seen as good fodder for fiction. *A Fool's Errand*, like a number of novels of the period, takes its time with procedural details, explaining, for instance, the circumstances surrounding the selection of a state constitutional delegate, the backroom strategies of a party thinking ahead to its next election, and the events of a county nominating convention. At first glance, these kinds of concerns might seem to place Tourgée within a growing trend in fiction that elsewhere I describe as novels of process,[12] including Mark Twain's *The Gilded Age* (1873), which came to name the era; Henry Adams's *Democracy* (1880); Frances Hodgson Burnett's *Through One Administration* (1883); Henry James's novella *Pandora* (1884); María Amparo Ruiz de Burton's *The Squatter and the Don* (1885); and Harold Frederic's *Seth's Brother's Wife* (1886). These and a host of others were all novels that made the day-to-day workings of government major features of their narratives. A focus on political dealing, absent or in spite of any questions of platform or policy, is what defines these novels of process as they replace the divisive conflicts of the war era with nonpartisan concerns for corruption and bureaucracy—over the manner and not the reason that political work is done. But while Tourgée, ever the jurist, does take some care in *A Fool's Errand* to delve into the civil procedures of the Reconstruction South, it is the uncivil ideologies that shaped this political climate that most concern him.

It is not, after all, a bit of bribery on one side and some vote tampering on the other that make the drama of the county nominating convention in *A Fool's Errand*; in fact, this gathering—as described in the chapter "Thrice Told Tale"— is at once a Democratic Party convention and a Klan meeting. The meeting is advertised as a chance for the southern Democrats to plot a course to take back their county (electorally) from the Republicans, but it quickly becomes a crime scene when a gang of Democrats murder John Walters, a popular Republican leader and a barrier to the restoration of their political supremacy. Tourgée's narrator relates the story through three sources—the pro-Democratic southern press, a sympathetic eyewitness, and an African American man who overhears a brazen confession. Importantly, as the truth is revealed with each account, the various perspectives matter less and less because they all are weighted with the narrative's larger ironic framing, such that the reader is asked to scoff at each claim that these ex-Confederates are somehow "respectable" or "honorable" or that the difference between them and the Republicans could be explained away with a new point of view. It is the difference between the parties and their platforms—between Walters's fearless organizing on behalf of Black citizens and the Democrats' terrifying response to their fall from power—that is made central in Tourgée's novel. But just after his own novels were gobbled up by tens of thousands of readers, Tourgée began to notice this partisan perspective falling out of literary fashion. We see in the example of two novels that Tourgée excoriates in *Our Continent* how quickly the broader literary world was moving away from concerns of this kind of fictional—and soon political—representation.

Written at the same time as Tourgée's ironic attack on "the wise men," Henry Adams's political satire *Democracy* (1880), which was also published

anonymously, created a national and international sensation that troubled Tourgée. Adams's novel tells the story of a young widow, Mrs. Madeleine Lightfoot
Lee, who comes to Washington to observe the political system in action. But this
investigation does not require either Madeleine Lee or the narrator to delve into
any of the violent oppositions that preoccupy Tourgée's novel; instead, what we
find in Adams's Washington is an insular world of men grasping to maintain and
advance nothing but their own power. Seemingly far from the party rancor of
Reconstruction, what we get in this 1880 novel is largely agreement that all politics, regardless of party, is a crooked business. Corrupt bargains and self-serving
backroom deals are the concern of both dinner parties and political meetings,
and the novel's ironic voice, wholly different than the cynical backward glance of
the Fool, lambasts the hapless president and the scheming congressional leaders,
offering a kind of comedy-of-no-manners. Adams spares no one, alluding to historical scandals that implicated both parties. Whereas in Tourgée's novel, written
at the same moment, the Democrats are in essence a white supremacist terrorist
organization and the Republicans, despite their foibles, the party of emancipation and the rule of law, in Adams's novel, they're simply all bums. This kind of
nonpartisan critique of corruption, far from unique to Adams—this commitment, in other words, to being uncommitted—is typical of the novel of process.

While written as a playful sendup of Washingtonian ugliness, this popular novel's implications were serious to Tourgée. In a November 1882 "Migma" column,
he quotes at length the rare reviewer who refused to fall for what he describes as
the "slurs and sarcasm" of the anonymously published spoof of Washington life.
The reviewer calls attention to the pettiness of the novel's attacks, wondering, for
instance, what sort of person could "write so bitterly about so small a matter as
the esthetic uncomeliness" of the president and First Lady. Although the reviewer
dismisses the novel partly for its poor taste, he, and by extension Tourgée, leaves
open the possibility that something more sinister is at stake in this novel's mass
appeal: "There is no doubt, some amount of truth in the author's satire, but a lie
that is a half-truth is the blackest of lies."[13] In this particular piece, Tourgée does
not reveal what he thinks this half-true takedown is dangerously obscuring, but
one can be sure that it was unlikely to have sat well with Tourgée that the one
supposedly unsullied man that Madeleine Lee finds in Washington is a pardoned
Confederate officer, Captain John Carrington. Carrington remains untouched by
the political system's corruptions simply because he practices law privately. The
idea that the South might be exonerated by overlooking the ideological distinctions of either the historical records or contemporary platforms of the parties for

some notion of personal virtue was a matter of substantial concern to Tourgée in the 1880s.

Once political fictions like *Democracy* had set the stage for politics to be imagined as a universally dirty business that stained anyone who touched it, a new kind of politics that looked not for the right thinking but for the right man started to emerge. In its short lifetime, *Our Continent* covers the way that fiction participates in this political reimagining. In a January 1884 "Migma" column, Tourgée rails against another anonymous novel, *The Bread-winners* (1883), which was causing a major sensation at the time. First published serially in the *Century*, the novel was later revealed to have been written by John Hay, who as a young man had been Abraham Lincoln's personal secretary during his presidency and later became Theodore Roosevelt's secretary of state. The political implications of this novel's setting—an industrial city during a major strike—combined with the secrecy of its authorship seemed guaranteed to generate buzz, and sure enough, newspapers soon filled with rumors about the mysterious writer. Tourgée, however, was not so much bothered by the question of its authorship as he was troubled about what the popularity of this work suggested about the new era.

In *The Bread-winners*, Hay tells the story of how the manipulative conman Andy Offitt incites an uprising among a group of workingmen against the wealthy business leaders of their city. Because of the corrupt association of local political bosses with labor agitators like Offitt, the real estate mogul Arthur Farnham is forced to defend his own property and that of his neighbors against a lawless mob. Farnham, a Civil War veteran, is scandalized by the corrupt entanglements of politicians and labor organizers and is compelled to action when this rotten alliance leads to violence. It might easily be assumed that by casting the pro-labor men as the bad guys and the rich man as the hero, the novel takes a firm stand in the era's raging political struggle between labor and capital. But when Tourgée calls the novel "faithless"[14] in *Our Continent*, it is important to consider this ascription in two senses. First, the novel, to Tourgée's mind, lacks a fidelity to what is real or true in life, and second, it lacks a guiding belief or purpose. Hay's novel structurally elevates a single heroic figure over a diverse assemblage of characters and in this way transforms the battle between labor and capital into a question of personal character. Hay's text then becomes the logical extension of works like Adams's *Democracy*: If the big political problem, according to Adams, is dishonest leaders, then the big political solution, according to Hay, is honest ones.

To understand the meaning of this literary moment for Tourgée, we must consider *The Bread-winners* both aesthetically and politically. Since it was first published, critics have tended to take up one or the other of these matters in their readings of this novel and much of the abundantly produced (and now rarely considered) political fiction of the era. For instance, in a contemporary review of Hay's novel, the prominent practitioner and theorist of American realism William Dean Howells separates *The Bread-winners'* aesthetic success from its political message.[15] Howells was generally more sympathetic to the plight of workers than his friend Hay, so while Howells describes *The Bread-winners* as "useless" as an economic commentary, he still praises it for advancing the kind of fictional truth telling that he himself advocated and attempted. Howells's aesthetic called for a dedication to an unflinching style that does not shy away from ugly inconsistencies or difficult subjects. What he appreciates most about Hay's novel, he says, is the array of imperfect characters that crowd his pages. From a woman seeking a patronage position at the public library to a rough-speaking business owner, there is, he says, "great merit in its characterizations."[16] In this regard, Howells writes effusively, Hay has "done the cause of art a service."[17] Interestingly, it is precisely the thing that Howells praises—the novel's fidelity to life—in some sense of the word, its realism—with which Tourgée takes issue in *Our Continent.*

Tourgée has long been understood as a critic of realism, but his departure from Howells's reading of Hay's popular novel raises an important question about what he meant by this term.[18] Considering his criticisms of the realists in the late-1880s essays "The South as a Field of Fiction" and "The Claim of Realism" and the fact that the Tourgée of *Our Continent* in no way spares Howells from the wrath of his critical eye, it might strike us as odd that his critique of Hay's work is primarily that it is unrealistic. Emblematic of this breach from reality is crucially Hay's hero, Arthur Farnham. As I have already suggested, the noble Farnham is at the center of the novel's political turn, so it is worth noting that Tourgée finds his characterization completely unconvincing and writes in the "Migma" column with searing irony, "Those who are not worth a million at the least are always the victims of some unfortunate defect of character or training." Here Tourgée picks up on a growing fictional trend wherein the hero is forced to confront a series of potentially compromising temptations, whether financial or sexual, and by fending off these threats to their reputation rises above the ugliness of democracy as the worthy leader. In the first pages of Hay's novel, Farnham is tested when Maud Matchin tries to woo her way into a job at the library, where Farnham sits on the board; he flirts but ultimately proves restrained and does not succumb to her sordid ploy. Tourgée attributes this trope not to a lapse in the novel's commitment to contemporary realism but rather as something constitutive of this popular form;

the conflation of riches and exemplary character, he says, "is a point on which the modern 'realistic' novelists are singularly unanimous." In addition to his quibble with the novel's verisimilitude, Tourgée points to a deeper problem with Farnham's heroic portrayal: The notion that a wealthy character like him "cannot be too good"[19] is, he claims, a damaging and particularly American phenomenon. Perhaps the reason we find this critique out of line with the way that Tourgée's literary criticism has been understood is because we have failed to appreciate how Tourgée's views on literary form were a highly contextual response to this emerging US trend of what he calls the "so-called realism" and not a totalizing indictment of the form. After all, his magazine regularly praises the work of British realists like Thackeray and Eliot.

Taking a cue from Tourgée, then, it is worth considering what Howells does not address about the form of his friend Hay's novel. It is indeed the case that, as Howells suggests, Hay places a variety of characters, many representing the seedier dimensions of democratic society, under the harsh fluorescence of his narrator's interrogation lamps. But the hero, Farnham, is set apart from their shortcomings and especially their unruly political commitments. In stark contrast to those around him, Farnham is temperate; amid a host of swearing ruffians, Farnham conducts himself with a "serious elegance," refusing to participate in loose talk, including both foul language and false demagogic appeals.[20] The coarse labor leader Offitt will use any tactic to recruit his dim-witted but mostly well-meaning workers to his cause, and when arguments about unfair wages fall flat, Offitt convinces workingman Sleeny that the rich Farnham is trying to steal his girlfriend. The violent standoff at Farnham's home becomes a chivalric battle, completely separate from the terms of any political claim. The incorruptibility of the protagonist supplants all other arguments that initially seem to fracture the text's landscape.

These fictions displaced divisive ideological conflicts with questions of personal character. Tourgée recognized the danger of this kind of political thinking first in the Gilded Age novel and then, by the end of the *Our Continent* years, in Gilded Age politics more generally. Certainly, as all readers of *A Fool's Errand* understand, Tourgée was not one to shy away from critiquing his elected representatives, but what he objects to again and again in the 1880s are narratives of widespread corruption advanced to the exclusion or the occlusion of significant ongoing debates, particularly over the meaning of the war and the ongoing civil rights crisis. As we have seen, such narratives had become central to the booming genre of political fiction since at least Twain's 1872 *The Gilded Age* and then were advanced in new ways by writers like Adams and Hay. But as the presidential election year of 1884 approached, this form of political thought was becoming increasingly formalized in the nonfictional political arena as well. Picking up from the failed insurgency of the 1872 Liberal Republicans, the Independents or Mugwump reformers emerged as a significant political factor in the lead-up to this election, when in their single most significant collective act, they refused to support their party's nominee, Republican James G. Blaine, and instead voted for Democrat Grover Cleveland.

Initially composed of primarily Boston Brahmin and New York intellectuals, the Mugwumps were an elite group with significant literary and cultural influence. Its prominent names included Mark Twain, Henry Adams, Harold Frederic, and several of Tourgée's publishing industry peers: members of the *Harper's Magazine* dynasty, editor of the *Nation* E. L. Godkin, the cartoonist Thomas Nast, and Richard Watson Gilder, then editor of the *Century*, which had published Hay's *The Bread-winners* serially. That these men were powerful in terms of their publishing influence is obvious—what issues they united around is less so. Mugwumps worked not so much from a political as a moral philosophy, choosing to support an individual candidate over a party or platform; "official integrity," according to the historian John Sproat, was their only issue.[21] In *Our Continent* and elsewhere, Tourgée describes them as possessing neither an animating "issue or idea."[22] With no substantial recommendation for what goals or priorities the Republican Party should have, their sole discernible principle was that Blaine, who had been implicated in some of the corruption scandals of the preceding decade, was not the right man to lead them.

Defining politics in terms of personal virtue is in keeping with what Sproat and others have described as the "best men" theory of governmental reform, which one can see playing out to Tourgée's dismay in a novel like Hay's. In general, this version of late-nineteenth-century liberalism proposed that the way to free politics from its partisan burdens and corruptions was to elect men of a certain moral and intellectual pedigree regardless of their ideological or party affiliation. Just as he does when he identifies the "realist" conflation of riches with morals, Tourgée condemns this understanding of political worth as necessarily elitist: "In plain words, it is a declaration that the man is better than the multitude—that a candidate is not a representative nor an exemplar but an independent political entity who will act on his own responsibility and utterly ignore the principles, policy and traditions of his party."[23] In the final months of his publication of *Our Continent*, Tourgée devotes most of his "Migma" pages to defend that which was indefensible in the novel of process—the meaningful difference between the historical goals of the major political parties. By this time, Tourgée had already seen his party begin to drift away from its legacy values, and he worried openly about this in the lead-up to the 1884 nomination. However, when faced with the defection of the Mugwumps, he was resolute in his opposition; bemoaning their publishing power, he writes unflinchingly, "The Republican party represents one line of thought, one class of mind, one theory of national existence, and the Democratic party another. Between these there is no middle ground. The one is progressive; the other obstructive. The one looks to the future for better things; the other worships a past long since dead."[24] Nevertheless, transforming structural conflicts like the demand for civil rights into a matter that might be solved by the instructive model of one good leader was a mode of political reform that was, by 1884 when Tourgée's magazine fully folded, the prevailing sentiment among the literary elite.

Tourgée considered the Mugwumps a significant threat, particularly after they contributed to the election of the first Democrat since the Civil War. He writes in the 1885 *Chicago Inter Ocean*, "A more serious peril could hardly threaten our republic. Already it has accomplished very great evils."[25] Tourgée's concern was that this shapeless movement would reinstate federally the "Solid South" of white supremacist Democratic power. Despite their indefinite platform, many Mugwumps believed themselves to be embarking on a great political revolution akin to the formation of the Free Soil Party. This is a point which Tourgée takes on directly in the final issues of *Our Continent*, which incidentally survived until just weeks before their greatest victory, Grover Cleveland's election. He rails against the supposition that the Mugwumps could be compared to the radical movements of the prewar era, claiming that "it does not come out of the cornfields or through the streets seeking advice and a leader. On the contrary, it has its origin in the clubs, and finds its John Baptists in rich men's palaces." Unlike the abolitionists, whose energy sprang from the oppressed, this band of the intelligentsia is "all head. . . . It is a movement that seems to have begun at the top."[26] Convinced of their moral superiority, the Mugwumps believed that they could dictate to the party without doing the work to organize consensus. In contrast, the abolitionists, he writes, were a group born in secret that suffered for their views, while the Mugwumps took no obvious risks. They "live on negations" alone—they knew only what they were not—whereas prewar heroes like John Brown and Frederick Douglass "declared themselves in great principles."[27]

Importantly, it was within the same clubs and circles that bred the Mugwump movement that the tenets and practitioners of literary realism also developed. While not professed Mugwumps, Howells and James are, when considered through Tourgée, whose columns on realism appeared side by side with those on the 1884 election, shaped by their proximity to Mugwumpery. Given this, I want to suggest that we might read Tourgée's literary critique as a political condemnation not just of substance but of form.

As we have seen, it was not a genuine concern for verisimilitude that bothered the author of *A Fool's Errand*; in fact, the truth and fidelity to the world and its histories was something he promoted as an editor, publishing the local-color work of committed realists such as Sarah Orne Jewett. But in columns adjacent to his screeds on the "so-called Independents," Tourgée decried the "so-called realists" whose work, he writes, flattens or equalizes the distinctions between once opposed ideas. Through a relentless accrual of detail, they make it impossible to imagine one thing as better than another. In novels like Hay's, one moral character rises above the corrupt masses, but as the "so-called realist school" developed from its origins in the novel of process, it loses even this moral focal point. In *Our Continent*, Tourgée explains how the realists had lost a crucial sense of purpose. He connects their aimlessness with an exclusive interest in complexity, a "morbid mental anatomy" that juxtaposed contradictions absent of any ordering priorities. "Keenness of observation," he writes, "is only thought to be evinced by the collection of contrarieties."[28] By picking apart their subjects without any larger principles, the realist's ambitions start to look a lot like the fictional version of the "negations" of the Mugwumps.

Relentless objectivity absent any partiality—or partisanship—defines this version of realism for Tourgée, and his resistance to this trend is evident throughout the *Our Continent* project. In this way, Tourgée's short-lived enterprise might help us understand the often-contested political stakes of the rise of this particular brand of American realism. It is, for instance, worth noting that Howells structures his realist masterpiece *A Hazard of New Fortunes* around the launch of Basil March's magazine *Every Other Week*, which attempts to print side by side and without editorial commentary the work of a socialist Union veteran and the work of an unreconstructed southerner. In this way, the fictional magazine, and by extension Howell's novel, becomes the epitome of the moral leveling project that Tourgée deplored, and it was precisely this effort that he overtly contested in what can now be understood as his second fool's errand, the failed magazine *Our Continent*. Comparing himself to the firebrand William Lloyd Garrison, Tourgée promises in one of the first issues that he would endeavor to be not a weathervane blowing "where the wind of public sentiment blows" but a signpost pointing the way.[29] But as the decade continued, the winds kept blowing, and the literary elite continued to turn away from the markers of partisanship, erasing the difference between what Douglass famously called the right side and the wrong side of the war. With every sentence of *Uncle Tom's Cabin*, Tourgée later writes, Stowe had exposed the wrongs of slavery;[30] this conviction shaped her words and the political work of her contemporaries. If for Tourgée Stowe's fiction helped sow the necessary division that began the work of the Reconstruction, the fiction of his own era, by obfuscating these same differences, helped end it.

Notes

1. "Salutatory," *Our Continent* 1 (February 15, 1882): 8.

2. Midway through its first year, a folio size is adopted.

3. Albion Tourgée, "Migma," *Our Continent* 2 (October 18, 1882): 477.

4. Mark Elliott, *Color-Blind Justice: Albion Tourgée and the Quest for Racial Equality from the Civil War to Plessy v. Ferguson* (New York: Oxford University Press, 2006), 204. Some of the most striking examples of the interplay between text and illustration come in those essays that focus on topics assertive of a certain kind of nationalist identity—such as the essays by Daniel Brinton on Americana or those by F. L. Oswald on the National Parks.

5. *Our Continent* 1 (February 15, 1882): 8. Early issues of *Our Continent* frequently featured considerations of Native American cultural production and history as part of the advancement of a non-European but unmistakably settler-colonial notion of national identity. We can see the dissonance of this brand of nationalism in the *Our Continent* frontispiece. The editors explain the *Our Continent* seal was designed for them by Louis Tiffany and based on the Aztec Calendar Stone (Figure 5). *Our Continent* 1 (February 15, 1882): 24. This stamp became the logo of the entire Our Continent Company. Despite this gesture to a pre-Columbian American identity, in the early editions of the magazine, the title "O" of the masthead is filled with an image of Columbus's ship, the Santa Maria (Figure 6). In later editions, Tourgée continued to use the Tiffany-designed logo but favored a more classical monumental font for the masthead.

6. *Our Continent* 1 (July 5, 1882): 328–29.

7. Jeannette Leonard Gilder and R. Gilder, *The Critic: A Weekly Review of Literature and the Arts* 4 (August 15, 1891): 82.

8. Elliott, *Color-Blind Justice*, 205.

9. *Our Continent* 1 (March 15, 1882): 72.

10. Qtd. in Elliott, *Color-Blind Justice*, 213.

11. While he had not yet turned his editorial focus to publishing fiction written by Black authors, as he would in a later 1890s venture, *Our Continent* did enjoy an inter-racial readership, as Carolyn Karcher has shown in her recent book.

12. I explain more about what I mean by "political novel"—novels that follow governmental or party politics specifically—and the genre of "novels of process" in "The Political Procedural," *American Literature* 89, no. 4 (December 2017): 669–95.

13. Albion Tourgée, "Migma," *Our Continent* 2 (October 25, 1882): 510.

14. "The Book Shelf," *Our Continent* 5, no. 6 (1884): 191.

15. Howells was one of the only people that Hay is known to have confided in about his secret authorship.

16. William Dean Howells, "John Hay in Literature," *North American Review* 181, no. 586 (1905): 346.

17. William Dean Howells, "The Bread-Winners: A Social Study," in *Criticism and Fiction and Other Essays*, ed. Clara Marburg Kirk and Rudolf Kirk (New York: New York University Press, 1965), 243.

18. See Ken Warren's essay in this volume.

19. Albion Tourgée, "Migma," *Our Continent* 5, no. 4 (1884): 125.

20. John Hay, *The Bread-winners* (New Haven, CT: College and University Press, 1973), 66.

21. David Tucker, *Mugwumps: Public Moralists of the Gilded Age* (Columbia: University of Missouri Press, 1998), 44. John G. Sproat, *"The Best Men": Liberal Reformers in the Gilded Age* (New York: Oxford University Press, 1968), 126.

22. Albion Tourgée, "Migma," *Our Continent* 6 (July 30, 1884): 152.

23. Albion Tourgée, "Letters to a Mugwump," *Daily Inter Ocean* (Chicago), November 19, 1885.

24. Albion Tourgée, "Migma," *Our Continent* 6 (July 2, 1884): 25.

25. Albion Tourgée, "Letters to a Mugwump," *Daily Inter Ocean* (Chicago), October 24, 1885.

26. Albion Tourgée, "Migma," *Our Continent* 6 (July 9, 1884): 61. Importantly, his story of bottom-up political formation is one that Tourgée tells vividly in *Hot Plowshares*, the novel that he publishes serially in *Our Continent*.

27. Albion Tourgée, "Migma," *Our Continent* 6 (August 13, 1884): 224.

28. Albion Tourgée, "Migma," *Our Continent* 4 (September 26, 1883): 411.

29. *Our Continent* 1 (March 15, 1882): 72.

30. Albion Tourgée, "The Literary Quality of *Uncle Tom's Cabin*," in *Undaunted Radical: The Selected Writings and Speeches of Albion W. Tourgée*, ed. Mark Elliott and David Smith (Baton Rouge: Louisiana State University Press, 2010): 229–34.

16

Tourgée on the Dangers of Reconciliation

Revenge in the Reconstruction-Era Novels

Gregory Laski

Time avenges wrongs which men forget.

—ALBION W. TOURGÉE, *An Appeal to Caesar* (1884)

It was April 1868, and the time must have felt out of joint. Three years after Robert E. Lee surrendered to Ulysses S. Grant, Albion W. Tourgée was immersed in his work to realize the promises of liberty and equality for all that were for him the Civil War's revolutionary aims. Tourgée had recently returned from the North Carolina Constitutional Convention, where he played a leading role in democratizing the political charter of his adopted state. The constitution was ratified by month's end, and the returns of the spring elections installed Tourgée as a Superior Court judge. If these developments augured the transformation that Tourgée wanted to effect in the South, sufficient signs of the enduring spirit of the Confederacy foretold a different future. One hit especially close to home: As March turned to April, George W. Ashburn—Tourgée's "old friend," fellow US army veteran, and collaborator in the fight for African American rights—had been murdered in Georgia by unrepentant rebels. This political assassination stood as an emblem of the forces of violent white terrorism that, combined with a steady federal retreat, would ultimately end the project of Reconstruction. As Tourgée wondered that April, was Ashburn's death not a declaration that "every white Republican should be hung higher than Haman, and every negro 'fossilized,' killed, or driven out of the country?"[1]

Putting pen to paper to contemplate these events, the writer composed in his notebook a brief but remarkable political-philosophical meditation on the prospect of justice in the Reconstruction-era United States. He titled it "Retribution or Revolution" and prophesied:

One or the other is (unavoidable) inevitable. Or rather retribution is ~~inevita~~ unavoidable either through revolution or otherwise. For three years, this fact has been staring the American people in the face, growing daily and hourly more plain and tangible. For three years we have been searching for a substitute for justice. We have tried to flatter ourselves with the idea of mercy and forbearance but the flimsy lie has long since lost its charm.

"Offence's gilded hand" can no more shove by Justice, when the people of a great nation are the jurors, than in the Courts above.[2]

Reading like a real-time record of Tourgée's evolving diagnosis of the course the nation should pursue in the wake of a war that continued to rage, "Retribution or Revolution" almost immediately overturns the certainty implied by the titular "or." By his second sentence, Tourgée decides that the question is not one of a choice between "revolution" or "retribution" but rather a question of *how* the retributive justice that is "unavoidable" would be secured ("through revolution or otherwise"). Tourgée calls it a "fact"—something obvious that "we" know yet cannot accept—but this second "or" suggests that the mode of redressing the matter is not at all clear, even as the endpoint is: "Offence's gilded hand" must not be able to "shove by justice." Tourgée takes this concluding line from *Hamlet*'s fratricidal King Claudius, who, in privately confessing the murder and usurpation of his brother, remarks that where "in the corrupted currents of this world, / Offense's gilded hand may shove by justice," no such evasion is possible in the heavenly realm "above." By contrast, Tourgée collapses above and below, the "courts" of heaven and those of earth. What the reconstructed United States urgently needed was a mode of democratic—because "universal"—justice that recognized and redressed the wrongs of secession and anti-Black violence with a clarity and commensurability that Claudius believes exceeds human capacity but Tourgée hopes does not. How, exactly, to bring this vision down to earth?[3]

Tourgée does not answer. But the citation from *Hamlet* invites an intriguing response: *revenge*. As Claudius kneels, attempting prayer after confessing, Hamlet enters. Drawing his sword, the prince prepares to avenge his father's murder, only to doubt the timing of his decision and the appropriateness of the circumstance. Hamlet's continual interrogation of what it would mean to "sweep to my revenge" must have held a special significance for Tourgée. If "mercy" and "forbearance" were "flimsy lies" that aided and abetted the Confederacy in evading the aims of Reconstruction, then what role might vengeance play as the nation navigated its commitments to African American inclusion and sought a genuine reunion of North and South? Tourgée explored these questions in his fictional output across the Reconstruction era. Not unlike Shakespeare's *Hamlet*, which questions the avenues and aims of revenge and expands the possibilities of vengeance beyond the notion of a single act of interpersonal violence, Tourgée never embraced a particular definition of vengeance or endorsed it as a singular path toward justice. Surely his personas as lawmaker and judge made him reticent on this score. As an author of fiction, however, his "legal imagination had free rein," as Brook Thomas argues in this volume, and in his Reconstruction trilogy Tourgée everywhere imagined the salutary force of vengeance as manifested variously in the forms of divine judgment, African American physical self-assertion, and biological disease. Taken together, *A Fool's Errand* (1879), *Bricks without Straw* (1880), and *Pactolus Prime* (1890) examine the possibilities of revenge as a tool in the fight for universal justice and—with the dawn of the nadir—as a necessary mode of salvaging the social and political transformation that the Civil War required and the abandoned project of Reconstruction sought to realize.[4]

When he wrote "Retribution or Revolution," Tourgée likely had Ashburn's assassination on his mind, but the killing of the Georgia Republican occasioned concerns that were neither new nor exclusively local. The question of April 1868 was also the question of April 1865: What would it mean to create a reconstructed nation, and specifically how should the Union deal with the Confederacy? A dominant answer emerged as early as Appomattox. When Lee surrendered his sword, some claimed that Grant returned it to his Confederate peer. Grant would later call this story "the purest romance." Invented as it may be, the narrative captured a real desire for reconciliation, whose risks Frederick Douglass decried. "Lee was spoken of with as much respect as General Grant," Douglass lamented in describing the national mood in early April, and "the whole North was meditating mercy towards the vanquished." The assassination of Abraham Lincoln on April 14, 1865, roused the North out of this conciliatory posture like the appearance of King Hamlet's ghost; it was as if "the graves opened at our feet and the sheeted dead walked forth," Douglass remarked. Americans both Black and white were prepared to reject their beloved leader's prescription for charity and embrace revenge in order to secure the ends for which the war had been waged. "On Slavery let vengeance fall," announced Charles Sumner in a eulogy for his fellow Republican in June. When Congress reconvened in Washington, DC, in December, the Massachusetts senator made good on this promise by seeking to destroy the racial inequality that was the remnant of slavery. "This is our only revenge," said Sumner early in 1866 in the course of advocating for equal rights, including the vote, for African Americans. He meant the phrase to counter any notion that the North was seeking a victor's vengeance; denying any revengeful feelings toward the former Confederacy had become de rigueur in the Thirty-Ninth Congress. But Sumner surely knew that for many Confederates, the prospect of Black equality—not to mention that of Black enfranchisement— constituted precisely the kind of revenge that he disavowed. And it was in response to the North's supposed revenge that acts of violence like the murder of G. W. Ashburn were justified by white supremacists in the South.[5]

Tourgée unraveled this tangled web of language and its effect on policy and action in his first Reconstruction novel, A Fool's Errand. Summarizing the result of this rhetorical inversion, Tourgée's narrator—Comfort Servosse, the "fool" who moves from North to South after the war—seems bemused, even a little envious: "One can not but admire the arrogant boldness with which they charged the nation which had overpowered them—even in the teeth of her legislators— with perfidy, malice, and a spirit of unworthy and contemptible revenge." Here "unworthy" and "contemptible" describe revenge as it was deployed by Confederates. Violent and regressive, this version of revenge, as the novel clarifies in the subsequent paragraph, was hardly supported by the circumstances. This unjust revenge should not define the concept.[6]

Another vision was possible. Unraveling the thread on which he pulled in "Retribution or Revolution," Tourgée imagined a vengeance that continued rather than contravened the aims of Civil War. This revolutionary revenge emerged from Tourgée's understanding of the war in which he himself fought. Writing as a member of the 105th Ohio Volunteer Infantry to his University of Rochester fraternity brothers in January 1863—the Emancipation Proclamation having decisively articulated the goals of the Civil War as a quest for racial liberation—Tourgée called for a "fundamental, thorough and complete revolution + renovation" of the nation. "I don't care a rag for 'the Union as it was.' I want and fight for the Union 'better than it was,'" he proclaimed. Significantly, the Civil War was only the start: "The Revolution is but just begun." This "better union" would need to be realized by the project of Reconstruction, the objectives of which Tourgée held were properly communicated by the term "construction." To build that new United States required the North to "rule as a conqueror," as Fool's puts it (171). It required military occupation, education for freedpeople as well as poor whites, and new political and economic structures. Often requiring force, violent and civil, this was a constructive revenge that a martial victor would exact, and it was precisely the kind of vocabulary that most in Congress, even many Republicans, wanted to avoid in the vision of Reconstruction they sought to publicize even as they endorsed radical measures. In their capacity as crafters of policy to reunite a divided nation, perhaps they had good reason; even today, it is difficult to hear Tourgée's insistence that the South was a "foreign country," a distinct "civilization," without thinking of the atrocity that many a colonizing force wrought while using similar logic to rationalize its aggression against a purported enemy. Why should such a paradigm be enacted if a restored union was the goal?[7]

And yet, any answer necessarily would turn on another question: what *kind* of Union? By the time Tourgée composed *Fool's*, the Union might have been restored, but the project of Reconstruction had been abandoned. In North Carolina, the former Confederate governor returned to power. Nationally, President Rutherford B. Hayes (whom Tourgée supported, as a Republican) committed to southern self-rule. The embrace of the conciliatory disposition by what the novel refers to mockingly as the "Wise Men" of the federal government resulted in devastation for democratically minded whites like Ashburn and Tourgée, and even more so for the freedmen and women who suffered the violent terrorism of the Ku Klux Klan and the routine economic and political dispossession that marked the final decades of the 1800s in the South. What Tourgée earlier termed the "flimsy lies" of "mercy" and Douglass called "maudlin magnanimity" enabled the triumph of the loser, not the victor, and amplified a reactionary, rather than revolutionary, revenge that corrupted the very ideas of forgiveness and charity as virtues. Not only was offense's gilded hand allowed to avoid justice, but the offending hand was aided and abetted by what *Fool's* calls "a reckless determination to forgive" (317). Simply put, revenge, which is the "original meaning of justice," was made to signify precisely the opposite.[8]

For someone who represents with such clarity the way that federal presentiment-turned-policy paved the way for the tragic fate of revenge in the Reconstruction era, it is intriguing that Tourgée spends little time thinking about how those same channels might redress the problem. The previously cited passages aside, *Fool's* focuses on the personal impact felt (often literally) by the humans who experience the kind of justice that revolutionary retribution can facilitate. One of the novel's most searching meditations on revenge comes by way of an extended exchange with one of the narrator's neighbors, Nathaniel Hyman, a white southerner and local magistrate. Hyman engages in extended conversations about the war, abolition, and the outcome of emancipation with Servosse and his wife, Metta. On the last score, he admits to a kind of agnosticism; as a "slaveholder from . . . youth" Hyman was taught to understand racial bondage as divinely sanctioned, but he admits that hearing Servosse speak positively about racial equality and Black citizenship has shaken that "faith" (87). If Hyman has been unsettled, his son, Jesse, has been converted. "He's heard the colonel speak once or twice," the character reports to Metta, "an' he's clean carried away" with the "notion" "that freein' the slaves is the best thing that's ever happened for the white folks of the South" (88). The younger Hyman puts his ideas into practice and joins the state's Radical Republicans.

Summarized thus, the episode would seem a progressive parable: Enslaver-father spawns radical son. But the story continues, with several twists, in a later chapter entitled "Footing up the Ledger." Jesse becomes the victim of political violence. "The Ku-Klux took out my boy Jesse last night, and beat him nigh about to death," the elder Hyman explains to Servosse; he has been terrorized for his "Radical" allegiances (197, 198). For the father, the assault conjures conflicted feelings about the white South and his relationship to it. To have his child subjected by "our own folks" to a punishment traditionally used by whites to abuse Black Americans strikes Hyman as a violation of an unwritten code of southern white solidarity (200). That the abuse was conducted under the cover of darkness, giving Jesse no chance to "get a gentleman's revenge" (199), brings this self-described "man of peace" close to contemplating violent retribution of his own. "But I swear to God," Hyman exclaims to Servosse, "if I knew who it was that had done this business, I'd let him know I could send a load of buckshot home yet: damned if I wouldn't" (200).

Tourgée pursues Hyman's recourse to divinity, but in a way that broadens the episode beyond the character's account of aggrieved white honor and an inter-personal—scarcely revolutionary—revenge. Heeding the request to find refuge for Jesse in the West, Servosse writes to the Reverend Theophilus Jones, an abolitionist preacher who, before the war, had been violently driven out of North Carolina, thanks in part to intelligence supplied by Nathaniel Hyman. Where the episode makes Hyman worry over the bonds of southern white fraternity, Jones stands amazed at evidence of divine "retribution." "My heart was hushed with holy awe when I read in your letter that the son of this man, who caused *us* to be scourged, had suffered a like chastisement at the hands of wicked men—perhaps the very hands by which we were smitten aforetime" (204, 203), explains Jones in the return letter that appears at the conclusion of the chapter. He is quick to clarify that "I had never entertained feelings of malice or revenge" (204), an allusion to the injunction against human vengeance in Romans 12:19: "Vengeance is mine; I will repay, saith the Lord." Yet the preacher has not renounced vengeance entirely. "Why not let him come hither," Jones reasons in the course of his decision to agree to aid, "and let me thank the good Father by succoring the son of him who persecuted me?" (204). This "act of praise and thanksgiving" (204) to an avenging God subtly recognizes that St. Paul's familiar teaching, rather than prohibiting human revenge entirely, simply shifts its valence. "Therefore if thine enemy hunger, feed him; if he thirst, give him drink," Romans continues, "for in so doing thou shalt heap coals of fire on his head." In taking in Jesse Hyman, that is, Jones experiences the pleasures of revenge "within the bounds of orthodoxy." Taking the moral high ground, he still takes revenge.[9]

Tourgée aligns himself neither with Jones nor Hyman. Although his narrator gets the last word, Servosse's sense that the preacher is a "fanatic" for his "ready assumption of the divine act as having been performed in his individual behalf" casts doubt more on the form that this "divine act" assumes than on the divinity of the act itself (204). In that regard, the chapter title provides the interpretive key. "Footing up the Ledger" refers to the work of adding up the columns in order to calculate the sum. This is the work of balancing, but it is also the work of reckoning. The elder Hyman laments that Jesse has spent his life "payin' his old father's debts," by which he means managing the family business, whose accounts fell out of balance after emancipation brought an end to their enslaved labor source (200). *Fool's* "Footing up the Ledger," however, suggests an even greater debt. That Jesse is made to pay it across generations, despite his Republican conversion, constitutes a revolutionary revenge that may serve the reckoning that the political ends of Reconstruction required but that is not finally defined by the limits of the political world or even within its control. As Tourgée explained in another context, God is "a good accountant who never shrinks from balancing his book with *red ink*. He finds a way too, of causing events to pass without the aid of human advice."[10]

In his 1880 novel *Bricks without Straw*, when Tourgée takes up African American revenge, he trains his sights squarely on humanity, revealing the great force and inevitable limitations embodied by the Black Americans who sought justice in Reconstruction. Nimbus, the novel's Black protagonist, stands as a case in point. He prefers peace but is ready to "hev blood fer blood" when his voting rights are threatened by whites. Nimbus delivers on this pledge later in the novel when the flourishing freedpeople's community of Red Wing comes under brutal attack by Klan members. Described as an "avenger" and "ebon angel of wrath," Nimbus wields a saber to defend his community; his wife, Lugena, takes up an axe as her weapon. Revealing the action in the scene cinematically, each sentence a shot from alternating perspectives, Tourgée delivers the retributive justice depicted in Quentin Tarantino's *Django Unchained* (2012) more than a century in advance.

Significantly, he not only shapes Nimbus as an African American superhero but also emphasizes the success of his efforts. Although the Black community has been devastated and the residents traumatized, the chapter concludes by focusing on the trouncing of the white terrorists. A group of invaders come to claim one of their own who is "prostrate" on the earth. For a "stretcher," they repurpose "the pieces of the coffin-shaped board which had been hung upon the gate two weeks before." The very object that the white terrorists earlier used to telegraph their threats has been transfigured, at least for the moment, into a symbol of their defeat.[11]

If, as one literary scholar has argued, the problem with the Black avenger figure is that it works against "racist oppression" but also against "collective agency," then *Bricks* unsettles this pattern: Red Wing withers, but not because of the hero's lack of commitment to the community. Rather, Tourgée explores other questions about Black retribution through this figure. What would it take to transform Nimbus's righteous revenge into a broader revolutionary revenge that might sustain more Red Wings? Tourgée clearly wanted to find an affirmative answer even as he didn't have it at the time. Reflecting on Reconstruction four years later, he wrote that African Americans "would have carried into effect plans of retributive justice which would have made those years memorable in all history for the terrible vengeance which an oppressed race executed upon their persecutors." Tourgée blames the "remonstrances of their recognized leaders" for holding this vengeance at bay, an indictment that perhaps extends even to his own modulating positions on resistance during the era and his stern sentences for African American attempts at retaliation. Still, through this episode he gave a glimpse of how justice might flourish, albeit episodically and unevenly, through a righteous revenge whose force necessarily challenged standards of the law.[12]

It is on that last score that Nimbus's vengeance finds some lasting vindication. In the novel's final pages, the narrator reports that no charges had been filed against him: "For some reason the law had not been appealed to to avenge the injuries of the marauders" (405). *Bricks* as a whole, however, suggests at least one clear reason: If the modern legal system historically has differentiated itself from mere revenge by claiming to serve as neutral arbiter of "justice," that distinction does not obtain here. In this case, "justice" is in fact "just revenge by another name," and it is only Nimbus who can legitimate any claim to that title.[13]

Published in book form in 1890, ten years after *Bricks* and in the wake of the retreat from Reconstruction, *Pactolus Prime* represents revenge not as an individual or interpersonal balancing, whether in the form of human self-assertion or divine reversal, but as an intergenerational biological punishment. In this novel that readers of Tourgée's day deemed "fanatical" and some contemporary critics have interpreted as a "dead end" in the author's lifelong quest to secure racial equality, revenge operates at the species level: Where Tourgée's Reconstruction novels give us the whipping of Jesse Hyman or the killing of a few Klan members, *Pactolus Prime* gives us revenge with a vengeance.[14]

Following the death of the title character, a formerly enslaved African American who passed as white to join the US Army but later lived as a Black man in Washington, DC, a conversation ensues between the white doctor who attended to Prime and the lawyer who manages the wealth Prime accrued after the Civil War as the owner of a South Carolina plantation and as an investor in DC real estate. His interest piqued by the mystery of Prime's racial identity and its back-stories, the doctor shares his theory of the "avenging spore" that travels across generations "to scourge the descendants" of the perpetrator of wrong. The particular wrong in this conversation is racial enslavement. Where earlier the doctor had expressed hope that the effects of slavery would end with abolition, here, after encountering Prime, he radically revises that notion. Instead, the character claims that the yellow fever, which "preys only on the white man," is a divinely sanctioned biological revenge for that system, "the scourge for the oppressor and those allied to him in blood and interest." Alluding to the Scottish doctor Charles Creighton's *Encyclopedia Britannica* entry on yellow fever, Tourgée's physician traces the deadly disease to the "unique unwholesomeness of the life summed up in the phrase 'the horrors of the middle passage.'" In an act of retributive justice that is "most beautiful and terrible," the sufferer of yellow fever experiences the very horrors—"nostalgia," "despair," "perpetual and overwhelming terror"—that the people who were the cargo of the transatlantic slave trade suffered more than two centuries ago. And, as the doctor clarifies in response to the attorney's legalistic question, whether a white person enslaved Africans or participated in its human trafficking is beside the matter: "The innocent suffer with the guilty." The lawyer, who has Prime's confidence in the novel and seems to have Tourgée's as well, deems the theory "strange" and yet "not impossible." "I do not like to think of it," he remarks at the end of the chapter.[15]

Through this vision, which readers must think of, coming as it does three chapters from the end of the book, Tourgée marks multiple returns. Without endorsing his character's incipient theory or Creighton's outmoded science, Tourgée invokes the notion of yellow fever as retribution for the sin of slavery, circulated by William Wells Brown and other antebellum authors, and he also revives the discredited belief that Africans were immune from the disease. That misinformation did much harm to Black Americans, particularly in the 1790s yellow fever epidemic in Philadelphia. Closer to Tourgée's time, the 1878 outbreak that plagued the South engendered kindly feelings among white northerners and southerners, allowing reunion without any admission of guilt on the part of the latter and thereby cultivating the attitudes of the mercy and forbearance that Tourgée decried as "lies" in 1868. In *Fool's*, this later yellow fever outbreak kills off Servosse literally and figuratively, ending his life and his errand. In *Prime*, however, Tourgée deploys the disease to wreak a revolutionary revenge for crimes committed by whites against African Americans—on both those who perpetrated the offense and those who did not. Intriguingly, according to the logic of the physician, Servosse, despite his good intentions, might have died at the hands of this "mysterious spore" (345) all the same.[16]

In this novel from the nadir, questions of justice have moved squarely into the scale of the macro, even the cosmic, a sign perhaps not of a "dead end" but a new kind of imaginative force required to deal with the various dispossessions of the era, whose original causes seemed to many Americans squarely in the past but whose effects lived on in other forms—and across time. The word "force" figures prominently in the title character's first-person narrative (293), which anticipates parts of the doctor's theory in that it becomes impossible to evaluate one person's life in isolation, for "its good and evil have not fruited, perhaps have hardly seeded, yet" (292). The "mysterious spore" lingers and, traversing timelines and family lines, might yet return a "multiplied avenger" (345, 334), wreaking its justice in ways that human law can hardly fathom. In what seems an echo of his own meditation on *Hamlet* from 1868, Tourgée has his judge remind Prime early in the novel that "there's no shuffling" in the "Heavenly Chancery" (92).

For all its brilliant daring, the force of Tourgée's imagination was too strong (or not strong enough) for his historical moment. Revenge in Reconstruction would be defined by another white writer, and it was hardly the revolutionary sort the author of *Fool's* imagined. With the publication of Thomas Dixon's Reconstruction trilogy, the very project of Black enfranchisement became unjust revenge; the only heroes in this oeuvre were Klansmen fighting to defend their lives against the supposed aggression of savage Black figures. Tourgée saw this future already in 1902. Asked by an old friend to comment on Dixon's *The Leopard's Spots*, he replied that "as a picture of the times, it is not worth discussing," but "as a delineation of the dominant thought of the southern white man of yesterday and today, it is of inestimable value." He still hoped for a Black-facilitated revenge that would raise the kind of revolution prophesied in his novels; referring to the Jim Crow order, and maybe recalling the spores of *Prime*, he wrote that "lynchings and burnings are sure seedlings of slaughter." But Tourgée left the letter unsigned and marked it confidential. His public fight for revolutionary revenge in his lifetime had ended. What about our own? If in the overturning of some Confederate statues in the summer of 2020 we witnessed Tourgée's ghost haunting the squares and streets of our United States, then the antidemocratic insurrection of January 6, 2021, when the Confederate flag floated in the Capitol, showed us the staying power of Dixon's vengeance. An American history in miniature, this twenty-first-century sequence of events entreats us to ask once again: What turn might the tragedy of Reconstruction take the next time?[17]

Notes

Thanks to Mark Elliott, Richard Johnston, Tess Chakkalakal, and especially Brook Thomas, who generously supported my research and thinking.

1. Albion W. Tourgée, "G. W. Ashburne," Albion W. Tourgée Papers (AWTP), item #1239, Chautauqua County Historical Society and McClurg Museum. Biographical details in Mark Elliott, *Color-Blind Justice: Albion Tourgée and the Quest for Racial Equality from the Civil War to* Plessy v. Ferguson (New York: Oxford University Press, 2006), 122–32; and Otto H. Olsen, *Carpetbagger's Crusade: The Life of Albion Winegar Tourgée* (Baltimore, MD: Johns Hopkins University Press, 1965), 114, 120. On Ashburn, see William A. Link, *Atlanta, Cradle of the New South: Race and Remembering in the Civil War's Aftermath* (Chapel Hill: University of North Carolina Press, 2013), chap. 4.

2. Albion W. Tourgée, "Retribution or Revolution," AWTP, item #1239. Written in Tourgée's own hand, "Retribution or Revolution" has no date, but internal evidence suggests April 1868. The meditation shared part of the same page with the memorial to "G. W. Ashburne," which he published, with some changes, under the pseudonym "Wenckar" in mid-April; see "G. W. Ashburn, of Georgia," *Weekly North Carolina Standard*, April 15, 1868. I have not been able to locate any published version of "Retribution or Revolution," which I have transcribed exactly as written, with one exception: in place of "starring," which appears in the original, I have silently substituted "staring."

3. William Shakespeare, *Hamlet*, ed. Barbara A. Mowat and Paul Werstine (New York: Simon & Schuster, 2012), 3.3.61–62, 64; Grégory Pierrot, *The Black Avenger in Atlantic Culture* (Athens: University of Georgia Press, 2019), 45.

4. Shakespeare, *Hamlet*, 1.5.37. Brook Thomas, "*With Gauge and Swallow, Attorneys*: Tourgée's Romance with the Law," in this volume.

5. Ulysses S. Grant, qtd. in Gregory P. Downs, *After Appomattox: Military Occupation and the Ends of War* (Cambridge, MA: Harvard University Press, 2015), 8. Frederick Douglass, "The Assassination and Its Lessons," speech delivered at the Brooklyn Academy of Music, January 29, 1866, *Brooklyn Daily Eagle*, January 30, 1866; Douglass, speech, October 24, 1865, Parker Fraternity Lecture, Musical Hall, Boston, *Boston*

Commonwealth, October 28, 1865. Charles Sumner, "Promises of the Declaration of Independence, and Abraham Lincoln," June 1, 1865, in *The Works of Charles Sumner* (Boston: Lee and Shepard, 1875), 9:422; *Congressional Globe*, 39th Cong., 1st sess., 686.

6. [Albion W. Tourgée], *A Fool's Errand: A Novel of the South during Reconstruction* (1879; Prospect Heights, IL: Waveland, 1991), 253. Hereafter cited parenthetically.

7. Albion W. Tourgée to "Brothers of the Union," AWTP, #454. Elliott discusses this letter in *Color-Blind Justice*, 88–89; he describes Tourgée's problem with "reconstruction" as a term on 102. Tourgée presents his theory that North and South were distinct civilizations in his essay collection *An Appeal to Caesar* (New York: Fords, Howard, and Hulbert, 1884), 41. On his later support for imperialism, see Brook Thomas, *The Literature of Reconstruction: Not in Plain Black and White* (Baltimore, MD: Johns Hopkins University Press, 2017), 114. My thinking draws on Gregory P. Downs's definition of "revolution" in *The Second American Revolution: The Civil War–Era Struggle over Cuba and the Rebirth of the American Republic* (Chapel Hill: University of North Carolina Press, 2019). On the tensions between the aims of reunion and revenge in Civil War–era discourse, see George C. Rable, "Fighting for Reunion: Dilemmas of Hatred and Vengeance," *Journal of the Civil War Era* 9, no. 3 (2019): 347–77.

8. Frederick Douglass, "The Assassination and Its Lessons," February 13, 1866, in *Frederick Douglass Papers*, ed. John W. Blassingame and John R. McKivigan, 1st series (New Haven, CT: Yale University Press, 1991), 4:109. Robert C. Solomon connects revenge and justice in *A Passion for Justice: Emotions and the Origins of the Social Contract* (Reading, MA: Addison-Wesley, 1990), 9. For the Civil War–era context, see Martha Hodes, *Mourning Lincoln* (New Haven, CT: Yale University Press), esp. 253. On the composition of *Fool's*, see Elliott, *Color-Blind Justice*, 166–67.

9. Emily L. King offers this reading of Romans 12:19–20 (King James Version) in *Civil Vengeance: Literature, Culture, and Early Modern Revenge* (Ithaca, NY: Cornell University Press, 2019), 53.

10. "foot, v.," OED Online, Oxford University Press, June 2020, https://oed.com/view/Entry/72684. Albion W. Tourgée, unsigned letter to E. H. Johnson, May 15, 1902, in *Undaunted Radical: The Selected Writings and Speeches of Albion W. Tourgée*, ed. Mark Elliott and John David Smith (Baton Rouge: Louisiana State University Press, 2010), 360.

11. Albion W. Tourgée, *Bricks without Straw: A Novel*, ed. Carolyn L. Karcher (1880; Durham, NC: Duke University Press, 2009), 187, 276, 280. Hereafter cited parenthetically.

12. Pierrot, *Black Avenger*, 10. Olsen, *Carpetbagger's Crusade*, 159–60, notes that as judge Tourgée "severely punished" any efforts of African Americans to retaliate against the Klan but clarifies that Tourgée struggled with this tactic as part of his larger strategy. Tourgée, *An Appeal to Caesar*, 214.

13. Thane Rosenbaum, *Payback: The Case for Revenge* (Chicago: University of Chicago Press, 2013), 13. Kate Masur explores the relationship between Black rights and law in "Law and Its Limits in Albion Tourgée's *Bricks without Straw*," in *Cannons and Codes: Law, Literature, and America's Wars*, ed. Allison L. LaCroix et al. (New York: Oxford University Press, 2021), 91–112.

14. Brook Thomas, *American Literary Realism and the Failed Promise of Contract* (Berkeley: University of California Press, 1997), 218; Carolyn L. Karcher, *A Refugee from*

His Race: Albion W. Tourgée and His Fight against White Supremacy (Chapel Hill: University of North Carolina Press, 2016), 77.

15. Albion W. Tourgée, *Pactolus Prime* (New York: Cassell Publishing Co., 1890), 333, 339, 341, 339, 336, 345, 346. Hereafter cited parenthetically. Charles Creighton, "Yellow Fever," in *The Encyclopaedia Britannica*, 9th ed., American Reprint (Philadelphia: J. M. Stoddart, 1889), 24:770–73. On *Prime*'s science, see Thomas, *American Literary Realism*, chap. 7.

16. On the early American history of yellow fever, see Sari Altschuler, *The Medical Imagination: Literature and Health in the Early United States* (Philadelphia: University of Pennsylvania Press, 2018), chap. 2. Edward J. Blum, *Reforging the White Republic: Race, Religion, and American Nationalism, 1865–1898*, updated ed. (Baton Rouge: Louisiana State University Press, 2015), chap. 5, treats the Reconstruction-era epidemic and records that some Black Americans saw the 1878 outbreak as divine vengeance. Brook Thomas supplies the context for Tourgée in *Literature of Reconstruction*, 279.

17. Dixon's Reconstruction trilogy included *The Leopard's Spots: A Romance of the White Man's Burden* (1902), *The Clansman: An Historical Romance of the Ku Klux Klan* (1905), and *The Traitor: A Story of the Fall of the Invisible Empire* (1907). Tourgée to Johnson, in *Undaunted Radical*, 356–57, 374.

17

Thomas Dixon, Albion Tourgée, and the False Balance of the Civil War

Alex Zweber Leslie

When Thomas Dixon Jr.'s *The Leopard's Spots* became a runaway best-seller in 1902, Albion Tourgée's publishers promptly reissued his own erstwhile bestselling novel of Reconstruction, 1879's *A Fool's Errand*. Both novels utilize conventions of historical romance to depict a nation still bit-terly divided in the wake of the Civil War, but they have little else in common. Dixon's novel advocates a virulent white supremacy; Tourgée's excoriates the southern regime of racial terror and disenfranchisement. If political idealism partly motivated the decision to reissue *A Fool's Errand*, however, the interplay between the two novels in the literary marketplace proved to be part of a more complex chain of effects. Despite the novels' diametrically opposed politics, peri-odicals recommended both approvingly—even in the same sentence. Publishers and reviewers treated *A Fool's Errand* as complementary to *The Leopard's Spots* rather than as an alternative to it. Readers were encouraged to read both nov-els, not in order to choose the correct account on their own but in order to re-main in a state of pseudoenlightened indecision, agnostic toward truth claims or moral judgment. This episode in print history illuminates the emergence of a now familiar practice of reading the Civil War and its cultural heritage. By trac-ing the intertwined publication and reception history of *A Fool's Errand* and *The Leopard's Spots*, I show how the unlikely pairing of Dixon and Tourgée prefigured our contemporary popular memory of the Civil War, which purports to be fair because it remains suspended in balance.

Progressive Era critics' treatment of Dixon and Tourgée exemplifies what media critics call "false balance" and social media users, more colloquially, call "both-sides-ism." This rhetorical device consists of the assertion that two op-posed positions should be treated as undecidable or equivalent because each has shortcomings, regardless of differences in degree. The underlying fallacy, of course, is all too familiar in contemporary clashes over the legacy of the Civil War and Reconstruction, from popular dramatizations pairing Robert E. Lee and

Ulysses S. Grant to the equivocation of public demonstrations by Confederacy sympathizers and Black Lives Matter protesters. The pervasiveness of this approach was neither immediate nor inevitable. Postbellum authors had previously achieved popular approval depicting the Civil War, but they often did so by utilizing one of two strategies designed to mitigate the conflicts comprising it: either by dwelling on accounts of particular figures and terrain to emphasize sterilized historical details or by deploying plot tropes like the romance of reunion to imaginatively surmount sociopolitical differences. Dixon and Tourgée seem to violently resist such polite restraint or compromise. Yet readers consumed these texts under the influence of turn-of-the-century print culture trends—the ideological diversification of publishers' lists, the fad for historical romance novels, and the symposium format in magazines—that promoted interpretive practices in which readers carried out the work of bringing together opposed positions themselves.

Fords, Howard, & Hulbert of New York reprinted *A Fool's Errand* in 1902. The same publishing house had brought out Tourgée's novels throughout his career, beginning with *Toinette* (1875). *A Fool's Errand*, his second novel, is a partly autobiographical narrative of the Union veteran Comfort Servosse, who moves to North Carolina for his health only to become involved in state politics and local efforts to educate and protect Black freedpeople. These activities earn Servosse—as they did his author—the fury of the Ku Klux Klan, and in the novel's climax he narrowly avoids being lynched. To this plot Tourgée somewhat unevenly grafted a romance between Servosse's daughter, Lily, and his political rival's son, Melville Gurney. The narrative is interspersed, however, with didactic chapters that critique the inadequacies of federal Reconstruction policy, northern indifference toward the plight of Black freedpeople, the racist manipulations of the southern press and officials, and the overall divergence of northern and southern society.

Fords, Howard, & Hulbert was unprepared for the phenomenal popularity of such a formally unusual novel. Though *A Fool's Errand* sold 84,889 copies in its first thirteen months, public commentary fueled demand that outstripped supply.[1] To meet and stimulate this demand, Fords, Howard & Hulbert quickly published a simultaneous expanded edition in 1880 that included illustrations and a new anti-Klan tract by Tourgée. These plates were reused for the 1902 edition. The firm's surprise at the success of *A Fool's Errand* is understandable. A large proportion of their list consisted of religious publications, most notably an extensive series of sermons and tracts by Henry Ward Beecher, one of the best-known preachers in America. As natural outgrowths from this base, they published art volumes of popular poetry with religious themes, such as versions of

Alfred Tennyson's *In Memoriam* and collections edited by William Cullen Bry-ant, as well as religious fiction, including late-career novels by Harriet Beecher Stowe and early-career novels by the reformer Helen Stuart Campbell. Tourgée's work, particularly his late novel *Murvale Eastman: Christian Socialist* (1890), fits with the firm's investment in social reform. Still, its initial decision to pub-lish Tourgée's Reconstruction novels was something of a fluke for both parties: Tourgée had hoped for a more prestigious placement for *A Fool's Errand* and *Figs and Thistles* (1879) before the latter was declined by Harper & Brothers, among others.[2]

Inspired by the success of *A Fool's Errand* and its immediate follow-ups, how-ever, Fords, Howard, & Hulbert thereafter expanded its offerings to include a considerable volume of material about the Civil War and its aftermath. Tourgée's influence and connections provided the source for many of their books on these topics and more.[3] In addition to novels like Tourgée's, Fords, Howard, & Hulbert published several soldiers' memoirs, a biography of Abraham Lincoln by former cabinet member William Stoddard, and Black editor-activist T. Thomas Fortune's *Black and White: Land, Labor, and Politics in the South* (1884). But their publica-tion that appears to have created the most buzz on the subject of postbellum race and politics was *An Appeal to Pharaoh* (1889) by Carlyle McKinley, a southern writer, newspaper editor, and instructor at the school that would become the Cit-adel. McKinley argues that no legislation could enact political equality between the races on the premise of a supposed fundamental social inequality beyond the possibility of redress. On this basis, he concludes that African Americans must be deported to Africa. This is a version of the argument that Dixon would make a decade later, and it comes from the house that Tourgée built.

Though *The Leopard's Spots* (and the advertising campaign for it) more explic-itly engaged Harriet Beecher Stowe's *Uncle Tom's Cabin* (1852)—turning its vil-lainous slave-owning Simon Legree into a scalawag Reconstructionist—Dixon's novel has more in common in tone and setting with *A Fool's Errand*, which critics had widely hailed at the time of its original publication as the successor to Stowe's novel.[4] *The Leopard's Spots* opens in Reconstruction North Carolina, which Dixon depicts as rife with misrule, financial ruin, and violent Black crime until Reverend John Durham helps form the Ku Klux Klan to fight back. The second part of the novel, set twenty years later, follows the political career of Durham's adoptive son Charlie Gaston. As in *A Fool's Errand*, the antagonists are apathetic northerners and opportunistic southerners, but in *The Leopard's Spots* the latter group consists of those who manipulate Blacks into contesting white sovereignty, often with ulterior motives. Charlie leads a crusade against Republican corrup-

tion, Black voting, and miscegenation that makes him a celebrity while also pit-
ting him against the aristocratic General Worth, whose daughter he loves. Like
Servosse, Gaston finds himself between the Scylla of mob rule and the Charybdis
of the Old South.

What *A Fool's Errand* did for Fords, Howard, & Hulbert, *A Leopard's Spots*
did for the new publishing house of Doubleday, Page & Co. Organized in 1900
with the experienced editor Walter Hines Page after Frank Nelson Doubleday's
split from Samuel McClure, the firm led the trend away from the courtesies of
gentleman publishing and toward more avowedly profit-driven business practices.[5] Publishing Dixon, and *The Leopard's Spots* in particular, proved foundational to Doubleday, Page's success. As Page noted in *A Publisher's Confession*
(1905), "half a dozen popular writers will build a publishing house," and by that
time Dixon had proven himself a popular writer three times over.[6] Doubleday,
Page moved one hundred thousand copies of *The Leopard's Spots* in its first
eleven months; the novel received top billing in almost all of the publisher's advertisements in leading trade journals from its February 1902 announcement until fall 1903, disappearing only when replaced by Dixon's next bestseller, *The One
Woman* (the first volume of his trilogy against socialism).[7] *The Clansman* (1905)
and *The Traitor* (1907), the subsequent volumes of his Reconstruction trilogy,
would also achieve bestseller status, while *Comrades* (1909), his second novel on
socialism, would fall just short. Of the forty-two times a Doubleday, Page book
made the *Bookman's* monthly top-six bestseller list in that publisher's critical first
decade, Dixon was its author thirteen times.[8] Only one other Doubleday, Page
author came close, with Ellen Glasgow at eleven appearances on the list. Dixon
may not have singlehandedly made a success of Doubleday, Page, but without
him the publisher's history would have been radically different.

Page accepted Dixon's manuscript not because he agreed with its politics but
because it advanced the new firm's strategy of prioritizing historical romance,
then the top-selling genre in trade publishing.[9] By the late 1890s, the Civil War
and Reconstruction had become regular backdrops for bestsellers in the genre,
including most notably Stephen Crane's 1895 *The Red Badge of Courage*, Thomas
Nelson Page's 1898 *Red Rock*, and Winston Churchill's 1901 *The Crisis*. The fad
came on so suddenly that George Washington Cable could reasonably defend
himself against charges of merely cashing in with his 1901 bestseller *The Cavalier* by professing that he had started writing it in 1893.[10] Indeed, the 1902 reissue of *A Fool's Errand* motivated by this wave of Civil War and Reconstruction
novels achieved considerably more press than an 1894 reissue that predated it.[11]
The Leopard's Spots wasn't even the only bestselling historical romance about the

war's impact on southern society that Doubleday, Page published in 1902: Ellen Glasgow's *The Battleground* vied for prominence in the firm's advertisements at the same time. It is certainly true that these novels represent a cultural concern for working through the conflicts of the Civil War and its aftermath. By utilizing the same conventions typical of historical romances across all settings, however, as a phenomenon these Civil War and Reconstruction novels render that conflict as another generic historical event. Within this context, Dixon's and Tourgée's novels were easily associated as belonging to the same genre.

Even so, Doubleday, Page published multiple books by Booker T. Washington, including *Up from Slavery* (1901), and advertised them alongside Dixon's novels.[12] In fall 1905, as *The Clansman* continued to blaze through new editions and the popular press, Page attempted to win over W. E. B. Du Bois as well. In a terse though inconclusive reply, Du Bois wrote that he was uncomfortable with the idea of publishing with "the exploiters of Tom Dixon."[13] Page, invoking a duty to facilitate "freedom of opinion," protested that "we are simply his publishers."[14] Page was voicing a growing opinion among publishers that the profession's service to the public lay in a greater willingness to put divergent opinions into print.[15] Here, too, Doubleday, Page was an industry bellwether, publishing Theodore Dreiser's *Sister Carrie* (1900) and Upton Sinclair's *The Jungle* (1906) after other houses had rejected them for reasons of propriety. As Du Bois understood, however, publishers exploited the professed ideal of ideological diversity out of financial interests, not societal interests. While Du Bois's contemporaneous publication choices demonstrate his willingness to appear alongside writers who disagreed over racial equality (as will be seen), his objection to sharing publishers with Dixon indicates his recognition that the damage caused by providing a platform for certain opinions undercut any benefits arising from the freedom to express them.

Postbellum publishers, then, pursued what were at the time both radically racist books and radically antiracist books. Fords, Howard, & Hulbert did so despite having a list that in many ways resembled the kind that would have included only abolitionist perspectives on race before the war, and Doubleday, Page did so despite owing their success to popular racism. The fact that the firm behind a Tourgée could be the same one behind a McKinley—indeed, that publishing Tourgée might in fact directly lead to a firm publishing an opposed position like McKinley's—played a vital role in shaping how *A Fool's Errand* circulated and what readers did with it as Reconstruction increasingly slipped from the realm of ongoing possibility to that of unpopular memory. The literary field was shifting over the 1880s and 1890s, such that publishing books like *A Fool's Errand* or

The Leopard's Spots no longer carried the meaning it once did. Publishing an ideologically fraught book no longer marked a publisher as having an ideological position. This shift would come to have an impact on reading practices as well.

Dixon's and Tourgée's careers overlapped only briefly—Tourgée died three years after *The Leopard's Spots* appeared—but comparisons between the two were common enough to regularly entangle them after Dixon's rise to fame, even plaguing Tourgée's obituaries. Dixon added fuel to the fire, incorporating what could only very generously be called his own Tourgée obituary into "The Story of Ku Klux Klan" that headlined the *Metropolitan Magazine* in September 1905. The article functioned as self-promotion for *The Clansman*, which had come out in January of that year; it was subsequently excerpted and reprinted in a number of newspapers, including the prominent Richmond *Times-Dispatch*.[16] Dixon blurs fact and fiction, mixing illustrations from his novel with portraits of historical figures. The article is a defense of the Klan that retells the attempt to lynch Tourgée as fictionalized in *A Fool's Errand*. Dixon shrewdly quotes at length one of the most flattering depictions of southerners in *A Fool's Errand*, a passage that testifies to the "indomitable spirit of the Southern people" who "scorned to yield to what they deemed oppression."[17] On this basis, he asserts that Tourgée "was a man the people of North Carolina would have been delighted to know under nobler conditions. He was one of the few men in our state government at the time who had any brains or conscience at all." This is clearly backhanded praise, but it possessed utility beyond its backhandedness. With this move, Dixon gives his readers the rhetorical warrant to believe both him and Tourgée. Indeed, this is a key point of the article: The Klan that tried to kill Tourgée was a different Klan, a mere "set of scoundrels," not Dixon's noble brotherhood.[18] Dixon had made the same appeal in *The Leopard's Spots*. Durham and others disband the original Klan because "it's too easy for vicious men to abuse it. Its power is too great. Besides, its work is done"; Gaston condemns the Klan when it is later reincarnated for its lack of principle and order.[19]

Dixon, then, presents Tourgée as a good guy who ended up on the wrong side of history: You may believe Tourgée as much as you want so long as you also believe Dixon. This seemingly conciliatory gesture may be surprising coming from someone as divisive and fundamentalist as Dixon, yet he had already treated Abraham Lincoln in a similar fashion in *The Leopard's Spots* to less than conciliatory ends. That novel praises a pro-southern "martyred Lincoln" for his "statesmanlike" bearing, "fraternity," and "charity," and it makes a sympathetic northerner profess that "the death of Mr. Lincoln was the most awful calamity that could possibly have befallen the South." Dixon rehabilitates Lincoln in order to invoke him as anti-Black via Durham, who remains one of the novel's primary mouthpieces: "Lincoln was right when he said, 'There is a physical difference between the white and the black races, which I believe will forever forbid them living together on terms of social and political equality.'"[20] Such a rhetorical move, reproducing structurally the segregation Dixon's argument calls for, asks readers to forgo any attempt at synthesizing rival accounts; it instead encourages readers to come away believing that Lincoln and truth claims can exist on both sides without overlapping.

Dixon is able to cite Tourgée to this end in "The Story of Ku Klux Klan" in part because *A Fool's Errand* provides similar openings for readers to straddle opposed positions in the interest of securing agreement. In one of the novel's didactic chapters, for example, Tourgée cycles between paraphrased paragraphs labeled "The Northern Idea," "The Southern Idea," "The Northern Idea of the Southern Idea," and "The Southern Idea of the Northern Idea" to illustrate how the two sections "played at cross-purposes" in their interpretations of the aims and impacts of the Civil War.[21] Each side is in turn criticized and vindicated. The North, justifiably associating the war with the abolitionist cause, insists out of blind self-interest that conditions will gradually improve on their own, while the South, justifiably diagnosing northern hypocrisy regarding the practical consequences of racial equality, insists out of blind self-interest that Blacks be dispossessed of any freedom that challenges their subordinacy. Such passages function as olive branches by leveraging the division they articulate rather than reconciling it. Like Dixon, Tourgée of course develops a nuanced account of right and wrong. Nonetheless, Tourgée strategically makes it possible along the way to agree with the perspective of his southern opponents so long as the reader also agrees with his assessment of Reconstruction's failure. Indeed, in the novel's final line a southern Unionist expresses regret at Servosse's imprudence. Critics put these openings to new use at the turn of the century.

The savvy publicist Dixon understood the potential value of curated opposition even better than Tourgée or Fords, Howard, & Hulbert in republishing him. Where *A Fool's Errand* has a chapter on the Union League titled "Citizens in Embryo," *The Leopard's Spots* counters with a chapter on the same titled "The Man or Brute in Embryo." Dixon's more distinctive positions in *The Leopard's Spots* often directly respond to Tourgée's most apt critiques. Halfway through the novel, the scheming MacLeod tempts Gaston to join the Republican Party by pointing out that "the Southern people have nothing in common with these Northern Democrats who make your platforms and nominate your candidate . . . you vote to enforce platforms that mean economic ruin to the South."[22] In *A Fool's Errand*,

Servosse argued similarly that white electoral partisanship hurt both races, professing that "the ignorant freedman [and] the ignorant poor-white man" were "the fruitage of slavery" and ongoing lack of government intervention.[23] Gaston's solution, for which the novel awards him the state governorship, is to flout both parties by combining Progressive statist reformism with even more radical segregation: "There is not room for both of us on this continent!"[24] Later parallels of *A Fool's Errand* in *The Clansman* and "The Story of Ku Klux Klan" likely stem from Dixon's recognition that such ties with Tourgée generated publicity and profit. A writer in the *Salt Lake Herald*, commenting on Dixon's "The Story of Ku Klux Klan," evinces how compelling the antagonism between the two authors could be. "In any question of veracity" between Dixon and Tourgée, the *Herald* posits, "it should be remembered that the two writers naturally view the situation differently. Judge Tourgee was a northern man and an extremely radical one. Dr. Dixon is an equally radical southerner. It is probable that both endeavored honestly to set forth the truth. And it is equally probable that both erred in some particulars."[25]

Pairing and balancing opposed opinions in this way drew on the logic of the symposium format, which had become popular in magazines over the preceding two decades. The phenomenon began when the *North American Review* printed a series of divergent opinions on the currency problem in November 1877. L. S. Metcalf, who made the symposium a regular feature of the *North American Review* when he became editor in 1878, instituted it as a cornerstone of the *Forum* when he left to found that magazine in 1886.[26] Other magazines of politics and public opinion adopted the format as well, perhaps most notably the *Arena* in 1889. Metcalf was succeeded at the *Forum* by none other than Walter Hines Page, who well understood the appeal of the practice. Page did not institute the symposium proper when he moved on to the *Atlantic* in 1898 in a short-lived bid to boost its perpetually disappointing circulation figures, but he did draw on his experience at the *Forum* to push for a timelier and more political periodical. In 1901, shortly after his departure to join Doubleday, Page & Co., his influence would bear fruit at the *Atlantic* in the form of a serial symposium on Reconstruction that included a variety of opposed viewpoints from, among others, Du Bois, Thomas Nelson Page, Woodrow Wilson, and William Dunning. Du Bois's contribution, along with several other articles he had published in the *Atlantic* dating back to Page's tenure, were adapted for *The Souls of Black Folk* (1903), which Page no doubt had in mind when soliciting a manuscript from Du Bois.

An array of newspaper commentaries and magazine reviews apply the logic of the symposium format to *A Fool's Errand* and *The Leopard's Spots*. E. H. Johnson, an erstwhile friend of Tourgée, wrote one particularly illustrative example for the *Watchman*, the nation's leading Baptist periodical.[27] The piece, titled "'The Leopard's Spots' and 'The Fools' Errand,'" begins by noting the authors' shared criticisms of Reconstruction policy. Though Tourgée's novel is two decades old, Johnson credits its prescience of subsequent sociopolitical events as more than sufficient cause to recommend it. A discerning catalog of the numerous conflicts between the two novels follows. Johnson is by no means a bad literary or social critic, but his conclusion demurs:

> Unlike as are these books, both ought to be read, if a lesson is to be accepted from either, and the new book certainly ought to revive the sale of the old. I think it will be felt that while Mr. Dixon shows unsurpassable intensity of conviction, Tourgée displays a more statesmanlike breadth. But neither writer can be called a whit more honest than the other, nor, what some will refuse to believe, neither means to be less humane than the other, or less patriotic.[28]

The article's obstinate refusal to square the contradicting positions it has spent a page outlining—"neither a whit more honest"—reveals not simply the difficulty of discerning right from wrong but an attempt to refrain from doing so. Readers aren't supposed to read both novels so that they may decide for themselves but rather so that they remain in a state of pseudoenlightened indecision.

The symposium format and the critical practices based on it did not inherently produce false balance. The *Arena*, for example, became known for espousing progressive reformism by using the symposium format to introduce new perspectives on contentious issues. When it came to evaluating Reconstruction through Dixon and Tourgée, however, even the *Arena* promoted the same reading practice as Johnson. The *Arena*'s review of *A Fool's Errand* was explicitly motivated by the success of *The Leopard's Spots*, which it had reviewed in its previous issue as a historically accurate though at times excessively prejudiced work of moderate literary success.[29] The review of Tourgée's reprinted novel notes that "the new [Civil War and Reconstruction] novels for the most part are the work of writers who view this period only from the standpoint of strong Southern sympathizers, and in some instances the writings have been very deeply tinged with a prejudice that destroys the judicial temper absolutely necessary to the historian or any one who would faithfully portray a given period"—though it does not so impugn *The Leopard's Spots*. The review continues that "it is well, therefore, that the rising generation should have the opportunity of hearing the other side, and in the handsome and newly published edition of 'A Fool's Errand.'" The *Arena* ultimately recommends the novel more safely on the basis of its fictionality rather than its claims to truthfulness: "Aside from its historical value, 'A Fool's Errand' is a beautiful romance and an important contribution to American fiction that merits a permanent place in literature."[30] Retroactively delimiting Tourgée's didactic and multimodal novel within the generic bounds of popular historical romance, the *Arena* underscores the pastness of the events—and concerns—that *A Fool's Errand* depicts.

If the *Arena* blunted *A Fool's Errand* by equating it with turn-of-the-century trends in historical romance, however, it did not defang the novel. The review praises Tourgée's prose and judgment, even so far as to proclaim *A Fool's Errand* the best novel of Reconstruction. Yet it nonetheless concludes that "we would not have the reader acquaint himself with but one side of the story. No author is wholly impartial, and he who reads 'A Fool's Errand' should also read 'Red Rock' or 'The Leopard's Spots.'"[31] The logic of false balance emerges again. The terminology employed in this review and those cited earlier, of "impartiality" or treating all parties as equal, is instructive. Both sides have agreeable points, yet both sides have uncomfortably partisan points; therefore, they are equivalent, and therefore we cannot choose between them. To believe one over the other would be a fault under this logic because it would encompass merely "one side of the story." In each review, breadth of perspective takes precedence over, or at least defines, other potential evaluative metrics like truthfulness or justness. *A Fool's Errand* and *The Leopard's Spots*, as two extremes of the political spectrum, come to encompass all possible positions in between like a symposium in microcosm. By emphasizing breadth and equivalence of perspective, these critics suggest how to approach not only Dixon and Tourgée but the wider gamut of Civil War and Reconstruction accounts, including those invoked in passing like Page's *Red Rock*. This approach to cultural memory differs from both reconciliation and forgetting. Its aim is to survey numerous disparate accounts not in order to subsequently evaluate them more effectively but in order to hold them all in a liminal state of belief.

A Fool's Errand and *The Leopard's Spots* are exceptional candidates for such readings precisely because of their insistence against reconciliation. Both novels use Jeremiah 13:23 to interpret a moral from the failure of Reconstruction: "Can the Ethiopian change his skin, or the leopard his spots?" For Tourgée, the "Ethiopian" represents southern whites, incapable of accepting equality even pragmatically. Comfort Servosse recognizes late in the novel that he has been a fool "to believe that the leopard *might* change his spots, while yet the Ethiopian retained his dusky skin." For Dixon, who adopts the allusion in his title, the "Ethiopian" represents African Americans, supposedly incapable of democratic citizenship, as well as the northerners who support them. Both misinterpret Jeremiah, whose logic parallels a more hopeful Reconstruction: With God's help the leopard can and must change his spots, doing good where accustomed to do evil, so that Israel may be reunified. Both authors imagine a degree of cooperation between the opposed sections late in their novels, Dixon in the Spanish-American War that unites Anglo-Saxon North and South under the banner of imperialism and Tourgée in the warm glow of retrospect that fills Servosse's antagonists as he lies dying. Yet these moments are overshadowed as both novels ultimately remain suspended in opposition. The marriage that concludes *The Leopard's Spots* further entrenches its sectional position by unifying Gaston's New South with the Old South of Sallie Worth. *A Fool's Errand* suggests a North-South romance of reunion between Lily and Melville only to defer it indefinitely. The novel instead concludes at Servosse's grave, where a sympathetic southern farmer reflects ambivalently on the persistence of political division: "Somehow it seemed as if his ideas wa'n't calkilated for this meridian."[32]

The Leopard's Spots proved more enduringly popular than most of its contemporaries for the same reason that *A Fool's Errand* proved enduringly relevant: not because more readers necessarily agreed with the perspectives of these respective novels—scholars have shown that many did not—but because their contentiousness evoked their opposites.[33] The two novels are doggedly radical relative to turn-of-the-century historical romances, but as their publishers and reviewers suggest, this makes them all the more effective for curating a supposedly balanced perspective. Whereas other Civil War and Reconstruction novels forged internal syntheses between representative opposed protagonists with tropes like the romance of reunion, the emergent practice of reading across disunion assimilated the thorny works of Dixon and Tourgée for comfortably relativized popular consumption. Much as publishing *A Fool's Errand* no longer marked an ideological position at the turn of the century, reading or even enjoying *A Fool's Errand* no longer entailed an ideological position. In the place of Reconstruction, we have false balance.

Notes

1. On Fords, Howard, & Hulbert's sales, see Roy F. Dibble, *Albion W. Tourgée* (New York: Lemcke & Buechner, 1921), 69. On their struggle meeting demand, see "Literary

and Trade Notes," *Publishers' Weekly* 18 (August 21, 1880): 213. As Dibble points out, given their drop-off after 1880, sales probably did not reach the oft-invoked 200,000 mark unless one assumes an inordinate number of pirated printings. Exaggerated sales reports were a mainstay of *A Fool's Errand*'s reception from the start: a widely reprinted 1881 notice claimed that it sold "260,000 or 270,000" copies, and Tourgée's *New York Times* obituary may have popularized the claim that it sold "probably 200,000 copies." *Emporia News*, April 29, 1881, 1; "Albion W. Tourgée Dead," *New York Times*, May 22, 1905, 7.

2. See Mark Elliott, *Color-Blind Justice: Albion Tourgée and the Quest for Radical Equality from the Civil War to* Plessy v. Ferguson (New York: Oxford University Press, 2006), 170.

3. Fords, Howard, & Hulbert published a series of works originally published in the magazine Tourgée edited, *Our Continent*. This arrangement sometimes yielded more popular authors than the firm typically secured, such as Julian Hawthorne's *Dust* (1883). Fords, Howard, & Hulbert itself only predated Tourgée's fiction by a few years: It was founded as J. B. Ford & Co. in 1867. "Notes," *Critic* 13 (November 17, 1888): 250. As Tourgée's literary star faded, so did his publisher's, exacerbated by the departure and death of the original Ford and his son, respectively. The firm auctioned off plates in February 1903 and thereafter did not appear in *Publishers' Weekly*'s exhaustive "Directory of American Publishers." "Clearance and Remainder Sale," *Publishers' Weekly* 63, no. 4 (January 24, 1903): 131; "Directory of American Publishers," *Publishers' Weekly* 65 suppl. (January 30, 1904). The 1902 printing of *A Fool's Errand* was one of their last.

4. See the account of *A Fool's Errand*'s original reception in Elliott, *Color-Blind Justice*, 170–71.

5. John Tebbel, *A History of Book Publishing in the United States*, vol. 2: *The Expansion of an Industry, 1865–1919* (New York: R. R. Bowker, 1975), 318–31. Page remarked in 1905 that "all these modern commercial methods have added to the publisher's expense or risk; and for these reasons his business has become more like any other manufacturing business." Walter Hines Page, *A Publisher's Confession* (New York: Doubleday, Page & Co., 1905), 65.

6. Page, *A Publisher's Confession*, 88.

7. "Books with Blood in Their Veins," *Publishers' Weekly* 63, no. 8 (February 21, 1903): 624. *The Leopard's Spots*' first half-page *Publishers' Weekly* ad was on February 22, 1902, shortly after its announcement.

8. See "Sales of Books during the Month" column in the *Bookman*. The *Bookman* was the first trade journal to collate bestseller figures. Though bestseller list methodology was and remains inexact, Dixon's success far exceeds uncertainty. A 1903 review of the previous year's bestsellers listed only one Doubleday, Page title, *The Leopard's Spots*, at 94,000 copies sold (6,000 copies behind the total then printed). "Chronicle and Comment. Great Sales," *Bookman* 17, no. 1 (March 1903): 17–19.

9. Page and Dixon met as students at Johns Hopkins University and again in Raleigh while Dixon served in the North Carolina state legislature and Page edited the *State Chronicle*, but Page ultimately took a more conciliatory approach to race issues. Anthony Slide, *American Racist: The Life and Films of Thomas Dixon* (Lexington: University Press of Kentucky, 2004), 32.

10. See Elaine Ware, "George W. Cable's *The Cavalier*, an American Best Seller and Theatrical Attraction," *Southern Literary Journal* 19, no. 2 (Spring 1987): 70–80.

11. See Elliott, *Color-Blind Justice*, 306.

12. "Books That Count," *Publishers' Weekly* 63, no. 12 (March 21, 1903): 751.

13. John David Smith, "'My Books Are Hard Reading for a Negro': Tom Dixon and His African American Critics, 1905–1939," in *Thomas Dixon Jr. and the Birth of Modern America*, ed. Michele K. Gillespie and Randal L. Hall (Baton Rouge: Louisiana State University Press, 2006), 46.

14. Smith, "'My Books Are Hard Reading for a Negro,'" 46.

15. See Paul S. Boyer, "Gilded-Age Consensus, Repressive Campaigns, and Gradual Liberalization: The Shifting Rhythms of Book Censorship," in *A History of the Book in America*, vol. 4: *Print in Motion: The Expansion of Publishing and Reading in the United States, 1880–1940*, ed. Carl F. Kaestle and Janice A. Radway (Chapel Hill: University of North Carolina Press, 2009); Donald Sheehan, *This Was Publishing: A Chronicle of the Book Trade in the Gilded Age* (Bloomington: Indiana University Press, 1952), chap. 5; and Tebbel, *A History of Book Publishing in the United States*, 2:170–74. Boyer, Sheehan, and Tebbel cite increases in the publication of books at odds with public orthodoxy, publisher attestations like Page's, and complaints from conservative commentators beginning around 1900.

16. Thomas Dixon Jr., "The Story of the Ku Klux Klan," *Times Dispatch* (Richmond, VA), October 29, 1905, C3, https://chroniclingamerica.loc.gov/lccn/sn85038615/1905-10-29/ed-1/seq-33/.

17. Albion W. Tourgée, *A Fool's Errand* (1879; New York: Fords, Howard, & Hulbert, 1902), 308.

18. Thomas Dixon Jr., "The Story of Ku Klux Klan," *Metropolitan Magazine* 22, no. 6 (September 1905): 662, https://babel.hathitrust.org/cgi/pt?id=mdp.39015039382489.

19. Thomas Dixon Jr., *The Leopard's Spots* (New York: Doubleday, Page & Co., 1902), 168.

20. Dixon, *The Leopard's Spots*, 35, 77, 459.

21. Tourgée, *A Fool's Errand*, 127–28.

22. Dixon, *The Leopard's Spots*, 192.

23. Tourgée, *A Fool's Errand*, 366.

24. Dixon, *The Leopard's Spots*, 439.

25. "The Ku Klux Klan," *Salt Lake Herald*, September 1, 1905, 4, https://chroniclingamerica.loc.gov/lccn/sn85058130/1905-09-01/ed-1/seq-4/.

26. See entries for the *Forum* and the *North American Review* in Frank Luther Mott, *A History of American Magazines*, vols. 2 and 4 (Cambridge, MA: Belknap, 1957–1968).

27. Tourgée's frustrated epistolary reply to Johnson provides insight into his feelings about Dixon. Albion Winegar Tourgée to E. H. Johnson, May 15, 1902, Chautauqua County Historical Society, NY, https://cdm16694.contentdm.oclc.org/digital/collection/NYCCH/id/765/.

28. E. H. Johnson, "'The Leopard's Spots' and 'The Fools' Errand,'" *Watchman* 84, no. 17 (April 24, 1902), 11, https://babel.hathitrust.org/cgi/pt?id=nyp.33433003180639.

29. See "Three Epochs of American History Mirrored in Fiction," *Arena* 28, no. 2 (August 1902): 215–18, https://babel.hathitrust.org/cgi/pt?id=uc1.$b200200.

30. "Books of the Day: A Fool's Errand," *Arena* 28, no. 3 (September 1902): 333–34, https://babel.hathitrust.org/cgi/pt?id=uc1.$b200200.

31. "Books of the Day: A Fool's Errand," 334.

32. Tourgée, *A Fool's Errand*, 323, 361.

33. See Brook Thomas, *The Literature of Reconstruction: Not in Plain Black and White* (Baltimore, MD: Johns Hopkins University Press, 2017).

Afterword

Mark Elliott

This volume of essays demonstrates how much the writings of Albion W. Tourgée remain a relevant and a valuable source for understanding the historical aspirations and shortcomings of American democracy. The themes of race, citizenship, and American nationalism that permeate his work continue to dominate our country's culture and politics as we continue to aspire, as he did, to achieve a more equal and just society. Over the years, scholars and general readers who encounter Tourgée in one context or another often react with surprise if not astonishment at the perspicacity of his analysis in his literature or editorials and wonder why he is not better known. Periodically, Tourgée enthusiasts have endeavored to redress this oversight. Each time, scholars seem to discover that there was more to Tourgée than we thought the last time we looked at him.

One difficulty in getting a handle on Tourgée is that his career crosses temporal and disciplinary categories, and so he has received attention in multiple scholarly fields that are not sufficiently in dialogue with one another. Since the 1960s, Tourgée has served as an eloquent primary source for historians studying Reconstruction because of his role as a participant and eyewitness who fought to transform the state of North Carolina. In the expansive literature on Civil War memory, Tourgée has received scholarly attention, especially from David Blight, who judged him second to only Frederick Douglass in his profound devotion to the emancipationist memory of the Civil War. More recently, in works by Carolyn Karcher, myself, and others, Tourgée's efforts to fight back against lynching and other forms of white supremacy in the 1890s have been more fully examined, especially his role as Homer Plessy's lead attorney in the now famous (but then ignored) US Supreme Court case of *Plessy v. Ferguson* (1896). But it is as a literary author where Tourgée's reputation has been the most unstable and in need of a more thorough reassessment.

Like the entire era of Reconstruction with which he was associated, Tourgée and his literary works were buried under an avalanche of vilification in the propagandistic distortion that served as an ideological foundation for Jim Crow

America. Repudiation of his work came from multiple angles. Reactionary forces rolled back the legal and constitutional revolution he had helped lead in the South. Two decades later, his constitutional theories were firmly rejected by the Supreme Court. His literary works suffered a gradual decline too, undermined both by their political message and their aesthetic forms—both of which seemed outdated to a new generation busily producing an outpouring of popular works devoted to the romanticization of the Old South, celebration of the Confederacy, and the denigration of Black people and Reconstruction. The rise of literary modernism in the early years of the twentieth century further contributed to the decline of his reputation as a novelist.

The long shadow of Reconstruction's failure makes it difficult to view Tourgée in a light other than that of explaining its reversal and attributing blame. Tourgée himself agonized and ruminated over that failure—his scathing assessments of the "wise men" leading the Republican Party who lacked the foresight to overcome the resistance to the democratization of southern life anticipated in many ways the modern scholarship of the period. By association, the stigma of his "fool's errand" still hovers around Tourgée and defines him. For him personally, an equally devastating setback was the failure of his literary magazine, *Our Continent*, which may have had just as lasting an impact on his literary career. In the early 1880s, Tourgée assumed a place within the literary establishment and tried to shape the direction of American fiction, particularly in regard to the monumental national drama of the Civil War and Reconstruction. Tourgée envisioned emancipation and its consequences at the center of the story—and he encouraged Black authors to find their voice in the telling of it. This volume endeavors to understand his larger literary project, which is shown to be an inclusive and nationalizing one, and use it to illuminate the politics of fiction in this time period.

One thing this volume makes clear is that Tourgée saw himself as a serious literary author. He was not a lawyer, journalist, or politician who merely dabbled in literature or used fiction as a tool for other aims. As his brief tenure editing *Our Continent* shows, Tourgée aspired to be a "man of letters" and an influential one at that. His work was inventive and artistic—sometimes even experimental and philosophical. These essays draw our attention to his range of forms, including the gothic romance of *Toinette*, the social realism of *A Fools' Errand* and *Bricks without Straw*, the Socratic dialogues of *Pactolus Prime*, and the dystopian *'89*. He blurred genres, borrowing literary devices from the likes of Hawthorne, Cooper, Stowe, and others, mixing realism with Victorian plot devices. These essays show that he fruitfully engaged a wider range of subject matter than has been previously recognized, such as his *Gauge and Swallow* stories on the legal profession, *Button's Inn*'s exploration of Mormonism, or *Murvale Eastman*'s meditation on the labor movement. Despite his declining sales and diminished reputation, he continued to write fiction until his final volume of short stories in 1898, after which he complained that he could no longer find a publisher for his fiction.

Several authors in this volume address Tourgée's vigorous defense of the novel written "with a purpose" and his harsh attacks on William Dean Howells's definition of "realism." Though his own works are replete with scenes and characters that arguably fit Howells's call for capturing unromanticized reality, Tourgée nevertheless insisted that the novel should aim at some level of moral instruction and not limit itself to subjective, self-absorbed introspections on inconsequential subjects. Just as with Reconstruction, Tourgée was on the wrong side of history, and Howells's standard often has been used to disparage Tourgée's work. Even during the first rediscovery of Tourgée in the 1960s, appreciative literary critics like Edmund Wilson described his fiction as didactically representative of a political viewpoint and marred by adherence to Victorian plot devices. Some even labeled his works propaganda disguised as fiction. Refreshingly, a common thread in these essays is an unapologetic approach to Tourgée's aesthetics, including his own version of realism, examining them on their own terms. Nor is it assumed that Howells's brand of realism was apolitical, while Tourgée's alone was shaped by political concerns. A more nuanced understanding of the "politics" of fiction allows us to see that Tourgée's technique of explicitly editorializing at certain moments in his novels does not invalidate other elements, such as the descriptive power and observational insights he provides throughout. The conflicts that drive the plots of his novels are rarely fully resolved, nor do his characters fit neatly in the roles of heroes and villains. Despite his habit of using characters to argue one of his own political or legal points, these editorial insertions are never the totality of the novel's purpose.

On the issue of his fidelity to the "novel with a purpose," it is worth considering why Tourgée turned to literature in the first place. His first novel, *Toinette*, was begun during the apex of Ku Klux Klan violence in North Carolina's Piedmont in 1868–1869, at the moment Tourgée was engaged in a life-or-death struggle to administer justice under the Reconstruction reforms. He later explained that he wanted to document the "unconscious evils" of slavery that continued to "shape and mold mental and moral qualities" of both the formerly enslaved and the former masters—noting it to be "especially" true for the master class. Tourgée recognized that he had a unique perspective on the postemancipation South in observing up close the changed relationship between former slave and master.

For him, it was essential to understand why *"Slavery still lives and dominates."*
The "evils" that he sought to describe "were a part of slavery that could not be
'abolished.' It was beyond the power of Military Proclamation, Constitutional
Amendment, or legal enactment."[1] Tourgée turned to fiction to meditate upon
the intangible cultural forces that presented the greatest challenge to the problem
of creating an interracial democracy in the South.

Tourgée never solved the dilemma of transforming the "mental and moral"
character of white southerners. By the time he wrote his Reconstruction novels,
he had embraced the cause of federally funded public educational systems in
the South, which he managed to advocate in several novels and tirelessly promote through extensive politicking and editorial writing. But it was clear from
his writings on this issue that while he hoped education would benefit white
southerners, he only believed with certainty that it would benefit Black southerners. This was no magic bullet; Black education would provide the tools for
self-advancement in American society, but there were no guarantees that whites
would ever acquiesce to racial equality. In the aftermath of the *Plessy* case and the
Wilmington Massacre, he renounced even that small hope. Tourgée's fiction on
the issues of race, slavery, and sectionalism were intended to present the problem
as faithfully as he could render it so that Americans could be equipped to better
deal with it in the future. No wonder he despaired when, after decades of effort,
he saw racism growing worse, not better.

In 1883, Tourgée explained his view of his purpose in writing fiction when he
published the last of a series of novels on the Civil War and Reconstruction that
he deemed, in retrospect, to be a six-volume historical epic. In the preface to that
final volume, *Hot Plowshares*, he wrote:

> Many years ago the author conceived the idea that he might aid some of his
> fellow-countrymen and countrywomen to a juster comprehension of these
> things by a series of works which should give, in the form of fictitious nar-
> rative, the effects of these distinct and contrasted civilizations upon various
> types of character.

By reading these works, he hoped that it would not only enlighten those who
lived through the "mighty drama" but that "our children should understand"
the causes of the conflict because their understanding was "essential to that homogeneity of sentiment on which our future prosperity and happiness so much
depend." In other words, he saw his historical fiction as doing antiracism work

through education and nationalization. He did not mean to suggest that the future meant complete national "homogeneity" but only that an agreement of sentiment might be reached on the underlying causes of the North-South conflict and, especially, the right and wrong of it. "There are many problems which the past has left unsolved. Some of them of the gravest possible character," he continued. "Their peaceful solution makes the fullest comprehension of the preexisting influences and developments a prime necessity on the part of all."[2]

Tourgée's fiction therefore undoubtedly had a purpose. His ability to enlighten and educate future generations about the consequences of slavery and emancipation depended not only on his literary powers but also his unique experience in the South as an intelligent observer. Few who lived through the Civil War and Reconstruction experienced and saw all of the things that Tourgée did. His novels on this topic are populated by a wide range of characters, white and Black, rich and poor, northern and southern. Tourgée brought his readers into contact with a wide range of Americans. He also attempted to discard popular caricatures of African Americans and portray a range of characters and a multiplicity of Black perspectives. *Bricks without Straw*, his 1880 sequel to *A Fool's Errand*, was his literary masterpiece in this effort. In it he details the tragic story of a prospering community of freedpeople ultimately destroyed by white violence. Vouching for the accuracy of his Black characters, Tourgée explained that they were composites constructed "out of actual Negro lives" based on people he knew or had observed.[3] Some essays in this collection find his Black characters more convincing than others do, but for the readers of his time those characterizations were a bold departure from the norm and inspired Black readers including Charles W. Chesnutt, Anna Julia Cooper, and Ida B. Wells-Barnett.

Another important insight shown in these essays is that the theme of citizenship unites a wide range of Tourgée's writings, both fiction and nonfiction. Like his editorials in the *Chicago Inter Ocean* and elsewhere, Tourgée's fiction addressed innumerable topics, but most could be viewed as part of a larger desire to reimagine national belonging and the rights of citizenship. Tourgée expressed a Tocquevillian understanding of democracy that located the culture of self-rule in the participatory activities of local government. Outspoken, active, involved citizens who recognize the equal rights of others were the essence of democratic society, and Tourgée's protagonists often exhibit these qualities. Corruption of society by powerful economic interests and the corrosive effect of the unrestrained individual pursuit of wealth are themes that repeat in novels such as *Figs and Thistles*, *Button's Inn*, and *Murvale Eastman*. Like John Dewey, Jane

Addams, and other progressive reformers of the early twentieth century, Tourgée ultimately believed democratic social ethics needed to become an ingrained part of our culture to keep our democracy vibrant.

For many reasons, the time is ripe to revisit Tourgée's literary work. Some current progressives have begun calling for a "Third Reconstruction" to rededicate the nation to the ideas of racial justice and equality. Just as the reforms of the First Reconstruction were rolled back with the rise of disenfranchisement and Jim Crow segregation, so the gains of the "Second Reconstruction" of the 1960s won by the civil rights movement have been significantly reversed in the past three decades. The deterioration of voting and civil rights, the rise of mass incarceration, the routine state-condoned violence against Black Americans, and the white supremacist takeover of the Republican Party have sounded an alarm and awoken a sense of urgency. Whether or not we ought to call for another "Reconstruction" (unless a third time is a charm), there is little doubt that another reckoning with the endemic inequalities of American life is badly needed, and it requires a reassessment of the rights of American citizenship and how to protect them.

Tourgée ought to be viewed as the foremost chronicler of the first Reconstruction. Like many others who went to the South after the Civil War, he imagined a new nation to be formed out of the wreckage of slavery that would be defined by equal citizenship for all, irrespective of race. Tourgée tried hard to realize that vision and then ruminated on its failure more deeply than most anyone. His works are full of the wisdom of that experience, which may be found useful to those who have a similar vision today. Speaking to a white audience on what is required to solve America's race problem, Tourgée once mused:

> During the fifteen of the early years of his freedom (1865 to 1880), I studied [the Negro] as an employer, a citizen, a lawyer, a judge. I was thoroughly familiar with his status in every portion of one of the Southern states . . . always keeping uppermost in my mind *his* view of his past and *his* hope for the future. . . . I have not always understood him. I am not certain anyone can who has not suffered with him. I have never been so sure as many of our friends what was the very best thing that *was to be done for* the colored man; but I have never doubted the most exact justice and fullest recognition of his equality of right must be the prime elements of any successful policy which has for its purpose the elevation of the race and the development of his individual manhood. Wrong is never cured by fresh injustice and manhood is never ennobled by being compelled to wear the brand of inferiority.[4]

This comment sums up the core of Tourgée's literary achievement exceedingly well. He observed, he listened, and he sought to understand the world from another's perspective. He never presumed to know or fully inhabit that perspective, but he could empathize with it and dignify it with respect. Moreover, he could represent it effectively to others. Here is an ethic that is both the basis for literary success and for a more truly democratic society.

Notes

1. Tourgée's emphasis. This description is taken from the preface to the 1881 revised version of *Toinette* retitled *A Royal Gentleman* (New York: Fords, Howard, & Hulbert, 1881).

2. These quotations are taken from the "Preface," dated May 2, 1883, to *Hot Plowshares: A Novel* (New York: Fords, Howard & Hulbert 1882), 2–3.

3. Albion W. Tourgée, "The Negro's View of the Race Problem" (1890), in *Undaunted Radical: The Selected Writings and Speeches of Albion W. Tourgée*, ed. Mark Elliott and John David Smith (Baton Rouge: Louisiana State University Press, 2010), 158.

4. Tourgée, "The Negro's View of the Race Problem," 198–99.

Albion W. Tourgée:
A Chronology

1838 Born May 2 in Williamsfield, Ohio.

1859 Enrolls at the University of Rochester.

1861 Withdraws from the University of Rochester to enlist in the Twenty-Seventh New York Infantry. Suffers serious back injury in the Battle of Bull Run.

1862 After a lengthy recovery period, reenlists in the Union Army as part of the 105th Ohio Volunteers.

1863 Captured near Murfreesboro, Tennessee, in January and held for four months as a prisoner of war in three Confederate prisons. Marries Emma L. Kilbourne in Columbus, Ohio, on May 14; ten days later rejoins the Ohio Volunteers. Fights at the battles of Chickamauga and Chattanooga. Reinjures back in December and resigns from the Union Army.

1865 Moves with Emma to Guilford County, North Carolina, in October.

1866 Serves as elected representative of Guilford County at the Southern Loyalist Convention in Philadelphia; Frederick Douglass speaks at the September convention. In December, publishes the first issue of a short-lived Republican newspaper, the *Union Register*.

1867 Elected as a Republican to North Carolina's state constitutional convention. Publishes the poem "Poll Tax Song" in the *National Anti-Slavery Standard*. Over the next three decades, he would publish poems in such places as the *Greensboro Patriot* (1873), *Our Continent* (1882), and *The Independent* (1896).

1868 Participates in the North Carolina state constitutional convention; elected judge of the Seventh District Superior Court in North Carolina.

1870 Writes the first of many reports on the terroristic activities of the Ku Klux Klan in North Carolina.

1874 Publishes first novel, *Toinette*, in September, under the pseudonym of Henry Churton. The novel is set in North Carolina.

1878 Defeated in run for a North Carolina congressional seat; Emma moves to Erie, Pennsylvania.

1879 Leaves North Carolina; joins Emma in Pennsylvania. Publishes *Figs and Thistles: A Romance of the Western Reserve* and *A Fool's Errand: By One of the Fools*. Published anonymously at first, *A Fool's Errand*, set in North Carolina, proves to be his most popular novel. Sales estimates range from 200,000 to 600,000 copies.

1880 Publishes new edition of *A Fool's Errand*, with an appendix on KKK atrocities titled *The Invisible Empire*. Later that year publishes *Bricks without Straw*. Attends the Republican national convention in Chicago and supports James A. Garfield. Garfield credits Tourgée's novels with helping him win the presidency. Tourgée sends Garfield letters advising him on policy.

1881   Purchases a home in Mayville, New York, near Chautauqua Institution, a Methodist summer community founded in 1874. Names the house "Thorheim," which he translates as "Fool's Home." Delivers "Christian Citizenship" at Chautauqua on August 11; the lecture is printed in the *Chautauquan* later that year. Collaborates on a stage version of *Fool's Errand*, which opens in Philadelphia on October 26. Taking advantage of his literary popularity, publishes a revised version of *Toinette*, now titled *A Royal Gentleman*. Garfield shot by assassin in July; dies in September.

1882   In February publishes the first issue of *Our Continent*, a weekly illustrated literary magazine. Publishes a volume with two novellas: *John Eax and Mamelon: The South without the Shadow*.

1883   Publishes *Hot Plowshares*, a historical novel about the antislavery movement that he had serialized in *Our Continent* from July 1882 to May 1883.

1884   Publishes *An Appeal to Caesar*, a nonfictional work on the importance of developing national policies of education. *Our Continent* fails financially, leaving Tourgée in debt.

1886   Publishes *The Veteran and His Pipe*, a collection of his newspaper columns first appearing in the *Daily Inter Ocean* (Chicago).

1887   Publishes *Button's Inn*, a historical novel that addresses capitalism and Mormonism.

1888   Begins a new newspaper column in the *Daily Inter Ocean* titled "A Bystander's Notes." The column runs off and on until 1898. Publishes in the journal *Forum* what would become his most widely cited work of literary criticism, "The South as a Field for Fiction." In it he attacks literary realists for focusing on small details instead of larger truths, and he predicts that great southern literature will be written by African Americans. Charles Chesnutt initiates a correspondence after reading Tourgée's essay. The two men develop a significant professional and personal relationship over the next several years.

1890   Publishes *Pactolus Prime*, a novel about passing and reparations first serialized in the *Advance* from December 1888 to March 1889; *Murvale Eastman, Christian Socialist*, a novel calling on churches to address class inequities and poverty; and *With Gauge and Swallow, Attorneys*, novelistically interconnected stories about a law office.

1891   Founds the National Citizens' Rights Association (NCRA); uses his columns in the *Daily Inter Ocean* to advocate for civil rights for all US citizens. Becomes interested in the *Plessy v. Ferguson* case challenging Jim Crow laws on railroad cars. He soon takes on the job of legal counsel representing Homer Plessy and other African Americans.

1892   Joins forces with fellow journalists Ida B. Wells (who applied for membership to the NCRA the previous year) and Harry C. Smith to combat lynching. Anna Julia Cooper includes a review of *Pactolus Prime* in *A Voice from the South*.

1893   Speaks on "Citizenship and Suffrage" at the Columbian Exposition in Chicago, as part of a week-long program including Frederick Douglass and Susan B. Anthony.

1895   Eulogizes Frederick Douglass at a November memorial service in Boston.

1896   Publishes *The Story of a Thousand. Being a History of the Service of the 105th Ohio Volunteer Infantry, in the War for the Union from August 21, 1862, to June 6, 1865.*

Presents legal arguments before the Supreme Court in the *Plessy* case; one month later, in May, the Supreme Court rules that the segregationist practice of "Separate but Equal" is legal.

1897   Appointed US consul to Bordeaux.

1898   Publishes *The Man Who Outlived Himself*, a collection of novellas.

1905   Dies in Bordeaux on May 21. Charles Chesnutt and Ida B. Wells eulogize Tourgée at a memorial service held November 14 in Mayville, New York. On Thanksgiving Day, W. E. B. Du Bois's newly formed Niagara Movement sponsors nationwide memorial services for three "friends of freedom": William Lloyd Garrison, Frederick Douglass, and Albion Tourgée.

Acknowledgments

We could not have produced this volume without the assistance we have received from a number of individuals. We are deeply grateful to the Tourgée scholars Mark Elliott, Carolyn Karcher, and Brook Thomas for their important work on Tourgée and for their contributions to this volume. Jon Schmitz, the archivist at Chautauqua Institution, provided essential support. The director of Fordham University Press, Fredric Nachbaur, offered invaluable advice and encouragement, and Rob Fellman provided expert copyediting. We would also like to thank Andrew L. Slap for championing the book for his Reconstructing America book series at Fordham. We were fortunate in our outside readers, Carrie Tirado Bramen and Shirley Samuels, who enthusiastically embraced the volume while offering keen suggestions for revision. Finally, we would like to thank our collegial and hardworking authors for their contributions to Tourgée studies.

Selected Bibliography

Criticism on Tourgée is still in its infancy. For biography, the best starting points are Mark Elliott's *Color-Blind Justice: Albion Tourgée and the Quest for Racial Equality from the Civil War to Plessy v. Ferguson* (New York: Oxford University Press, 2006) and Carolyn L. Karcher's *A Refugee from His Race: Albion W. Tourgée and His Fight against White Supremacy* (Chapel Hill: University of North Carolina Press, 2016). Karcher's book gives greater attention to the literary. On Tourgée in the literary context of Reconstruction, see Brook Thomas's *The Literature of Reconstruction: Not in Plain Black and White* (Baltimore, MD: Johns Hopkins University Press, 2017). Also useful is Carolyn L. Karcher's edition of Tourgée's 1880 novel *Bricks without Straw* (Durham, NC: Duke University Press, 2009), the first fully annotated edition of a Tourgée novel. For an introduction to a wide range of Tourgée's writings, see *Undaunted Radical: The Selected Writings and Speeches of Albion W. Tourgée*, ed. Mark Elliott and John David Smith (Baton Rouge: Louisiana State University Press, 2010).

1. Tourgée's Writings

Tourgée published numerous novels, novellas, short stories, and nonfiction works. He also published hundreds of articles and letters. For a list of his article publications in particular, see the more comprehensive bibliography in Mark Elliott and John David Smith's *Undaunted Radical*. Dean H. Keller's *Checklist of the Writings of Albion W. Tourgée (1838–1905)* is still useful. (See Section 2 for citation information on Keller.)

Below we provide a chronological list of Tourgée's major works, focusing on the fiction.

Toinette: A Novel. New York: J. B. Ford & Company, 1874.
Figs and Thistles: A Romance of the Western Reserve. New York: Fords, Howard, & Hulbert, 1879.
A Fool's Errand. By One of the Fools. New York: Fords, Howard, & Hulbert, 1879.
A Fool's Errand; By One of the Fools; The Famous Romance of American History. New, Enlarged, and Illustrated Edition. To Which Is Added, by the Same Author, Part II. The Invisible Empire: A Concise Review of the Epoch on Which the Tale Is Based. New York: Fords, Howard, & Hulbert, 1880.
Bricks without Straw: A Novel. New York: Fords, Howard, & Hulbert, 1880.
A Royal Gentleman [revised version of *Toinette*]. New York: Fords, Howard, & Hulbert, 1881.
John Eax and Mamelon; or, The South without the Shadow. New York: Fords, Howard, & Hulbert, 1881.
Hot Plowshares: A Novel. New York: Fords, Howard, & Hulbert, 1883.

An Appeal to Caesar. New York: Fords, Howard, & Hulbert, 1884.
Button's Inn. Boston: Roberts Brothers, 1887.
Black Ice. New York: Fords, Howard, & Hulbert, 1888.
With Gauge and Swallow, Attorneys. Philadelphia: J. P. Lippincott, 1889.
Pactolus Prime. New York: Cassell Publishing Co., 1890.
A Son of Old Harry: A Novel. New York: Robert Bonner's Sons, 1891.
The Story of a Thousand. Being a History of the Service of the 105th Ohio Volunteer Infantry in the War for the Union. Buffalo, NY: McGerald & Son, 1896.
The Man Who Outlived Himself. New York: Fords, Howard, & Hulbert, 1898.

2. Biographical Studies and Resources

Mark Elliott's *Color-Blind Justice* and Carolyn L. Karcher's *A Refugee from His Race* are the essential biographical studies. The Albion W. Tourgée Papers are located at the Chautauqua County Historical Society, McClurg Museum, Westfield, New York, and are also available online: http://www.nyheritage.org/collections/albion-winegar-tourgee -collection. The following biographical and bibliographical studies are also useful.

Current, Richard Nelson. *Those Terrible Carpetbaggers.* New York: Oxford University Press, 1988.
Ealy, Marguerite, and Sanford E. Marovitz. "Albion Winegar Tourgée (1838–1905)." *American Literary Realism* 8, no. 1 (1975): 52–80.
Karcher, Carolyn L. "Albion W. Tourgée." Oxford Bibliographies, 2018. Online, by subscription.
——. "Albion W. Tourgée and Louis A. Martinet: The Cross-Racial Friendship behind *Plessy v. Ferguson.*" *MELUS: The Journal of the Society for the Study of the Multi-Ethnic Literature of the United States* 38, no. 1 (2013): 9–29.
Keller, Dean H. "A Checklist of the Writings of Albion W. Tourgée (1838–1905)." *Studies in Bibliography* 18 (1965): 269–79.
Luxenberg, Steve. *Separate: The Story of Plessy v. Ferguson, and America's Journey from Slavery to Segregation.* New York: Norton, 2019.
Olson, Otto H. *Carpetbagger's Crusade: The Life of Albion Winegar Tourgée.* Baltimore, MD: Johns Hopkins University Press, 1965.

3. Literary and Historical Studies of Tourgée

Some of the best work on Tourgée has appeared in book chapters and articles. Brook Thomas's *The Literature of Reconstruction*, which focuses on Tourgée's fiction, is an excellent starting point. In addition, see the following critical works.

Aaron, Daniel, *The Unwritten War: American Writers and the Civil War*, 193–205. New York: Knopf, 1973.
Biggio, Rebecca Skidmore. "Violent Fraternities and White Reform: The Complementary Fictions of Albion Tourgée and Thomas Dixon." *Arizona Quarterly* 67, no. 2 (2011): 73–100.
Blight, David W. *Race and Reunion: The Civil War in American Memory.* Cambridge, MA: Harvard University Press, 2001.

Caccavari, Peter. "Reconstructing Reconstruction: Region and Nation in the Work of Albion Tourgée." In *Regionalism Reconsidered: New Approaches to the Field*, ed. David Jordan, 119–138. New York: Garland, 1994.

Carter, Everett. "Edmund Wilson Refights the Civil War: The Revision of Albion Tourgée's Novels." *American Literary Realism* 29, no. 2 (1997): 68–75.

Finseth, Ian. "The Realists' Civil War." In *A History of American Civil War Literature*, ed. Coleman Hutchison, 62–76. New York: Cambridge University Press, 2016.

Gilmore, Michael T. *The War of Words: Slavery, Race, and Free Speech in American Literature*, 199–213. Chicago: University of Chicago Press, 2010.

Gordon-Smith, George M. "Albion Tourgée and the Politics of Disability and Race in Reconstruction-Era Literature." *Studies in American Fiction* 42, no. 1 (2015): 103–22.

Gross, Theodore L. *Albion W. Tourgée*. New York: Twayne, 1963.

Gustafson, Sandra M. "Democracy and Discussion: Albion Tourgée on Race and the Town Meeting Ideal." *J19: The Journal of Nineteenth-Century Americanists* 5, no. 2 (2017): 389–96.

Hardig, Bill. "Who Owns the Whip? Chesnutt, Tourgée, and Reconstruction Justice." *African American Review* 36, no. 1 (2002): 5–20.

Kelley, Mark B. "Reconstructing the Racial Politics of Disability and Literary History in *Bricks without Straw*." *American Literary Realism* 49, no. 1 (2016): 21–36.

Kennedy-Nolle, Sharon D. *Writing Reconstruction: Race, Gender, and Citizenship in the Postwar South*, 76–122. Chapel Hill: University of North Carolina Press, 2015.

Levine, Robert S. "Isabel Wilkerson, Albion Tourgée, and the Problem of Caste in the United States." *Literary Imagination* 23, no. 2 (2021): 151–60.

Miller, Jeffrey W. "Redemption through Violence: White Mobs and Black Citizenship in Albion Tourgée." *Southern Literary Journal* 35, no. 1 (2002): 14–27.

Schmidt, Peter. *Sitting in Darkness: New South Fiction, Education, and the Rise of Jim Crow Colonialism, 1865–1920*, 55–63. Jackson: University of Mississippi Press, 2008.

Short, Gretchen. "The Dilemmas of Reconstructing the Nation in Albion W. Tourgée's *A Fool's Errand* and Charles W. Chesnutt's *The Marrow of Tradition*." *REAL: The Yearbook of Research in English and American Literature* 14 (1998): 241–67.

Thomas, Brook. *American Literary Realism and the Failed Promise of Contract*, 191–229. Berkeley: University of California Press, 1997.

———. "Of Mules and Men, Fathers and Husbands, Schools and Suffrage: African American Manhood and the Paradox of Paternalism in Law and Literature after Emancipation." *Arizona Quarterly* 70, no. 1 (2014): 1–27.

———. "*Plessy v. Ferguson* and the Literary Imagination." *Cardoza Studies in Law & Literature* 9, no. 1 (1997a): 45–65.

Warren, Kathryn Hamilton. "Empathetic Persuasion in Albion Tourgée's *A Fool's Errand*." *American Literary Realism* 44, no. 1 (2011): 44–67.

Wilson, Edmund. *Patriotic Gore: Studies in the Literature of the American Civil War*, 529–48. New York: Oxford University Press, 1966.

Contributors

Molly Ball is a Post-Doctoral Associate in American Studies at the University of Minnesota, Twin Cities. She has published on women's slave narratives, seduction novels, and pedagogy, and her work has appeared in journals such as *ESQ* and *Early American Literature*. She is currently revising a book-length project titled "Writing out of Time," which examines how nineteenth-century populations deemed to have "no future" within the progressing nation both represent and dispute that temporal status through experiments with forward-moving narrative forms.

Nancy Bentley is Donald T. Regan Professor of English at the University of Pennsylvania. Her publications include *The Ethnography of Manners* and *Frantic Panoramas: Mass Culture and American Literature, 1870–1920*. She coauthored Volume 3 of *The Cambridge History of American Literature* (2005) and is currently writing a book entitled "New World Kinship and American Literature," a study of the way the novel and other genres mediated the multiple forms of kinship in the Americas in the nineteenth century.

Tess Chakkalakal is Associate Professor of Africana Studies and English at Bowdoin College. She is the author of *Novel Bondage: Slavery, Marriage, and Freedom in Nineteenth-Century America*. She is the coeditor of *Jim Crow, Literature, and the Legacy of Sutton E. Griggs* and *Imperium in Imperio by Sutton E. Griggs: A Critical Edition*. She is currently at work on a biography of Charles W. Chesnutt, a portion of which has been published in *J19*. She serves on the editorial team for *The Complete Writings of Charles W. Chesnutt*, forthcoming from Oxford University Press.

Sarah E. Chinn is Professor of English at Hunter College, CUNY. She is the author of three books: *Technology and the Logic of American Racism: A Cultural History of the Body as Evidence* (2000); *Inventing Modern Adolescence: The Children of Immigrants in Turn-of-the-Century America* (2007); and *Spectacular Men: Race, Gender, and Nation on the Early American Stage* (2017), which won the 2017 George Freedley Prize for Outstanding Work of Theatre History; as well as a scholarly edition, *Nine Plays of Early America* (Early American Reprints, 2018). Her work has appeared in such journals as *American Literature, Signs, GLQ, WSQ*, and *Nineteenth-Century Literature*. She is currently working on a manuscript that explores representations of amputation during Reconstruction, especially as deployed by white antiracist radicals.

Mark Elliott is Associate Professor of History at the University of North Carolina, Greensboro. He is the author of *Color-Blind Justice: Albion Tourgée and the Quest for Racial Equality from the Civil War to* Plessy v. Ferguson (2006). The book won the Avery O.

Craven Award from the Organization of American Historians. He also coedited *Undaunted Radical: The Selected Writings and Speeches of Albion Tourgée* (2010) with John David Smith. His current research focuses on ideas of human rights and American nationalism in the nineteenth century.

John Ernest is Judge Hugh M. Morris Professor and Chair of the Department of English at the University of Delaware. He is the author or editor of twelve books and over forty journal articles and book chapters. His books include *Liberation Historiography: African American Writers and the Challenge of History, 1794–1861* (2004); *Chaotic Justice: Rethinking African American Literary History* (2009); *A Nation within a Nation: Organizing African American Communities before the Civil War* (2011); *The Oxford Handbook of the African American Slave Narrative* (2014); *Douglass in His Own Time: A Biographical Chronicle of His Life, Drawn from Recollections, Interviews, and Memoirs by Family, Friends, and Associates* (2014); and *Race in American Literature and Culture* (2022). With Joycelyn K. Moody, he serves as editor of Regenerations: African American Literature and Culture, a series devoted to undervalued works by early African American writers.

Annemarie Mott Ewing is a PhD candidate in the English Department at the University of Maryland. Her dissertation, "Citizenship and the Counterfactual Imagination: Race, Exclusion, and Redress in the Literature of the Long Reconstruction," explores the way Reconstruction writings use the counterfactual to depict the undecided, malleable nature of citizenship.

Jennifer Rae Greeson is Associate Professor of English and Chair of the Department of American Studies at the University of Virginia. She is the author of *Our South: Geographic Fantasy and the Rise of National Literature* (2010) and coeditor of *Keywords for Southern Studies* (2016) and of the Norton Critical Edition of Charles Chesnutt's *Conjure Stories* (2011).

Sandra M. Gustafson is Professor of English and Concurrent Professor of American Studies at the University of Notre Dame. Her books include *Imagining Deliberative Democracy in the Early American Republic* (2011); *Eloquence Is Power: Oratory and Performance in Early America* (2000); and the coedited volume *Cultural Narratives: Textuality and Performance in American Culture before 1900* (2010). She is the editor of *The Norton Anthology of American Literature*, Vol. A, and past editor of the MLA-affiliated journal *Early American Literature*. In 2019, she codirected an NEH summer seminar for college and university professors at Cornell University that devoted a session to Tourgée and was lead organizer for the conference "Literary Tourgée." Tourgée and Charles Chesnutt figure in *Peace in the US Republic of Letters, 1840–1900* (forthcoming 2023), on nineteenth-century American fiction and the early peace movement.

Mary B. Hale is Assistant Director of Scholarly and Undergraduate Programs at the Newberry Library in Chicago. She holds a PhD from the University of Illinois at Chicago, where she wrote a dissertation titled "Democratic Conventions: The Form of Politics in the Gilded Age." She has won numerous awards, including a fellowship from the Massachusetts Historical Society to support her work on Henry Adams. Her work has appeared in journals such as *American Literature* and the *New Americanist*. Her current project is a consideration of the political fiction of Ellen Glasgow in the post-Populist South.

DeLisa D. Hawkes is an Assistant Professor of Africana Studies specializing in African American literature and an affiliate faculty of the Women, Gender, and Sexuality Program at the University of Tennessee, Knoxville. She is currently working on her first book project, which examines representations of Black and Indigenous relationships in African American print culture and their impact on narratives of racial identity and kinship in the United States. Her work has appeared in *J19*, *MELUS*, *Langston Hughes Review*, *Studies in the Fantastic*, *North Carolina Literary Review*, and *21st Century US Historical Fiction: Contemporary Responses to the Past* (2020).

Christine Holbo is Associate Professor of English at Arizona State University. Her work investigates the intersections of law, literature, philosophy, and politics in the late nineteenth and early twentieth centuries. She is the author of *Legal Realisms: The American Novel under Reconstruction* (Oxford, 2019), which explores the transformation of the realist novel in the age of the Fourteenth Amendment. Her publications on literary realism, poetic and novelistic modernism, and sentimental aesthetics have appeared in journals including *ELH*, *American Literary History*, *American Literary Realism*, and *Early American Literature*.

Carolyn L. Karcher is Professor Emerita of English, American Studies, and Women's Studies at Temple University. She is the author of *A Refugee from His Race: Albion W. Tourgée and His Fight against White Supremacy* (2016) and the editor of Tourgée's novel *Bricks without Straw*. She is also the author of *The First Woman in the Republic: A Cultural Biography of Lydia Maria Child* (1994) and *Shadow over the Promised Land: Slavery, Race, and Violence in Melville's America* (1980).

Almas Khan is Assistant Professor of Law at the University of Arkansas at Little Rock William H. Bowen School of Law. She is a literary and legal historian who analyzes how intellectual movements in law and literature have shaped conceptions of US citizenship since the Civil War. Khan's work draws on her PhD in English from the University of Virginia and her JD with a concentration in constitutional history from the University of Chicago. Her current book project, "An Intellectual Reconstruction: American Legal Realism, Literary Realism, and the Formation of Citizenship," construes legal realism (a progenitor of critical race theory) in relation to literary realism. Her work has appeared in the anthology *Critical Insights: Social Justice and American Literature* and *Clio: A Journal of Literature, History, and the Philosophy of History*.

Gregory Laski is the author of *Untimely Democracy: The Politics of Progress after Slavery* (2018), which won the American Literature Association's 2019 Pauline E. Hopkins Society Scholarship Award. Formerly a visiting faculty member at Carnegie Mellon University,

Laski is currently a civilian Associate Professor of English at the United States Air Force Academy. A Mellon Fellow at the Newberry Library in 2021–2022, he is at work on a new book project: an intellectual history of revenge in the long Reconstruction era. An overview of the study's primary argument appeared in the December 2019 number of *American Literature*; this article was awarded the journal's Norman Foerster Prize for best essay of the year as well as the 1921 Prize, given annually by the American Literature Society.

Alex Zweber Leslie received his PhD from Rutgers University in 2021. His book project, "Reading Regions: American Literature and Cultural Geography, 1865–1925," shows how extensive regional differences in circulation and reception shaped authorial production and the literary marketplace. His work has appeared in *American Literary History* and *J19*.

Robert S. Levine is Distinguished University Professor of English at the University of Maryland. His most recent books include *The Lives of Frederick Douglass* (2016), *Race, Transnationalism, and Nineteenth-Century American Literary Studies* (2018), and *The Failed Promise: Reconstruction, Frederick Douglass, and the Impeachment of Andrew Johnson* (2021). He has edited and coedited a number of editions and collections, including *Hemispheric American Studies* (2008), *The New Cambridge Companion to Herman Melville* (2014), and the Norton Critical Edition of Melville's *Pierre* (2017). He is the general editor of *The Norton Anthology of American Literature*.

Brook Thomas is Chancellor's Professor, Emeritus, at the University of California, Irvine. A scholar of law and literature, he has written about Tourgée for thirty years, including in Plessy v. Ferguson: *A Brief History with Documents* (1997); *American Literary Realism and the Failed Promise of Contract* (1999); *Civic Myths: A Law and Literature Approach to Citizenship* (2007); and, most recently, *The Literature of Reconstruction: Not in Plain Black and White* (2017), which won the 2018 C. Hugh Holman Award from the Society for the Study of Southern Literature. His essay "Albion W. Tourgée on Race, Class, and Caste" is forthcoming in *ELH*.

Kenneth W. Warren is Fairfax M. Cone Distinguished Service Professor at the University of Chicago. He is the author of *What Was African American Literature?* (2010); *So Black and Blue: Ralph Ellison and the Occasion of Criticism* (2003); and *Black and White Strangers: Race and American Literary Realism* (1993) and coeditor of *Renewing Black Intellectual History: The Material and Ideological Foundations of African American Thought* (2010); *Jim Crow, Literature, and the Legacy of Sutton E. Griggs* (2013); and *Imperium in Imperio by Sutton E. Griggs: A Critical Edition* (2022).

Index

Note: Illustrations are indicated by page numbers in *italics*.

RECONSTRUCTING AMERICA
Andrew L. Slap, series editor

Hans L. Trefousse, *Impeachment of a President: Andrew Johnson, the Blacks, and Reconstruction.*

Richard Paul Fuke, *Imperfect Equality: African Americans and the Confines of White Ideology in Post-Emancipation Maryland.*

Ruth Currie-McDaniel, *Carpetbagger of Conscience: A Biography of John Emory Bryant.*

Paul A. Cimbala and Randall M. Miller, eds., *The Freedmen's Bureau and Reconstruction: Reconsiderations.*

Herman Belz, *A New Birth of Freedom: The Republican Party and Freedmen's Rights, 1861 to 1866.*

Robert Michael Goldman, *"A Free Ballot and a Fair Count": The Department of Justice and the Enforcement of Voting Rights in the South, 1877–1893.*

Ruth Douglas Currie, ed., *Emma Spaulding Bryant: Civil War Bride, Carpetbagger's Wife, Ardent Feminist—Letters, 1860–1900.*

Robert Francis Engs, *Freedom's First Generation: Black Hampton, Virginia, 1861–1890.*

Robert F. Kaczorowski, *The Politics of Judicial Interpretation: The Federal Courts, Department of Justice, and Civil Rights, 1866–1876.*

John Syrett, *The Civil War Confiscation Acts: Failing to Reconstruct the South.*

Michael Les Benedict, *Preserving the Constitution: Essays on Politics and the Constitution in the Reconstruction Era.*

Andrew L. Slap, *The Doom of Reconstruction: The Liberal Republicans in the Civil War Era.*

Edmund L. Drago, *Confederate Phoenix: Rebel Children and Their Families in South Carolina.*

Mary Farmer-Kaiser, *Freedwomen and the Freedmen's Bureau: Race, Gender, and Public Policy in the Age of Emancipation.*

Paul A. Cimbala and Randall Miller, eds., *The Great Task Remaining Before Us: Reconstruction as America's Continuing Civil War.*

John A. Casey Jr., *New Men: Reconstructing the Image of the Veteran in Late-Nineteenth-Century American Literature and Culture.*

Hilary Green, *Educational Reconstruction: African American Schools in the Urban South, 1865–1890.*

Christopher B. Bean, *Too Great a Burden to Bear: The Struggle and Failure of the Freedmen's Bureau in Texas.*

David E. Goldberg, *The Retreats of Reconstruction: Race, Leisure, and the Politics of Segregation at the New Jersey Shore, 1865–1920.*

David Prior, ed., *Reconstruction in a Globalizing World.*

Jewel L. Spangler and Frank Towers, eds., *Remaking North American Sovereignty: State Transformation in the 1860s.*

Adam H. Domby and Simon Lewis, eds., *Freedoms Gained and Lost: Reconstruction and Its Meanings 150 Years Later.*

Sandra M. Gustafson and Robert S. Levine, eds., *Reimagining the Republic: Race, Citizenship, and Nation in the Literary Work of Albion W. Tourgée.*

Brian Schoen, Jewel L. Spangler, and Frank Towers, eds., *Continent in Crisis: The U.S. Civil War in North America.*

www.ingramcontent.com/pod-product-compliance
Lightning Source LLC
Chambersburg PA
CBHW020356110726
47899CB00006B/1736